Wissenschaftliche Untersuchungen
zum Neuen Testament · 2. Reihe

Herausgeber/Editor
Jörg Frey

Mitherausgeber / Associate Editors
Friedrich Avemarie · Judith Gundry-Volf
Martin Hengel · Otfried Hofius · Hans-Josef Klauck

170

Lidija Novakovic

Messiah, the Healer of the Sick

A Study of Jesus
as the Son of David in the Gospel of Matthew

Mohr Siebeck

LIDIJA NOVAKOVIC, born 1955; 2002 Ph.D. in Biblical Studies (New Testament) from Princeton Theological Seminary; currently Assistant Professor of Biblical and Theological Studies at Bethel College, St. Paul.

BS
2575.52
.N68
2003

ISBN 3-16-148165-8

ISSN 0340-9570 (Wissenschaftliche Untersuchungen zum Neuen Testament 2. Reihe)

Die Deutsche Bibliothek lists this publication in the Deutsche Nationalbibliographie; detailed bibliographic data is available in the Internet at *http://dnb.ddb.de*.

The book was printed by Druckpartner Rübelmann GmbH in Hemsbach on non-aging paper and bound by Buchbinderei Schaumann in Darmstadt.

Printed in Germany.

Preface

This book represents a revision of my doctoral dissertation "Messiah, the Healer of the Sick: A Study of the Origins of Matthew's Portrayal of Jesus as the Son of David," submitted to the Faculty of Princeton Theological Seminary and defended in November of 2001. In this project, I examine the background of the Matthean link between Jesus' messianic identity and his healing ministry. I explore Scriptural quotations and allusions that have informed Matthew's understanding of Jesus' messiahship, as well as various passages from the early Jewish writings, such as the Old Testament Pseudepigrapha, the Dead Sea Scrolls, and Josephus. My conclusion is that Matthew's understanding of Jesus as the healing Davidic Messiah should be seen as an outcome of Christian midrashic interpretation of Scripture in light of the conviction that Jesus is the Messiah. This study is intended to advance the discussion focused on the development of early Christology and to offer a reconstruction of the exegetical methods used by Jewish believers in Jesus' messiahship.

My research received assistance and encouragement from many scholars. First of all, I am deeply indebted to Professor Donald Juel for his enthusiastic and proficient supervision of the writing of this thesis. His Ph.D. seminar on the use of the Old Testament in the New Testament inspired me to undertake this project. His insightful comments, helpful suggestions, and continuous encouragement made the writing of the dissertation the most rewarding and enjoyable scholarly experience. He received the news that my work was accepted for publication in the WUNT 2. Series with great joy, but unfortunately did not live long enough to see it in a published form. His premature death in February of 2003 will remain an immense loss for me personally and professionally.

I want to offer special thanks to Professor James H. Charlesworth who opened to me the world of Early Judaism and introduced me to its literature and history. His scholarly expertise and enthusiasm became invaluable resources for the completion of this project. Working under his supervision in the PTS Dead Sea Scrolls Project offered me the first-hand experience with the Qumran writings, and I am deeply grateful for his professional guidance and support.

I wish to extend thanks to the entire faculty in Biblical Studies at Princeton Theological Seminary for creating such a stimulating academic environment for study and research. Besides the doctoral seminars I had with Professors Juel and Charlesworth, those with Professors Ulrich W. Mauser, Beverly

Roberts Gaventa, A. K. M. Adam, Brian K. Blount, and Patrick D. Miller proved to be especially helpful. In addition, I am indebted to many of my friends and colleagues from the PTS Dead Sea Scrolls Project, with whom I was able to share my ideas and discuss my findings. Among them are Michael T. Davis, Professor Casey D. Elledge, John B. F. Miller, Cory P. Hall, and Professor Henry W. Rietz. I also remember with appreciation my former teachers at the Baptist Theological Seminary in Rüschlikon, Switzerland, who stimulated my interest in New Testament studies and supported my academic pursuits. I am especially grateful to Dr. Günter Wagner for instigating my love for the Gospel of Matthew, and Dr. Samuel Byrskog for calling my attention to the intriguing relationship between the Son of David and Jesus' miracles of healing.

I also wish to express appreciation to Professor Dr. Carsten Claussen, a visiting scholar at Princeton Theological Seminary, for his initial interest in my work, and to Professor Dr. Jörg Frey from the Evangelisch-Theologische Fakultät, University of Munich, who accepted it for publication and offered various helpful suggestions for revision. A special thanks is extended to Ms. Sarah Jacobson from Bethel College, St. Paul, who has read and edited the final version of the manuscript.

Finally, I wish to thank my husband Ivo, and my children Andreja and Matthew for their love and encouragement during the writing of this book. Numerous thought-provoking discussions with my husband enabled me to complete this project in the first place. I dedicate this work to him.

Table of Contents

Abbreviations

AB	Anchor Bible
ABD	*Anchor Bible Dictionary*
ABRL	Anchor Bible Reference Library
AGJU	Arbeiten zur Geschichte des antiken Judentums und des Urchristentums
ALGHJ	Arbeiten zur Literatur und Geschichte des hellenistischen Judentums
AnBib	Analecta biblica
ANRW	*Aufstieg und Niedergang der römischen Welt: Geschichte und Kultur Roms im Spiegel der neueren Forschung*
ANTJ	Arbeiten zum Neuen Testament und Judentum
ArBib	The Aramaic Bible
ArOr	*Archiv Orientální*
ASNU	Acta seminarii neotestamentici upsaliensis
ATA	Alttestamentliche Abhandlungen
BAR	*Biblical Archaeology Review*
BETL	Bibliotheca ephemeridum theologicarum lovaniensium
BEvT	Beiträge zur evangelischen Theologie
BFCT	Beiträge zur Förderung christlicher Theologie
Bib	*Biblica*
BIOSCS	*Bulletin of the International Organization for Septuagint and Cognate Studies*
BIS	Biblical Interpretation Series
BJRL	*Bulletin of the John Rylands UniversityLibrary of Manchester*
BRev	*Bible Review*
BTB	*Biblical Theology Bulletin*
BThSt	Biblisch-theologische Studien
BWANT	Beiträge zur Wissenschaft vom Alten und Neuen Testament
BZ	*Biblische Zeitschrift*
BZNW	Beihefte zur Zeitschrift für die neutestamentliche Wissenschaft
CBQ	*Catholic Biblical Quarterly*
CBQMS	Catholic Biblical Quarterly Monograph Series
CCWJCW	Cambridge Commentaries on Writings of the Jewish and Christian World
CJAS	Christianity and Judaism in Antiquity Series
CNT	Commentaire du Nouveau Testament
ConBNT	Coniectanea neotestamentica or Coniectanea biblica: New Testament Series
DJD	Discoveries in the Judaean Desert
DSD	*Dead Sea Discoveries*
EHS.T	Europäische Hochschulschriften. Reihe 23: Theologie
EtB	Études Bibliques
EtB.NS	Études Bibliques; nouvelle série
ExpTim	*Expository Times*
FAT	Forschungen zum Alten Testament
FB	Forschung zur Bibel
FRLANT	Forschungen zur Religion und Literatur des Alten und Neuen Testaments

HAR	*Hebrew Annual Review*
HBS	Herders Biblische Studien
HDR	Harvard Dissertations in Religion
HNT	Handbuch zum Neuen Testament
HSM	Harvard Semitic Monographs
HSS	Harvard Semitic Studies
HTR	*Harvard Theological Review*
ICC	International Critical Commentary
IEJ	*Israel Exploration Journal*
Imm	*Immanuel*
Int	*Interpretation*
JAOS	*Journal of the American Oriental Society*
JBL	*Journal of Biblical Literature*
JJS	*Journal of Jewish Studies*
JQR	*Jewish Quarterly Review*
JSNT	*Journal for the Study of the New Testament*
JSNTSup	Journal for the Study of the New Testament: Supplement Series
JSP	*Journal for the Study of the Pseudepigrapha*
JSPSup	Journal for the Study of the Pseudepigrapha: Supplement Series
KomNT	Kommentar zum Neuen Testament
LCL	Loeb Classical Library
MTZ	*Münchener theologische Zeitschrift*
NCB	New Century Bible
Neot	*Neotestamentica*
NovT	*Novum Testamentum*
NovTSup	Novum Testamentum Supplements
NRTh	*La nouvelle revue théologique*
NTAbh	Neutestamentliche Abhandlungen
NTD	Das Neue Testament Deutsch
NTL	New Testament Library
NTOA	Novum Testamentum et Orbis Antiquus
NTS	*New Testament Studies*
OBO	Orbis biblicus et orientalis
OTP	*Old Testament Pseudepigrapha*
OTS	Old Testament Studies
OTS	*Oudtestamentische Studien*
RB	*Revue biblique*
RevQ	*Revue de Qumran*
RGG	*Religion in Geschichte und Gegenwart*
SANT	Studien zum Alten und Neuen Testaments
SBEC	Studies in the Bible and Early Christianity
SBLDS	Society of Biblical Literature Dissertation Series
SBLEJL	Society of Biblical Literature Early Judaism and Its Literature
SBLMS	Society of Biblical Literature Monograph Series
SBLSCS	Society of Biblical Literature Septuagint and Cognate Studies
SBT	Studies in Biblical Theology
ScEs	*Science et esprit*
SDSSRL	Studies in the Dead Sea Scrolls and Related Literature
SEÅ	*Svensk exegetisk årsbok*
SEAJT	*South East Asia Journal of Theology*
Sem	*Semitica*
SNTSMS	Society for New Testament Studies Monograph Series

SSN	Studia semitica neerlandica
SSS	Semitic Study Series
ST	*Studia theologica*
STDJ	Studies on the Texts of the Desert of Judah
SUNT	Studien zur Umwelt des Neuen Testaments
TDNT	*Theological Dictionary of the New Testament*
ThViat	*Theologia viatorum*
TS	Texts and Studies
TS	*Theological Studies*
TSAJ	Texte und Studien zum antiken Judentum
TUGAL	Texte und Untersuchungen zur Geschichte der altchristlichen Literatur
TZ	*Theologische Zeitschrift*
UNT	Untersuchungen zum Neuen Testament
VT	*Vetus Testamentum*
VTSup	Supplements to Vetus Testamentum
WBC	World Biblical Commentary
WMANT	Wissenschaftliche Monographien zum Alten und Neuen Testament
WUNT	Wissenschaftliche Untersuchungen zum Neuen Testament
YJS	Yale Judaica Series
ZAW	*Zeitschrift für die alttestamentliche Wissenschaft*
ZDMG	*Zeitschrift der Deutschen Morgenländischen Gesellschaft*
ZNW	*Zeitschrift für die neutestamentliche Wissenschaft und die Kunde der älteren Kirche*
ZTK	*Zeitschrift für Theologie und Kirche*

Abbreviations for biblical books and other primary sources follow the guidelines set forth in *The SBL Handbook of Style: For Ancient Near Eastern, Biblical, and Early Christian Studies*, ed. P. H. Alexander *et al.* (Peabody, Mass.: Hendrickson Publishers, 1999).

Chapter 1

Introduction

1.1 The Problem

To those even slightly familiar with Jewish messianic expectations, the title of this book might sound odd. It is a well-known axiom accepted by every reputable scholar that the Messiah was neither expected to do miracles nor to be a healer. The subtitle of my project, however, immediately clarifies that I am dealing with the Gospel of Matthew and the portrayal of Jesus as the Son of David presented there. It does not require much research to see that the Matthean Jesus is addressed with the messianic title "Son of David" almost exclusively within the context of his healing activity. Thus the title of my project expresses a unique phenomenon that characterizes Matthew's Gospel only. To say this, however, does not explain anything. It merely circumscribes a tangible fact, but it does not make it any more intelligible for the modern reader.

My initial interest in this topic was born out of the conviction that this strange link between the Davidic Messiah and the activity of healing made sense for Matthew and the audience for which he wrote. This is not something that can be directly proven but represents an assumption based on what we know about the first-century world in general and Matthew's Gospel in particular. There was more logic in the way early Jewish and Christian interpreters presented certain phenomena than we today are ready to give them credit for. They did not arbitrarily associate unrelated concepts. Jewish and Christian interpretative traditions were primarily intellectual activities, which presupposed a recognizable shared hermeneutical framework. Moreover, the Gospel of Matthew is well known for its high organization of traditional material, redaction, and profound theology. If so, it is to be expected that behind the portrayal of Jesus as the healing Messiah lies a discoverable purpose and method. All of this led me to believe that it is worth trying to find a link between two disparate traditions, messianic expectations and attitudes towards healing, which inform the Matthean narrative about the Son of David who heals the sick.

1.2 A Review of Previous Research

There is no doubt that Matthew takes pains to present Jesus as the Son of David who acts as a healer. Apart from the infancy narrative in Matt 1 and the dialogue about Davidic sonship in Matt 22:41–46, all other occurrences of the title "Son of David" appear almost exclusively in the healing contexts (the only exception is Matt 21:1–11). Most of them are individual healings (9:27–31; 12:22–24; 15:21–28; 20:29–34), with the climax being the healing of the blind and the lame in the Temple (21:14–17), a scene that is described only in Matthew. In spite of this phenomenon, however, no comprehensive treatment of Matthew's combination of the "Son of David" title and Jesus' healing ministry has been offered so far.

In some important works on Matthew's portrayal of Jesus as the Son of David, the link between the title "Son of David" and Jesus' healings has not been treated at all. Thus, in his article "Purpose and Pattern in Matthew's Use of the Title 'Son of David',"[1] James M. Gibbs argued that Matthew used this title with the purpose of delineating a development in the crowd's recognition of Jesus as the royal, messianic Son of David. In his view, this development begins in chapter 9 and culminates in chapter 21. The crowd would have come to accept Jesus completely if the perverse Pharisees and other Jewish leaders had not influenced them. The title itself, as understood by Matthew, is inadequate in comparison with the recognition of Jesus as the Son of God.

In an article published a few years later,[2] Alfred Suhl disagreed with Gibbs' proposal and argued that the title "Son of David" is an inadequate response to Jesus by the crowd. The presence of the definite article in the crowd's use of the title indicates that they use it falsely, in contrast to the devoted individuals who by this title claim his help on the basis of his sending.

According to Brian M. Nolan's study of Matthew's Christology in the first two chapters of his Gospel,[3] the first-century Davidic mystique determined Matthew's presentation of Jesus. The private persona of David, the prophet-king who became a model of piety and fidelity in first-century Judaism, gave sensitivity and language to the title "Son of David," which enabled it to assimilate the motif of the Son of God. In Nolan's view, the royal, Davidic motifs pervade the Matthean narrative from the beginning to the end and integrate all other titles and roles of Jesus into a unified whole.

---

[1] J. M. Gibbs, "Purpose and Pattern in Matthew's Use of the Title 'Son of David,'" *NTS* 10 (1963/64): 446–464.

[2] A. Suhl, "Der Davidssohn in Matthäus-Evangelium," *ZNW* 59 (1968): 57–81.

[3] B. M. Nolan, *The Royal Son of God,* OBO 23 (Göttingen: Vandenhoeck & Ruprecht, 1979).

Jack D. Kingsbury developed his view on the title "Son of David" in Matthew in his book *Matthew: Structure, Christology, Kingdom*[4] and his subsequent article "The Title 'Son of David' in Matthew's Gospel."[5] In his view, Matthew used this title theologically (to affirm that Jesus is the expected Jewish Messiah) and apologetically (to emphasize the guilt of Israel). He contrasts the use of this title on the lips of no-accounts in Jewish society with Israel's blindness. However, despite Kingsbury's affirmation that Matthew uses this title positively, he argued that its scope is limited and its significance subordinated to Jesus' divine sonship. Furthermore, he believed that the Matthean community has "outgrown" this title, because "Son of David no longer adequately captures these Christians' understanding of the person of Jesus."[6]

In an article published several years later,[7] William R. G. Loader further elaborated Kingsbury's idea concerning Israel's guilt in rejecting Jesus. In his view, the title "Son of David" is developed primarily within the motives that are concerned with Israel's unbelief. Loader's conclusion is that this title "is the appropriate term of response to the Messiah of Israel rather than a term designated to allude to the healing function of Jesus."[8]

To this series of short studies on the Son of David in Matthew, which were not primarily interested in the relationship between this title and Jesus' healing ministry, we can add two articles by Donald J. Verseput. In "The Role and Meaning of the 'Son of God' Title in Matthew's Gospel,"[9] he stressed the importance of the title "Son of David" for Matthew. In his view, the evangelist shows that Jesus is indeed the Messiah who was hoped for by Israel and defends this Davidic claim against all those who want to deny it. After investigating Jesus' divine sonship, Verseput reconsidered Jesus' Davidic messiahship, bringing the two into an "inextricable relation," which offers, in his view, "the ultimate explanation of the 'unmessianic' messianic mission" of Jesus.[10] In his SBL 1995 paper,[11] Verseput argued that the presentation of the Davidic Messiah in Matthew's Gospel was not detached from its Jewish

---

[4]J. D. Kingsbury, *Matthew: Structure, Christology, Kingdom* (Philadelphia: Fortress Press, 1975).

[5]J. D. Kingsbury, "The Title 'Son of David' in Matthew's Gospel," *JBL* 95 (1976): 591–602.

[6]Ibid., 592.

[7]W. R. G. Loader, "Son of David, Blindness, Possession, and Duality in Matthew," *CBQ* 44 (1982): 570–585.

[8]Ibid., 585.

[9]D. J. Verseput, "The Role and Meaning of the 'Son of God' Title in Matthew's Gospel," *NTS* 33 (1987): 532–556.

[10]Ibid., 544.

[11]D. J. Verseput, "Davidic Messiah and Matthew's Jewish Christianity," in *SBL 1995 Seminar Papers*, ed. E. Lovering, Jr., SBL Seminar Papers Series 34 (Atlanta: Scholars Press, 1995), 102–116.

origins. Rather, it incorporates a sufficient number of traditional themes that
were typical for Matthew's Jewish compatriots. They were, in Verseput's
view, related to the hope that God's people will be "restored from the
affliction of divine retribution imposed since the time of the exile."[12]

The most important *traditionsgeschichtliche* study of Davidic messiahship
in the New Testament in general, and the Gospel of Matthew in particular, can
be found in Christoph Burger's dissertation *Jesus als Davidssohn*.[13] Burger
was the first to call attention to the Matthean connection of the title "Son of
David" and Jesus' healings. According to his reconstruction, Matthew's
Gospel shows an independent development of this title. This happened
because Mark before Matthew added the title "Son of David" to the episode
about the healing of the blind Bartimaeus, just before Jesus' entry into
Jerusalem. Mark did it because he wanted to prepare his readers for the
acclamation of Jesus as the Davidic Messiah by the crowd, and not because he
made a conscious link between the title and the act of healing. Matthew, in
turn, found this connection already established in his *Vorlage* and developed it
further with the purpose of expressing the healing function of the Son of
David. In Burger's view, the Matthean presentation of Jesus as the Son of
David represents a distinctive Christian development that is far removed from
any early Jewish concept of the Davidic Messiah.

In the early 1970s, several authors explored a possible link between the
Matthean Son of David and the traditions about Solomon who acts as an
exorcist found in certain fragments of the Dead Sea Scrolls Psalms, Pseudo-
Philo, Josephus, the *Testament of Solomon*, and the Aramaic incantation
bowls.[14] The most recent contribution to this discussion is the essay "Solomon
and Jesus: The Son of David in Ante-Markan Traditions (Mark 10:47)" by
James H. Charlesworth,[15] who argued that the title "Son of David" in Mark is
not messianic. Thus, when the blind Bartimaeus addressed Jesus as the Son of

---

[12]Ibid., 115.

[13]C. Burger, *Jesus als Davidssohn: Eine traditionsgeschichtliche Untersuchung*, FRLANT
98 (Göttingen: Vandenhoeck & Ruprecht, 1970).

[14]L. R. Fisher, "Can This Be the Son of David?" in *Jesus and the Historian*, ed. F. T.
Trotter, FS E. C. Colwell (Philadelphia: Westminster, 1968), 82–97; E. Lövestam, "Jésus Fils
de David chez les Synoptiques," *ST* 28 (1974): 97–109 [Swedish original: "David-son-
kristologin hos synoptikerna," *SEÅ* 15 (1972): 198–210]; K. Berger, "Die königlichen
Messiastraditionen des Neuen Testaments," *NTS* 20 (1973/74): 1–44; D. C. Duling, "Solomon,
Exorcism, and the Son of David," *HTR* 68 (1975): 235–252; idem, "The Therapeutic Son of
David: An Element in Matthew's Christological Apologetic," *NTS* 24 (1977–78): 392–410.

[15]J. H. Charlesworth, "Solomon and Jesus: The Son of David in Ante-Markan Traditions
(Mark 10:47)," in *Biblical and Humane*, ed. L. B. Elder, D. L. Barr, and E. S. Malbon, FS J.
F. Priest (Atlanta: Scholars Press, 1996), 125–151.

David, he "was certainly thinking of Jesus as a healer, after the order of Solomon."[16]

In view of the brevity of various treatments of the Matthean link between the Son of David and the miracles of healing, it is not surprising that this topic did not receive sufficient attention so far. Apart from the interest in the connection with the traditions about Solomon who acts as an exorcist, Jewish roots of Matthew's portrayal of Jesus as the Son of David have been largely neglected. The view that Matthew's characterization of the Son of David as a healing Messiah is a distinctive Christian development that is far removed from any early Jewish concept of the Davidic Messiah cannot be justified in view of Matthew's obvious tendency to demonstrate that the whole of Jesus' life represents the fulfillment of Scriptures. Similarly to other early Christian exegetes, Matthew had to solve the problem of how to present Jesus' life and death in light of the conviction that he is indeed the expected Davidic Messiah.

1.3 The Thesis

The concluding statement of the previous paragraph needs to be explicated with greater precision because it contains the working hypothesis concerning the development of early Christology adopted in this study. Following the original proposal of Nils A. Dahl,[17] endorsed and further developed by Donald Juel,[18] I presume that the confession of Jesus as the Messiah is the presupposition of New Testament Christology, not its content. Several studies have convincingly demonstrated that within a relatively short period after Jesus' resurrection, his followers expressed his significance by confessing him as χριστός.[19] It is outside of the scope of this study to examine the origins of

---

[16]Ibid., 147.

[17]N. A. Dahl, *The Crucified Messiah and Other Essays* (Minneapolis: Augsburg, 1974).

[18]D. Juel, *Messianic Exegesis: Christological Interpretation of the Old Testament in Early Christianity* (Philadelphia: Fortress Press, 1992).

[19]N. A. Dahl (*The Crucified Messiah*, 25) notes that in the Greek-speaking Christianity "within a few years of the crucifixion, the name Christ as applied to Jesus must have been firmly established. This presupposes that Jesus was already designated 'the Messiah' and 'Jesus the Messiah' in the Aramaic-speaking regions. To this extent the Christology of the primitive community from the very first must have been a Messiah-Christology." M. Hengel ("Jesus, the Messiah of Israel," in *Studies in Early Christology* [Edinburgh: T&T Clark, 1995], 10) also claims that "the striking pre-eminence of the Christ name (or title) in the letters, that is, outside the gospels, in which the linguistic usage of the earthly Jesus has left more trace than is commonly recognized, can only be explained if from the beginning – indeed, especially *at the beginning* [emphasis his] – it was fundamental for the post-Easter community." Similarly, D. Juel (*Messianic Exegesis*, 2) contends that "what stands at the beginning of that [Christian] reflection and provides a focus and a direction for scriptural exegesis is the confession of Jesus as Messiah."

this startling declaration, given the fact there is no evidence that any version of early Jewish messianic hopes contained a notion of a suffering Messiah or a human being who would achieve messianic status through resurrection.[20] Regardless of whether we can discover the basis of this declaration in Jesus' own self-understanding or in other versions of Jewish messianic expectations triggered by Jesus' words and deeds,[21] all four Gospels agree that he was crucified as the messianic pretender, i.e. as the "King of the Jews."[22] The early Christian confession of Jesus' messiahship cannot be separated from this historical background.

Equally important for our understanding of the development of early Christology is the traditional material found in 1 Cor 15:3–4, which declares that Christ (χριστός)[23] died and was raised "according to the Scriptures" (κατὰ τὰς γραφάς). This pre-Pauline formula demonstrates that Jesus' messiahship was from the very beginning inseparable from a dialogue with Israel's Scripture. The crucified Messiah, a stumbling block to the Jews and foolishness to the Gentiles (1 Cor 1:23), had to be explained and vindicated in light of scriptural evidence. The order of these two processes, however, should not be reversed. Scriptural study cannot explain the origin of the confession of Jesus' messiahship. Rather, to use Dahl's formulation, "the messiahship of the crucified Jesus is . . . the presupposition that lies at the root of all the scriptural evidence *de Christo*."[24] Consequently, I presume that reflecting upon and deepening one's faith, rather than wining new converts, was the primary purpose of this exegetical activity.[25]

Such an endeavor enabled early Christian interpreters to further explicate Jesus' significance with the help of other titles and imageries, which went far beyond the initial messianic conceptions. Thus the confession of Jesus' messiahship has not only chronological but also exegetical and logical priority. One of the tasks of this study is to demonstrate the likelihood of this hypothesis. By the time the Gospel of Matthew was written, several decades of

---

[20]Cf. Dahl, *The Crucified Messiah*, 25; Juel, *Messianic Exegesis*, 13; Hengel, "Jesus, the Messiah of Israel," 12.

[21]M. Hengel ("Jesus, the Messiah of Israel," 14) rightly insists that "if Jesus never possessed a messianic claim of divine mission, rather sternly rejected every third-hand question in this regard, if he neither spoke of the coming, or present 'Son of Man', nor was executed as a messianic pretender and alleged king of the Jews – as is maintained with astonishing certainty by radical criticism unencumbered by historical arguments – then the emergence of christology, indeed, the entire early history of primitive Christianity, is completely baffling, nay, incomprehensible."

[22]For a defense of the historicity of this charge, see Dahl, *The Crucified Messiah*, 23–24, and Hengel, "Jesus, the Messiah of Israel," 41–58.

[23]The term χριστός, which here appears without a definite article, probably functions as a name, but its messianic connotations are unmistakable; cf. Juel, *Messianic Exegesis*, 8–9.

[24]Dahl, *The Crucified Messiah*, 28.

[25]Cf. Juel, *Messianic Exegesis*, 1–29.

intensive exegetical efforts had passed. The evangelist himself applies various titles to Jesus, which stand in a very complex relationship. Yet, this is the first Christian writing, which tries to present Jesus' healings as the messianic deeds performed in his capacity as the Davidic Messiah.

This study will try to demonstrate that despite the fact that none of the various messianic figures in Judaism were expected to perform healing miracles, Matthew's portrayal of Jesus as the Son of David is nevertheless firmly anchored in the messianic traditions of the Second Temple period. My main argument, however, is not that Jewish traditions contain certain antecedents of a healing Messiah, but rather that they offered to early Christian communities a sufficient number of interpretative possibilities for constructing such a figure. I will try to show that Matthew fulfilled this task by quoting or alluding to the scriptural passages which had the potential for a messianic interpretation within the parameters found in various Jewish messianic texts preceding or contemporary with Matthew's Gospel. Although I am fully aware that the history of ideas cannot offer a complete explanation of the origins of Matthew's Christology, I am convinced that an examination of Matthew's employment of traditional imagery drawn from Scripture along the lines of early Jewish interpretations found in the post-biblical literature can offer a good starting point for an assessment of Matthew's presentation of Jesus as the healing Davidic Messiah.

One should be aware, however, that the terms "Messiah" and "messianic" possess a certain degree of ambiguity that remains even when the most rigorous scrutiny is applied. In the past, scholars had a tendency to read every eschatological text as "messianic," without regard to whether a savior figure that can be properly called "the Messiah" is mentioned.[26] However, there are end-time visions which do not include any eschatological deliverer at all, or if they do, such a figure can be a prophet, priest, king, or God himself. Moreover, even when the term משיח(ה) (Greek [ὁ] χριστός) appears, it does not have to refer to the future messianic deliverer. This word can be translated as "an anointed one" (without a definite article), "the Anointed One," "the Anointed One of" (if in construct), or "the Messiah." Generally, the latter should be reserved for an anointed eschatological redeemer who is actually called "the Messiah" in the original text. The application of this criterion, however, should not be mechanical. Pre-Christian documents are quite diverse and contain various designations for a future deliverer. Such a figure can still be regarded as "messianic" if we possess the evidence that the actual designation has been associated with the term "Messiah." The messianic redeemer is

---

[26]See the critique by M. de Jonge, "The Use of the Word 'Anointed' in the Time of Jesus," *NovT* 8 (1966): 132–133.

mentioned for the first time in post-biblical literature,[27] but his specific characteristics vary considerably from document to document.

The term "Christian" will be used in this study for the sake of convenience, even though it can be occasionally misleading and anachronistic. This designation is, I believe, broad enough to encompass various forms of the Palestinian Jesus Movement, from the first believers who claimed that Jesus of Nazareth is the Messiah to more institutionalized groups to which the Matthean community probably belongs.

1.4 Methodology

Because of my interest in the origins of Matthew's portrayal of Jesus as the Son of David, I will predominantly use a tradition-history approach. The main task of this method, as it has been developed by Gerhard von Rad, is to trace the history of a particular tradition and demonstrate how it has been adapted and reformulated in subsequent changing historical situations. The objective is to detect both the points of continuity and discontinuity in this process. My goal, however, is not only to trace the development of the traditions related to the Davidic Messiah, but also to explain them in light of the present state of research regarding Jewish scriptural interpretations and Christological interpretations of the Old Testament in early Christian communities.

On the other hand, my interest in the way Matthew portrays Jesus as the Davidic Messiah within his narrative requires the application of a narrative-critical approach as developed within literary theory. This method has proved to be useful in the analysis of Matthew's narrative.[28] However, in order to discover Matthew's *Tendenzen*, which characterize him not only as an author but also as an interpreter of the received tradition, I will also pay attention to

---

[27]Cf. A. S. van der Woude, "Messias," in *Biblisch-Historisches Handwörterbuch: Landeskunde, Geschichte, Religion, Kultur, Literatur*, ed. B. R. Reicke and L. Rost, vol. 2 (Göttingen: Vandenhoeck & Ruprechet, 1964), cols. 1197–1198; J. H. Charlesworth, "Messianology in the Biblical Pseudepigrapha," in *Qumran-Messianism: Studies on the Messianic Expectations in the Dead Sea Scrolls*, ed. J. H. Charlesworth, H. Lichtenberger, and G. S. Oegema (Tübingen: Mohr Siebeck, 1999), 21–23.

[28]The conventional literary categories can be found in S. Chatman, *Story and Discourse: Narrative Structure in Fiction and Film* (Ithaca/London: Cornell University Press, 1978); M. H. Abrams, *A Glossary of Literary Terms*, 6th ed. (Fort Worth: Harcourt Brace Jovanovich, 1993). Some major works on Matthew that apply narrative criticism are: R. A. Edwards, *Matthew's Story of Jesus* (Philadelphia: Fortress Press, 1985); J. D. Kingsbury, *Matthew as Story* (Philadelphia: Fortress Press, 1986); W. G. Thompson, *Matthew's Story: Good News for Uncertain Times* (New York: Paulist Press, 1989); D. B. Howell, *Matthew's Inclusive Story: A Study in the Narrative Rhetoric of the First Gospel*, JSNTSup 42 (Sheffield: JSOT Press, 1990).

his modifications and adaptation of the material which he had at his disposal.[29] Yet, in contrast to the traditional redaction-critical approach, I will disregard a great number of changes that could be ascribed to Matthew the redactor and mention only those that are relevant for the subject matter of this study.

Narrative criticism is based on the theoretical model of the narrative that differentiates between real author, implied author, real reader, and implied reader.[30] The real author is the historical author of the text.[31] The implied author is a theoretical construct of a "creative intellect at work in the narrative."[32] One real author can produce several literary works, each having a different image of the implied author.[33] When we read Matthew's Gospel, we meet only the implied author, whom we infer from the narrative. The nature of Matthew's Gospel, however, leads to the supposition that there is no reason to assume that the real author is different from the implied author. Even if on certain occasions Matthew might have been aware that he was creating fiction,[34] his story world contains a diachronical aspect intended to be read as a historical dimension of the story. It is therefore hard to imagine that under the presupposition that the sources available to him were the same, the real author of Matthew's Gospel would have produced another, different narrative of Jesus' life. This is the reason that the name Matthew will be used here to refer to the real, as well to the implied author, though this does not mean that on the theoretical level the distinction between them has been dissolved.

The real reader is any actual reader of the narrative. The implied reader is a literary construct, the reader "created by the text"[35] and as such presupposed by the text. The real reader is to be differentiated from the implied reader because the specific historical context in which s/he lives significantly impacts the reading process. Even the first readers/hearers of Matthew's Gospel should not be identified with the implied reader. Since, however, Matthew obviously had his fellow believers in mind when he was writing, we can assume that they come very close to the image of the implied reader. Consequently, the term "Matthew's reader" will be used here to designate both the implied reader and the real reader/hearer in Matthew's community, though the theoretical difference between them will not be dismissed.

---

[29]This study is based on the premises of the Two-Document hypothesis.

[30]The full diagram of this model can be found in Chatman, *Story and Discourse*, 267.

[31]The identity of the real author of Matthew's Gospel is irrelevant for the purpose of this study.

[32]R. A. Culpepper, *Anatomy of the Fourth Gospel: A Study in Literary Design*, New Testament Foundations and Facets (Philadelphia: Fortress Press, 1983), 16.

[33]Chatman, *Story and Discourse,* 148.

[34]Cf. U. Luz, "Fiktivität und Traditionstreue im Matthäusevangelium im Lichte griechischer Literatur," *ZNW* 84 (1993): 153–177.

[35]Culpepper, *Anatomy of the Fourth Gospel*, 205.

The book consists of three major chapters, each being defined through the structural categories of Matthew's narrative. Chapter 2 deals with the framework of the segment of the plotted story in which Jesus is addressed as the Son of David. Since this title does not appear in the passion narrative, its last occurrence in Jesus' dispute with the Pharisees in the Temple marks the end of that part of the story in which Matthew applies this designation to Jesus. I will try to show that in the framing portions of this section Matthew wants to demonstrate that Jesus possesses the required prerequisites for a Davidic Messiah as they are defined in Nathan's promise to David in 2 Samuel 7. Chapter 3 will be focused on the content of the segment of Matthew's narrative in which various characters address him with the Davidic messianic title either in the expectation of a healing or on the basis of the healing that he has just performed. In search for an explanation of this phenomenon, I will explore Matthew's indebtedness to the Solomonic traditions, as well as the traditions about the eschatological prophet like Moses. At the end of this chapter, I will create the basis for the approach that I will adopt in chapter 4, which will examine the scriptural basis of Matthew's portrayal of the Davidic Messiah who heals the sick. The results of the entire investigation will be summarized in the final summary of conclusions.

Chapter 2

Jesus and Davidic Messianism

2.1 Introduction

The designation "Son of David" appears already in the first verse of Matthew's Gospel as part of the introductory phrase βίβλος γενέσεως Ἰησοῦ Χριστοῦ υἱοῦ Δαυὶδ υἱοῦ Ἀβραάμ, followed by Jesus' genealogy (Matt 1:2–17) and its "enlarged footnote"[1] (Matt 1:18–25). The fact that Matthew recounts the genealogy before the narrative proper and not at some later point of the story, as for example Luke, testifies to its importance for the narrative that follows. Not surprisingly, the genealogy is often regarded as the key to Matthew's entire Gospel.[2] Equally significant is the fact that Jesus' dispute with the Pharisees about the origin of the Messiah (Matt 22:41–46) concludes Matthew's account of the conflict between Jesus and the Jewish leaders, which was so bitter and deep that it eventually led him to the cross.

In this chapter, I intend to show that Matt 1:1–25 and 22:41–46, which create the framework of the segment of Matthew's narrative in which Jesus is called the Son of David, serve to establish Jesus' messianic prerequisites by demonstrating that both his ancestry and activity fulfill three major elements of God's promise to David in 2 Samuel 7: (a) that he is a royal figure of the Davidic line, (b) that he stands in a father-son relationship with God, and (c) that he grants the permanence of the Davidic dynasty. This task will be accomplished through several interdependent stages. After reviewing major biblical, post-biblical, and early Christian texts which are related to God's promises to David in 2 Samuel 7, I intend to demonstrate that, on the one hand, Matt 1:1–25 and 22:41–46 establish Jesus' royal Davidic messianic

---

[1] This phrase comes from K. Stendahl, "Quis et Unde? An Analysis of Mt. 1–2," in *Judentum, Urchristentum, Kirche*, ed. W. Eltester, FS J. Jeremias, BZNW 26 (Berlin: Alfred Töpelmann, 1960), 102.

[2] Cf. D. E. Nineham, "The Genealogy in St. Matthew's Gospel and Its Significance for the Study of the Gospels," *BJRL* 58 (1975–76): 433; H. C. Waetjen, "The Genealogy as the Key to the Gospel according to Matthew," *JBL* 95 (1976): 205–230; J. M. Jones, "Subverting the Textuality of Davidic Messianism: Matthew's Presentation of the Genealogy and the Davidic Title," *CBQ* 56 (1994): 256–272.

identity in terms of his origin, whereas on the other hand, Matt 1:21 establishes Jesus' royal Davidic messianic identity in terms of his activity.

2.2 God's Promises to David and the Davidic Messiah

The thesis that there was "a fairly consistent, compact, yet expanding and developing promise tradition which is founded on the promises to David," proposed by Dennis C. Duling in one of his articles,[3] is certainly easily defensible. His conclusion, however, that in numerous passages in the Hebrew Scripture and early Jewish literature, God's promises to David were referred or alluded to through a cumulative set of metaphors, but not through the title Son of David as such, needs further assessment. As much as the scarcity of the usage of the title "Son of David" might speak in favor of such a conclusion, this does not necessarily imply that the designation "Son of David" was not an outcome of the same promise tradition. In the following, the tradition centered around God's promises to David will be reviewed with the purpose of demonstrating that the hope for a Davidic Messiah called the Son of David was a direct result of the application of Davidic promises to the changed political situation under the Hasmonean rulers and the Roman occupation of Palestine.[4]

Nathan's oracle to David preserved in 2 Sam 7:12–16 undoubtedly represents the primary[5] biblical text for the early Jewish tradition of the Davidic ancestry of the Messiah.[6] According to Nathan's prophecy in 2 Sam

---

[3]D. C. Duling, "The Promises to David and Their Entrance Into Christianity – Nailing Down a Likely Hypothesis," *NTS* 20 (1973–74): 55.

[4]Cf. J. H. Charlesworth, "From Messianology to Christology: Problems and Prospects," in *The Messiah*, ed. J. H. Charlesworth (Minneapolis: Fortress, 1992), 24.

[5]The word "primary" is used here not to indicate chronological but only logical priority. For the present research, it is of no importance to determine the precise dating or interrelationship between various biblical passages. Early Jewish exegetes read these texts synchronically, as parts of sacred Scriptures available to them independently of their origin.

[6]J. J. Collins calls 2 Sam 7:12–16 "the Magna Carta of Davidic messianism" ("Jesus, Messianism and the Dead Sea Scrolls," in *Qumran-Messianism: Studies on the Messianic Expectations in the Dead Sea Scrolls*, ed. J. H. Charlesworth, H. Lichtenberger, and G. S. Oegema [Tübingen: Mohr Siebeck, 1998], 110). Cf. also the comprehensive treatment of the Davidic dynasty tradition in early Judaism by K. E. Pomykala, *The Davidic Dynasty Tradition in Early Judaism: Its History and Significance for Messianism*, SBLEJL (Atlanta: Scholars Press, 1995), esp. p. 13. It has been long recognized that the development of messianic expectations in early Judaism cannot be limited to the Hebrew word Messiah (משיח) because, as J. J. M. Roberts notes, "not one of the thirty-nine occurrences of משיח in the Hebrew canon refers to an expected figure of the future whose coming will coincide with the inauguration of an era of salvation" ("The Old Testament's Contribution to Messianic Expectations," in *The Messiah: Developments in Earliest Judaism and Christianity,* ed. J. H. Charlesworth [Minneapolis: Fortress, 1992], 39).

7:12–16, God's promise to David consists of three main elements:[7] (1) the Davidic descent ("and I will raise up your seed after you" [וַהֲקִימֹתִי אֶת־זַרְעֲךָ אַחֲרֶיךָ; καὶ ἀναστήσω τὸ σπέρμα σου μετὰ σέ LXX] – v. 12), (2) the father-son relationship with God ("I will be a father to him, and he shall be a son to me" [אֲנִי אֶהְיֶה־לּוֹ לְאָב וְהוּא יִהְיֶה־לִּי לְבֵן]; ἐγὼ ἔσομαι αὐτῷ εἰς πατέρα, καὶ αὐτὸς ἔσται μοι εἰς υἱόν LXX] – v. 14), and (3) the perpetuity of Davidic dynasty ("Your house and your kingdom shall be made sure forever" [וְנֶאֱמַן בֵּיתְךָ וּמַמְלַכְתְּךָ עַד־עוֹלָם; καὶ πιστωθήσεται ὁ οἶκος αὐτοῦ καὶ ἡ βασιλεία αὐτοῦ ἕως αἰῶνος LXX] – v. 16).[8]

2.2.1 The Davidic Descent

2.2.1.1 Biblical Writings

The promise of a Davidic offspring is the element that has been most frequently repeated or alluded to in various references to the promises to David. Among them, especially prominent are various metaphors, such as the "lamp" (נר – 2 Sam 21:17; 1 Kgs 11:36; 15:4), "tribe"[9] (שבט – 1 Kgs 11:13, 32, 36), and the "horn" which God causes to branch out (אצמיח קרן – Ps 132:17, combined with the metaphor of the lamp, Ps 89:25; Ezek 29:21). The horn which branches out can be easily associated with plant and tree imagery, so that it is not surprising to find various "vegetative metaphors"[10] for the promised David's offspring, such as the "twig from the stump of Jesse" (חטר

---

[7]Duling also adds two subsidiary elements: (4) the 'house' = dynasty in v. 13a, and (5) David's temporary chastisement ("The Promises to David," 56). Since they do not play any significant role for the present research, they will not be explicitly treated in this study.

[8]In the Deuteronomistic history, king David is presented as the one who is elected by Yahweh to rule over Israel (cf. 2 Sam 6:21). David is chosen not for his own sake, however, but for the sake of Israel as a nation, or, to use the formulation of J. A. Fitzmyer, he has "corporate salvific significance for the history of Israel" ("The Son of David Tradition and Matthew 22,41–46 and Parallels," *Concilium* 20 [1967]: 78). Nathan's prophecy to David in 2 Sam 7:12–16 makes this point particularly obvious. David is promised an offspring who will establish the Davidic kingdom and rule forever. God's promise shows that Yahweh's favor is not limited to David, but extends to his descendant who will come after him and who will bring the task which David started to its fulfillment. It is noteworthy that the term משיח does not appear in Nathan's words in 2 Sam 7:12–16, but in the introduction (2 Sam 23:1) to David's "last words" in 2 Sam 23:2–7. As in the most cases where the term משיח appears in the Hebrew Scripture, it is a singular nominalized adjective in construct followed by the reference to the deity משיח אלהי יעקב. The promise to David is here interpreted in covenantal terminology: as an everlasting covenant made with his house (2 Sam 23:5). Historically, Nathan's prophecy had an important impact on the stability of the Davidic dynasty in the Southern Kingdom. J. Becker speaks about Nathan's prophecy as a legitimating document of the Davidic monarchy (*Messianic Expectation in the Old Testament*, trans. D. E. Green [Edingburgh: T.&T. Clark, 1980], 25–31).

[9]This term can be also translated as the "scepter"; cf. Balaam's oracle in Num 24:17.

[10]Duling, "The Promises to David," 58.

מגזע ישי) and "shoot out of his roots (נצר משרשיו) in Isa 11:1, and the "righteous branch" (צמח צדיק) for David in Jer 23:5, the latter being a noun from the same root as the verb צמח in Ps 132:17.

In contrast to these metaphors, which regularly allude to the tenacity of the promise, a certain number of references employ the same reproductive term "seed" (זרע; σπέρμα LXX) as 2 Sam 7:12, such as Ps 89:4, 30, 37 (Ps 88:5, 30, 37 LXX)[11] and Ps 18:51 (Ps 17:51 LXX). Their dominant characteristic is the descent itself. A similar function is performed by the references to the offspring "coming from your inward parts" (יצא ממעיך; ἐκ τῆς κοιλίας σου LXX) in 2 Sam 7:12, such as "the fruit from your womb" in Ps 132:11 (מפרי בטנך; ἐκ καρποῦ τῆς κοιλίας σου[12] – Ps 131:11 LXX), and "your/their sons" in Ps 132:12 (בניך / בניהם; οἱ υἱοὶ σου / οἱ υἱοὶ αὐτῶν – Ps 131:12 LXX).[13]

Later biblical texts further elaborate or modify the promise tradition. Thus, for example, in Isa 11:10 the "root" metaphor no longer designates the source of the shoot of David, as in Isa 11:1 (נצר משרשיו) but is transferred to the promised descendant of David (שרש ישי).[14] The "branch" metaphor from Jer 23:5 reappears in Zech 6:12 in the reference to a man whose name is "Branch" (איש צמח שמו)[15] who will "branch out" (יצמח) and build the temple of the Lord. Similarly, Jer 33:14–26 interprets God's promises to David in a strongly futuristic sense with the help of the "branch" metaphor that has been slightly modified: the "righteous branch" (צמח צדיק) from Jer 23:5 becomes in Jer 33:14 the "branch of righteousness" (צמח צדקה) which God will cause to "branch out" (אצמיח). In the same context, in Jer 33:22 we find a reference to the "seed" of David (זרע דוד), while Jer 33:21 uses the term "son" (בן), both of which allude to the actual Davidic descent of a royal figure.

---

[11]For the cultic affinities and synoptic relationships of Psalm 89 to 2 Samuel 7, see J. L. McKenzie, "The Dynastic Oracle: II Samuel 7," *TS* 8 (1947): 201–202. For a pre-exilic dating of this psalm, see F. M. Cross, *Canaanite Myth and Hebrew Epic* (Cambridge, MA: Harvard University Press, 1973), 260; S. Mowinckel, *The Psalms in Israel's Worship*, vol. 1 (Nashville: Abingdon, 1962), 70; J. L. McKenzie, "Royal Messianism," *CBQ* 19 (1957): 27–31; N. Sarna, "Psalm 89: A Study in Inner Biblical Exegesis," in *Biblical and Other Studies*, ed. A. Altmann (Cambridge: Harvard University Press, 1963), 29–46. The question of the historical relationship between 2 Samuel 7 and Psalm 89 (i.e. which text preserves the oldest form of the promise) is not essential for this study. By the first century, both versions were available in the textual form and were at the disposal of early Jewish and Christian interpreters.

[12]The LXX translates both Hebrew words, מעה and בטן with the same Greek word κοιλία, which makes the connection between Ps 131:11 and 2 Sam 7:12 more explicit.

[13]Duling ("The Promises to David," 59) ascribes Ps 132:11–12 to the same category as the references which do possess the actual word "seed," but fails to notice that the language here is that of sonship.

[14]Cf. Duling, "The Promises to David," 60. The "root" metaphor is also applied to the servant in Isa 53:2.

[15]The LXX translates צמח in Jer 23:5 and Zech 3:8, 6:12 with the noun ἀνατολή. This could be the result of the use of the verb ἀνατέλλω for translating צמח in Zech 6:12, which also appears (combined with the "star") in Num 24:17 and (with the "horn") in Ps 132:17.

The Book of Chronicles contains a further development of the Davidic tradition. David was idealized, and his reign schematized. He was described not as he was, but as he should have been. The modification of Nathan's promise is also significant. While 2 Sam 7:16 indicates that the word "your offspring" (זרעך) used in 2 Sam 7:12 has a collective meaning, in 1 Chr 17:11 the word offspring has been interpreted as "one of your sons" (מבניך).[16]

2.2.1.2 Early Jewish Writings

In the post-biblical literature, God's promises to David belong to prominent themes of theological reflection, especially in the documents composed after the occupation of Palestine by the Romans. Chapter 17 of *Psalms of Solomon*, written most probably after Pompeus' conquest of Jerusalem in 63 B.C.E.,[17] contains a prayer for a future messianic deliverer called the "Son of David." This is both the only pre-Christian Jewish source and the earliest Jewish document that applies the titles "Son of David"[18] and χριστός as a *terminus technicus*, i.e. without a modifier, to the future deliverer of Israel – the Messiah.[19] This work can be understood as a direct Jewish reaction to the disappointment with the Hasmonean rulers, the Roman conquest, and the hellenizing policy of the Herods.

Psalms of Solomon explicitly link the hope for the Davidic Messiah to God's promise to David (*Pss. Sol.* 17:4). The psalmist reminds God of that fact because the promise has not yet been fulfilled and, in hope and expectation that this will be done in the future, continues with the prayer to

---

[16]Cf. also the use of the third person singular personal pronoun in 1 Chr 17:14 which interprets 2 Sam 7:16. This difference between the collective and individual sense is particularly emphasized by Fitzmyer ("The Son of David Tradition," 81).

[17]The entire composition might be dated sometime between 80–40 B.C.E.; cf. M. de Jonge, "The Psalms of Solomon," in *Outside the Old Testament,* ed. M. de Jonge, CCWJCW 4 (Cambridge: Cambridge University Press, 1985), 161; R. B. Wright, "Psalms of Solomon," in *The Old Testament Pseudepigrapha*, ed. J. H. Charlesworth, vol. 2 (Garden City, NY: Doubleday, 1985), 641.

[18]Rabbinic literature uses the title "Son of David" much more frequently. Davidic royal tradition is particularly prominent in Talmud. Thus, e.g., *b. Sanh.* 97b–99a presents the discussion of the rabbis concerning the conditions of the coming of the Son of David, the time when he will come, the names which he will have, and the length of his rule. Despite not knowing how early the rabbinic tradition actually is, it is at any rate a witness to the fact that the expectation of the Son of David was a legitimate continuation of the pre-Christian Jewish Davidic tradition. This in turn means that, despite the fact that apart from the Psalms of Solomon the title "Son of David" does not appear in any other pre-Christian document, it would be incorrect to presuppose that its occurrence in *Pss. Sol.* 17:21 is a Christian interpolation, because, as R. H. Fuller emphasizes, "it is hardly likely that the rabbis would have adopted it after it had become current in the Christian Church" (*The Foundations of New Testament Christology* [New York: Scribner's Sons, 1965], 33).

[19]*Pss. Sol.* 17 and 18 are usually regarded as the *locus classicus* of a pre-Christian expectation of the messianic figure called the "Son of David."

God to raise the promised Davidic king, the Son of David (*Pss. Sol.* 17:21). The connection between *Pss. Sol.* 17:4, 21 and 2 Samuel 7 is also linguistically strengthened: τὸ σπέρμα αὐτοῦ in *Pss. Sol.* 17:4 echoes τὸ σπέρμα σου in 2 Sam 7:14 (LXX); εἰς τὸν αἰῶνα in *Pss. Sol.* 17:4 echoes the same phrase found in 2 Sam 7:13, 16 (LXX); βασίλειον αὐτοῦ (*Pss. Sol.* 17:4) stands for ἡ βασιλεία αὐτοῦ in 2 Sam 7:12, 16 (LXX); and ἀνίστημι in *Pss. Sol.* 17:21 also appears in 2 Sam 7:12 (LXX). This clearly demonstrates that from the very beginning, the hope for the Davidic Messiah was directly linked to God's promise to David in 2 Sam 7:12–16. Even though in all likelihood the designation υἱὸς Δαυίδ in *Pss. Sol.* 17:21 has a titular force, its primary function is to designate David's promised descendant, his seed (τὸ σπέρμα αὐτοῦ – 17:4). There is therefore no reason to regard this document as an exception in the development of the promise tradition.[20] *Pss. Sol.* 17 associates the term "seed" from 2 Sam 7:12 with the designation "Son of David." Although the latter does not appear in this form in any text prior to the *Psalms of Solomon*, the concept of the "son" as a reference to David's offspring can be found already in Ps 132:12 and Jer 33:21.[21]

Additional confirmation for the thesis that the Davidic promises have been incorporated into the early Jewish messianic texts can be found in the Dead Sea Scrolls. Column 5 of 4Q252 (4QCommGen A),[22] a document that can be paleographically dated to the second half of the first century B.C.E.,[23] contains an extended reference to God's covenant with David.[24] It begins with a quotation of Gen 49:10a (line 1) and continues in line 2 with the quotation (with minor modifications) of Jer 33:17b, which says that "[there will not] be cut off one sitting (on) the throne for David" (לדויד כסא יושב יכרת]לוא י[). In lines 3–4, after the *vacat*, the text mentions "the righteous Messiah" (משיח הצדק) who is identified as "the Branch of David" (דויד צמח). The explanation

---

[20]In Duling' view, *Pss. Sol.* 17 and 18 represent a certain deviation from the non-titular, metaphorical evolution of the promise tradition ("The Promises to David," 68–69).

[21]It is therefore unlikely that the designation "Son of David" represents a Greek translation of an original metaphor such as Shoot of David, as Duling proposes (ibid., 69).

[22]The text of this column is supplied by fragment 6, which also contains the beginning of column 6; cf. *The Dead Sea Scrolls: Hebrew, Aramaic, and Greek Texts with English Translations*, ed. J. H. Charlesworth, vol. 6B: *Pesharim, Other Commentaries, and Related Documents* (Tübingen: J. C. B. Mohr [Paul Siebeck], 2002), 216–219.

[23]Cf. J. L. Trafton, introduction to "*Commentary on Genesis A* (4Q252 = 4QPBless)," in *The Dead Sea Scrolls: Hebrew, Aramaic, and Greek Texts with English Translations*, ed. J. H. Charlesworth, vol. 6B, 204.

[24]The messianic character of this column prompted J. M. Allegro to publish it already in 1956 under the name "4QPatriarchal Blessings"; see J. M. Allegro, "Further Messianic References in the Qumran Literature," *JBL* 75 (1956): 174–175. For the official publication of the whole document see G. J. Brooke, "4QCommentary on Genesis A," in *Qumran Cave 4*, vol. 18: *Parabiblical Texts*, part 3, ed. VanderKam, DJD 22 (Oxford: Clarendon Press, 1997), 185–207.

that follows in line 4, which recounts God's promise to David in 2 Sam 7:12–16, clarifies that the "Branch of David" is in fact David's "seed" (זרעו) to whom "has been given the covenant of the kingdom (over) his people for everlasting generations." The text thus creates a chain of multiple identifications: "the righteous Messiah" = "the Branch of David" = "David's seed." The significance of 4Q252 for the study of Jewish messianism lies in the fact that it contains, together with the *Psalms of Solomon,* the earliest known evidence for an explicit application of the term משיח to the expected Davidic king.[25]

A reference to the Davidic promise can be also found in 4Q174 (4QFlor), a document which can be paleographically dated to the first century B.C.E.[26] Fragments 1–2 and 21 1.1–13 contain a midrash on 2 Sam 7:10–14, whereas fragments 1–3 and 21 1.14–2.6 preserve a midrash on Pss 1–2.[27] The term David's "seed" (זרע) appears in the actual quotation of 2 Sam 7:12b (והקימותי את זרעכה אחריכה [frgs. 1–2 and 21 1.10]),[28] but in the commentary it is

---

[25]Cf. J. Zimmermann, *Messianishe Texte aus Qumran: Königliche, priesterliche und prophetische Messiasvorstellungen in den Schriftfunden von Qumran,* WUNT II/104 (Tübingen: Mohr Siebeck, 1998), 124. In Zimmermann's view "diese Texte zeigen, dass die Bezeichnung des erwarteten Davididen als משיח im Judentum bereits vor 70 n. Chr. erfolgte" (ibid., 125).

[26]For a proposal that 4Q174 and 4Q177 belong to a single composition, see A. Steudel, *Der Midrasch zur Eschatologie aus der Qumrangemeinde (4QMidrEschat^{a.b}): Materielle Rekonstruktion, Textbestand, Gattung und traditionsgeschichtliche Einordnung des durch 4Q174 ("Florilegium") und 4Q177 ("Catena A") repräsentierten Werkes aus den Qumranfunden,* STDJ 13 (Leiden, New York, Köln: E. J. Brill, 1994). Steudel offers a new, more precise arrangement of individual fragments within this integrated document, which she calls an "eschatological midrash" (4QMidrEschat^{a.b}). In her arrangement, the extant text of 4Q174 (4QMidrEschat^a) is used for reconstructing columns 1–6, and the extant text of 4Q177 (4QMidrEschat^b) for reconstructing columns 8–12 of this hypothetical, originally 18-columns large scroll. Even though Steudel presents a compelling argument for a new rearrangement of fragments, the references in this study will, for the sake of convenience, follow the traditional layout of 4Q174 as presented in *The Dead Sea Scrolls: Hebrew, Aramaic, and Greek Texts with English Translations,* ed. J. H. Charlesworth, vol. 6B, 250–263.

[27]Cf. Y. Yadin, "A Midrash on 2 Sam. vii and Ps. i–ii (4Q Florilegium)," *IEJ* (1959): 95–98. In contrast to *pesharim,* which represent verse-by-verse commentaries on individual biblical books, 4Q174 is a thematic commentary on selected biblical texts gathered around a central idea. A distinction between *pesher continu* and *pesher thématique* was proposed by J. Carmignac, "Le document de Qumran sur Melkisédek," *RevQ* 7 (1969–71): 360–361. A. Steudel calls 4Q174 "ein thematischer Midrasch mit Parallelen zu den (frühen) Pescharim" (*DerMidrasch zur Eschatologie aus der Qumrangemeinde,* 191).

[28]The quotation of 2 Sam 7:12b is directly followed by a quotation of 2 Sam 7:13b–14a. Omitted is, among other things, a reference that David's offspring shall come forth from his body. This is most likely done in order to avoid any association with Solomon. The interpretation that follows clearly shows that this offspring is an eschatological figure who will appear "[in the] latter days" (ב[אחרית הימים] – line 12); cf. Zimmermann, *Messianishe Texte aus Qumran,* 111.

identified with the "Branch of David" (צמח דויד [frgs. 1–2 and 21 1.11]), who will appear in the latter days, and associated with the fallen "booth of David" (סוכת דויד [frgs. 1–2 and 21 1.12]) from Amos 9:11a.[29] Even though the actual term משיח does not appear in the text, its messianic character is unmistakable.

Both Qumran documents, 4Q252 and 4Q174, demonstrate not only the importance of God's promises to David for the rise of the messianic hope, but also the messianic significance of the "branch" metaphor taken from Jeremiah and Zechariah. Also, similar to Jer 33:14–26, both texts combine the metaphor that connotes the persistency of the promise with the metaphor that connotes the actual Davidic descent.

A few other writings roughly contemporaneous with the rise of Christianity also contain references to the Messiah of the Davidic lineage. Thus a prayer for the Messiah of the Davidic descent can be found in *The Eighteen Benedictions* or *Shemoneh Esreh*. The 15th Benediction of the Palestinian version contains the prayer for the restoration of the Davidic dynasty coupled with the petition for the rebuilding of Jerusalem.[30] Similarly, *4 Ezra*, an apocalyptic document composed by the end of the first century,[31] also contains a passage[32] which claims that the Messiah whom God has kept until the end of days will arise from the posterity of David (*4 Ezra* 12:31–32). He is called "the seed" (Syr: *zr'h*) of David" and identified as the Messiah (Lat: *unctus*; Syr: *mšyḥ'*).[33]

This does not mean that all early Jewish messianic references include the notion that the Messiah will be a Davidid, even less that the future deliverer

---

[29]The association between 2 Sam 7:12b and Amos 9:11a is established through a *gezerâ šawâ* technique – raising up (והקימותי) of David's offspring in line 10 is interpreted as raising up (והקימותי) of the booth of David that is fallen; cf. Zimmermann, *Messianische Texte aus Qumran*, 111.

[30]The Babylonian version divided this Benediction into two parts, thus creating altogether nineteen benedictions.

[31]Cf. M. E. Stone, *Fourth Ezra*, Hermeneia (Minneapolis: Fortress, 1990), 10; B. M. Metzger, "The Fourth Book of Ezra," in *The Old Testament Pseudepigrapha*, ed. J. H. Charlesworth, vol. 1 (Garden City, NY: Doubleday, 1985), 520.

[32]The Davidic descent of the Messiah is mentioned in the interpretation of the fifth vision (also called the "Eagle Vision") that begins in *4 Ezra* 11:1 and ends in 12:3.

[33]M. E. Stone ("The Question of the Messiah in 4 Ezra," in *Judaisms and Their Messiahs at the Turn of the Christian Era*, ed. J. Neusner, W. S. Green, and E. S. Freirichs [Cambridge: Cambridge University Press, 1987], 215) notes that messianic figure does not appear in the role of a king who reigns over people. He merely announces judgment and has a legal function only. For the messianic passages in *4 Ezra*, see idem, *Features of the Eschatology of IV Ezra*, HSS 35 (Atlanta: Scholars Press, 1989), 131–133. K. E. Pomykala (*The Davidic Dynasty*, 221) points out that *4 Ezra* 11–12 and *Pss. Sol.* 17 share many similarities, such as the judging function of the Messiah, restoration of Israel, the underlying influence of Isaiah 11, and the Davidic descent, even though in *4 Ezra* the latter is not a central feature as in *Pss. Sol.* 17.

expected by some groups had to be a messianic figure.[34] However, the hope for a royal Messiah of the Davidic lineage,[35] despite not being a standard form of Jewish messianic expectations, is, as Juel notes, "fairly consistent."[36] It has its basis in Nathan's oracle in 2 Samuel 7, which remains its constant reference point. It is therefore not surprising that the confession of Jesus as the Messiah who has been accused as a messianic pretender, crucified as the "King of the Jews," and as such vindicated by God, coupled with the never questioned affirmation that Jesus came from the Davidic family, almost naturally led into the royal Davidic framework for the understanding of Jesus' messiahship.

2.2.1.3 New Testament Writings

Some of the earliest New Testament confessions include the affirmation that Jesus was of the Davidic family. These formulations, as Duling has noted, regularly employ metaphorical language that is similar to the biblical and post-biblical allusions to God's promise to David.[37] Thus, the pre-Pauline confession formula in Rom 1:3–4 asserts that Jesus Christ was born[38] ἐκ σπέρματος Δαυίδ according to the flesh (κατὰ σάρκα) and designated the Son of God in power according to the spirit of holiness since the resurrection of the dead. The first of these two parallel clauses,[39] which is our interest at this point,[40] affirms Jesus' human descent from David, or, to use a well-known

---

[34] A good survey of various messianic and other eschatological expectations in Judaism can be found in J. J. Collins, *The Scepter and the Star: The Messiahs of the Dead Sea Scrolls and Other Ancient Literature*, ABRL (New York: Doubleday, 1995). For an informed discussion of Qumran messianism, see J. H. Charlesworth, H. Lichtenberger, and G. S. Oegema, eds., *Qumran-Messianism: Studies on the Messianic Expectations in the Dead Sea Scrolls* (Tübingen: Mohr Siebeck, 1998); Zimmermann, *Messianishe Texte aus Qumran*.

[35] The attribute "royal" should not be equated with the "Davidic." There were other royal messianic figures, such as the Messiah of Israel and the Prince of the Congregation in Qumran writings, the Messiah of Judah in the *Testaments of the Twelve Patriarchs*, and Simon bar Giora in Josephus, who were never explicitly related to the Davidic lineage. K. E. Pomykala points out that "messianism rooted in the davidic dynasty tradition . . . must be understood as one among several types of royal messianism" (*The Davidic Dynasty*, 264; for the entire discussion of the non-Davidic royal messianic figures, see pp. 231–264).

[36] Juel, *Messianic Exegesis*, 11.

[37] Duling, "The Promises to David," 70–77.

[38] Cf. R. H. Fuller, "The Conception/Birth of Jesus as a Christological Moment," *JSNT* 1 (1978): 38–40.

[39] The apparent *parallelismus membrorum*, which betrays the Semitic origin of this early Christian confession, in addition to non-Pauline vocabulary, indicates not only that this is traditional material, but also that it comes from the Jewish speaking Christian community; cf. P. Stuhlmacher, *Biblische Theologie des Neuen Testaments*, vol. 1 (Göttingen: Vandenhoeck & Ruprecht, 1992), 187.

[40] For a discussion of the second part of this confession, see section 2.2.2.3.

expression, his earthly existence in humiliation,[41] in contrast to his exalted state achieved at the resurrection.[42]

The phrase ἐκ σπέρματος Δαυίδ appears also in 2 Tim 2:8 in reference to Jesus Christ, and in John 7:42 in reference to the expected Messiah. Rom 15:12 quotes Isa 11:10, which speaks about the "root" of Jesse (ἡ ῥίζα τοῦ Ἰεσσαί) in a series of citations whose purpose is to demonstrate that the Gentiles should glorify God for his mercy. Also, according to Heb 7:14, it was a common knowledge that Jesus descended from Juda (ἐξ Ἰούδα). Jesus' Davidic ancestry is assumed in Peter's argument for his messiahship in Acts 2:29–36 and in Paul's speech in Acts 13:23.

Even though Rom 1:3–4 and 2 Tim 2:8 make a connection between Jesus' Davidic descent and his resurrection, it is highly questionable whether this represents a shift from the "coming forth" imagery to the "raising up" of the Davidic descendant.[43] The idea of "raising up" of the Davidic offspring, despite its apparent relatedness to the idea of "raising up" of Jesus from the dead, is usually transmitted with the help of the verbs קום / ἀνίστημι, while Jesus' resurrection is regularly referred to with ἐγείρω.[44] Moreover, Rom 1:3–4, Act 2:29–36, and Acts 13:32–37 clearly indicate that early Christian interpreters understood Jesus' resurrection as God's fulfillment of the promises to David either because it established his divine sonship or because it represented God's ultimate victory over corruption and decay, which secured the permanency of the dynasty.[45]

2.2.2 The Father-Son Relationship with God

2.2.2.1 Biblical Writings

In contrast to the promise of the Davidic descent, the promise of a father-son relationship between David's offspring and God declared in Nathan's oracle (2

---

[41]The participle γενομένου indicates that human existence as such is meant, rather than the actual birth, for which the verb γεννάω would have been more suitable; cf. J. D. G. Dunn, *Romans 1–8*, WBC 38A (Dallas: Word Books, 1988), 12. Since the phrase κατὰ σάρκα most likely belongs to the pre-Pauline material, it should not be interpreted within the framework of a typically Pauline opposition between σάρξ and πνεῦμα, i.e. as having a somewhat negative overtone, as Dunn proposes (ibid., 13). It is also inappropriate to understand the phrase τοῦ γενομένου ἐκ σπέρματος Δαυίδ as a reference to Jesus' human nature, in contrast to his divine nature, as C. E. B. Cranfield (*A Critical and Exegetical Commentary on the Epistle to the Romans*, vol. 1, ICC [Edinburgh: T.&T. Clark Ltd., 1975], 60) argues, because this represents an anachronistic use of categories; for a critique, see Dunn, *Romans 1–8*, 15.

[42]Cf. Stuhlmacher, *Biblische Theologie des Neuen Testament*, vol. 1, 187.

[43]Duling, "The Promises to David," 74.

[44]The proposal of H. E. Tödt (*The Son of Man in the Synoptic Tradition*, trans. D. M. Barton [Philadelphia: Westminster Press, 1965], 101–103) that ἀνίστημι might be the earliest Greek term for the resurrection of Jesus is only a conjecture.

[45]See E. Lövestam, *Son and Savior*, ConBNT 8 (Lund: C. W. K. Gleerup, 1961), 41–48, 81–83.

Sam 7:14) is infrequently mentioned in other biblical passages. In a close proximity to 2 Sam 7:14, Ps 89:27–28 speaks about the f 'her-son relationship between God and David's seed. The major difference is that, unlike 2 Sam 7:14 which contains only a divine promise that this relationship will be established, in the psalm God first expects human response based on the recognition of this relationship, and then makes a divine declaration that this will really take place. Thus, after the king makes a confession that God is his father (הוא יקראני אבי אתה אלי [Ps 89:27], αὐτὸς ἐπικαλέσεταί με πατήρ μου εἶ σύ θεός μου [Ps 88:27 LXX]), God responds by affirming that he will make him the firstborn (אף־אני בכור אתנהו; κἀγὼ πρωτότοκον θήσομαι αὐτόν [Ps 88:28 LXX]).

In the Book of Chronicles, Nathan's promise of the father-son relationship between David's offspring, interpreted here as one of his sons, and God is repeated *verbatim*. As in 2 Sam 7:14, so also in 1 Chr 17:13 God declares, "I will be a father to him, and he shall be a son to me" (אני אהיה־לו לאב והוא יהיה־לי לבן; ἐγὼ ἔσομαι αὐτῷ εἰς πατέρα καὶ αὐτὸς ἔσται μοι εἰς υἱόν [LXX]).

Finally, a reference to the father-son relationship between a king and God can be found in Psalm 2. The psalm speaks about the enthronement of a royal figure called God's "anointed" (משיחו, τοῦ χριστοῦ αὐτου [LXX] – Ps 2:2), who is installed at the position of God's son through an act of divine adoption. This act is completed through the divine recognition of the new status of the king (בני אתה, υἱός μου εἶ συ [LXX] – Ps 2:7a) and the act of divine begetting through which this has been accomplished (אני היום ילדתיך, ἐγὼ σήμερον γεγέννηκά σε [LXX] – Ps 2:7b). These words were probably said at the coronation of the king, thus making him God's representative among the people.[46] Since, however, Psalm 2 does not mention David's offspring as such, it cannot be directly linked to the tradition rooted in God's promises to David.[47]

2.2.2.2 Early Jewish Writings

We have seen that 2 Sam 7:12–16 played an important role in the development of royal Davidic messianism. A review of relevant texts shows that early

---

[46]Cf. R. E. Brown, *The Birth of the Messiah: A Commentary on the Infancy Narratives in Matthew and Luke* (Garden City, NY: Doubleday & Company, 1979), 136.

[47]However, although there is no direct link provided by the text itself between Psalm 2 and 2 Samuel 7, it is quite possible that this psalm "dramatises the oracle of Nathan (2 Sam 7:5–16) recalling the exploits of the dynasty's founder as a guarantee of the future stability and permanance of his line" (M. Daly-Denton, *David in the Fourth Gospel: The Johannine Reception of the Psalms*, AGJU 47 [Leiden/Boston/Köln: Brill, 1999], 49). The connection between the two is clearly established in *Pss. Sol.* 17:23–27, which shows that "when it could no longer be sung in honour of an incumbent king, it continued to foster Israel's conviction that God would honour the covenant with David" (ibid.).

Jewish interpreters were mostly interested in the Davidic descent of the expected royal deliverer. It cannot be denied that God's promise to David about the father-son relationship with his descendant was largely ignored in the early Jewish literature. From this, however, does not necessarily follow that one must express a "considerable caution in supposing any first-century Jewish use of the title "Son of God" for the expected Messiah.""[48] Although not many, certain passages in early Jewish writings betray that this aspect of God's promise to David was not entirely forgotten.[49]

Thus 4Q174 frgs. 1–2 and 21 1.10–11 explicitly apply this promise to the eschatological "Branch of David." More precisely, the author does not identify David's seed (זרע) in 2 Sam 7:12, which is quoted in line 10, as the "Branch of David" (צמח דויד) mentioned in the commentary in line 11, before repeating, word for word, Yahweh's promise in 2 Sam 7:14 "I shall be his father, and he shall be my son" (אני אהיה לוא לאב והוא יהיה לי לבן) in the first part of line 11. Even though there is no explicit commentary on this verse, the interpretation that immediately follows (הואה צמח דויד) clearly assumes that this aspect of the promise to David equally applies to the messianic figure[50] called the "Branch of David."[51] There are no indications that the author(s) of *Florilegium*

---

[48]Verseput, "The 'Son of God' Title," 538. The thesis that there is nothing in the Palestinian Jewish tradition that supports the view that "Son of God" was understood as a messianic title has been advanced by J. A. Fitzmyer, *The Gospel According to Luke I–IX*, AB 28 (Garden City: Doubleday, 1981), 206. For a critique, see J. J. Collins, "The 'Son of God' Text from Qumran," in *From Jesus to John: Essays on Jesus and New Testament Christology in Honour of Marinus de Jonge*, ed. M. C. de Boer, JSNTSup 84 (Sheffield: JSOT, 1993), 65–82, esp. 80.

[49]Recent studies on messianism show a revived interest in this topic; cf. the following essays published in *Qumran-Messianism*, ed. Charlesworth, Lichtenberger and Oegema: Collins, "Jesus, Messianism and the Dead Sea Scrolls" (107–112), C. A. Evans, "Are the 'Son' Texts at Qumran Messianic? Reflections on 4Q369 and Related Scrolls" (135–153), and J. Zimmermann, "Observations on 4Q246 – The 'Son of God'" (175–190).

[50]Evans aptly says that "we have in this instance a messianizing of a 'father-son' passage" ("Are the 'Son' Texts at Qumran Messianic?" 141)

[51]The fact that midrash on Psalms 1–2 follows the messianic midrash of 2 Samuel 7 could indicate that Psalm 2 might have been understood messianically by the Qumran community. It is, however, impossible to build anything certain on this basis since the extant text only contains a citation of Ps 2:1–2 followed by a commentary which merely mentions "the chosen ones of Israel in the latter days."

The translation of the phrase אם יוליד [אלה את] המשיח found in another Qumran document, 1QSa 2.11–12, as "when [God] will have begotten the Messiah" is based on a dubious reading of the last consonant in the verb יוליד as ד, which was originally proposed by D. Barthélemy, "Règle de la Congrégation (1QSa)," in *Qumran Cave I*, ed. D. Barthélemy and J. T. Milik, DJD 1 (Oxford: Clarendon, 1955), 108–118, and pl. XXIV. Cf also P. W. Skehan ("Two Books on Qumrân Studies," *CBQ* 21 [1959]: 74) who claims that the verb should be translated as "causes to be born, begets." After Milik (DJD 1, p. 117) amended the text to יוליד, Barthélemy, and later F. M. Cross accepted Milik's restoration. Cf. also J. H. Charlesworth and L. T. Stuckenbruck, introduction to the "*Rule of the Congregation* (1QSa),"

tried to correct the text of the quotation, which is certainly significant especially when compared with targums of 2 Sam 7:14 and 1 Chr 17:13, which use the phrase (כאב)א ("like a father") instead of לאב, thus obviously attempting to show that this relationship should be understood either symbolically or as a figure of speech.[52]

The term "son of God" appears in another Qumran text, 4Q246 (4QapocrDan ar) 2.1, but its meaning has been highly debated among the interpreters. Even though several scholars understand the Aramaic expressions ברה די אל ("Son of God") and בר עליון ("Son of [the] Most High"), which appear in the first line of the second column, as the references to the Davidic Messiah,[53] other solutions are also possible, such as the Son of Man from Dan 7[54] (positive figure), or Antiochus IV Epiphanes[55] and anti-Christ[56] (negative figures).[57] In general, the negative proposals are based upon internal criteria provided by the context.[58] The section in which the titles "Son of God" and "Son of the Most High" appear is preceded and followed by descriptions of wars. Only after the *vacat* in 2.4, the appearance of universal peace and dominance of Israel is described. A positive understanding of the term "Son of God" within such a context would be an anomaly difficult to explain. The unsolvable problem for this interpretation, however, is the lack of negative

---

in *The Dead Sea Scrolls: Hebrew, Aramaic, and Greek Texts with English Translations*, vol. 1 (Tübingen: J. C. B. Mohr [Paul Siebeck], 1994) 109. Recently Evans argued again for Barthélemy's original restoration by claiming that it is "completely in step with Ps 2:2, 7" ("Are the 'Son' Texts at Qumran Messianic?" 139).

[52]For a discussion of the targumic reading see D. Juel, *Messiah and Temple: The Trial of Jesus in the Gospel of Mark* (Missoula, Mont.: Scholars Press, 1977), 108–109.

[53]H.-W. Kuhn, "Röm 1,3f und der davidische Messias als Gottessohn in den Qumrantexten," in *Lese-Zeichen für Annelis Findeiss zum 65. Geburtstag am 15. März 1984*, ed. C. Burchard and G. Theissen (Heidelberg: Carl Winter, 1984), 103–113; J. J. Collins, "A Pre-Christian 'Son of God' Among the Dead Sea Scrolls," *BRev* (1993): 34–38; idem, "The 'Son of God Text from Qumran," 65–82; Zimmermann, *Messianische Texte aus Qumran*, 159–168. A variation of this view is offered by J. A. Fitzmyer ("4Q246: The 'Son of God' Document from Qumran," *Bib* 74 [1993]: 153–174), who sees here a royal figure who will be a successor of the throne of David, but he does not believe that he is the Messiah.

[54]F. García Martínez, "Messianic Hopes in the Qumran Writings," in *The People of the Dead Sea Scrolls*, ed. F. García Martínez and J. Trebolle Barrerra (Leiden: Brill, 1995), 159–189.

[55]É. Puech, "Fragment d'une apocalypse en araméen (4Q246 = pseudo-Dan[d]) et le 'Royaume de Dieu'," *RB* 99 (1992): 98–131.

[56]D. Flusser, "The Hubris of the Antichrist in a Fragment from Qumran," *Imm* 10 (1980): 31–37.

[57]For a detailed review of various proposals see Zimmermann, *Messianische Texte aus Qumran*, 153–158.

[58]Ibid., 158.

parallels of the aforementioned titles in early Jewish literature.[59] This critique becomes an asset and the starting point for the positive proposals. They are based upon external criteria, i.e. positive parallels in early Jewish and Christian writings. Among the examples, which include the Old Testament passages that speak about divine adoption of the enthroned king, such as 2 Sam 7:14 and Ps 2:7, an astoundingly similar text is found in Luke 1:32–35. Luke's text not only contains the exact Greek equivalents of the Aramaic titles ברה די אל (υἱὸς θεοῦ – Luke 1:35) and בר עליון (υἱὸς ὑψίστου – Luke 1:32), but also the passive verb forms.[60] Such a high correspondence between these two texts can be taken not only as an indication that both of them originate from a common tradition,[61] but also that both have clear messianic implications.[62] If so, 4Q246 offers a compelling evidence that the title "Son of God" was applied to the expected Messiah in pre-Christian Judaism.

In *4 Ezra*, the Davidic Messiah is called God's son (*filius meus christus*) (*4 Ezra* 7:29). In chapters 13 and 14, the language of divine sonship completely replaces the language of messiahship. However, even though the technical term "the Messiah" does not appear (only the designation "my son" [*filius meus*] does), its messianic connotations are apparent because it is clear that the author has in mind the Messiah who was identified as "my son" in chapter 7. It has been sometimes objected that the term "son," which appears in both Latin and Syriac version, is a translation of the original Hebrew "servant" rather than "son."[63] However, as John J. Collins notes, the final scene in chapter 13 where the Messiah standing on a mountain repudiates the attack of the Gentiles with his blazing breath, echoes Psalm 2, where God's anointed, called God's son, being set by God on Zion, God's holy mountain, terrifies the nations.[64]

---

[59]Cf. Collins, "The 'Son of God' Text from Qumran," 67; Zimmermann, *Messianische Texte aus Qumran*, 160.

[60]For a comparison of both texts see J. A. Fitzmyer, "The Contribution of Qumran Aramaic to the Study of the New Testament," in *A Wandering Aramean: Collected Aramaic Essays*, SBLMS 25 (Missoula: Scholars Press, 1979), 91–94; Zimmermann, *Messianische Texte aus Qumran*, 159. Zimmermann understands the passive verb forms as *passivum divinum*, whose background can be found in Ps 2:7 (ibid., 160).

[61]Cf. Collins, "A Pre-Christian 'Son of God'," 35.

[62]One of the most convincing arguments for the messianic interpretation of the "Son of God" passage in 4Q246 has been presented by J. Zimmermann, *Messianische Texte aus Qumran*, 161–169. Zimmermann not only demonstrates the importance of the positive parallels for our understanding of the "Son of God" designation in this Qumran document, but also offers a plausible solution to the problem of internal coherence of the text itself. In his view, 2.1 concludes with a break that thematically separates it from the text that follows. Hence, 1.7–2.1 contrasts the Son of God to the hostile kings (1.4–6) and the short-lived kingdoms of various nations (2.1–3), until finally the eternal kingdom of God prevails (2.4–9).

[63]Stone, *Features of the Eschatology of IV Ezra*, 71–75; idem, *Fourth Ezra*, 207.

[64]Collins, *The Scepter and the Star*, 165.

2.2.2.3 New Testament Writings

New Testament writers show a considerable interest in the concept of divine sonship that originates in the promise tradition. This is especially evident in the combination of the citations of 2 Sam 7:14 and Ps 2:7 in Heb 1:5. Even though the pre-Christian Jewish sources do not provide enough evidence for an unambiguous confirmation of the thesis that Psalm 2 was messianically interpreted in Judaism prior to the rise of Christianity, the New Testament and later Jewish writings[65] show that this psalm had a potential for messianic interpretation.

The earliest Christian reference can be found in the pre-Pauline confession preserved in Rom 1:3–4, which applies the royal language of enthronement to Jesus' resurrection. The text is significant because it contains both a reference to Jesus' Davidic descent and a reference to his installation to the position of the Son of God, i.e. two constitutive elements of God's promise to David in 2 Samuel 7.[66] Even though these parallel clauses build a formal antithesis, one referring to Jesus' state of humiliation (κατὰ σάρκα) and the other to his state of exaltation (κατὰ πνεῦμα), the contrast between them should not be exaggerated. The former points to a quality that characterized Jesus' earthly existence (Davidic descent), and the latter to a quality that characterizes his post-resurrected existence (divine sonship in power). The passive ὁρισθέντος most likely implies that the implied subject is God (divine passive). If so, it should be translated "appointed" or "installed."[67] Even though this pre-Pauline confession does not contain any direct scriptural quotation, it probably alludes to Ps 2:7 with its royal enthronement ideology.[68] Such an assumption is even more plausible if the designation "in power" belonged to the original wording.[69] According to Rom 1:4, Jesus was appointed the Son of God in power (υἱὸς θεοῦ ἐν δυνάμει)[70] since[71] the resurrection of the dead.[72] If the

---

[65]Psalm 2 is interpreted messianically in the rabbinic literature; see *Midr. Ps.* 2:9 [on Ps 2:7] and *b. Sukkah* 52a; cf. C. A. Evans, *Jesus and His Contemporaries: Comparative Studies*, AGJU 25 (Leiden: Brill, 1995), 97.

[66]Cf. Stuhlmacher, *Biblische Theologie des Neuen Testaments*, vol. 1, 187.

[67]Cf. J. D. G. Dunn, *Christology in the Making: A New Testament Inquiry into the Origins of the Doctrine of Incarnation*, 2nd ed. (London: SCM, 1989), 34; Cranfield, *The Epistle to the Romans*, 61; J. A. Fitzmyer, *Romans: A New Translation with Introduction and Commentary*, AB (New York: Doubleday, 1992), 234–235. Other translations are also possible, such as "designated" or "declared," as long as they convey the sense that Jesus achieved a status he did not have before.

[68]Cf. L. C. Allen, "The Old Testament Background of (*pro*)*horizein* in the New Testament," *NTS* 17 (1970–71): 104–108; J. H. Hayes, "The Resurrection as Enthronement and the Earliest Church Christology," *Int* 22 (1968): 337–345.

[69]This is the position of Lövestam, *Son and Savior*, 47.

[70]There is a scholarly consensus that here the prepositional phrase ἐν δυνάμει refers to a noun and not to a verb.

original formula did not contain the phrase "in power," it declared that Jesus' divine sonship stemmed from his resurrection, i.e. that he was installed to a status and was assigned prerogatives he did not have before. If the phrase "in power" belonged to the pre-Pauline confession, it affirmed that Jesus' divine sonship *in power* stemmed from his resurrection, i.e. that the divine sonship which Jesus already possessed[73] was enhanced by a quality it did not have before.[74] In either case, the text assigns the crucial role to the resurrection, either as determining his divine sonship, or installing him to the status that he had not enjoyed before. It is therefore not surprising that the resurrection is sometimes regarded as the most likely point of entry of the promise tradition into Christianity.[75]

Acts 13:33–34 is another passage which clearly associates Jesus' resurrection, his divine sonship and his messiahship. Although this speech, like other speeches in Acts, is most likely a Lukan composition, it testifies to the significance of this link in certain early Christian circles. What connects it with Rom 1:3–4 is the idea that Jesus' resurrection brought about the fundamental change in his relationship to God. According to Acts 13:33–34, Paul makes two claims and supports them with three scriptural quotations. For our purposes here only the first claim is significant. In verse 33, Lukan Paul says that God fulfilled the promise to the fathers by raising Jesus (ἀναστήσας Ἰησοῦν) and supports this by quoting Ps 2:7 (υἱός μος εἶ σύ, ἐγὼ σήμερον γεγέννηκά σε). Although the word ἀναστήσας could mean "let appear" (like

---

[71]It is more likely that the Greek preposition ἐκ is temporal than causal, because, as Cranfield aptly notes, "Christ's resurrection was scarcely the ground of His exaltation; but it was the event which was the beginning of His exalted life." (*The Epistle to the Romans*, 62)

[72]Even though the phrase ἐξ ἀναστάσεως νεκρῶν undoubtedly refers to Jesus' resurrection, its formulation indicates that this event represents the beginning of general resurrection; cf. Stuhlmacher, *Biblische Theologie des Neuen Testaments*, vol. 1, 187; Dunn, *Romans 1–8*, 15–16; Cranfield, *The Epistle to the Romans*, 62. A similar understanding of the significance of this event can be found in 1 Cor 15:20, 23; Col 1:18, and Rev 1:5. The critique of J. A. Fitzmyer (*Romans*, 237) that this view "does not echo Pauline teaching otherwise, which sees the resurrection of Christ itself as the source of human justification," disregards the fact that this is a pre-Pauline formulation whose subject matter is not justification but Jesus Christ's messianic identity.

[73]Fitzmyer (*Romans*, 235) remarks that "before the resurrection Jesus Christ was the Son of God in the weakness of his human existence."

[74]Cf. Dunn, *Christology in the Making*, 35. Dunn notes that in this case, the confession affirms that Jesus shares not only in status, but also in "executive authority" of God; cf. Dunn, *Romans 1–8*, 14.

[75]Cf. Duling, "The Promises to David," 70–74. It should be noted, however, that the exegetical activity, to which the traditional material preserved in Rom 1:3–4 testifies, cannot explain the origin of the confession of Jesus as the Messiah, because the resurrection as such was not a constitutive element of Jewish messianic expectations. However, it gave to Jesus' followers a significant point of departure for a specifically Christian adaptation of the promise tradition.

in Acts 3:22, 26 or in *Pss. Sol.* 17:21), Lövestam has shown that such an interpretation would produce the break in the context and argued that the word should be understood as a reference to Jesus' resurrection.[76] Acts 13:33 then states that through Jesus' resurrection God appointed Jesus as the Messiah and adopted him as his son by giving him universal dominion and lordship. Both the peculiar language of "begetting" and the time-specification ("today") emphasize the point (event) at which Jesus became God's son.

Both texts, Rom 1:3–4 and Acts 13:33–34, indicate that one possible source of the understanding of Jesus' divinity should be sought in the royal enthronement ideology found in Psalm 2, which is explicitly or implicitly referred to in these texts. Whether this Christology could be called "adoptionist" is highly questionable. James D. G. Dunn calls attention to the danger inherent in this label, because this is a technical term for a later concept that has been developed in the opposition/denial of Jesus' pre-existence – its claim is that Jesus was only a human being who was adopted by God.[77] There is no evidence that the New Testament passages which speak about Jesus' becoming God's son at his resurrection consciously want to deny his divine sonship before the resurrection.

2.2.3 The Perpetuity of the Davidic Dynasty

2.2.3.1 Biblical Writings

God's promise of the permanent endurance of Davidic dynasty appears in the Old Testament in two basic forms: unconditional and conditional. Its basic formulation found in 2 Samuel 7 and Psalm 89 is unconditional.[78] In 2 Sam 7:14–16, God promises to David the eternal reign (עַד־עוֹלָם) of his offspring on the throne of the kingdom of Israel. The fulfillment of this promise, however, does not depend on the obedience of the king, because it is given without qualifications. The consequence of his disobedience will be his temporary chastisement, but the permanency of his reign will not be threatened. The sole guarantor of the promise is God's steadfast love (חֶסֶד), which does not depend on the behavior of the receiver of the promise. The standard pattern of this

---

[76]Lövestam, *Son and Savior,* 8–11.

[77]Dunn, *Christology in the Making,* 62. For a comprehensive critique of an alleged two-stage adoptionist Christology behind Rom 1:3–4, see Stuhlmacher, *Biblische Theologie des Neuen Testaments,* vol. 1, 187–187. In contrast to Stuhlmacher, Dunn (*Romans 1–8,* 14) accepts the term "two-stage Christology" but quickly adds that he does not use this term in an adoptionist sense.

[78]Cf. E. T. Mullen, "The Divine Witness and the Davidic Royal Grant: Ps 89:37–38," *JBL* 102 (1983): 207–218. Sarna, "Psalm 89," 29–46; P. E. Satterthwaite, "David in the Books of Samuel: A Messianic Hope?" in *The Lord's Anointed: Interpretation of Old Testament Messianic Texts,* ed. P. E. Satterthwaite, R. S. Hess, and G. J. Wenham (Exeter: Paternoster Press; Grand Rapids: Baker, 1995), 41–65. T. Veijola, *Die ewige Dynastie* (Helsinki: Academia Scientiarum Fennica, 1975).

essentially unconditional promise to David is the negative formulation in 2 Sam 7:15 that God will not take away his steadfast love from David and his descendants: וחסדי לא־יסור ממנו; τὸ δὲ ἔλεός μου οὐκ ἀποστήσω ἀπ' αὐτοῦ (LXX).

Ps 89:34 contains a similar version of this "prophetic perpetuation formula."[79] God promises that he will not remove his steadfast love from David: וחסדי לא־אפיר מעמו – τὸ δὲ ἔλεός μου οὐ μὴ διασκεδάσω ἀπ' αὐτοῦ [Ps 88:34 LXX]).[80] Similarly to 2 Samuel 7, the promise about the eternal endurance of the Davidic reign (Ps 89:5, 29, 37, 38) appears in the unconditional form. God assures that he will establish David's descendants on the throne forever (Ps 89:5, 29, 37, 38). Transgressions will be punished with the rod and iniquities with scourges (vv. 30–33), but the promise itself will not be annulled. The idea of the temporary chastisement can also be found in 1 Kgs 11:39 – David's descendants will be punished, but not forever.

Jer 33:14–25 contains the most elaborate version of the unconditional promise. The "branch of righteousness" (צמח צדקה) which God will cause to "branch out" (אצמיח) in verse 15 is presented as the fulfillment of God's promise to the house of Israel and the house of Judah. Verse 17 is the affirmation of the permanency of the Davidic dynasty expressed through the negative formulation: David shall never lack a man to sit on the throne of the house of Israel (לא־יכרת לדוד איש ישב על־כסא בית־ישראל). This formulation does not mention God's חסד which will not be taken away from David,[81] but promises that God will not "cut off" a man on the Davidic throne. In Jer 33:19–22, 25–26, God's promise is guaranteed by the order of creation. Yahweh's covenant with day and night assures that he will not reject the offspring of Jacob and his servant David.

All these unconditional formulations of the promise to David could be regarded as various expressions of the Davidic covenant, even though the word "covenant" does not always appear in these texts. Its basic characteristics are that it is made with the house of David and that it is eternal and unconditional.[82] This covenant stands in tension with the Sinaitic covenant,

---

[79]The term has been coined by Duling, "The Promises to David," 56. It refers to various prophecies about the perpetuation of the Davidic descendant on the throne of Israel.

[80]In addition to 2 Samuel 7 and Psalm 89, Isa 55:3 also mentions an everlasting covenant (ברית עולם) and God's steadfast sure love for David (חסדי דוד הנאמנים). However, O. Eissfeldt has demonstrated that this passage represents a transfer of God's promises to David to Israel as a whole ("The Promises of Grace to David in Isaiah 55:1–5," in *Israel's Prophetic Heritage*, ed. B. W. Anderson and W. Harrelson [London: Harper & Brothers, 1962], 196–207).

[81]Cf. 2 Sam 7:15 and Ps 89:34.

[82]J. Plastaras (*The God of Exodus: The Theology of the Exodus Narratives*, Impact Books [Milwaukee: The Bruce Publishing Company, 1966], 248–252) notes that since Davidic covenant is made once for ever, there is no place for the concept of the "new" covenant.

which was made with all of Israel and knew no unconditional promises. It was based on God's saving actions, but it expected from the nation obedience to the divine commandments and threatened penalties for failure to do so.[83]

The conditional form of the promise, which appears in deuteronomistic history in all subsequent references to 2 Sam 7:12–16, represents a deuteronomistic combination of these two covenants.[84] All three major passages where this conditional form appears apply the promise to Solomon. Thus in his last instructions to Solomon before his death, David recounts God's promise which he received in the conditional form: only if his [David's] heirs are obedient will God fulfill his promise that his dynasty will be eternal (1 Kgs 2:4). The standard negative pattern characteristic of the unconditional form appears here also (לא־יכרת לך איש מעל כסא ישראל) but now firmly coupled with the conditional particle אם. Similarly, the negative pattern in 1 Kgs 8:25 formulated as לא־יכרת לך איש מלפני ישב על־כסא ישראל is again accompanied by the conditional אם. The third passage in 1 Kgs 9:4–5, on the other hand, does not employ the negative pattern, but rather contains the positive formulation that God will establish Solomon's royal throne over Israel, under the condition that he walks before God in the same way David did.

Ps 132:12 contains the classical formulation of the conditional form of the promise outside deuteronomistic history. God promises to David that, if his sons keep God's covenant and his decrees, their sons will also forevermore sit on David's throne.[85] In the book of Chronicles, both forms can be found. Like 2 Samuel 7, 1 Chr 17:13–14 recounts God's promise to David unconditionally. The text even omits the disciplinary chastisement from 2 Sam 7:14b in the case of king's disobedience. God will not take his steadfast love from him, and

---

[83]Cf. J. Bright, *Covenant and Promise: The Prophetic Understanding of the Future in Pre-Exilic Israel* (Philadelphia: Westminster Press, 1976), 28–43. Plastaras (*The God of Exodus*, 248–252) contends that the Sinai covenant could be annulled because of Israel's transgressions, but also renewed, as in Jer 31:31–33.

[84]According to Bright (*Covenant and Promise,* 133), the deuteronomistic historian "places the very existence of the institution of kingship under the terms of the Mosaic covenant," which finds its clearest expression in Samuel's speech to Saul in 1 Sam 12:1–15. When J. R. Porter (*Moses and Monarchy: A Study in the Biblical Tradition of Moses* [Oxford: Basil Blackwell, 1963], 11–13) denies a sharp distinction between the Davidic and Sinaitic covenant, he regularly refers to these passages, which certainly demonstrate that the tension between the unilateral promise to David and the bilateral covenant with all the people has been overcome.

[85]Bright (*Covenant and Promise,* 64–65) calls attention to the fact that "in the psalm in its present form the conditional element is somewhat blunted" because it is followed in vv. 13–16 by Yahweh's announcement of his choice of Mt. Zion as his eternal dwelling, and in vv. 17–18 by further unconditional promises of prosperity, enduring dynasty, and victory over enemies.

his throne shall be established forever. However, 2 Chr 6:16[86] and 7:17–18 recapitulate the promise in the conditional form.

Even such a brief survey of various forms of the Davidic promise allows several conclusions. The recipients are David and his descendants, not Israel as a whole, so that "the divine election narrows from the sons of Israel and their land to the son of David and his city."[87] The unconditional version of the promise, which contains only the concept of the everlasting covenant with David, seems to undermine the obligation of the king to keep the law. It is opposed to the deed-consequence schema, which is at the core of the Sinaitic covenant. Its ground is God's faithfulness to the promise expressed through his steadfast love and mercy, not the king's obedience to God's commandments. Since the covenant with David was basically unilateral and guaranteed by God's חסד, it is not surprising that the reality which contradicted God's assurance gave rise to both the lamenting question "Why?"[88] and the expectation of the eventual realization of the promise.

2.2.3.2 Early Jewish Writings

In *Pss. Sol.* 17:21, the expectation of the fulfillment of the promise given to David takes the form of a prayer: ἰδέ κύριε καὶ ἀνάστησον αὐτοῖς τὸν βασιλέα αὐτῶν υἱὸν Δαυιδ. The language of "raising up" comes from 2 Sam 7:12 (καὶ ἀναστήσω τὸ σπέρμα σου μετὰ σε [LXX]; והקימתי את־זרעך אחריך [MT]). It is taken over again in Amos 9:11, a text which assumes the termination of Davidic dynasty but still promises that God he will raise up the booth of David that is fallen: ἀναστήσω τὴν σκηνὴν Δαυιδ τὴν πεπτωκυῖαν (LXX); אקים את־סכת דויד הנפלת (MT).

Early Jewish writings show that Amos 9:11 became an especially suitable text for the messianic interpretation in a situation when there was no Davidic ruler on the throne. One of the clearest references can be found in 4Q174 frgs.1–2 and 21 1.12–13. The citation of Amos 9:11 directly follows the midrashic interpretation of 2 Sam 7:12–14 preserved in lines 11–12. The quotation of Amos 9:11a in line 12 is introduced with the formula "as it is written" (כאשר כתוב) and followed by the interpretation, "He is the booth of David that is falle[n w]ho will arise to save Israel." CD MS A 7.15–16 contains another citation of Amos 9:11. The interpretation, which follows in lines 17–21, shows that Amos' prophecy was also here understood as a reference to the appearance of the Davidic Messiah, who is then identified as the "scepter" from Num 24:17 who will, together with the "star" who

---

[86]Note the change which Chronicler introduces into his source material by stating the condition of obedience not in terms of "walking before me" (1 Kgs 8:25), but as "walking in my Law" (2 Chr 6:16). Otherwise, the conditions of the continuity of Davidic dynasty are generally defined in terms of the obedience to the Mosaic Law.

[87]Nolan, *The Royal Son of God*, 225.

[88]Cf. Ps 89:46–51.

interprets the law, shatter Israel's enemies (represented here through the sons of Sheth).

The conditional version of the promise, on the other hand, offered an explanation for the incongruity between the reality and God's word: its realization depended on the obedience of the Davidic kings. Thus, for example, Sir 49:4–5 concludes that the Davidic dynasty came to an end because all Davidic kings, except David, Hezekiah, and Josiah, sinned (כלם חשחיתו) and abandoned the Torah of the Most High. Also, according to Josephus, the Davidic dynasty, which comprised twenty-one kings, has ended,[89] and there are no indications that he expected its re-establishment. The time of the Davidic dynasty was glorious, but it was conditional depending on the faithfulness of its kings to the Mosaic law.[90] Josephus never mentions that part of the promise that speaks about the eternity of the Davidic line.[91] It is therefore not surprising that there is no Davidic messianism in Josephus' writings.

Other early Jewish texts, however, demonstrate that this answer was not sufficient as a rational explanation of the current predicament, which was understood not only in terms of the termination of the Davidic dynasty, but also general national and personal suffering. The question of responsibility understood as human failure to keep God's commandments was broadened: no

---

[89]*Ant.* 5.9.4 and 10.8.4.

[90]According to H. W. Attridge (*The Interpretation of Biblical History in the Antiquitates Judaicae of Flavius Josephus*, HDR 7 [Missoula, MT: Scholars Press, 1976], 78–80, 83), Josephus replaces the covenantal terminology from the biblical text with benefactor/alliance terminology which has its basis in God's retributive justice explained as a reward of the righteous and a punishment of the wicked. He applies the criterion of retributive justice not only to the Davidic dynasty, but to the Jewish people as a whole. Attridge points out that this idea can be found in deuteronomistic history and Chronicles, but in Josephus it has been reinforced. See also Pomykala, *The Davidic Dynasty*, 226–227.

[91]*Ant.* 6.8.1 contains a description of David's anointing by Samuel narrated in 1 Sam 16:13 and Josephus' closing comment that David's obedience was required in order that his kingship endures. *Ant.* 7.4.4 represents Josephus' account of Nathan's promise in 2 Sam 7:11–16. He mentions that God would punish David's son Solomon, if he sinned, with sickness and barrenness of soil. David's kingdom will be preserved for Solomon's posterity instead. Despite the prevalent positive tone of Nathan's oracle, the unconditional nature of promise is not mentioned. Similarly, in *Ant.* 7.14.8 Josephus again specifies that the kingdom will prosper only if Solomon shows himself to be pious and just, and observes his country's laws. The conditional nature of God's promise to David is especially emphasized in *Ant.* 7.15.1, where Josephus refers to David's last words to Solomon in 1 Kgs 2:1–4. David charges Solomon to be righteous, because only in this way the kingdom will be guaranteed to the Davidic line. A similar comment can be found in *Ant.* 8.4.6, where Josephus, by discussing God's promise to Solomon in 1 Kgs 9:4–9, again underscores the conditional nature of the Davidic dynasty. K. E. Pomykala (*The Davidic Dynasty*, 228) notes that "this portrait of the davidic dynasty tradition fits Josephus' theological conception of divine providence and his moralizing and apologetic purposes in the Antiquities."

longer Davidic kings alone, but the entire nation of Israel was blamed for the miserable condition. This, however, does not mean that a clear and acceptable explanation was ever found. The literature of the time demonstrates much confusion and bewilderment in handling the question of theodicy.[92] A concise review of the texts which contain the references to the Davidic Messiah shows

---

[92]The liability of human sins for the lack of the fulfillment of God's promises is a prominent theme in post-70 writings. The author of *4 Ezra*, being faced with the depth of the national catastrophe in 70 C.E., cannot easily find an answer to the question of "why." He is not able to reconcile the fact that God said that he will be faithful to his promises to Adam, Noah, Abraham, and David (note that in addition to the promise to David, Ezra mentions only those which unilaterally oblige God, because they were not made subjects to conditions) and the reality which is quite opposite: the Temple is burned and the land devastated because a pagan, idolatrous nation has defeated Israel. Ezra is neither able to explain the present situation on the basis of some historical experience nor to assign sins to some particular group. Rather, he universalizes the problem by reaching back to the first human transgression done by Adam. In a series of dialogues between Ezra and Uriel, the text presents two different views of human responsibility. Ezra's position is characterized by tension between Adam's and each individual's responsibility for sinning, and between the concept of hereditary sinfulness and the freedom of moral choice. For further discussion, see W. Harnisch, *Verhängnis und Verheissung der Geschichte: Untersuchungen zum Zeit- und Geschichtsverständnis im 4. Buch Esra und in der syr. Baruchapokalypse*, FRLANT 97 (Göttingen: Vandenhoeck & Ruprecht, 1969), 54–56; Stone, *Fourth Ezra*, 65; J. R. Levison, *Portraits of Adam in Early Judaism from Sirach to 2 Baruch*, JSPSup 1 (Sheffield: JSOT Press, 1988), 123.

Uriel's answer is a strong rebuttal of Ezra's determinism. By affirming the existence of the free will in every human being (*elige tibi uitam ut uiuas*), Uriel stresses human capacity to decide whether s/he will live a sinful life resulting in damnation, or a righteous life resulting in salvation. Also, Uriel claims that the world to come is the solution to the problem of universal human sinfulness. According to *4 Ezra* 7:113–114, in this new and immortal age "corruption has passed away, sinful indulgence has come to an end, unbelief has been cut off, and righteousness has increased." Even though this final period is not a messianic, but rather post-messianic age, its functionality depends on how the problem of human sinfulness has been solved. It requires the removal of sin (even the change of human heart), holiness, and righteousness of the participants.

In contrast to *4 Ezra*, *2 Baruch* is much less pessimistic. This document affirms individual responsibility and promises eternal reward to the righteous. Similarly to *4 Ezra*, *2 Baruch* addresses the problem of suffering, because it calls God's promises into question. Nevertheless, his message is that "despite appearances to the contrary, God's promises to Abraham have not been nullified" (G. B. Sayler, *Have the Promises Failed? A Literary Analysis of 2 Baruch*, SBLDS 72 [Chico, CA: Scholars Press, 1984], 86). *2 Bar.* 54:13–19 clarifies that the consequence of Adam's sin for all humanity should be clearly distinguished from the consequence that affects only those who deliberately chose to repeat Adam's behavior. The strengthening of individual responsibility most likely represents Baruch's response to a deterministic view advocated by the character of Ezra in *4 Ezra*, who insisted on hereditary sinfulness. For the relationship between *2 Baruch* and *4 Ezra*, see G. E. W. Nickelsburg, *Jewish Literature Between the Bible and the Mishnah* (Philadelphia: Fortress, 1981), 288–293; Harnisch, *Verhängnis und Verheissung der Geschichte*, 19–87; Sayler, *Have the Promises Failed?* 123–134.

that the problem of human sin was one of the most fundamental issues raised in these writing.

Pss. Sol. 17 contains the most articulate treatment of the problem of non-realization of the promise to David. The most unusual feature of this text is the tension between the unconditional version of the promise in 17:4 and the comment in 17:5 that the promise is not fulfilled "because of our sins" (ἐν ταῖς ἀμαρτίαις ἡμῶν). The Hasmonean usurpation of the throne, which is interpreted as the threat to the fulfillment of God's promise because they were not its receivers (οἷς οὐκ ἐπηγγείλω – 17:4b),[93] is understood as a consequence of people's sins. This universal acceptance of blame is most eloquently expressed in 17:20, which specifies that all, from rulers to common people, were ἐν πάσῃ ἀμαρτίᾳ. However, even though the text does not explicitly refer to the responsibility of the Davidic kings, which was an essential element in various versions of the conditional forms of the promise, there is a sign that the author was familiar with this conception. One of the characteristics of the future ideal king, the Son of David, will be his sinlessness. 17:36 specifies that he will be free from sin, in order to rule a great people (καὶ αὐτὸς καθαρὸς ἀπὸ ἀμαρτίας τοῦ ἄρχειν λαοῦ μεγάλου), which suggests by implication that due to the sinfulness of previous Davidic rulers they were not able to rule the people and lost the throne. Thus, the sinlessness of the Messiah functions as a guarantor that the promise of the permanency of Davidic dynasty will be realized.

4Q252 5.1–5 is another text from this period which implicitly addresses the question of the responsibility of the Davidic kings for the loss of the throne. Here is the quotation of and commentary on Gen 49:10a (line 1) directly associated with the promise in Jer 33:17b that "[there will not] be cut off one sitting (on) the throne for David" (לוא י[כרת יושב כסא לדויד]) (line 2). The righteous Messiah called the "Branch of David" and his seed are said to be the receivers of the covenant which has been given "for everlasting generations" (עד דורות עולם) (line 4). This clear reference to the everlasting perseverance of the Davidic dynasty is then, somewhat surprisingly, followed by a comment about the character of the promised Davidic heir, "who kept °[. . .] the Torah with the men of the Community" (lines 4–5). Thus, similarly to the sinlessness of the Messiah in *Pss. Sol.* 17, his obedience to the Law guarantees the fulfillment of God's promise about the perpetuity of the Davidic dynasty.

The evidence considered so far shows that God's promise of the eternal Davidic reign, which appears in the biblical writings in two basic forms, conditional and unconditional, became the object of intensive theological

---

[93]K. E. Pomykala notes that "the davidic dynasty tradition did not generate disappointment with the Hasmoneans; rather, disappointment with the Hasmoneans generated this appropriation of the davidic dynasty tradition (*The Davidic Dynasty*, 167).

reflection especially around the turn of the era and during the rise of messianism. In view of what we know about the diversity of messianic expectations in early Judaism, the following statement of Gerhard von Rad sounds like a gross simplification, but it certainly applies to those circles which favored the Davidic Messiah: "The Nathan prophecy became highly creative in the tradition; for this promise of Yahweh was never forgotten, but in the ages following it was constantly interpreted anew and made relevant to the present. In it also lie the historical origin and legitimization of all messianic expectations."[94] The relevance of this insight is especially visible in *Pss. Sol.* 17, a psalm that tries to solve the problem of incongruity between Scripture and actual experience. The solution which was envisioned was God's raising of the Son of David, the ideal king of the Davidic line.[95] The unendurable circumstances in which people lived had to be changed.[96] For this reason the Messiah, when his role is explicated, was regularly expected to rescue people from their present calamities. This task, however, cannot be detached from the reasons that caused the current predicament, which were in most cases identified as national and individual sins.

2.3 The Origin of Jesus, the Son of David

2.3.1 Jesus' Genealogy (Matthew 1)

2.3.1.1 The Structure of the Matthean Infancy Narrative

A reconstruction of the hypothetical sources which Matthew used for the infancy narrative in chapters 1–2 seems to be a hopeless endeavor. The entire material belongs to Matthew's *Sondergut*, and hence any comparison among the synoptic Gospels brings little, if any result. It has been often argued that the material in these two chapters comes from the oral tradition, and that Matthew was the first who put it into written form. However, the degree of Matthew's intervention in reshaping the traditional material when he

---

[94]G. von Rad, *Old Testament Theology*, trans. D. M. G. Stalker, vol. 1: *The Theology of Israel's Historical Traditions* (London: SCM Press, 1975), 311.

[95]It should be noted, however, that the continuation of the Davidic dynasty through the appearance of the Davidic Messiah was only a partial solution to the problem. This is evident in *4 Ezra* and *2 Baruch* which treat the lack of the fulfillment of the Davidic promise in broader terms, as the lack of the blessings which were promised, without being focused on the actual continuation of the Davidic line.

[96]J. D. Levenson (*Creation and the Persistence of Evil: The Jewish Drama of Divine Omnipotence* [San Francisco: Harper & Row, 1988], xvii) perceptively notes that "the overwhelming tendency of biblical writers as they confront undeserved evil is not to *explain* it away but to call upon God to *blast* it away. This struck me as a significant difference between biblical and philosophical thinking that had not been given its due either by theologians in general or by biblical theologians in particular." [emphasis his]

incorporated it into his Gospel is still an open question. Did he only change the vocabulary and style, or did he make more radical changes in the structure and the composition? Scholarly opinions vary, from those who assume that Matthew was only a redactor of the received tradition,[97] to those who speak about Matthew's authorship.[98] In the absence of any conclusive evidence on the basis of which the scope of Matthew's editorial activity can be judged, it will be assumed in this study that Matthew is responsible for the present text of the infancy narrative, without any further specifications regarding the character of that activity.

Recent studies focus much more on the structure of Matthew 1–2 than on its pre-history. Opinions, however, differ again. Proposals are made that the material in these chapters presents the pentatych, consisting of five different stories apart from the genealogy.[99] Others opt for a triptych, i.e. the genealogy followed by three scenes (Matt 1:18–25; 2:1–12; 2:13–23),[100] or a diptych, i.e. the genealogy followed by its "enlarged footnote" (Matt 1:18–25) on the one side, and Matt 2:1–23 on the other side.[101]

---

[97]Cf. G. D. Kilpatrick, *The Origins of the Gospel according to St. Matthew* (Oxford: Clarendon Press, 1946), 52–55, 93; W. L. Knox, *The Sources of the Synoptic Gospels,* vol. 2: *St. Luke and St. Matthew,* ed. H. Chadwick (Cambridge: University Press, 1957), 121–128; and G. Strecker, *Der Weg der Gerechtigkeit: Untersuchung zur Theologie des Matthäus,* 3rd ed., FRLANT 82 (Göttingen: Vandenhoeck & Ruprecht, 1971), 51–55.

[98]Cf. R. Bultmann, *The History of the Synoptic Tradition,* trans. K. Grovel (Oxford: Basil Blackwell, 1963), 291–296, 304, 443–444; C. T. Davis, "Tradition and Redaction in Matthew 1:18–2:23," *JBL* 90 (1971): 404–421; G. M. Soares Prabhu, *The Formula Quotations in the Infancy Narrative of Matthew: An Inquiry into the Tradition History of Matt 1–2,* AnBib 63 (Rome: Biblical Institute Press, 1976), 294–300; Brown, *The Birth of the Messiah,* 105–119, 192; A. Vögtle, *Messias und Gottessohn: Herkunft und Sinn der matthäischen Geburts- und Kindheitsgeschichte,* Theologische Perspektiven (Düsseldorf: Patmos, 1971), 16–27, 54–60, 81–88.

[99]Knox, *The Sources of the Synoptic Gospels,* vol. 2, 121; E. Lohmeyer, *Das Evangelium des Matthäus,* ed. W. Schmauch, 3rd ed., MeyerK (Göttingen: Vandenhoeck & Ruprecht, 1962), 9.

[100]T. Zahn, *Das Evangelium des Matthäus,* 3rd ed., KomNT 1 (Leipzig:A. Deichert, 1910), 44–105; J. Schniewind, *Das Evangelium nach Matthäus,* 11th ed., NTD 2 (Göttingen: Vandenhoeck & Ruprecht, 1964), 12–20.

[101]Probably the best known representative of a diptych is K. Stendahl, who interprets Matthew's division into two parts as an effort to "substantiate and defend the decisive names (ch. 1) and the locale (ch. 2) of the messianic event," with the goal of providing answers to the questions "Quis et Unde?" ("Quis et Unde?" 104). H. Milton believes that the main theme of chapter 1 is the paradox of the person of Jesus, while chapter 2 narrates the triumph over suffering and thus foreshadows the destiny of Jesus (paradox of his work) ("The Structure of the Prologue to St. Matthew's Gospel," *JBL* 81 [1962]: 175–181). According to A. Vögtle, however, there is no significant difference between the messages of chapters 1 and 2. He argues for their common theme which is the announcement of the messiahship of Jesus, attested through his origin (chapter 1) as well as God's providential care for his destiny

A careful analysis of Matthew's vocabulary and style reveals that he wanted to give a formal unity to the first two chapters of his Gospel. Various catchwords and inclusions indicate a strong cohesion of the text in chapter 1,[102] as well as in chapter 2.[103] It can also be shown that Matthew connected both chapters in such a way that they belong together.[104] However, the differences between them in regard to names, vocabulary and themes with which they deal are so numerous that we can simultaneously speak about their distinctiveness and relative independence. Thus, for example, it can be noticed that chapter 1 is full of personal names, while chapter 2 describes journeys and place names; chapter 1 addresses the relationship between Joseph and Mary (1:16 identifies him as the husband of Mary, and 1:18–25 identifies Mary as the γυνή of Joseph) and specifies that Jesus is Mary's υἱός, while chapter 2 ceases to speak about the relation between Joseph and Mary, and mentions only the relation between Mary and Jesus: the phrase τὸ παιδίον καὶ μήτηρ αὐτοῦ occurs five times in the second chapter; there are also differences between the Joseph scene in chapter 1 and the Joseph scenes in chapter 2 in terms of fulfillment and the obedience formula. In his article "Quis et Unde?" Krister Stendahl particularly stresses the difference between the two chapters in terms of their theme: chapter 1, being dominated by personal names, answers the question *quis* of the Messiah, while chapter 2, being dominated by geographical names, answers the question *unde* of the Messiah.[105] It seems, therefore, that the distinction between the first chapter with its major theme centered around the origin of Jesus, and the second chapter with its major

---

(chapter 2) ("Die Genealogie Mt 1,2–16 und die matthäische Kindheitsgeschichte," *BZ* NF 8 [1964]: 45–58, 239–262; 9 [1965]: 32–49).

[102]Since the word γένεσις appears in Matt 1:1 and 1:18, it connects the genealogy with the narrative about Jesus' origin. Γεννηθέν in 1:20 recalls the puzzling passive ἐγεννήθη from 1:16. The name Ἰησοῦς, which appears in 1:1, 16, 18, 21, leads toward the final climax of giving the name of the newborn child in 1:25.

[103]Chapter 2 is framed by 2:1 and 3:1, both of them containing τῆς Ἰουδαίας, ἐν ἡμέραις, and the verb παραγίνομαι. Further, there is also an *inclusio* between 2:12 and 2:22 (χρηματίζειν κατ' ὄναρ . . . ἀναχώρειν), a chiasm between 2:12 and 2:13 (κατ' ὄναρ . . . ἀναχώρησαν / ἀναχωρησάντων . . . κατ' ὄναρ), and the ending of the chapter which reminds of the ending of chapter 1 because of the use of the verb καλέω.

[104]Thus, for example, U. Luz (*Matthew 1–7: A Commentary*, trans. W. C. Linss [Minneapolis: Augsburg Fortress, 1989], 102 n.1) calls attention to various interconnections between the two chapters: the appearance of the angel of the Lord to Joseph in a dream in 1:20 and 2:13, 19; the use of the verb παραλαμβάνω in 1:20, 24 and 2:13, 19; the use of ἐγερθείς in 1:24 and 2:13, 21. B. M. Nolan emphasizes the similarity between the prophetic quotations in contrast to the formula applied in the rest of the Gospel (*The Royal Son of God*, 100).

[105]It can be noticed, however, that the theme of the geographical origin of Jesus the Messiah is not limited to chapter 2, but continues to be an issue up to 4:16. Cf. W. B. Tatum, "'The Origin of Jesus Messiah' (Matt 1:1, 18a): Matthew's Use of the Infancy Traditions," *JBL* 96 (1977): 530, 532–533; Luz, *Matthew 1–7*, 102 n.2.

theme centered around the destiny of the newborn child and his departure from Bethlehem to Nazareth, can be fully justified.

2.3.1.2 Jesus' Davidic Lineage

Christoph Burger introduced his comprehensive tradition-historical study of the title "Son of David" in the New Testament by noticing that in contrast to other confessions, the designation "Son of David" represents an assertion which is susceptible to historical proof.[106] Matt 1:1–17 is the oldest document where this genealogical aspect of the title comes to full expression.[107] The only pre-Christian document where this title appears, *Psalms of Solomon*, does not contain any genealogy, which is quite understandable in light of the futuristic character of the expected messianic figure called the Son of David. The Gospel of Mark, which contains the oldest Christian usage of this title and its application to Jesus, does not have Jesus' family tree. The genealogy of Jesus in Luke 3:23–38, on the other hand, is not linked up with this title, similar to other New Testament documents which refer to Jesus' Davidic ancestry without associating it with the messianic title "Son of David."

All New Testament references undoubtedly possess the historical aspect to which Burger refers in his introduction, and there is compelling evidence in the history of New Testament research that this question caught a considerable scholarly attention.[108] It should be noted, however, that the historical question is not an essential topic for the treatment of Jesus' Davidic descent.[109] Many

---

[106]Burger, *Jesus als Davidssohn*, 9.

[107]The heading of Matthew's genealogy is βίβλος γενέσεως Ἰησοῦ Χριστοῦ υἱοῦ Δαυὶδ υἱοῦ Ἀβραάμ.

[108]Cf. W. Wrede, "Jesus als Davidssohn" in *Vorträge und Studien* (Tübingen: J. C. B. Mohr, 1907), 148; W. Heitmüller, "Jesus Christus," in *RGG*, vol. 3 (1912), 364; H. Conzelmann, "Jesus Christus," in *RGG*, vol. 3, 3rd ed. (1959), 627; F. Hahn, *The Titles of Jesus in Christology: Their History in Early Christianity*, trans. H. Knight and G. Ogg (London: Lutterworth Press, 1969), 240–246; W. Michaelis, "Die Davidssohnschaft Jesu als historisches und kerygmatisches Problem," in *Der historische Jesus und der kerygmatische Christus*, ed. H. Ristow and K. Matthiae (Berlin: Evangelische Verlagsanstalt, 1961), 317–330.

[109]B. M. Nolan (*The Royal Son of God*, 149–154), however, thinks that "the question whether Jesus really was of David's blood merits investigation" (ibid., 154), although he admits that, from a theological viewpoint, the Son of David need not necessarily be a son of David. He is certainly correct by pointing out that the actual Davidic ancestry was not a prerequisite for someone to be hailed as the Messiah, as Josephus' examples of the messianic pretenders in the first century and Rabbi Akiba's renaming of Bar Kosiba to Bar Kokhba demonstrate. From this he draws the conclusion that the New Testament evidence about Jesus' Davidic ancestry refers to the actual fact, not a theological statement. It is, however, questionable whether this reasoning carries enough weight to persuade a historian that Jesus actually was of a Davidic family. None of the messianic pretenders which he mentions were remembered as carrying the messianic title "Son of David." As it will be shown below, this title encompasses both a messianic connotation and a Davidic ancestry of this type of messianic figure.

New Testament passages simply assume that Jesus was of the Davidic family[110] and do not offer enough material for a sound historical judgment.[111]

The inappropriateness of historical inquiry becomes especially apparent in the analysis of Jesus' family trees in Matthew and Luke. In the past, both genealogies were often compared with the purpose of harmonizing them in order to confirm their historical integrity.[112] But, as Marshall D. Johnson points out, all such attempts are unconvincing and do not do justice to the first-century milieu, in which the "midrashic character of genealogical speculation"[113] was a customary practice in both Judaism and Christianity.[114] The comparison of Matthew's and Luke's genealogies, however, has its merits because, as Johnson notes, "the two genealogies of Jesus in the NT are the only extant messianic genealogies which are written to prove that the Messiah has come."[115] In the following analysis, Matthew's genealogy will be compared with Luke's with the only purpose of demonstrating its peculiarity, and not its historicity.

Matthew's genealogy follows the basic pattern of the Old Testament genealogies, which are mainly tables of male descendants. Its first part presents the least difficulty. The names in Matt 1:2–6a agree with those in Luke 3:31–34. The only difference is that Matthew has Ἀράμ (1:3c), while Luke has two names, Ἀρνί and Ἀδμίν (3:33). The agreement between them can be explained by the assumption that both use 1 Chr 2:1–15 or Ruth 4:18–22 as source. These texts are in harmony with Matthew in regard to the name Ἀράμ.[116] Matthew also follows the texts in 1 Chr 2:1–15 and Ruth 4:18–22 in the construction of the verses (ἐγέννησεν) instead of Luke's genitive and the reverse order of names. Consequently, the first group of fourteen generations from Abraham to David agrees with the Old Testament texts. The addition of the phrase "and his brothers" (καὶ τοὺς ἀδελφοὺς αὐτοῦ) after the name of Judah in verse 2c alludes to all the tribes of Israel.

---

[110]As Juel notes, there are no indications in the New Testament that Jesus' Davidic descent has been brought into question or attacked (*Messianic Exegesis,* 143).

[111]Cf. Wrede, "Jesus als Davidssohn," 149–155; J. Jeremias, *Jerusalem zur Zeit Jesu: Kulturgeschichtliche Untersuchung zur neutestamentlichen Zeitgeschichte* (Göttingen: Vandenhoeck & Ruprecht, 1962), 308–331.

[112]An excellent overview and critique of these attempts can be found in M. D. Johnson, *The Purpose of Biblical Genealogies, with Special Reference to the Setting of the Genealogies of Jesus,* SNTSMS 8 (Cambridge: University Press, 1969), 140–145.

[113]Ibid., 145.

[114]Because of the midrashic character of early Jewish and Christian genealogical speculations, it is unlikely that Jesus' genealogies were constructed with the purpose of providing the historical verification of the theologumenon that Jesus was the Son of David, as H. Conzelmann assumed ("Jesus Christus," *RGG³,* vol. 3, 627).

[115]Johnson, *The Purpose of the Biblical Genealogies,* 208.

[116]1 Chr 2:9–10; Ruth 4:19. Luke's source for the two names Ἀρνί and Ἀδμίν is difficult to identify. Perhaps this is due to different MSS traditions.

The names that appear in the second group, generations from David to Jechoniah (vv. 6b–11) cannot be found in Luke's Gospel. Luke not only mentions twenty generations for the same period for which Matthew has fourteen, but presents a completely different Davidic branch. By following the line of David's son Nathan, Luke shows that Jesus' ancestors were insignificant people, which is in agreement with his concern for those who are poor and marginalized. Matthew, on the other hand, presents the list of David's royal descendants, which begins with Solomon. Matthew seems to follow 1 Chr 3:10–15, but he apparently omits the names of Ὀχοζία, Ἰώας, and Ἀμασίας.[117] At the end Matthew also omits the king Jehoiakim, thus making Josiah the father of his grandson Jechoniah.[118]

The names in the third division, generations from Jechoniah to Jesus (vv. 12–16) differ again from Luke's genealogy, with the exception of verses 12 and 16: both Matthew and Luke have Σαλαθιήλ and Ζοροβαβέλ (v. 12) and both have Ἰωσήφ and Ἰησοῦς (v. 16). The agreement in Matt 1:12 is probably due to the use of 1 Chr 3:17–19. It should be noted, however, that only the LXX mentions Shealtiel as the father of Zerubbabel, in contrast to the MT which has Pedaiah. The main disagreement between Matthew and Luke is that for the same period Matthew claims to have fourteen,[119] while Luke has twenty-two generations.[120] It is almost impossible to discover why some names were eliminated, and some not. Johnson has shown that all of them can be found in the Old Testament but never in a genealogical order.[121] Matthew thus covers the period of more than five centuries with only fourteen generations, leaving over forty years for each of them.

---

[117]Different answers could be given concerning the question of why Matthew omitted exactly these names and not the others. One possibility is that these kings were omitted because all three were accused by God: Ἰώας as murderer (2 Chr 24:22), Ἀμασίας as idolatrer (2 Chr 25:14, 16) and Ὀχοζία as Baal-worshiper (2 Chr 22:3–4) who died by violent death (2 Chr 22:7–9). Cf. G. Kuhn, "Die Geschlechtsregister Jesu bei Lukas und Matthäus, nach ihrer Herkunft untersucht," *ZNW* 22 (1923): 221–222. Kuhn also notices that the king Aman, who also died violently, has been included into the genealogy. A more convincing interpretation, however, is the one which ascribes this omission to a scribal mistake due to the similarity of the names Ὀχοζία and Ὀζίας. The fact that Ἀζαρία is known in the Old Testament also as Ὀζίας (cf. 2 Kgs 15:1 and 2 Chr 26:1), could have easily led to the scribal confusion; cf. Johnson, *The Purpose of the Biblical Genealogies*, 180; Burger, *Jesus als Davidssohn*, 94; and Luz, *Matthew 1–7*, 107.

[118]Cf. 2 Kgs 23:30, 34 and 24:6, 17.

[119]A disagreement between the factual evidence (thirteen generations) and Matthew's claim (fourteen generations) will be discussed below.

[120]Other disagreements are: according to Matthew, Shealtiel is the son of Jechoniah, while according to Luke, he is the son of Neri; if Ματθάν in Matt 1:15c and Μαθθάτ in Luke 3:24a are identical, Matthew regards Eleazar, while Luke names Levi as his father; according to Matt 1:16 Jacob was the father of Joseph, while according to Luke 3:23 Joseph's father was Heli.

[121]Johnson, *The Purpose of the Biblical Genealogies*, 180.

This inevitably suggests that Matthew's genealogy is artificially composed with the goal of fitting the pattern three times fourteen, which clearly betrays its midrashic character. The numbering of generations itself is not surprising, because it was an ancient habit that we find in many biblical and post-biblical Jewish texts. Thus, for example, Genesis 5 lists ten generations from Adam to Noah; Gen 11:10–26 has ten generations from Noah to Abraham; Dan 9:1–27 divides the history of the people into 70 year-weeks; *1 En.* 93:1–10 and 91:12–17 divides the history of the world into 10 units of 7, i.e. 10 times 7 generations, which is further developed in *T. Levi* 17. What is surprising, however, is the fact that Matthew deliberately structured his genealogy in a threefold division, each containing 14 generations.

The reasons for Matthew's arrangement are not easy to discern. According to one view, Matthew adopted the number fourteen from the first division from Abraham to David, as he had found it in the Old Testament sources.[122] This interpretation, however, does not offer the explanation of why the number fourteen is artificially applied to the second and the third group of generations.

One of the most popular opinions is that the number fourteen comes from *gematria*, a custom of counting the numerical value of consonants in a certain word, which was very common in the first century, particularly in the apocalyptic circles. Thus the grouping of generations into three fourteens may be due to the fact that in the Hebrew name David (דוד), there are three letters whose numerical value is 4+6+4=14.[123] This theory, however, presupposes either that the genealogy was originally composed in Hebrew or Aramaic, or that Matthew, being familiar with both Hebrew and Greek, applied the numerical value of Hebrew name דוד to the genealogy composed in Greek. The weakness of the former is that there are indications of a strong dependence of Matthew's genealogy on the LXX, because some of the changes he made do not work in Hebrew. The weakness of the latter is that it is based on too many assumptions. It presupposes, namely, not only a bilingual author, but also a bilingual audience, since otherwise Matthew readers would not be able to grasp *gematria*. Indeed there are two instances in Greek documents where *gematria* was used. In *Sib. Or.* 1:324–330, *gematria* was based on the numerical value of Greek letters, while in Rev 13:18 *gematria* was probably based on the Hebrew transliteration of the Greek name Νέρων Καῖσαρ. Matthew's *gematria*, however, would be quite unique, because it is based on the Hebrew name which was given in Greek transliteration. All of this

---

[122]Zahn, *Matthäus*, 51.

[123]Cf. G. H. Box, "The Gospel Narratives of the Nativity and the Alleged Influence of Heathen Ideas," *ZNW* 6 (1905): 80–81; Johnson, *The Purpose of the Biblical Genealogies*, 192–193; Waetjen, "The Genealogy," 210. D. Hill emphasizes that "as well as providing an aid to memory, this schematization would strengthen the already clear emphasis on the Davidic character of Jesus" (*The Gospel of Matthew*, NCB [London: Marshall, Morgan and Scott, 1972], 74).

suggests that *gematria* was probably a "coincidence"[124] which additionally supported the division into three fourteens.

More convincing than *gematria* are parallels which can be found in the apocalyptic literature. A comparison with the "Messiah Apocalypse" in *2 Bar.* 53–74 is particularly illuminating. This text, which divides world history into fourteen epochs, shows that number fourteen was considered in some apocalyptic circles as a pointer to the coming of the expected eschatological age. Another striking parallel to Matthew's genealogy is the "Ten-week apocalypse" in *1 En.* 93:1–10 (first seven weeks) and 91:12–17 (last three weeks). According to Strack and Billerbeck,[125] *1 En.* 93:3 indicates that each week was composed of seven days or generations. Weeks 4–5 would thus encompass the fourteen generations between Isaac and Solomon, weeks 6–7 fourteen generations between Solomon and exile, while weeks 8–9 encompass fourteen generations which would pass until the coming of the eschatological age.

In any case, it is difficult to decide which, if any, of these texts contains the key to Matthew's arrangement of three times fourteen. What can be said with greater certainty is that Jewish parallels indicate that divisions of world history into periods and their numbering according to a certain pattern are often done with the purpose of speculating about the coming of the final eschatological age. Even though in some of these visions of the future the Messiah is present (*2 Bar.* 53–74)[126] while in some not (*1 En.* 93:1–10 and 91:12–17), it is likely that Matthew's strong insistence on the numeric structure of the history between Abraham and Jesus in 1:17 serves as a reference to the eschatological significance of the last name mentioned in the succession of generations. Its purpose is to signal that the long awaited deliverer has been born. The difference between Matthew 1 and other early Jewish messianic texts which assert that only God knows when the Messiah will appear, such as *Pss. Sol.* 17:21; *4 Ezra* 12:31–32; 13:26, is the changed perspective: while the latter look into the future which is yet to come, the former claims that the Messiah has already appeared. Jesus' name at the end of the genealogy in Matthew 1 denotes the turning point of the history of God with his chosen people, which began with Abraham, indicating the end of the old and the beginning of the new era.

---

[124]M. J. Lagrange, *Évangile selon Saint Matthieu*, 4th ed., EtB (Paris: Lecoffre/Gabalda, 1927), 3.

[125]H. L. Strack and P. Billerbeck, *Kommentar zum Neuen Testament aus Talmud und Midrasch*, vol. 1 (München: C. H. Beck'sche Verlagsbuchhandlung, 1924), 44–45.

[126]Another similar passage can be found in *4 Ezra* 7, which divides the time into "this world" and "the world to come." This world is then divided into three periods, at the end of which the Messiah will appear. However, the Messiah does not inaugurate a messianic age, but will die after four hundred years (*4 Ezra* 7:28–29).

Matthew's genealogy therefore fulfills a double task. On the one hand, it demonstrates that Jesus, as any other member of the genealogy, is David's descendant and therefore rightly called a son of David. On the other hand, its numeric structure indicates that Jesus is not only *a* son of David, as for example Joseph (Matt 1:20), but that he is *the* Son of David. As the last member of the series of three times fourteen generations, Jesus[127] is the goal of history – the long awaited Davidic Messiah.

Jesus' Davidic lineage, however, contains two odd features: it enumerates four women along their male partners, and it abruptly ends between Joseph and Jesus. If the former is strange,[128] the latter is certainly problematic and requires further elaboration.

---

[127]Cf. Matt 1:17 which does not mention Jesus' name, but only Christ. However, in order to avoid any confusion of the reader, v. 16 (Ἰησοῦς ὁ λεγόμενος χριστός) clearly identifies that both expressions refer to the same person.

[128]The inclusion of women in someone's pedigree was not a customary feature of Jewish genealogies. A woman is mentioned in scriptural genealogies only when there is an irregularity of pedigree, or if her name has noteworthy associations, as in Gen 22:20–24; 25:1–6; 35:22b–26; 1 Chr 2:3–4, 18–20, 46–47; 7:24. Surprisingly, Matthew's genealogy includes only the women who had a questionable reputation in Israel's history; cf. Strack and Billerbeck, *Kommentar*, vol. 1, 15–18, 20–30; Johnson, *The Purpose of the Biblical Genealogies*, 152–179. Thamar (v. 3a) dressed herself as a harlot in order to conceive a child with her father-in-law Judah; Rahab (v. 5a) was known as a harlot, and nowhere in the Old Testament or Jewish literature can we read about her marriage to Salma or parentage of Boas; cf. R. Bauckham, "Tamar's Ancestry and Rahab's Marriage: Two Problems in the Matthean Genealogy," *NovT* 37 (1995): 323, who ponders that Rahab's marriage to Salma reflects the midrashic desire to connect various biblical characters, as well as to find husbands for those female figures whose husbands are not specified in the Bible. Matt 1:5a would be then a midrash on 1 Chr 2:54–55; Ruth (v. 5b) was a foreigner who spent the night with Boas, which might at least provoke a suspicion that she has sinned, and Bathsheba (v. 6b) committed adultery with David. These women appear only in the first division of the genealogy, so that none of Matthew's contemporaries could have denied that they belong to David's and thus ultimately messianic lineage. Deciphering Matthew's motives for mentioning their names, however, is a difficult task. A good overview of various interpretations is given by Brown, *The Birth of the Messiah*, 71–74. For a feminist critique of traditional explanations see A.-J. Levine, *The Social and Ethnic Dimensions of Matthean Salvation History: "Go nowhere among the Gentiles . . ." (Matt. 10:5b)*, SBEC 14 (Lewiston/Queenston/Lampeter: The Edwin Mellen Press, 1988), 59–80; and E. M. Wainwright, *Towards a Feminist Critical Reading of the Gospel according to Matthew*, BZNW 60 (Berlin: Walter de Gruyter, 1991), 63–67. Some commentators, for example, see here an apologetic interest on the part of Matthew, who might have wished "to disarm criticism by showing that irregular unions were divinely countenanced in the Messiah's legal ancestry" (A. H. McNeile, *The Gospel According to St. Matthew: The Greek Text with Introduction, Notes, and Indices*, Thornapple Commentaries [London: Macmillan and Company, 1915], 5). Another common opinion is that these four women in the genealogy prepare the reader for the inclusion of Mary, i.e. that the strangeness in their pregnancies prepares for the divine irregularity of the birth of Jesus; cf. E. Klostermann, *Das Matthäusevangelium*, 4th ed., HNT 4 (Tübingen: J. C. B. Mohr, 1971), 2; Jeremias, *Jerusalem zur Zeit Jesu*, 327; Hill, *The Gospel of Matthew*, 74. The plausibility of this interpretation is

2.3.1.3 The Engrafting of Jesus into the Davidic Line

The anomaly of Jesus' Davidic lineage is that the unbroken chain of generations does not continue beyond Joseph. Instead of fathering Jesus, Joseph appears in the role of the husband of Mary, ἐξ ἧς ἐγεννήθη Ἰησοῦς ὁ λεγόμενος Χριστός (Matt 1:16).[129] The text which follows, Matt 1:18–25, is sometimes incorrectly called "the account of the birth of Jesus."[130] The birth as such is not even mentioned but only implied at the end. The verses narrate how the problem of discontinuity has been solved.[131] It is a drama in which Joseph

---

supported by the fact that in the post-biblical Jewish literature, these women were often seen as instruments of God's plan for Israel, and their initiative and courage were interpreted as means of divine providence. Equally popular is the view that these women were included into Jesus' genealogy because they were all non-Jews. Rahab was Canaanite, Ruth was Moabite, Tamar was a "daughter of Aram" (*Jub.* 41:1; *T. Jud.* 10:1), while the omission of the personal name of Bathsheba (ἐκ τῆς τοῦ Οὐρίου) might suggest that she was also considered non-Israelite. This was the dominant position of the church fathers, such as Origen, Chrysostom, Jerome, and Ambrose, as well as Luther; cf. also Y. Zakowitch, "Rahab als Mutter des Boas in der Jesus-Genealogie," *NovT* 17 (1975): 1–5; H. Stegemann, "'Die des Uria': Zur Bedeutung der Frauennamen in der Genealogie von Matthäus 1,1–17," in *Tradition und Glaube: Das frühe Christentum in seiner Umwelt*, ed. G. Jeremias, H.-W. Kuhn, and H. Stegemann, FS K. G. Kuhn (Göttingen: Vandenhoeck & Ruprecht, 1971), 246–276; Nolan, *The Royal Son of God*, 62–63. Although Bauckham ("Tamar's Ancestry and Rahab's Marriage," 313–320) argued that *Jub.* 41:1 and *T. Jud.* 10:1 should be no longer taken as a proof to support a view that Tamar was a Canaanite, he did not deny that Philo's presentation of Tamar as a proselyte from Palestinian Syria (*Virt.* 220–222) provides a clear evidence that Tamar could have been considered a Gentile by the first-century Jews. The usual objection to this view is that despite their pagan origin, these women were regarded as proselytes in later Jewish tradition. The weakness of this proposal is usually seen in its inability to explain the connection between these four women and Mary; cf. Brown, *The Birth of the Messiah,* 73. Since, however, there is no compelling reason for assuming that they have to be linked to Mary only, it is quite plausible to see them as foreshadowing Jesus' life and ministry, especially its broadening from the Jewish toward the Gentile world. After all, it cannot be a coincidence that Matthew added the title "Son of David" to the story of the Canaanite woman in 15:21–28. In his capacity as the Son of David Jesus was asked for and eventually offered help to a person of Gentile origin, who, interestingly enough, happened to be a woman, like the four female characters mentioned in Jesus' family tree.

[129]The variant reading, Ιωσηφ, ω μνηστευθεισα ην Μαριαμ παρθενος, εγεννησεν Ιησουν τον λεγομενον χριστον, found in *Sinaitic Syriac*, is most likely a declaration of Joseph's legal, not biological paternity. For a discussion of this reading see A. S. Lewis, *Light on the Four Gospels from the Sinai Palimpset* (London: Williams & Norgate, 1913), 31–44.

[130]For some authors, like Lohmeyer (*Matthäus*, 12), and Strecker (*Der Weg der Gerechtigket*, 53–54) the meaning of γένεσις in 1:18 is "birth" in contrast to the meaning of the same word in 1:1.

[131]Cf. the comment of H. C. Waetjen: "On the one hand, the procreation of Jesus the Christ is not simply a matter of the continuity of history. The greatest anomaly of the entire genealogy occurs here [v. 16]! But on the other hand, Joseph must be the father of Jesus or the entire preliminary history of Jesus' origin and his relationship to the Davidic dynasty is irrelevant and useless" ("The Genealogy," 216).

plays the main role. With the introductory sentence τοῦ δὲ Ἰησοῦ Χριστοῦ ἡ γένεσις οὕτως ἦν (v. 18a), Matthew first clarifies that he is now going to explain the origin of Jesus, which remained obscure at the end of the genealogy. This means that οὕτως should not be understood in isolation, i.e. as an introduction to the miracle of Jesus' birth, but rather as an introduction to the narrative about circumstances which made it possible to regard Jesus as the legitimate son of Joseph and therefore the heir of David's throne.

The text that follows describes the situation in which Joseph found himself after discovering Mary's pregnancy. Matthew reports about Joseph's inner decision after he realized that Mary was expecting a baby (he resolved to divorce her quietly), and immediately gives a comment about his character (he was a just man) which is meant to explain his decision to divorce her (he was not willing to put her to shame). His intentions are altered through the utterance of an angel. By addressing him as a son of David, the angel gives him guidance for his conduct (he should not fear to take Mary) by explaining to him what the reader already knows from verse 18, namely that Mary is pregnant by the Holy Spirit. Besides referring to the past, the angel reveals to him the future (Mary will bear a son), again gives him instructions of what to do (he should give the name Jesus to the newborn child), and explains to him the meaning of the name (he will save his people from their sins).

The last two verses (Matt 1:24–25) describe the events after Joseph's vision. Joseph obeyed the command of the angel, took his wife and named the child after it was born. With this act, "Joseph, by exercising the father's right to name the child (cf. Luke 1:60–63), acknowledges Jesus and thus becomes the legal father of the child."[132] Joseph's adoption of Jesus restores the broken chain of generations from verse 16. With this, Matthew has demonstrated that Jesus could be rightly called the son of David and the son of Abraham.

The designation "son of Abraham" is significant in many ways. Jewish literature, especially many New Testament passages, emphasize that Abraham is the father of the Jewish nation. Yet, in Jewish tradition Abraham was remembered not only as the subject of God's election,[133] but also as the recipient of God's promise that in his seed all the nations will be blessed. The latter aspect is emphasized and the former one broadened in the other three

---

[132]Brown, *The Birth of the Messiah,* 138–139. Legal paternity, as Brown suggests, is probably a better term than adoption, which was, as G. H. Box notes, an institution "evidently unfamiliar in Palestine during the NT period" ("Adoption [Semitic]," in *Encyclopaedia of Religion and Ethics,* ed. J. Hastings, vol. 1 [Edinburgh: T.&T. Clark, 1908], 115). Cf. also Jones, "Subverting the Textuality of Davidic Messianism," 259–260. I will nevertheless continue to use the term "adoption" because it is so widely used in the literature, though I am aware that it is an interpretation of Joseph's act which reveals Hellenistic influence.

[133]Cf. F. E. Wieser, *Die Abrahamvorstellungen im Neuen Testament,* EHS.T 317 (Bern: Peter Lang, 1987), 14–16, who interprets Matthew's genealogy as "eine zentrale Aussage des erwählungsgeschichtlichen Modells zur Deutung Abrahams im NT" (ibid., 16).

passages outside chapter 1, where Matthew mentions Abraham. In 3:7–10, John the Baptist warns the Pharisees and Sadducees that God is able to raise up children to Abraham from stones. In 8:10–12, Jesus says that Gentiles will share in the eschatological banquet with the patriarchs, while the sons of the kingdom will be judged. In 22:29–33, Abraham, Isaac and Jacob prefigure the resurrection of the just. The main thrust of these texts is strengthened by the fact that at the end of his Gospel, Matthew presents Jesus sending his disciples to all nations (28:19). Matthew's designation of Jesus as the son of Abraham announces the fulfillment of the eschatological promise given to Abraham and thus widens the narrowness of the nationalistic horizon connected with the name David.[134] "In a hidden way"[135] the universalistic significance of Jesus as the Son of David is predicted.

Although the universalistic aspect of Jesus' messiahship appears to be very important for Matthew, it seems, that his primary goal in chapter 1 is to establish the royal identity of the newborn child Jesus. This conclusion is supported not only by the fact that in 1:1 he mentions the designation "son of David" before the designation "son of Abraham," but also by the fact that the term "son of David" occurs again in verse 20, but here applied to Joseph. This indicates that the crucial point is the continuity of the Davidic line. The adoption of Jesus by Joseph made him a legal descendant of David, the king. This is the reason for the shift towards Joseph as a central figure in Matthew's explanation of Jesus' origin, because Jesus' identity as the son of David is established only in his relationship to Joseph and not to his mother Mary.

Since the purpose of the designation "son of David" in Matthew 1 is to demonstrate Jesus' Davidic ancestry, it belongs to the same category as the term "seed of David." It is even possible to regard it as a genealogical elaboration of the latter. It explicates an important aspect of the title "Son of David" – the actual Davidic descent of its bearer. It is therefore absolutely legitimate to regard it as a further development of the promise tradition that has been discussed above.

---

[134]Psalm 2, which was read as a messianic text in some early Christian circles (see section 2.2.2.3), offers a potential link between the promises given to Abraham and to David. In Ps 2:8, God says to His Anointed, "Ask of me, and I will make the nations your heritage and the ends of the earth your possession" (שאל ממני ואתנה גוים נחלתך ואחזתך אפסי־ארץ; αἴτησαι παρ' ἐμοῦ καὶ δώσω σοι ἔθνη τὴν σου καὶ τὴν κατάσχεσίν σου τὰ πέρατα τῆς γῆς [LXX]). This promise resembles the promise given to Abraham in Gen 22:18, "And by your offspring shall all the nations of the earth be blessed" (והתברכו בזרעך כל גויי הארץ; καὶ ἐνευλογηθήσονται ἐν τῷ σπέρματί σου τὰ ἔθνη τῆς γῆς [LXX]). D. Juel notes that this "psalm not only provides the scriptural justification for a messianic interpretation of Abraham's 'seed' but offers evidence of such an interpretation within the Bible itself" (*Messianic Exegesis*, 87).

[135]Luz, *Matthew 1–7*, 110.

2.3.1.4 The Divine Sonship of Jesus

Even though Matthew explicitly claims that Jesus' genealogy is structured after the pattern of three fourteens, in reality the number fourteen applies only to the first two divisions, but not to the generations between the deportation to Babylon and the Christ. This phenomenon has long been noted and different solutions have been offered, such as that Jesus should be counted as the thirteenth and the Christ as the fourteenth generation,[136] that Jesus Christ should be counted twice,[137] that Matthew probably counted Jehoiakim in the second group although his name was omitted, and started counting the third group with Jechoniah,[138] while some feminist interpreters argue that Jesus is an illegitimate child and that the thirteenth place belongs to his biological father.[139]

However, despite the fact that neither is God explicitly said to be Jesus' father nor is Jesus called the "Son of God,"[140] there are three main reasons for assuming that the missing link between Joseph and Jesus should be assigned to God, Jesus' divine father. First, the passive ἐγεννήθη in v. 16b (repeated in the participial form in v. 20), which suddenly replaces formula "x ἐγέννησεν y," is most likely the divine passive, which was often used in Judaism to describe God himself.[141] Second, the phrase ἐκ πνεύματος ἁγίου (Matt 1:18), which

---

[136]K. Stendahl, "Matthew," in *Peake's Commentary on the Bible*, ed. M. Black (London: Thomas Nelson and Sons, 1962), 770–771.

[137]Waetjen, "The Genealogy," 213.

[138]Brown, *The Birth of the Messiah*, 83–84.

[139]J. Schaberg, *The Illegitimacy of Jesus: A Feminist Theological Interpretation of the Infancy Narratives* (San Francisco: Harper & Row, 1987), 36–41.

[140]The absence of the title "Son of God" in Matthew 1 is usually taken as a strong argument against the Son of God Christology in the birth narrative. Thus, for example, W. D. Davies points out that the wording of v. 18a is τοῦ δὲ Χριστοῦ ἡ γένεσις οὕτως ἦν and not τοῦ δὲ υἱοῦ τοῦ θεοῦ ἡ γένεσις οὕτως ἦν ("The Jewish Sources of Matthew's Messianism," in *The Messiah*, ed. J. H. Charlesworth [Minneapolis: Fortress, 1992], 494). A careful reader, however, will notice that Davies equates Son of God Christology with incarnation, which certainly cannot be found in Matthew. None of the New Testament writings associate virginal conception with the idea of incarnation; cf. Brown, *The Birth of the Messiah*, 141; Fuller, "The Conception/Birth of Jesus," 47. The absence of the title can be explained as the result of Matthew's emphasis on Jesus' Davidic descent, which is problematized and endangered. Jesus' divine sonship is assumed and never questioned. The only problem is human inability to recognize it without divine revelation. Moreover, the first occurrence of the title in Matt 2:15 in the fulfillment citation from Hos 11:1 certainly does not have the purpose of marking Jesus' departure to Egypt as a Christological moment. The divine voice recognizes the state of affairs that has been already established, not the migration to Egypt as *the* moment when Jesus acquired the status of the Son of God. The curious lack of any reference in chapter 2 to Joseph's relationship to the newborn child, after he has obeyed the divine order and adopted the child, and the constant repetition of the phrase "the child and his mother" point in the same direction.

[141]Cf. Nolan, *The Royal Son of God*, 223.

indicates God's creative power, implies a divine sonship of Jesus.[142] Third, it is very likely that the deliberate use of the verb γεννάω[143] is Matthew's allusion to God's begetting the Messiah in Ps 2:7 LXX (υἱός μου εἶ σύ ἐγώ σήμερον γεγέννηκά σε), which was understood especially in early Christian writings as a reference to the promise of a father-son relationship between God and David's offspring in 2 Samuel 7. The second and third reason require more elaborate explications.

The idea that a human being could be conceived with the help of God's creative power was not strange in Judaism. Thus, for example, *Gen. Rab.* 47 (29c); 63 (39c) and *Midr. Ruth* 4:12 (137a) reflect upon Gen 17:17; 18:11–14; 21:1–7; 25:21, by asserting that Sarah, Rebekah and Ruth were able to conceive their children only through a miraculous intervention of God who created their uterus. The idea, however, that a human being could be conceived only through the divine action and without the participation of the male partner cannot be found in the literature of early Judaism. Consequently, it is not surprising that Jews never expected that the promised Messiah would be born through the intervention of supernatural forces.[144] The concept of a virgin birth is thus something absolutely new in comparison to the Jewish way of thinking.

Matthew, however, presents the citation of Isa 7:14 as a scriptural confirmation for the idea of virginal conception. The style of Matt 1:22–23, the appearance of a different name (not Jesus but Emmanuel), the change from "you" to "they," and the fact that the name Emmanuel is translated indicate that these verses contain Matthew's interpretation of the preceding episode. Because of the introductory formula in 1:22, this citation belongs to the group of the so-called Matthean formula quotations.[145] Matt 1:23 (ἰδού ἡ παρθένος ἐν

---

[142]Many scholars trace the Son of God Christology back to the birth narrative. Among them are: Fuller, *The Foundations of New Testament Christology,* 192; O. Cullmann, *The Christology of the New Testament,* trans. S. C. Guthrie and C. A. M. Hall, rev. ed., NTL (Philadelphia: Westminster, 1963), 294; Hahn, *The Titles of Jesus in Christology,* 306–307; R. Pesch, "Der Gottessohn im matthäischen Evangelienprolog (Matt 1–2). Beobachtungen zu den Zitationsformeln der Reflexionzitate," *Bib* 48 (1967): 395–420; Vögtle, *Messias und Gottessohn,* 16–17; Soares Prabhu, *The Formula Quotations,* 52–53; Brown, *The Birth of the Messiah,* 133–138; Dunn, *Christology in the Making* (London 1980), 49–50.

[143]Cf. Luke's genealogical formula x τοῦ y (Luke 3:23–38).

[144]*Pace* P. Sigal, who claims that 1QSa 2.11–15 contains the idea of divine conception of the Messiah ("Further Reflections on the 'Begotten' Messiah," *HAR* 7 [1983]: 221–233); cf. also M. Smith, "'God's Begetting the Messiah' in 1QSa," *NTS* 5 (1958–59): 218–224. However, the reading יוליד in 1QSa 2.11 is, first of all, highly questionable. Moreover, even if such a reading were accepted, the idea of divine conception of the Messiah would be, as Evans notes, an overinterpretation of the text ("Are the 'Son' Texts at Qumran Messianic?" 140).

[145]Cf. 2:15, 17, 23; 4:14; 8:17; 12:17; 13:35; 21:4; 27:9. Matthew's formula quotations were the object of extensive scholarly research. The most important studies are: K. Stendahl, *The School of St. Matthew and Its Use of the Old Testament,* ASNU 20 (Lund: C. W. K. Gleerup, 1954), 97–127, 183–206; Strecker, *Der Weg der Gerechtigkeit,* 49–85; R. H. Gundry, *The Use of the Old Testament in St. Matthew's Gospel with Special Reference to the*

γαστρὶ ἕξει καὶ τέξεται υἱόν, καὶ καλέσουσιν τὸ ὄνομα αὐτου Ἐμμανουήλ) is
the only Matthew's fulfillment citation that offers a text which is almost
identical with the LXX. In all other cases the text of a citation differs
substantially from the LXX.

It should be noted that the Hebrew text of this verse does not speak about a
"virgin," but about a "young woman" (העלמה). This, however, does not mean
that the early church developed the idea of virginal conception on the basis of
the LXX translation of Isa 7:14. Raymond E. Brown rightly insists that "there
was nothing in the Jewish understanding of Isa 7:14 that would give rise to
such a belief nor, *a fortiori,* to the idea of a begetting through the creative
activity of the Holy Spirit."[146] Even the LXX translators perhaps did not have a
virginal conception in mind, but only that a girl who is now a virgin will, by
natural means, conceive a child in the future.

It is neither possible nor necessary to deal here with the development of the
doctrine of the virginal conception. The only thing that matters is that
Matthew's text presupposes such a belief, which the author equally shares with
his audience. The LXX text of Isaiah is then additionally used as a scriptural
confirmation of this concept. Matthew's exegesis follows the rules of
midrashic exegesis of the first century C.E. He was not looking for the literal
sense of Isa 7:14, but for words which he could use. Isa 7:14 LXX, containing
the term παρθένος, was the most suitable text for the purpose he wanted to
accomplish. Also, the change from λήμψεται to ἕξει might be an indication
that the evangelist wanted to avoid any association with the male originator of
the pregnancy.[147] With this the emphasis switches from the process of
becoming pregnant to the state of pregnancy. The combination of the term
παρθένος and ἐν γαστρὶ ἕξει leads to the conclusion that Matthew had in mind
a virgin who will be pregnant as a virgin.[148]

Matthew apparently takes pains to demonstrate that the fatherless
conception belongs to the same realm of God's relationship to the world as his
act of creation described in Genesis 1. William D. Davies calls attention to the
use of the word γένεσις in Matt 1:1 which evokes the first book of the Tanak,

---

Messianic Hope, NovTSup 18 (Leiden: E. J. Brill, 1967), 89–127; W. Rothfuchs, *Die
Erfüllungszitate des Matthäus-Evangeliums: Eine biblisch-theologische Untersuchung,*
BWANT 88 (Stuttgart: W. Kohlhammer Verlag, 1969), 27–44; Soares Prabhu, *The Formula
Quotations,* 18–161.

[146]Brown, *The Birth of the Messiah,* 149.

[147]Waetjen ("The Genealogy," 223) has shown that in the LXX, "the preposition ἐκ
conveys the agency of the male principle only in conjunction with the clause ἐν γαστρὶ
λαμβάνεσθαι, never with the clause ἐν γαστρὶ ἔχειν."

[148]Cf. J. Nolland, "No Son-Of-God Christology in Matthew 1.18–25," *JSNT* 62 (1996): 7
n.18.

and connotes an act of a new creation.[149] His assumption, however, that the genitive Ἰησοῦ Χριστοῦ in Matt 1:1 is subjective is highly questionable. There are no indications that "Jesus is the initiator of a new creation parallel with the first."[150] Rather, through his Spirit, God is the only subject of the new creative act.[151] The role of the Holy Spirit in virgin birth parallels the role of the Spirit at the first creation. Matthew's association of the role of the Holy Spirit in the virginal conception and the repetition of the word γένεσις in Matt 1:18 additionally strengthen this conclusion. As *4 Ezra* 7:31 demonstrates, the idea of a new creation has found an easy entrance into Jewish messianology. Its potential lies in the parallelism between the commencement of the world and the inauguration of the anticipated messianic time, better known as the parallelism between *Urzeit* and *Endzeit*.[152]

The weakness of the idea that there is a connection between the virgin birth as an act of a new creation and the beginning of the messianic time lies in its inability to offer a convincing explanation of the notion of Jesus' divine sonship.[153] The answer for the origin of this conception must be sought elsewhere. The language of "begetting" (ἐγεννήθη) suggests a link with Ps 2:7 (γεγέννηκα). It also shares certain similarities with the New Testament enthronement language discussed above.[154] It alludes to the divine begetting from Ps 2:7, now understood in a more literal sense. Even though the Holy Spirit does not function as a male principle, but as an agent of God's creative power, the passive construction of the verb γεννάω insinuates the divine subject of the process. Jesus' divine sonship is thus directly linked to his Davidic sonship, similar to the Jewish and Christian texts considered earlier.[155]

---

[149]Davies conjectures that Philo's application of the word "Genesis" to the first book of Tanak in *Post.* 127, *Abr.* 1, *Aet.* 19 shows that this usage could have been known to Matthew ("The Jewish Sources of Matthew's Messianism," 496–498).

[150]Ibid., 497.

[151]E. Schweizer (*The Holy Spirit*, trans. Reginald H. and I. Fuller [Philadelphia: Fortress Press, 1980], 54–55) interprets this act of a new creation as "a direct act of the creator himself such as never happened before in the case of any other human being . . . . God, in his free, underivative action, causes Jesus to be born, who, entirely under the control of his Spirit, will accomplish the saving presence of God."

[152]Cf. Davies, "The Jewish Sources of Matthew's Messianism," 498.

[153]See the critique of Nolland, "No Son-Of-God Christology in Matthew 1:18–25," 8.

[154]This feature of Matthew's infancy narrative has been especially emphasized by Brown, *The Birth of the Messiah*, 29–32, 134–137, 140–142, 181–183. However, his thesis that this proves that the post-resurrection Christology of Jesus' enthronement as the Son of God has been pushed back first to his baptism and then to his conception/birth must be seriously questioned. See the critique by Fuller, "The Conception/Birth of Jesus," 37–52.

[155]According to Brown, Jesus' divine conception and his adoption by Joseph are for Matthew "a most literal fulfillment of the promise of God to David through Nathan: 'I shall raise up *your son* after you . . . . I shall be his father, and he will be *my son.*'" (*The Birth of the Messiah*, 137). Brown is, however, slightly imprecise here. 2 Samuel 7 does not use the word

The major difference, however, is the way these two sonships relate to each other. In Matthew, Jesus' divine sonship precedes his Davidic sonship, with the consequence that the idea of adoption becomes associated with his Davidic lineage, not his status as the Son of God.

Matthew takes pains to show that Jesus' messiahship is inseparable from his identity as the Son of God. He is the only evangelist who links Peter's confession of Jesus' messiahship in Cesarea Philippi to his confession that Jesus is the son of the living God (σὺ εἶ ὁ Χριστὸς ὁ υἱὸς τοῦ θεοῦ τοῦ ζῶντος – Matt 16:16; cf. Mark 8:29, Luke 9:20, and John 6:69). An almost identical wording appears in Matthew's version of the question of the high priest: σὺ εἶ ὁ χριστὸς ὁ υἱὸς τοῦ θεοῦ; (Matt 26:63) in contrast to Mark 14:61 (σὺ εἶ ὁ χριστὸς ὁ υἱὸς τοῦ εὐλογητοῦ;) and Luke 22:67 (σὺ εἶ ὁ χριστός;). Finally, the answer to Jesus' question about David's son in Matt 22:41–46 presupposes an inseparable link between Jesus' Davidic and divine sonship. The argument for this thesis will be offered in the next section.

2.3.2 The Question about David's Son

2.3.2.1 The Question about David's Son in Mark 12:35–37

The main theme of Jesus' dialogue with the Pharisees in Matt 22:41–46 is the sonship of the Messiah (Τί ὑμῖν δοκεῖ περὶ τοῦ Χριστοῦ; τίνος υἱός ἐστιν;). This is the reason that even though this text appears almost at the end of Jesus' career and serves to conclude his conflict with the Pharisees, it directly refers to the question of Jesus' origin.

Matthew's text represents an adaptation of the question about David's son found in Mark 12:35–37, which has been the object of an extended scholarly debate.[156] Disputable questions are whether this text preserves a genuine Jesus saying[157] or is a church interpolation,[158] and whether there is a difference between its original meaning and its meaning in the Gospel of Mark.[159]

"son" for David's descendant, but "seed which shall come forth from your body." Nevertheless, the latter clearly refers to David's son Solomon.

[156]An excellent overview of different opinions can be found in G. Schneider, "Die Davidssohnfrage (Mk 12,35–37)," *Bib* 53 (1972): 65–90.

[157]Those who hold this position offer various reasons for it. Thus R. Gagg ("Jesus und die Davidssohnfrage: Zur Exegese von Markus 12,35–37," *TZ* 7 [1951]: 18–31) regards this as a *Streitgespräch* of the historical Jesus who did not use the terms κύριος and υἱὸς Δαυίδ as "theologisch gefüllte Begriffe," but who wants to stop the controversy with his opponents (ibid., 24). E. Lohmeyer (*Das Evangelium des Markus*, 4th ed. [Göttingen: Vandenhoeck & Ruprecht, 1954], 261–263) interprets this passage as a polemical argument of Jesus that the Messiah does not have to be Davidide, because both statements, i.e. that the Messiah is David's son and that he is David's Lord, cannot be true. According to Lohmeyer, Jesus did not speak of himself, but of somebody else. O. Cullmann (*The Christology of the New Testament*, 130–133) uses Mark 3:33 as the hermeneutical key and interprets Mark 12:35–37 as a genuine Jesus' saying in which Jesus did not deny his Davidic sonship, but rather rejected "the

D. Daube[160] was among the first to insist that here we have a special case of *haggadha*, composed according to the rabbinic pattern of the fourfold

---

Christological significance the Jews attached to this descent for the work of salvation he had to accomplish . . . . Jesus argues against the idea that the Messiah must be of the physical lineage of David" (p. 131), because this idea emphasizes "the political Messianic ideal" which Jesus rejects (p. 132). Cullmann argues that the saying must go back to the historical Jesus, because, otherwise it is not explainable why the church would include it in its canon in light of Rom 1:3 and other texts which reflect the early Christian confession of Jesus' descent from David.

[158]R. Bultmann (*The History of the Synoptic Tradition*, 136–137; idem, *Theology of the New Testament,* trans. K. Grobel, vol. 1 [New York: Charles Scribner's Sons, 1954], 28) is probably the best known proponent of the opinion that the passage is the formulation of the early church. He reached this conclusion on the basis of his interpretation of the meaning of the passage. In his view, the pericope denies Davidic origin of Jesus, and stands therefore in opposition to Paul (Rom 1:3). The fact that Paul presupposes Davidic origin of Jesus suggests that this idea could be traced back to the historical Jesus. This in turn means that Jesus himself could not have denied the Davidic origin of the Messiah, so that the pericope in Mark 12:35–37 cannot be ascribed to him, but to the church. G. Bornkamm (*Jesus of Nazareth,* trans. I. and F. Mcluskey [New York/ Evanston/London: Harper & Row, 1960], 227–228) also does not ascribe the passage to the historical Jesus, but regards it as the formulation of the early church which has the purpose of disputing the applicability of the title "Son of David" to Messiah. Hahn (*The Titles of Jesus in Christology*, 103–105) analyses the passage within the schema of two-stage Christology. In Mark 12:35–37, he sees a development from the identification of the Son of David with the Messiah toward the identification of the latter with the Kyrios. According to him, this identification cannot originate in the Palestinian church and cannot therefore be the authentic word of Jesus.

[159]O. Cullmann (*The Christology of the New Testament,* 132–133), for example, thinks that the historical Jesus denied the Christological significance of Davidic origin of the Messiah, but since Mark did not know how to interpret it, he did not understand this as a denial of Jesus' Davidic origin. A. Suhl (*Die Funktion der alttestamentlichen Zitate und Anspielungen im Markusevangelium* [Gütersloh: Gerd Mohn, 1965], 91) assumes the existence of the pre-Markan tradition of the saying, but thinks that it is difficult to reconstruct it. He believes that in the Markan pericope the Son of David question is unequivocally negatively answered. Burger (*Jesus als Davidssohn,* 71) denies the authenticity of the saying and regards it rather a formulation of such Christian group which was not able say that Jesus was of Davidic origin. Burger, however, disagrees with Suhl that the pericope in its present Markan context represents a denial of Jesus' Davidic origin and argues that it signifies the latter's overcoming through the title Son of God. Burger emphasizes the similarity between Mark 12:35–37 and Rom 1:3, because in both cases the Son of David represents only one temporary stage which is exceeded by Jesus' installation to the position of the Son of God. The only difference to Romans is, in his view, the time of the installation: in Romans, it is the resurrection, while in Mark, it is the adoption at baptism, the proclamation at the transfiguration, and the acclamation at the resurrection (ibid., 64).

[160]D. Daube, "Four Types of Question," in *The New Testament and Rabbinic Judaism.* The Jewish People: History, Religion, Literature (New York: Arno Press, 1973), 158–169. Daube's primary concern was Mark 12:35–37 in its Markan context, but he discusses its Matthean and Lukan parallels as well.

grouping of exegetical questions.[161] The basis of Jesus' dialogue with the Pharisees about the sonship of the Messiah is an apparent contradiction between two scriptural passages which must be resolved. According to Daube, the task is to discover the viewpoint which will bring both statements into agreement.

Daube's analysis opened the door for a more comprehensive comparison of Mark 12:35–37 with the rabbinic material. It has been noticed that this pericope, even if taken out of its present context, follows the rabbinic pattern of an apparent contradiction between two scriptural passages. The hermeneutical rule which was to be applied in these cases was formulated by R. Ishmael as the last of his thirteen *middoth,* which speaks about "two scriptural passages which contradict one another until a third passage comes and decides between them."[162] According to Nils A. Dahl, both the rabbinic practice and the older formulation of this rule ascribed to R. Akiba,[163] which advises that the conflicting scriptural passages "should be upheld in their place until a third passage comes and decides between them,"[164] indicate that the apparent contradiction is to be principally solved by an exegetical distinction, i.e. by attempting to find the proper context for each scriptural passage which will preserve their validity. If, however, a third passage demands another resolution of the discord, contextual exegesis must be repudiated.[165] In Dahl's view, Mark 12:35–37 is a classic example of the apparent contradiction between two scriptural passages, whose solution is to be found in the career of Jesus of Nazareth, who was of David's lineage, and who was seated at the right hand of God.[166]

A more elaborate investigation of the relationship between Davidic sonship and the lordship of the Messiah in Mark 12:35–37 (and its Matthean and Lukan parallels) along the lines of Daube's and Dahl's inquiry was undertaken

---

[161]These four groups are: *hokhma* ("wisdom," i.e. halakic interpretation of legal texts), *boruth* ("vulgarity," i.e. questions designed to ridicule a belief), *derekh 'eres* ("way of the land," i.e. the principle of moral conduct), and *haggadha* ("legend," i.e. the interpretation of biblical passages with apparent contradictions). Daube's approach was followed by J. Jeremias (*Jesus' Promise to the Nations,* SBT 24 [London: SCM, 1958], 52–53), Fitzmyer ("The Son of David Tradition," 86–87), and Schneider ("Die Davidssohnfrage [Mark 12,35–37]," 81–90).

[162]Translated by N. A. Dahl, "Contradictions in Scripture," in *Studies in Paul: Theology for the Early Christian Mission* (Minneapolis: Augsburg, 1977), 162. Dahl insists that this is a more literal translation of R. Ishmael's rule than the free paraphrase proposed by H. J. Schoeps, "If two verses contradict one another, one seeks a third to set aside the contradiction" (*Paul: The Theology of the Apostle in the Light of Jewish Religious History,* trans. H. Knight [London: Lutterworth Press, 1961], 177–178).

[163]*Mek. Pisha* 4; *Sipre Num.* 58; see J. Z. Lauterbach, *Mekilta de-Rabbi Ishmael,* vol. 1 (Philadelphia: Jewish Publication Society of America, 1933), 32.

[164]The translation by Dahl, "Contradictions in Scripture," 162.

[165]Ibid., 161–162.

[166]Ibid., 161.

by Evald Lövestam.[167] In searching for a solution to the conflicting scriptural references, Lövestam first investigated other New Testament passages in which the relationship between Jesus' Davidic sonship and his exaltation in reference to Ps 110:1 are treated: Acts 2:29–35, 13:23–39, and Heb 1:5–13. He came to the conclusion that all three passages wish to demonstrate that God's promise to David in 2 Sam 7:12 has been completed in Jesus' exaltation according to Ps 110:1. In other words, divine promises are viewed from the perspective of their completion (*Vollendung*) which took place in Jesus' resurrection and exaltation.[168] With the help of this insight into the early Christian treatment of the relationship between the Davidic descent of the Messiah and his lordship, Lövestam interpreted the question about David's son in Mark 12:35–37, Matt 22:41–46, and Luke 20:41–44, and concluded that these two characteristics are neither put in opposition to each other, nor presented as two stages in which the second surpasses the first. Rather, they are mutually interdependent, because the promises to David have found their fulfillment precisely in Jesus' resurrection and exaltation.[169]

Lövestam's analysis is highly instructive and illuminating. It represents a perceptive inquiry of early Christian interpretation of Scripture in light of the conviction that Jesus is indeed the promised Messiah. A closer examination, however, reveals that two out of his three New Testament examples of the treatment of the relationship between Jesus' Davidic sonship and his exaltation in reference to Ps 110:1 do not contain both elements which seemingly contradict each other in the question about David's son in the Synoptics. Thus in the argument of Acts 13:23–39, despite the fact that there is a clear reference to David's posterity, Ps 110:1 plays no role. This connection can be made only indirectly, by linking the role of the resurrection as a prerequisite of the fulfillment of the promise given to David in Paul's speech in Acts 13:23–39 to the similar role of the resurrection in Peter's speech in Acts 2:29–35, where it is interpreted as the exaltation in a direct reference to Ps 110:1. The situation is exactly the opposite in Heb 1:5–13. Even though the argument for Jesus' superiority to angels starts with the citations of Ps 2:7 and 2 Sam 7:14 and concludes with the quotation of Ps 110:1, the reference to the promise to David does not have in view David's descendant, but his status as God's son. Finally, Lövestam's final conclusions are too general and do not reflect the differences among the Synoptics in handling the question of David's son. Nevertheless, his approach has much to recommend it, especially his attention to the treatment of Ps 110:1 in other NT texts which either quote or allude to

---

[167]E. Lövestam, "Die Davidssohnfrage," *SEÅ* 27 (1962): 72–82.

[168]Ibid., 78.

[169]Ibid., 80. Juel further qualifies Lövestam's conclusion by pointing out that the solution of the apparent contradiction serves to make a point "that death and resurrection are not incompatible with what the Scriptures have to say about the Christ" (*Messianic Exegesis,* 144).

it. In the following, some of his insights will be further developed, especially with attention to Matthew's presentation of the apparent conflict between the Davidic sonship and the lordship of the Messiah.

2.3.2.2 The Argumentative Structure of Matt 22:41–46

By comparing Matthew's text with Mark 12:35–37, it can be noticed that Matthew made some significant changes to his Markan *Vorlage*. First of all, he reworked the Markan monologue into a dialogue between Jesus and the Pharisees. He not only left the Pharisees on the scene, but also assigned them a different role: Jesus is the one who charges, and they are those who have to defend themselves. Further, instead of starting with the polemical inquiry: Πῶς λέγουσιν οἱ γραμματεῖς ὅτι ὁ Χριστὸς υἱὸς Δαυίδ ἐστιν, Jesus begins with a simple and quite neutral question: Τί ὑμῖν δοκεῖ περὶ τοῦ Χριστοῦ; τίνος υἱός ἐστιν? The answer of the Pharisees is equally simple: Τοῦ Δαυίδ. Matthew further divides Jesus' second question into two parallel questions, each being introduced by πῶς, by reformulating the Markan statement αὐτὸς Δαυίδ λέγει αὐτὸν κύριον (Mark 12:37a) into a protasis of a conditional clause, and by altering the curious word order αὐτοῦ ἐστιν υἱός[170] into υἱὸς αὐτοῦ ἐστιν.

The weight of these modifications can be determined only through the analysis of the argumentative structure of the pericope. The leading question of the dialogue is the question about the sonship of the Messiah. The question is asked by Jesus, and the answer given by the Pharisees: the Messiah is the son of David. This statement has a double reference point: it pertains both the titular usage of this designation and its non-titular usage in the sense of David's descendent. As noted earlier, the titular application of the phrase "Son of David" to the expected Davidic Messiah is not attested in Hebrew Scripture, but appears for the first time in *Pss. Sol.* 17:21. The non-titular usage refers to the promised offspring of David in 2 Sam 7:12 and its various scriptural references which have been messianically interpreted in early Jewish literature. There is no explicit scriptural citation supplied for supporting the affirmation that the Messiah is the son of David, but in view of the fact that the "Son of David" title strongly resembles God's promise to David, explicitly in *Pss. Sol.* 17 and implicitly in Matthew, it is very likely that it functions as "a shorthand substitution for the actual citation of a passage like 2 Sam 7:12–14."[171] Its truthfulness is accepted and the text presupposes that both the Pharisees (who make this statement) and Jesus (who does not reject it) share the same affirmative attitude toward it.

---

[170] Already Wrede noticed a striking placement of αὐτοῦ in the sentence: instead of the expected καὶ πόθεν ἐστὶν υἱὸς αὐτοῦ, Mark has καὶ πόθεν αὐτοῦ ἐστιν υἱός ("Jesus als Davidssohn," 175).

[171] Juel, *Messianic Exegesis,* 143.

The second statement is that David called the Messiah lord, and its validity is supported by the scriptural quotation of Ps 110:1 (109:1 LXX).[172] However, the word "Messiah" does not appear in the actual citation of the psalm. Rather, God (יהוה in the Hebrew text, κύριος in the LXX[173]) speaks to someone whom David, as the presumed author of the psalm,[174] calls his lord (לאדני in the Hebrew text, τῷ κυρίῳ μου in the LXX). The quotation of the psalm in Matt 22:44 makes sense only under the presupposition that both dialogue partners share the view that the recipient of God's utterance (second κύριος) should be understood as a reference to the Messiah.[175]

Jewish literature does not unequivocally support this interpretation. David M. Hay has demonstrated that there is only a sparse evidence in pre-Christian literature with a clear reference or even an allusion to Ps 110:1, and that even this scarcity testifies to the variety of interpretations attached to this psalm.[176]

---

[172]The closing phrase of the quotation (ὑποκάτω τῶν ποδῶν σου) betrays the influence of Ps 8:7 LXX (ὑποκάτω instead of ὑποπόδιον). A full quotation of Ps 8:7 LXX can be found in Heb 2:8. In 1 Cor 15:25–27, Paul makes an explicit connection between Ps 110:1 and Ps 8:7. Although he does not make use of the first line of Ps 110:1, which explicitly mentions the title κύριος, he links the second line of this psalm with Ps 8:7b by associating the phrases ὑπὸ τοὺς πόδας αὐτοῦ. A combination between these two scriptural texts can be also found in Eph 1:20–22 and 1 Pet 3:22.

[173]Even though the New Testament writings show that early Christian interpreters had copies of the LXX in which God's ineffable name יהוה was translated with κύριος, it is uncertain how widespread this practice really was in the first century C.E. In some early manuscripts, such as 4QLXXLev[b], יהוה has been replaced by the term Ιαω. In other instances, such as the fragments of Deutoronomy from the 1st cent. B.C.E. (see P. Fouad Inv. 266), the divine name is presented in a normal Jewish script of the time. In the oldest copy of the Greek Minor Prophets scroll published by D. Barthélemy (*Les devanciers d'Aquila*, VTSup 10 [Leiden: Brill, 1963]) the Tetragrammaton is represented in the paleo-Hebrew script. For further evidence and discussion see P. W. Skehan, "The Divine Name at Qumran, in the Masada Scroll, and in the Septuagint," *BIOSCS* 13 (1980): 14–44. This means that one can no longer suppose that early Christian interpreters had at their disposal only the Greek manuscripts that contained the term κύριος for God's ineffable name and then applied it to Jesus, because he is according to Ps 110:1 also called κύριος. The latter has been most eloquently argued by Hahn, *The Titles of Jesus in Christology*, 104–110. For a critique of this view, see Juel, *Messianic Exegesis*, 148.

[174]By the time the Gospel of Matthew was written, Davidic authorship of the psalms was generally accepted by both Jews and Christians. After carefully examining the literature of the Second Temple period, M. Daly-Denton (*David in the Fourth Gospel*, 59–113) concludes that even though the earliest unambiguous Jewish declarations of Davidic authorship of the Psalter postdate the New Testament period, the supposed Davidic authorship was universally accepted by the end of the first century. She further adds that "this presupposition was the basis for the use of the psalms in early Christianity" (ibid., 318). The phrase ἐν πνεύματι (Matt 22:43) points to an inspired speech; cf. U. Luz, *Das Evangelium nach Matthäus*, vol. 3, EKK I/3 (Zürich, Düsselforf: Benziger; Neukirchen-Vluyn: Neukirchener, 1997), 287.

[175]Cf. Luz, *Matthäus*, vol. 3, 287.

[176]D. M. Hay, *Glory at the Right Hand: Psalm 110 in Early Christianity*, SBLMS 18 (Nashville: Abingdon, 1973), 21–33; see also Juel, *Messianic Exegesis*, 137–139.

In *T. Job* 33.3, it is understood as a reference to the exoneration of a righteous sufferer. In Dan 7:9–14, it is probably applied to a humanlike figure who was enthroned beside God.[177] Descriptions of the heavenly enthronement of the messianic figure called "The Elect One" or "The Son of Man" in the *Similitudes of Enoch*[178] might be allusions to Ps 110:1.[179] Psalm 110 as a whole might have been understood messianically by the translators of the Greek Psalter.[180] There is a possibility that the portrait of Melchizedek as a heavenly eschatological warrior in 11Q13 (11QMelch) echoes Ps 110:1, even though the actual psalm is not quoted. Only in some later passages from rabbinic literature,[181] such as *Midr. Ps.* 18, sec. 29, the second lord in the psalm is unambiguously understood as a messianic designation.

The New Testament evidence shows that early Christian interpreters made use of potential messianic implications of the psalm and applied it to Jesus of Nazareth in order to present him as the vindicated Messiah exalted to the right hand of God.[182] The messianic interpretation of Ps 110:1, however, was only

---

[177]This conclusion is not so certain. In later rabbinic interpretation, such as *b. Sanh.* 38b, we find a clear association between Ps 110:1 and Dan 7, but whether this was the case already in the pre-Christian Judaism is, in Juel's words, "difficult to determine" (*Messianic Exegesis,* 138).

[178]*1 En.* 45:3; 51:3; 55:4; 61:8; 69:29.

[179]According to M. Hengel, the affinity between Ps 110:1 and the figure of the son of man has been "broadly developed in the Similitudes" ("'Sit at My Right Hand!' The Enthronement of Christ at the Right Hand of God and Psalm 110:1," in *Studies in Early Christology* [Edinburgh: T&T Clark, 1995], 186).

[180]This has been argued by J. Schaper, *Eschatology in the Greek Psalter*, WUNT II/76 (Tübingen: J. C. B. Mohr [Paul Siebeck], 1995), 101–107. Shaper's reconstruction is based on a careful analysis of the translation of Ps 110:3 (109:3 LXX) from Hebrew to Greek, which indicates, in his view, that this verse was understood as a reference to a pre-existent transcendent Messiah. He dates this process to the reign of Hyrcanus I (ibid., 141). A messianic interpretation of Ps 110:3 (109:3 LXX) in the Greek translation of the Psalter in the sense of a pre-existent figure is also accepted by W. Horbury, *Jewish Messianism and the Cult of Christ* (London: SCM Press, 1998), 95–96.

[181]According to Hay (*Glory at the Right Hand*, 28), the earliest messianic interpretation of the psalm in the rabbinic sources is not attested before the second half of the third century C.E.

[182]Cf. Acts 2:33–36; 7:55–56; Rom 8:34; 1 Cor 15:25; Eph 1:20; Col 3:1; 1 Pet 3:22; Heb 1:3, 13; 12:2, etc. For a comprehensive analysis of the use of Ps 110:1 in early Christianity, see M. Gourgues, *A la Droite de Dieu. Résurrection de Jésus et Actualisation du Psaume 110,1 dans le Nouveau Testament*, EtB (Paris: Lecoffre/Gabalda, 1978); Hay, *Glory at the Right Hand*; M. Hengel, "'Sit at My Right Hand!'" 119–225; cf. also T. Callan, "Ps 110,1 and the Origin of the Expectation that Jesus will come again," *CBQ* 44 (1982): 622–635; W. R. G. Loader, "Christ at the Right Hand – Ps. CX in the New Testament," *NTS* 24 (1978): 199–217. It is beyond the scope of this study to trace the development of Christian application of Ps 110:1 to the exalted Christ. D. Juel (*Messianic Exegesis*, 139–141) believes that this psalm was originally read and interpreted as a messianic text. Once applied to Jesus in this way, it opened other possibilities of application to the risen Christ. Unfortunately, explicit evidence about the earliest stages of this process is lacking. What can be asserted with relative certainty

one among several interpretative possibilities, so that it could not have been unambiguously used for apologetic purposes.[183] Christian understanding of this psalm as messianic is a consequence of a prior conviction that Jesus is indeed the expected Messiah, and not the other way around.

Even though Ps 110:1 might be the scriptural passage that is most frequently directly or indirectly referred to in the New Testament,[184] it is actually quoted only in the question about David's son (Matt 22:41–46; Mark 12:35–37; Luke 20:41–44), Peter's Pentecost speech (Acts 2:34), and at the end of the argument for Jesus' superiority over angels constructed as a series of scriptural quotations (Heb 1:13).[185] Among them, only the first two applications make the connection between the psalm and the promise of David's descendant. Furthermore, only in Acts 2:34, Ps 110:1 is used for apologetic purposes as part of the argument for Jesus' messiahship. Jesus' resurrection and exaltation are viewed as the literal fulfillment of the psalm, whose messianic connotations are taken for granted.

Similarly, in Matt 22:41–46, the messianic interpretation of the psalm is presupposed, but in contrast to Peter's speech, its function is not to demonstrate that Jesus can be rightly called κύριος and χριστός, but to show that the Messiah can be called David's lord. However, even though there is no explicit application of the psalm to Jesus, its implicit applicability to Jesus' career is meant to be the solution of the apparent conflict between two scriptural passages. Matthew's editorial activity is instructive at this point. In contrast to Mark (and Luke) who seem to take the complete wording of Ps 110:1 as a description of the dignity of the Messiah, Matthew's emphasis falls on κύριος only.[186]

The text presumes that the statement that the Messiah is David's lord contradicts the statement that the Messiah is David's son. Yet the reason for this contradiction is not so apparent, especially if the reader presupposes that υἱός Δαυίδ and κύριος are the titles which can be legitimately applied to the Messiah. Thus in *Pss. Sol.* 17 we find both titles, υἱός Δαυίδ (17:21) and χριστός κύριος (17:32), peacefully coexisting next to each other. Similarly, in Acts 2:29–35, the only other New Testament text containing both affirmations

---

is that this interpretative endeavor of the primitive church can be traced back to the first few years after Jesus' death and resurrection. If so, it was "a claim of fanatic boldness," as Hengel notes ("Sit at My Right Hand!" 174), because it declared that Jesus, an alleged Messiah who died a shameful death by crucifixion, was subsequently resurrected and exalted to God's very presence.

[183]See Juel's critique of B. Lindars' approach in his *New Testament Apologetic* (*Messianic Exegesis*, 140).

[184]Cf. Lövestam, *Son and Savior*, 32; Hengel, "Sit at My Right Hand!" 133.

[185]The list of Hay (*Glory at the Right Hand*, 163–65) also includes thirteen allusions.

[186]Matthew introduces the quotation with πῶς οὖν Δαυίδ ἐν πνεύματι καλεῖ αὐτὸν κύριον λέγων (Matt 22:43).

which appear in Matt 22:41–46 (and parallels), Ps 110:1 plays a crucial role in the complex argument that Jesus is the Messiah, David's descendant promised to sit upon his throne. As noted above, Jesus' resurrection, viewed here as his exaltation to the right hand of God in reference to Ps 110:1, represents the fulfillment of God's promise that David will continually have a descendant sitting upon his throne.

It is therefore somewhat surprising that the Davidic descent and the lordship of the Messiah have the seemingly contradicting role in the question about David's son. Exegetical literature is remarkably silent at this point. The contradiction, which the text presupposes, is usually taken for granted, without much effort to spell it out. The main difficulty comes from the fact that the premise under which this apparent discrepancy makes sense is not explicated, but must be deduced. The contradiction works only under the condition that both designations, David's son and David's lord, are understood literally, and under the premise shared by all participants, that fathers do not call their sons lords.

As a result of Matthew's editorial activity, the conflicting role of both affirmations is clearly articulated through two parallel questions asked by Jesus, which have the following structure:

1. *Question* (v. 43): If the Messiah is David's son[187] (assuming that fathers do not call their sons lords), how (πῶς)[188] can the Messiah be called David's lord?
2. *Question* (v. 45): If the Messiah is called David's lord (assuming that fathers do not call their sons lords), how (πῶς) can the Messiah be David's son?

Both questions ask about the condition, under which the realization of the statement in the *apodosis* will be possible, if the condition in the *protasis* is fulfilled. Grammatical structure and the tenses which are used (all of them are present indicatives) show that here we are dealing with the special case of the real conditional sentences.[189] However, since they are shaped as questions, it becomes clear that in each of them another condition must be fulfilled in order for the statement in the *apodosis* to become a fact.

---

[187]Despite the fact that Jesus does not say εἰ ὁ Χριστὸς υἱὸς Δαυίδ ἐστιν, it is clear from his argument that the truthfulness of the Pharisees' answer is not problematized, but taken as a real condition for the first πῶς question.

[188]πῶς can also be translated "In what way?" See R. H. Gundry, *Matthew: A Commentary on His Handbook for a Mixed Church under Persecution,* 2nd ed. (Grand Rapids, Michigan: William B. Eerdmans Publishing Company, 1994), 452.

[189]For this group of conditional clauses see F. Blass and A. Debrunner, *A Greek Grammar of the New Testament and Other Early Christian Literature.* A Translation and Revision of the ninth-tenth German edition incorporating supplementary notes of A. Debrunner by R. W. Funk (Chicago and London: The University of Chicago Press, 1961), 189 § 372.

Grammatically speaking, in this type of sentence emphasis is on the reality of the assumption in the *protasis*, and "not of what is being assumed,"[190] i.e. the speaker assumes the reality of the assumption without giving his/her subjective judgment concerning the relationship of the assumption to the reality.[191] However, since we are dealing here with an apparent contradiction between the two scriptural passages, it is clear that Matthew's questions are not ambivalent in regard to the truthfulness of the assumptions on which they are based. The problem which must be solved is to discover the viewpoint that will bring both statements into agreement.

2.3.2.3 The Resolution of the Conflicting Statements in Matt 22:41–46

The analysis of the argumentative structure of Matt 22:41–46 has shown that the crucial question of the dialogue is not about the relationship between the designations Son of David and κύριος,[192] but about the condition under which both qualifications can be simultaneously applied to the same person. In agreement with the rabbinic practice discussed above, the solution should be first looked for in exegetical distinction, i.e. by attempting to find the context in which both statements can remain valid. Matthew's concluding comment that no one among Jesus' dialogue partners was able to answer him a word reveals that the solution is to be found in the realm for which the characters in the story, the Pharisees, remain blind – in the identification of David's son and David's lord with Jesus of Nazareth.[193]

Notwithstanding this primary solution, there are two elements that indicate that Matthew wanted to suggest a more precise resolution of the conflicting statements in reference to Jesus' true identity. First, he reformulated Jesus'

---

[190]Ibid., 188 § 371.

[191]R. Kühner and B. Gerth, *Ausführliche Grammatik der Griechischen Sprache,* vol. 2, part 2 (Hanover: Hahnsche Buchhandlung, 1904), 464.

[192]Some scholars think that the main issue in Matt 22:41–46 is the question of the relationship between the Son of David and κύριος; see Duling "The Therapeutic Son of David," 406–407; Strecker, *Der Weg der Gerechtigkeit,* 119–120. Behind such a proposal is usually the conviction that Matthew does not offer a choice "either . . . or," but wants to affirm both attributes, Son of David and κύριος. Thus I. Broer ("Versuch zur Christologie des ersten Evangeliums," in *The Four Gospels 1992,* ed. F. Van Segbroeck, C. M. Tuckett, G. Van Belle, and J. Verheyden, FS F. Neirynck, vol. 2 [Leuven: University Press, 1992], 1258–1259) insists on the relationship between the designations Son of David and κύριος because he disagrees with those scholars who, like J. D. Kingsbury ("The Title 'Son of David'," 595–596) and H. Geist (*Menschensohn und Gemeinde: Eine redaktionskritische Untersuchung zur Menschensohnprädikation im Matthäusevangelium,* FB 57 [Würzburg: Echter Verlag, 1986], 377–378), introduce the title Son of God into the interpretation of the text with the purpose of asserting that Jesus' Davidic sonship is overcome by his divine sonship. Broer's thesis that "die Perikope bejaht mit dem ganzen Evangelium die Davidssohnschaft Jesu" is confirmed by the study undertaken here, in spite of a disagreement concerning the way the problem in Matt 22:41–46 is formulated.

[193]See Dahl, "Contradictions in Scripture," 161.

question into a double question, which first takes Davidic sonship, and then Davidic lordship as the assumption, thus suggesting that the solution has to enable simultaneously the truthfulness of both assumptions.[194] Second, he indicated the area in which the answer should be sought by starting the dialogue with Jesus' question τί ὑμῖν δοκεῖ περὶ τοῦ χριστοῦ; τίνος υἱός ἐστιν; Such formulation of the initial question suggests that more than one sonship is possible. For the reader of Matthew's narrative this cannot be surprising, because both Jesus' Davidic sonship and his divine sonship were established already in the first chapter of Matthew's Gospel and consistently affirmed throughout the narrative.[195]

The postulation that Jesus' divine sonship represents the solution to the conflict between two scriptural statements in Matt 22:41–46 is supported not only by the link between Jesus' Davidic and divine sonship, but also by a cogent association between Ps 110:1 and Jesus' divine sonship, attested both in other New Testament passages and in the Gospel of Matthew. In Acts 2:32–36, Jesus' resurrection is interpreted as his exaltation to God's right hand and presented as the fulfillment of Ps 110:1, while in Acts 13:33, Jesus' resurrection is understood as his elevation to the position of the Son of God and presented as the fulfillment of Ps 2:7. The association between Jesus' divine sonship in light of Ps 2:7 and his exaltation to God's right hand is

---

[194]This is the reason for the deficiency of the solution proposed by Daube ("Four Types of Question," 163), in whose view the Messiah is David's son up to a certain moment in history, but is Lord from that moment on. Already Jeremias (*Jesus' Promise to the Nations,* 53), who followed Daube's proposal concerning the haggadic question, limited this solution to the Gospel of Mark only. Many scholars agree that Jesus' questions as formulated by Matthew do not imply any chronological division between these titles, i.e. that Matthew does not presuppose any kind of two-stage Christology. Even the thesis of G. Bornkamm that this "paradoxal combination of the two titles" can be resolved in such a way that "in his earthly lowliness he [Jesus] is David's son, but as the Exalted One he is Lord" ("End-Expectation and Church in Matthew," in *Tradition and Interpretation in Matthew,* ed. G. Bornkamm, G. Barth, and H. J. Held [London: SCM, 1963], 33) is an affirmation of the simultaneous application of both titles to Jesus; See Strecker, *Der Weg der Gerechtigkeit,* 120 n.2. Strecker himself is clear at this point: "Es kann sich also nur um ein gleichzeitiges Nebeneinander handeln" (p. 120), but in contrast to Bornkamm he sees the solution in the different context of application of both titles: the title "Son of David" expresses Jesus' sending to Israel, while the title "Kyrios" expresses Jesus' universal significance which goes beyond the national boundaries of Israel. Apart from the question whether κύριος should be treated as a fixed title in Matthew, the problem with this interpretation is that Jesus' universal significance has not become obvious to the reader at this point in the narrative but will be revealed fully at the end of Matthew's Gospel (Matt 28:16–20). On the other hand, since the closure of the narrative sheds light on the events narrated before, the reader will grasp the full implications of Jesus' question in 22:41–46 only at the end; cf. U. Luz, "Eine thetische Skizze der Matthäischen Christologie," in *Anfänge der Christologie,* ed. C. Breytenbach and H. Paulsen, FS F. Hahn (Göttingen: Vandenhoeck & Ruprecht, 1991), 225.

[195]Cf. Luz, *Matthäus,* vol. 3, 288.

especially evident in Heb 1:5–13, where the former starts and the latter concludes the argument for Jesus' superiority over angels. Finally, in all synoptic accounts (Matt 26:63–65; Mark 14:61–63; Luke 22:67–71), Jesus' reply to the question of the high priest in the trial scene associates the designation "Son of God" with two scriptural passages, Ps 110:1 and Dan 7:13.[196] In Matthew, Jesus answers the question of the high priest whether he is χριστός ὁ υἱὸς τοῦ θεοῦ, which ironically echoes Peter's confession in Matt 16:16, by referring to Ps 110:1 combined with Dan 7:13.

This evidence suggests that both apparently conflicting assumptions in Matt 22:41–46, that the Messiah is David's son and that he is also David's lord, can be associated with Jesus' divine sonship. Moreover, a closer examination of their role in Jesus' πῶς questions shows that the resolution of the conflict represents a uniquely Matthean understanding of the relationship between Jesus' Davidic and divine origin. It is usually assumed that Jesus' questions are two equivalent versions of one and the same question. However, this can be said only for Mark, who presents a single question two times.[197] In Matthew, both questions are quite distinct and point in opposite directions.[198] First πῶς asks about the possibility for the truthfulness of the statement that the Messiah is David's lord under the condition that he is David's son. This question can be rephrased in this way: How can somebody who is according to his position inferior to David (his son) be at the same time superior to him (David's lord)? Assuming the knowledge of the reader about Jesus' dual sonship, the only answer which could be given is that this is possible only if that one is in reality the son of somebody higher than David, i.e. God.

The second πῶς asks about the possibility for the truthfulness of the statement that the Messiah is David's son under the condition that he is David's lord. This question can be rephrased in this way: How can somebody who is according to his position superior to David (David's lord) be at the same time inferior to him (David's son)? This question reverses the poles as they were formulated in the first question. The answer therefore cannot be identical with the first one, because it will be a confirmation of what is already assumed. Somebody who is superior to David can be his son only if he becomes his son. This answer suggests an act by which his Davidic sonship is established.[199] For Matthew's reader this can be nothing else but an allusion to

---

[196]In *Midr. Ps.* 2:9 (14b), Ps 2:7 is associated with Exod 4:22, Isa 52:13, Isa 42:1, Ps 110:1, and Dan 7:13; cf. Lövestam, *Son and Savior,* 108.

[197]The first question: πῶς λέγουσιν οἱ γραμματεῖς ὅτι ὁ Χριστὸς υἱὸς Δαυίδ ἐστιν (Mark 12:35b) is in fact repeated again: αὐτὸς Δαυὶδ λέγει αὐτὸν κύριον, καὶ πόθεν αὐτοῦ ἐστιν υἱός (Mark 12:37a).

[198]The distinctiveness of both questions has been emphasized by Verseput, "The 'Son of God' Title," 546.

[199]A. Schlatter interpreted Jesus' question similarly by pointing out that "die Frage ist die, wie der von David als sein Herr Erkannte ihm gegenüber in die Stellung des Sohnes komme."

the way the newborn child Jesus became a legal descendant of David through Joseph's acknowledgment of his paternity. This connects Jesus' question directly to chapter 1 where Jesus' origin was presented to the reader and where Matthew explained how the Son of God became the Son of David.[200] However, although both of Jesus' questions go in opposite directions, the first one pointing toward Jesus' divine sonship, and the second one toward his Davidic sonship, they imply the same fact – a unique combination of both sonships which was realized only in one person, Jesus Christ, already at his birth.[201]

2.3.3 Conclusions

The argument of this section is that Matthew's designation of Jesus as the Son of David and the genealogy that follows should be understood in light of God's promises to David in 2 Samuel 7. Jesus' Davidic descent and his divine sonship, which are linked together in the promise tradition, are also associated in Matthew 1 and referred to in Matt 22:41–46. Since Jesus is both a son of David and God's son, he completely fulfills the first two elements of Nathan's promise to David and therefore possesses both attributes expected of the Davidic Messiah.

Yet, the peculiarity of Matthew's presentation of Jesus' Davidic and divine sonship is the notion that the continuity in Jesus' Davidic lineage is achieved through its brokenness. Jesus' divine sonship is presented as a feature that endangers Jesus' Davidic ancestry, which has been overcome by his "engrafting" into the Davidic line through the adoption by Joseph. This does not mean that Jesus is more than the Son of David, because he is in the first line the Son of God.[202] Rather, he became the Son of David despite the fact he was the Son of God. The title "Son of David" incorporates in this way the

---

Schlatter calls this process of entering into a father-son relationship with David "die Erniedrigung des Christus," and continues: "Damit ist der Kommende in die jüdische Geschichte und Gemeinschaft hineingestellt mit allen ihren ihn beengenden Schranken" (*Der Evangelist Matthäus: Seine Sprache, sein Ziel, sein Selbständigkeit,* 6th ed. [Stuttgart: Calwer, 1963], 660).

[200]B. M. Nolan does not link Matt 22:41–46 to Matthew 1 because he wants to avoid the conflict between his own interpretation of Matt 22:41–46 which, in his view, denies the Davidic sonship of Jesus, and Matthew 1, which affirms Jesus' Davidic origin: "The evangelist so dissociates the Christ from the Son of David in 22:42–45 that he can hint at the transcendence of the former without depreciating the descent from David" (*The Royal Son of God,* 149).

[201]A similar conclusion is reached by Strecker, *Der Weg der Gerechtigkeit,* 119–120; R. Walker, *Die Heilsgeschichte im Ersten Evengelium,* FRLANT 91 (Göttingen: Vandenhoeck und Ruprecht, 1967) 52 n.34; Hay, *Glory at the Right Hand,* 118.

[202]The superiority of Jesus' divine sonship has been particularly emphasized by J. D. Kingsbury, "The Title 'Son of God' in Matthew's Gospel," *BTB* 5 (1975): 3–31; idem, "The Figure of Jesus in Matthew's Story," *JSNT* 21 (1984): 3–22.

newness of Jesus' origin and introduces into the continuity of the Davidic line its radical discontinuity.

The Christology in Matthew 1 is thus not only an answer to but in some sense exactly the reverse of those streams of the Old Testament and early Jewish messianic traditions which connect Davidic and divine sonship. Although 2 Sam 7:12–14 and other related texts do not clarify the relationship between these two sonships, they clearly presume the chronological priority of the Davidic descent. Similarly, God's utterance to his anointed in Ps 2:7 "You are my son, today I have begotten you" insinuates that the royal figure was expected to become God's son by an act of divine adoption. Yet, instead of asking how David's offspring came to be the Son of God, Matthew shows how the Son of God, the One conceived by the Holy Spirit, came to be the Son of David. Matthew thus does not present Jesus as the Son of David who has been installed to the position of the Son of God by an act of divine adoption, but as the Son of God who became the Son of David by an act of human adoption.

2.4 The Task of Jesus, the Son of David

2.4.1 Jesus' Task According to Matt 1:21

It has been argued so far that the main task of the first chapter of Matthew's Gospel is to establish the messianic identity of the child to be born to Mary. This still holds true with one important qualification. In Matt 1:21, the angel announces Jesus' task in relationship to his people: He will save them from their sins. Strictly speaking, this is not a statement about who Jesus is, but about what he will do, and by implication, not about his identity but about his activity. On the other hand, one should not forget Jewish understanding of the close connection between one's name and one's identity.[203] The fact that Matt 1:21 interprets Jesus' name through his future activity closely ties Jesus' identity to his activity.

In Matt 1:21, Matthew uses the naming of the child as an opportunity to offer an explanation of the meaning of the name "Jesus." With this, he directly associates Joseph's act of adoption, which secured Jesus' incorporation into the Davidic line, with the succinct summary of the role Jesus was going to play in the future of his people. The programmatic significance of this verse has been generally recognized. Thus, for example, George W. Buchanan underscores that saving people from their sins is "a basic theme of the entire Gospel according to Matthew."[204] Similarly, Donald J. Verseput stresses that

---

[203]This is most clearly expressed in Abigail's words to David in 1 Sam 25:25 in regard to the character of her husband Nabal: "as his name is, so is he" (כשמו כן־הוא).

[204]G. W. Buchanan, *The Gospel of Matthew*, vol. 1, The Mellen Biblical Commentary New Testament Series [Lewiston, NY: Mellen Biblical Press, 1996], 82.

Matt 1:21 has the key position at the outset of the story, because it is important for deciphering the remainder of the narrative.[205] The problematic point, however, is the apparent link which Matt 1:21 makes between Jesus' saving from sins and his messianic identity. It has been often observed that "the fact that he will save his people from their sins is not a univocal mark of the Davidic savior."[206] Equally problematic is the frequently emphasized remark that "forgiveness of sins is the prerogative of God alone."[207]

These questions, however, cannot be addressed before a preliminary analysis of Matt 1:21 and its supposed scriptural *Vorlage*. In Matt 1:21, Matthew apparently alluded to the Hebrew version of Jesus' name (Joshua), which was according to popular etymology related to the Hebrew verb "to save" (ישע) and to the Hebrew noun "salvation" (ישועה). Philo[208] confirms that the etymology of the name "Joshua" was also known outside of Palestine.[209] Strictly speaking, the name Jesus means "Yahweh is salvation." However, Matthew ascribes the salvific activity not to God but to the bearer of the name, Jesus, and explains it as a salvation from the sins of "his," i.e. Jesus' people. Since Ps 130:8 (129:8 LXX) contains a similar wording, it is usually assumed that Matt 1:21 represents an adaptation of this psalm. Nevertheless, it should be noted that the formula τοῦτο δὲ ὅλον γέγονεν ἵνα πληρωθῇ τὸ ῥηθὲν ὑπὸ κυρίου διὰ τοῦ προφήτου λέγοντος introduces the citation of Isa 7:14 LXX in Matt 1:22–23, but not the citation of Ps 129:8 LXX in Matt 1:21.[210] The

---

[205]Verseput, "Davidic Messiah and Matthew's Jewish Christianity," 108. See also M. A. Powell, "The Plots and Sublots of Matthew's Gospel," *NTS* 38 (1992): 195.

[206]Nolan, *The Royal Son of God,* 205.

[207]W. D. Davies and D. C. Allison, *The Gospel According to Saint Matthew,* vol. 1, ICC (Edinburgh: T.&T. Clark, 1988), 210. Cf. also Nolan, *The Royal Son of God,* 129; J. Michl, "Sündenvergebung in Christus," *MTZ* 24 (1973): 25–35. For a different view see J. M. Allegro, *Die Botschaft vom Toten Meer: Das Geheimnis der Schriftrollen* (Frankfurt/ Hamburg: Fischer Verlag, 1957), 132. Allegro mentions Matt 1:21 in order to argue that the Davidic Messiah and the Messiah of Israel in Qumran refer to the same political-apocalyptic figure. This has been criticized by H. Braun, *Qumran und das Neue Testament,* vol. 1 (Tübingen: J. C. B. Mohr [Paul Siebeck], 1966), 7–8. Braun contends that salvation from sins is in Qumran, as otherwise in Judaism, God's and not Messiah's task. Very rarely one finds a statement that "sowohl der Name 'Jesus' wie auch seine Begründung sind durchaus vom atl und jüdischen Verständnis her erklärbar – ohne eine christliche Transformierung" (H. Frankemölle, *Jahwebund und Kirche Christi: Studien zur Form- und Traditionsgeschichte des "Evangeliums" nach Matthäus,* NTAbh 10 [Münster: Aschendorff, 1974], 214).

[208]Philo, *Mut.* 12.121, on Num 13:16.

[209]For the evidence of the knowledge of the meaning of Jesus' name in Hellenistic Christianity see Justin, *1 Apol.* 33.7; *2 Apol.* 6; Eusebius, *Dem. ev.* 4.10, 17; Epiphanius, *Haer.* 29.4.

[210]G. D. Kilpatrick argued that the introductory formula in Matt 1:22 originally belonged to Matt 1:21 (*The Origins of the Gospel According to St. Matthew,* 57). For a critique of this view see Stendahl, *The School of St. Matthew,* 99. In Stendahl's view, the credibility of

reason for this might have been a significant number of modifications
Matthew introduced in the scriptural quotation.

Matt 1:21	Ps 129:8 LXX
αὐτὸς γὰρ σώσει	καὶ αὐτὸς λυτρώσεται
τὸν λαὸν αὐτοῦ	τὸν Ἰσραηλ
ἀπὸ τῶν ἁμαρτιῶν αὐτῶν	ἐκ πασῶν τῶν ἀνομιῶν αὐτοῦ

It is clear from the context of both verses that despite the identity of both
personal pronouns (αὐτός), their antecedents are different: in Ps 129:8 LXX it
is God (κύριος), while in Matt 1:21 it is Mary's son who is to be named Jesus.
The change from λυτρώσεται into σώσει is best explainable as an adaptation
of the verse to the etymology of Jesus' name, whose Hebrew root ישע is in the
LXX most commonly translated with σῳζω.[211] The noun ἁμαρτία was probably
chosen because it was already an established constituent of Christian
vocabulary.[212] Also, the fact that in Matthew's Gospel the term ἀνομία
functions exclusively as a polemical term[213] might provide an additional
reason for its replacement with ἁμαρτία.[214]

The most puzzling change is the substitution of Ἰσραήλ with ὁ λαὸς αὐτοῦ,
given the fact that throughout Matthew's narrative the word ὁ λαός always
means Israel. This led some interpreters to maintain that ὁ λαὸς αὐτοῦ in Matt
1:21 also denotes Israel.[215] The difficulty with this interpretation is that the
reason for Matthew's alteration of the original wording Ἰσραήλ remains
obscure, especially in view of the fact that otherwise Matthew does not find it
difficult to mention or even stress Jesus' mission to Israel.[216] If Israel was
meant in 1:21, why didn't Matthew leave the word Ἰσραήλ from Ps 129:8
LXX?

Kilpatrick's argument is weakened by the fact "that the Hebrew equivalent of Matthew's
σώσει is not ישע but פדה (LXX: λυτρώσεται)."

[211]G. Fohrer, "σῳζω and σωτερία in the Old Testament," in *TDNT* 7 (1971), 970–971.

[212]Cf. primitive confessional statements in 1 Cor 15:3 and 1 Pet 3:18.

[213]Cf. Matt 7:23; 13:41; 23:28; 24:12. Also, the concept of ἀνομία is never associated with
the idea of forgiveness.

[214]Gundry (*Matthew,* 23) aptly notes that behind the redactional changes in Matt 1:21 is the
same tradition as behind Luke 1:77 (τοῦ δοῦναι γνῶσιν σωτηρίας τῷ λαῷ αὐτοῦ ἐν
ἀφέσει ἁμαρτιῶν αὐτῶν). Nonetheless, three most important differences between Matt 1:21
and Luke 1:77 are: (1) the text in Luke speaks about John, not Jesus; (2) the term ἁμαρτία is
directly linked to ἄφεσις, not to σωτηρία; (3) even though both texts contain the same phrase
ὁ λαὸς αὐτοῦ, in Luke it denotes God's, not Jesus' people.

[215]R. Hummel, *Auseinandersetzung zwischen Kirche und Judentum im Matthäusevangelium,* 2nd ed., BEvT 33 (München: Christus Kaiser, 1966), 136; Luz, *Matthew 1–7,*
121; Frankemölle, *Jahwebund und Kirche Christi,* 214.

[216]Cf. Matt 15:24 which represents Matthew's addition to Markan material: οὐκ
ἀπεστάλην εἰ μὴ εἰς τὰ πρόβατα τὰ ἀπολωλότα οἴκου Ἰσραήλ.

In search for an explanation, it can be noticed that apart from Matt 2:6[217] the word ὁ λαός never appears accompanied by a genitive of a noun or a pronoun. Matthew speaks about Jesus' church (μου τὴν ἐκκλησίαν – Matt 16:18) or his kingdom (ἡ βασιλεία αὐτοῦ – Matt 13:41; 16:28; 20:21). When to this we add the observation that in 21:43 only Matthew speaks about the kingdom of God which will be taken from the unbelieving Jews[218] and given to a nation (ἔθνος) which produces fruit,[219] it is very likely that ὁ λαός αὐτοῦ in Matt 1:21 refers to Jesus' church composed of both Jews and Gentiles.[220] The church thus represents the group which differentiates itself from Israel at large.[221] This sectarian understanding is comparable to the sectarian understanding of other Jewish groups around the turn of the era, such as the Qumran covenanters, the group behind the *Psalms of Solomon*, etc.

Nevertheless, Matthew's changes in 1:21, important as they might be, do not warrant the conclusion that the understanding of the relationship between redemption and sins in the quoted verse has been basically changed. This can be easily confirmed through a comparison of the concepts of deliverance and sinning in this psalm and the Gospel of Matthew.

Even though the expectation of salvation in Ps 130:8 (129:8 LXX) (and the parallel Ps 25:22 [24:22 LXX]) is preceded by a petition for forgiveness, it

---

[217]Matt 2:6 is a direct quotation from 2 Sam 5:2. The phrase τὸν λαόν μου designates God's, not Jesus' people, and it is followed by the qualifier τὸν᾽ Ισραήλ.

[218]The phrase "from you" (ἀφ᾽ ὑμῶν) is addressed to Jesus' listeners, the chief priests and the Pharisees, not to Israel as a whole.

[219]Contrast Mark 12:1–12 and Luke 20:9–19. Cf. a much harsher treatment of the sinful Jews than the treatment of the Gentiles in the future kingdom of the Son of David described in *Pss. Sol.* 17. K. E. Pomykala (*The Davidic Dynasty*, 163) calls attention to the modification of Ps 2:9 in the text of the psalm. While in the psalm the nations are broken by the iron rod, in *Pss. Sol.* 17:25 the sinners are condemned. Also, while the Gentiles will have a certain role in the messianic kingdom, "there appears to be no place for errant Jews."

[220]For this interpretation see Gundry, *Matthew*, 23–24; Davies and Allison, *Matthew*, vol. 1, 208; D. A. Hagner, *Matthew 1–13*, WBC 33A (Dallas, TX: Word Books, 1993), 19–20. The inclusion of the Gentiles into the people over whom the expected Davidic Messiah shall rule is convincingly attested in Ps Sol 17:32. The content of the verse ("There will be no unrighteous among them in his days, for all shall be holy, and their king shall be the Lord Messiah") refers to the Gentiles, not to the Jews. G. L. Davenport ("The 'Anointed of the Lord' in Psalms of Solomon 17," in *Ideal Figures in Ancient Judaism: Profiles and Paradigms*, ed. J. J. Collins and G. W. E. Nickelsburg, SBLSCS 12 [Chico: Scholars Press, 1980], 79) notes that "one of the most surprising things of all is that the one place in the psalm in which the designation 'anointed' appears for the king is the section describing his gracious rule over the Gentiles." Also, in *1 En.* 48:4, the Son of Man, identified as the Messiah in 48:10, is presented as "the light of the Gentiles" and "the hope of those who are sick in their hearts."

[221]The parable of the wedding feast in Matt 22:1–14 has a similar message. Those originally invited to the banquet (Israel at large) have refused. Then the others were invited, good and bad (*corpus mixtum*), and they responded positively.

should not be identified with it. Deliverance from iniquities is rather understood as a deliverance from the consequences of sins, which becomes a visible sign that the sins have been forgiven.[222] The link between deliverance and forgiveness can be found in many other psalms, such as Pss 40, 85, and 90. Especially noteworthy, however, is the fact that in the verse which precedes the one quoted in Matt 1:21, Ps 130:7 (129:7 LXX), Yahweh's steadfast love is paralleled to his redemption of Israel from her iniquities: כי עִם־יהוה החסד והרבה עמו פדות; ὅτι παρὰ τῷ κυρίῳ τὸ ἔλεος καὶ πολλὴ παρ' αὐτῷ λύτρωσις (LXX). Katharine D. Sakenfeld notes that an "important nuance of *ḥesed* in the psalms . . . is Yahweh's faithfulness given expression in his forgiveness," but underscores that "this aspect of *ḥesed* cannot be completely divorced from deliverance and the willingness to deliver, for misfortune was often regarded as an indication of God's displeasure and change of fortune was in turn seen as an expression or sign of forgiveness."[223]

A similar understanding of the relationship between salvation and forgiveness can be found in the Gospel of Matthew. Apart from 1:21, nowhere else in Matthew we can find a direct link between salvation and sins. Aside from four occurrences of the verb σῴζω in Jesus' eschatological speeches,[224] this verb appears almost exclusively in either the context of Jesus' miracles[225] or his crucifixion.[226] The noun ἁμαρτία, on the other hand, is in nearly all

---

[222]Similarly, L. C. Allen (*Psalms 101–150*, WBC 21 [Waco, TX: Word Books, 1983], 192) notes that פדה "refers to deliverance as the visible sign of divine forgiveness, rather than actually to forgiveness of sins." H. W. Robinson also contends that "here we must not unduly spiritualize. The cry for help *de profundis* is partly, at least, a cry for deliverance from the calamities brought by sin. The ransoming means the escape from them. The outward sign of 'forgiveness' is restoration to prosperity, though forgiveness undoubtedly meant more than this to the devout Israelite" (*Redemption and Revelation In the Actuality of History* [London: Nisbet & Co., 1942], 223). W. H. Schmidt ("Gott und Mensch in Ps. 130: Formgeschichtliche Erwägungen," *TZ* 22 [1966]: 252), however, does not distinguish between salvation and forgiveness and believes that the deliverance in v. 8 should be understood exclusively as the forgiveness of sins. He nevertheless notes that this understanding is quite exceptional, because this is the only passage in the Old Testament which speaks directly and unequivocally about salvation from sins. The fact that this is an exception, hardly supports Schmidt's view, because, as H. W. Robinson notes, the word פדה is "nowhere . . . used of redemption from sin alone; it always means deliverance from some tangible and visible menace, which may or may not be regarded as a consequence of the supplicant's sin" (*Redemption and Revelation*, 223).

[223]K. D. Sakenfeld, *The Meaning of Hesed in the Hebrew Bible: A New Inquiry*. HSM 17 (Missoula, Montana: Scholars Press, 1978), 226.

[224]Matt 10:22; 19:25; 24:13, 22.

[225]Matt 8:25; 9:21, 22; 14:30

[226]Matt 27:40; 27:42; 27:49. P. Luomanen, *Entering the Kingdom of Heaven: A Study of the Structure of Matthew's View of Salvation*, WUNT II/101 (Tübingen: J. C. B. Mohr [Paul Siebeck], 1998), 38, treats these references together with those which refer to Jesus' miracles under the category "saving from affliction or disease." My division of this group into two subcategories is done merely on the basis of who is the recipient of salvation: various

instances[227] coupled with the verb ἀφίημι.[228] Yet these two seemingly unrelated spheres are firmly linked together in Matt 9:2–8, which testifies to the close connection between the forgiveness and salvation/healing, as well as to the necessity of forgiveness for the actual experience of deliverance.

After these preliminary considerations, it is possible to address the question of the messianic implications of Matt 1:21. The close proximity between Matt 1:21 and Jesus' messianic identity does not yet explain the messianic connotation of this verse. The starting point of investigation can be *Pss. Sol.* 17, the only Jewish text prior to the Gospel of Matthew which employs the title "Son of David." It should be noted that the main purpose of the recollection of God's promise to David in *Pss. Sol.* 17:4 is the eternal perseverance of the Davidic kingdom: "You swore to him about his seed forever that his Kingdom should not fail before you" (σὺ ὤμοσας αὐτῷ περὶ τοῦ σπέρματος αὐτοῦ εἰς τὸν αἰῶνα τοῦ μὴ ἐκλείπειν ἀπέναντί σου βασίλειον αὐτοῦ). In a somewhat surprising manner the psalmist then continues in v. 5: "But because of our sins, sinners rose up against us, they set upon us and drove us out" (καὶ ἐν ταῖς ἁμαρτίαις ἡμῶν ἐπανέστησαν ἡμῖν ἁμαρτωλοί ἐπέθεντο ἡμῖν καὶ ἔξωσαν ἡμᾶς). The author thus not only contrasts the content of the promise with the reality which seemingly denies its validity, but also offers an explanation – "because of our sins."[229] Similarly, he concludes the section in which he describes the present situation with the comment that the people were in sin (ὁ λαὸς ἐν ἁμαρτίᾳ – v. 20), which is then immediately followed by the petition for the Son of David.[230]

---

individuals in the case of Jesus' miracles, and Jesus himself in the crucifixion scene. The contrast between two groups is especially evident in Matt 27:42: ἄλλους ἔσωσεν, ἑαυτὸν οὐ δύναται σῶσαι.

[227]The only exception is Matt 3:6 which speaks about confessing the sins.

[228]9:2, 5, 6; 12:31; 26:28.

[229]Other passages from the *Psalms of Solomon*, however, demonstrate that the recognition of the corporate guilt of the nation is in fact not a satisfying answer to the question of theodicy. After all, the psalmist regards himself and his own devout companions as relatively guiltless. The suffering of the righteous individual cannot be so easily explained. Nevertheless, in a somewhat unsystematic manner several explanations have been offered, from the idea that justice has been delayed, to the idea that the present suffering represents some sort of divine discipline. Despite these attempts to rationally explain suffering, as R. B. Wright notes in his introduction in *OTP* 1, 639–650, "there is nothing approaching a 'theology of suffering' as found in other Jewish and Christian ruminations of the problem of evil. The psalmist believes that suffering is purgative and salutary (10:1–3) and will say that the righteous are singled out for especially exacting discipline, but he never moves toward assigning a positive meaning to suffering or of making it the sign of election. For the psalmist, suffering remains suffering for sin" (ibid., 644).

[230]J. Tromp ("The Sinners and the Lawless in Psalm of Solomon 17," *NovT* 35 [1993]: 352) notes that there are "two motives brought forward to move God to mercy: (1) the recognition of the sinfulness of the people as the cause of the present miserable situation; (2)

This raises the question of the relation between the promise of the permanent endurance of Davidic dynasty and human sins. It will be argued below that, similar to *Pss. Sol.* 17, Matt 1:21 represents an attempt to cope with the problem of reality which ostensibly contradicts the content of the promise as formulated in 2 Samuel 7,[231] and likewise understands national and individual sins as a cause of the current predicament.[232]

2.4.2 The Davidic Messiah and Salvation from Sins

The idea of salvation indeed belonged to the realm of the messianic expectations of early Judaism. By seeing the Messiah as God's instrument of redemption, the Old Testament and later Jewish literature were able to ascribe the idea of deliverance itself to Messiah's mission. Thus, for example, in an almost identical wording, Jer 23:6 and 33:16 describe the reign of the "righteous branch" that God will raise up for David as a time when Judah will be saved and Israel will live in safety (בימיו תושע יהודה וישראל ישכן לבטח; ἐν ταῖς ἡμέραις αὐτοῦ σωθήσεται Ιουδας καὶ Ισραηλ κατασκηνώσει πεποιθώς – Jer 23:6 LXX).

4Q174 frgs. 1–2 and 21 1.13 speaks about the Davidic Messiah called the "Branch of David" (צמח דויד) who shall arise to save (להושיע) Israel. Even though the text does not qualify this task with any closer designation,[233] it associates two aspects which are also recognizable in Matthew 1. On the one

---

the miserable situation itself, which is described in order to show that the chastisement has been executed and the punishment fulfilled."

[231] If this is correct, Matthew's "messianism" might support the claim that messianism in general represents an answer to the problem of theodicy. This is most obvious in *Pss. Sol.* 17 & 18, because the question of theodicy is central to the entire collection of these psalms, but it holds true even for the theodicy of *4 Ezra*. One might, of course, concur with M. E. Stone that "the Messiah and his kingdom . . . cannot be the final resolution of the writer's problems" ("The Question of the Messiah in 4 Ezra," 215), but J. H. Charlesworth is probably more accurate when he says that even though messianic ideas are not sufficient to counterbalance the force of Ezra's devastating questions, they are certainly on the side of the answers ("From Jewish Messianology to Christian Christology: Some Caveats and Perspectives," in *Judaisms and Their Messiahs at the Turn of the Christian Era,* ed. J. Neusner, W. S. Green, and E. S. Frerichs [Cambridge: University Press, 1987], 243).

[232] It should not be overlooked that among the "foreign" elements in Matthew's genealogy are his addition of τὸν βασιλέα to τὸν Δαυὶδ in 1:6, which indicates that with David a qualitatively new period, the period of monarchy, has begun, and the mentioning of the exile as the marker between the second and the third division of the genealogy (ἐπὶ τῆς μετοικεσίας Βαβυλῶνος – 1:11, and μετὰ δὲ τὴν μετοικεσίαν Βαβυλῶνος – 1:12) as a pointer to the fact that the period of monarchy has come to an end.

[233] K. E. Pomykala (*The Davidic Dynasty,* 196) contends that "based on the use of ישע elsewhere in Qumran literature, we may suppose it means that the Branch of David will deliver Israel from its enemies." Since, however, in Qumran literature the verb ישע can also denote redemption from external oppression by the wicked in a broader sense, as well as inner individual conflicts, it is probably better to leave the concept of salvation in 4Q174 undefined.

hand, by linking the quotations from 2 Sam 7:12–14 and Amos 9:11, 4Q174 addresses the problem of the incongruity between the promise and reality. On the other hand, this document defines the messianic duty as the salvation of Israel, just as Matt 1:21.

In *4 Ezra* 12:34, Uriel explains to Ezra that the Messiah who will arise from the posterity of David "will deliver in mercy the remnant of my people, those who have been saved throughout my borders." Later, in 13:26, he clarifies that the Messiah ("the Man from the Sea") "will himself deliver his creation."

Matthew, however, defines the redemptive task of Jesus as the salvation from sins, which has been traditionally ascribed to God alone. Apart from Ps 130:8 (129:8 LXX), the motifs of redemption, purification, and iniquities are linked together in Ezekiel 36–37. Some of the combinations that can be found in the LXX are: καθαρίζω + ἀπὸ τῶν ἀκαθαρσιῶν (Ezek 36:25), σώζω + ἐκ πασῶν τῶν ἀκαθαρσιῶν (Ezek 36:29), καθαρίζω + ἐκ πασῶν τῶν ἀνομιῶν (Ezek 36:33), and ῥύομαι + ἀπὸ πασῶν τῶν ἀνομιῶν αὐτῶν, ὧν ἡμάρτοσαν ἐν αὐταῖς (Ezek 37:23). In Ezekiel 36–37, the restoration of the nation and gathering of the dispersed people are associated with purification of sins and, by implication, forgiveness,[234] with the purpose of the re-creation of the holy people who will follow God's statutes. Only then can the promise of life in the promised land be fulfilled (Ezek 36:28). This process is summarized in 36:29a: "I will save you from all your uncleannesses" (καὶ σώσω ὑμᾶς ἐκ πασῶν τῶν ἀκαθαρσιῶν ὑμῶν), followed by the promise of life of abundance (36:29b–30). Purification from wickedness functions here as a condition for the experience of blessings. The same order of events is repeated in Ezek 36:33–35: first comes the cleansing of sins (καθαριῶ ὑμᾶς ἐκ πασῶν τῶν ἀνομιῶν ὑμῶν), and then the promise that the desolate places will be rebuilt until the land becomes like the garden of Eden. In Ezek 37:23–24, the appearance of the promised Davidic ruler called "my servant David" is associated with God's cleansing of the apostasies into which the people have fallen (ῥύσομαι αὐτοὺς ἀπὸ πασῶν τῶν ἀνομιῶν αὐτῶν ὧν ἡμάρτοσαν ἐν αὐταῖς καὶ καθαριῶ αὐτούς – v. 23).

These biblical references certainly confirm the assumption that purification from sins is a divine activity. Notwithstanding this conclusion, there is evidence that the final victory over sin (though not the actual act of forgiveness) could have been assigned to angelic or human figures, such as "a new priest" (*T. Levi* 18:9), Melchizedek (11Q13 2.6–8), or the angel Michael (*1 En.* 10:20–22). Moreover, certain texts associate the purification from defilement with messianic activity. Thus according to *Pss. Sol.* 17:22–25, the Son of David has the task "in wisdom and righteousness to drive out the sinners," "to destroy the unlawful nations with the word of his mouth,"[235] and

---

[234]Neither the verb ἀφίημι nor the noun ἄφεσις actually appear in the text.

[235]Cf. Isa 11:4.

"to condemn sinners by the thoughts of their hearts." Verse 30 emphatically concludes that "he will purge Jerusalem and make it holy as it was even from the beginning." A possible objection is certainly the fact that the Messiah does not actually purify the sins of Israel, but rather purifies Jerusalem (καθάρισον Ἰερουσαλήμ – 17:22b; καθαριεῖ Ἰερουσαλήμ – 17:30b) from the Gentiles and thus performs an act of "ethnic cleansing." Also, 18:5 clearly assigns the purification of Israel to God himself (καθαρίσαι ὁ θεὸς Ἰσραήλ).[236] It is nonetheless significant that the language of cleansing has been applied to the Son of David, who otherwise actively participates in the implementation of holiness.

This observation contributes to the overall impression of the close proximity between Messiah's and God's activity in *Pss. Sol.* 17 & 18. First of all, both the appearance of the ideal king who is a successor to David's throne and his acts of deliverance of Israel from the sinners and foreign occupation are the signs "that God has forgiven the nation for its sin and that he has turned his face toward them once again in love."[237] Everything that the Messiah does both presupposes and is enabled by an act of divine forgiveness. Furthermore, as James H. Charlesworth points out, the emphasis falls on God who will eventually accomplish the messianic goals. "God is clearly the actor . . . and the Messiah is God's agent."[238] The royal language which is used to describe the Messiah (βασιλεὺς αὐτῶν χριστὸς κύριος – 17:32) is also applied to God (κύριος αὐτὸς βασιλεὺς αὐτοῦ – 17:34; κύριος αὐτὸς βασιλεὺς ἡμῶν – 17:46).[239] Also, while 17:42 asserts that the Son of David should discipline Israel (παιδεῦσαι αὐτόν), 18:4 claims that God is the one who uses discipline toward his people (ἡ παιδεία σου ἐφ' ἡμᾶς). Finally, the phrase τοῦ βασιλεῦσαι ἐπὶ Ἰσραηλ παῖδά σου in 17:21b, can grammatically refer to either God or the expected king.[240]

A similar ambiguity exists in *1 En.* 48:7, which claims that "the righteous will be saved in his name and it is his good pleasure that they have life." Charlesworth notes that it is not clear whether "his" refers to the Messiah[241] or

---

[236]The parallelism between the concepts of cleansing and forgiving in *Pss. Sol.* 9:6–7 (καθαρίσει ἐν ἁμαρτίαις . . . ἀφέσει ἁμαρτίας) shows that purification here refers to forgiveness.

[237]Davenport, "The 'Anointed of the Lord' in Psalms of Solomon 17," 82.

[238]J. H. Charlesworth, "The Concept of the Messiah in the Pseudpigrapha," *ANRW* II.19.1 (1979), 199.

[239]M. de Jonge contends that "in no way does the kingship of the son curtail the kingship of God. Psalm 17 begins and ends with a hymn of praise on the kingship of God" ("The Expectation of the Future in the Psalms of Solomon," *Neot* 23 [1989]: 101). However, the reverse is also true: God's kingship is expressed through an earthly king.

[240]Noted by M. de Jonge, ibid., 112 n.29.

[241]The Son of Man in the parables of Enoch is in 48:6 equated with the Chosen One, and in 48:10 with the Messiah.

the Lord of the Spirits.[242] In the Qumran literature, the verb ישע always, but once, refers to God's redemptive activity. The exception is 4Q174 frgs. 1–2 and 21 1.13, which asserts that the "Branch of David" will save Israel. The apparent ambiguity should be probably resolved in light of 1QM 11.1–3, which declares that God's deliverance is achieved through human agency.

Yet, this similarity, even ambiguity, between descriptions and activities of God and the Messiah[243] should not obscure the apparent tendency in these passages, especially *Pss. Sol.* 17, to see God's own engagement behind everything the Messiah is supposed to do. Does Matt 1:21 represent a drift that runs opposite to this proclivity? Does he transfer to Jesus the responsibilities which belong to the divine sphere, instead of eventually ascribing to God the responsibilities which belong to the messianic sphere? Such a conclusion comes close, especially in view of Matt 9:2–8, which betrays Matthew's knowledge of Christian tradition that Jesus' declaration of forgiveness to the paralytic was a blasphemy in the eyes of his contemporaries. On the other hand, the fact that only Mark 2:7 and Luke 5:21 report the question of the scribes: "Who can forgive sins but God alone?" while Matt 9:3 deliberately omits it, indicates that he is working within the framework which permits the interchangeability between human and divine activity. Also, he is the only evangelist who underscores that this is the authority which God has given to human beings (9:8).[244]

However, it should not be forgotten that in 1:21 Matthew does not speak about the forgiveness of sins, but the salvation from sins. The idea of salvation presupposes divine forgiveness, but should not be identified with it. This further means that Jesus' salvific activity, despite being expressed through the language that comes from Ps 129:8 LXX where it refers to divine activity, eventually belongs to the messianic sphere. Furthermore, it is certainly not accidental that the citation about Emmanuel from Isa 7:14 has been introduced with the formula, τοῦτο δὲ ὅλον γέγονεν ἵνα πληρωθῇ τὸ ῥηθὲν ὑπὸ κυρίου διὰ τοῦ προφήτου λέγοντος (Matt 1:22), which refers not only to the preceding narrative, but most directly to 1:21. Krister Stendahl is certainly right when he claims that "the title Emmanuel underscores the messianic function of Jesus, who is to set his people free from their sins."[245] The name Emmanuel itself

---

[242]Charlesworth, "From Jewish Messianology to Christian Christology," 241.

[243]The source of this similarity and partial overlapping can be probably found in Israel's understanding of monarchy. In the same way the king functions as the earthly representative of Yahweh, the supreme king, so the royal Messiah. Cf. the transferability of descriptions and functions between God and David in Ezekiel 34: v. 11 says that God is shepherd, while v. 23 calls David the shepherd; in v. 13 God will feed the sheep, while in v. 23 this is David's duty.

[244]Cf. Matt 16:17–19 where Jesus actually gives this authority to his followers.

[245]Stendahl, "Quis et Unde?" 68. Frankemölle also underscores that Matt 1:21 and 1:23 are closely interrelated because they say the same thing: Jesus saves his people from their sins

connects the divine and human sphere. It points to the presence of the divine among the humans. In an astonishing similarity to *Pss. Sol.* 17, Emmanuel points toward God who stands behind Jesus' activity.[246] Jesus' salvific mission is in fact God's own mission and a sign of divine forgiveness. Jesus as Emmanuel is the embodiment of God's presence on earth. In that sense he has an eschatological significance. In a similar way as he begins his Gospel saying that Emmanuel means "μεθ' ἡμῶν ὁ θεός," Matthew closes his narrative with Jesus' promise to be always with his disciples: ἐγὼ μεθ' ὑμῶν εἰμι. These phrases, which form an *inclusio* of Matthew's Gospel, suggest that the whole of Matthean Christology should be seen within the framework of Emmanuel-Christology.

2.4.3 The Programmatic Significance of Matt 1:21

It has already been mentioned above that nowhere else after 1:21 does Matthew directly combine the verb σώζω with the noun ἁμαρτία.[247] Apart from a few instances when this verb is used to denote the eschatological salvation, it regularly refers to Jesus' salvation of his contemporaries from affliction and disease, or to his refusal to save his life on the cross. The noun ἁμαρτία, however, is regularly linked to forgiveness.

This, however, does not mean that the two spheres are unrelated. Matt 9:2–8 shows that Matthew, similar to other Synoptics, saw a close connection between sickness and sin. It is therefore highly likely that Jesus' healing ministry is viewed by Matthew as saving his people from their sins. This interpretation could shed some light on the question of why Matthew presents Jesus being addressed as the Son of David almost exclusively in the context of his therapeutic miracles, a phenomenon otherwise difficult to account for because in Jewish tradition the Davidic Messiah was not expected to do miracles.

The second sphere where Matthew associates the motifs of salvation and forgiveness of sins is Jesus' death on the cross. The combination between

---

(through which they ceased to be God's people) and is therefore the earthly Emmanuel, i.e. God among his (i.e. Jesus') people (*Jahwebund und Kirche Christi*, 217).

[246]Emmanuel is not an ontological category. It does not refer to Jesus' divine nature, even less to his identity with God. Cf. the recognition of Jesus in the "little ones" who suffer in Matt 25, or the experience of his presence among his followers in Matt 28:20.

[247]This combination is otherwise quite rare in the New Testament. Moreover, the only three passages where σώζω and ἁμαρτία are linked together do not have Christological implications. Thus in Luke 1:77, these two concepts are applied to John the Baptist, while two verses in James 5:15, 20 relate them to the community of believers. It is noteworthy that James, like Matthew, does not combine σώζω and ἁμαρτία directly, but uses the former to denote the healing of the sick, and the latter to express the idea of forgiveness. It is therefore not surprising that in his categorization of the occurrences of the verb σώζω in the Gospel of Matthew, P. Luomanen (*Entering the Kingdom of Heaven*, 39) treats Matt 1:21 as an exeptional case which does not fit into any identifiable category.

ἁμαρτία and ἀφίημι[248] appears for the last time in Matthew's narrative in his account of the Last Supper (26:26–29). Matthew deleted the phrase εἰς ἄφεσιν ἁμαρτιῶν from the preaching of John the Baptist (cf. Matt 3:2 and Mark 1:4) and added it to Jesus' saying about the cup.[249] The whole phrase is thus directly linked to τὸ περὶ πολλῶν ἐκχυννόμενον. The participle ἐκχυννόμενον as the attribute of τὸ αἷμα μου points towards Jesus' death on behalf of many. In the same direction points the paradox between Jesus' readiness to save others and his refusal to save himself, emphasized so eloquently in the mocking scene in Matt 27:41–43. By connecting the concepts of salvation and forgiveness of sins to Jesus' death and by defining Jesus' messianic task as the salvation of his people from their sins, Matthew is able to present Jesus' messianic mission within the royal Davidic framework not despite his death on the cross, but exactly as being fulfilled on the cross.

It is therefore not surprising that Matthew's programmatic statement in 1:21 is often understood either as a pointer to Jesus' healings[250] or his crucifixion.[251] The evidence of the usage of σῴζω and ἁμαρτία, however, suggests that the emphasis on the one side at the expense of the other cannot be justified. It is more likely that Matthew's programmatic statement in 1:21 introduces both aspects of Jesus' career – his healing ministry and the atoning death, neither of which can be directly explained as a messianic act on the basis of what we know about Jewish messianic expectations. By anchoring the statement in 1:21 in the traditions which in the first century flourished in those circles which expected the royal Messiah of the Davidic line, Matthew establishes the ground to make another step, to present Jesus' healing activity and his death on the cross as the messianic salvation of his people from their sins. The former is developed through the traditional connection between sickness and sin, and the latter through the concept of ransom and the atoning sacrifice. While the former represents the affirmation of the traditional

---

[248]Although Mt 26:28 contains the noun ἄφεσις, and not the verb ἀφίημι, both words have the same root.

[249]In this way, Matthew has assigned the task of forgiving sins exclusively to Jesus. In Mark 1:4 and Luke 1:77 and 3:3 the forgiveness of sins was part of the message of John the Baptist. Other passages, such as Luke 24:47; Acts 2:38; 5:31; 10:43; 13:38; 26:18; Col 1:14; Heb 10:18, which link the concept of forgiveness to Jesus, represent various forms of Christian proclamation of the significance of Jesus, especially his death and resurrection/exaltation. In Matthew, however, the forgiveness of sins is part of Jesus' own message.

[250]P. Luomanen quite radically asserts that in "Matthew's view, Jesus was not sent to die for his people, but to heal their diseases, preach repentance and lead them into eternal life through his authoritative interpretation and proclamation of the law . . . . Jesus saves like a healer" (*Entering the Kingdom of Heaven*, 226).

[251]J. D. Kingsbury, "The Significance of the Cross within the Plot of Matthew's Gospel: A Study in Narrative Criticism," in *The Synoptic Gospels: Source Criticism and the New Literary Criticism*, ed. C. Focant, BETL 110 (Leuven: University Press, 1993), 272–279; Hagner, *Matthew 1–13*, 19; Verseput, "Davidic Messiah," 116.

understanding of salvation (deliverance from death), the latter paradoxically represents its denial (delivery to death).[252]

The salvation from sins in Matt 1:21 should be therefore primarily understood as salvation from the consequences of sins that is made possible through their forgiveness. In the Gospel of Matthew, this salvation is presented as salvation from human fragility, perishability, suffering, and ultimately death. This understanding of salvation, however, is fundamentally threatened on the cross. Jesus' refusal to save himself seemingly challenges his salvation of others. Ultimately, his death functions as a threat to the lasting validity of God's promise to David.[253] For Matthew, however, Jesus' death paradoxically represents the fulfillment of the promise because it is death for the forgiveness of sins that hinder the realization of the promise and therefore death that opens the possibility for the creation of the holy community along the lines of *Pss. Sol.* 17 and 18.

2.4.4 Conclusions

In biblical and post-biblical writings, which address the relationship between God's promise of the eternal Davidic dynasty and human obedience to God's commandments, sin was viewed as problematic from two standpoints: (1) from the standpoint of the fulfillment of the promise (no Davidide on the throne), and (2) from the standpoint of the quality of people's life (national and personal suffering).

The solution to the first problem was found in the hope that God's faithfulness to his promise will be demonstrated through his sending of the Messiah of the Davidic descent. In its core lies the understanding of the unconditional nature of God's promises and the interpretation of the present predicament as a temporary chastisement. This type of hope can be recognized behind the unbroken chain of David's descendants in Matthew's genealogy and the identification of Jesus as the legitimate royal pretender of the Davidic line.

The solution to the view that sins have caused the present misery is found in the hope that the Messiah will save Israel from the consequences of her sins. To be sure, Jewish literature demonstrates that there were various versions of

---

[252]Davies and Allison also recognize the polyvalence of Matthew's programmatic statement in 1:21, and underscore that it refers to both Jesus' atoning death and his healing ministry. Their conclusion is that "perhaps, then, Matthew thought that Jesus saved his people from their sins in a variety of ways" (*Matthew,* vol. 1, 210).

[253]A comparison with Acts 2 and 13 can be illuminating. In both speeches, Jesus' resurrection (not his death) is understood as the confirmation of the lasting validity of Davidic promises (2:30–31 and 13:34–35) and contrasted with David's corruptibility and death (2:29 and 13:36–37). Resurrection as a victory over death is understood as God's fulfillment of the promise about the eternal permanency of the Davidic dynasty. Jesus Christ in his resurrected state at the right hand of God does not belong any more to the finite world of decay.

eschatological hope, which either do not mention any messianic figure at all, or if they do, do not contain any reference to the Davidic Messiah. Nevertheless, a number of documents which do mention the Davidic Messiah and assign him a certain role, see his activity as a salvation from the consequences of people's sins. The latter presupposes, explicitly or implicitly, purification or forgiveness, but it is primarily oriented toward blessings, which are presently hindered by human sins. In the core of this hope, however, lies the conditional understanding of God's promises, because the responsibility for the present predicament has been put on people's shoulders. This understanding of human sins can be recognized behind the promise that Jesus will save his people from their sins, announced in Matt 1:21.

Chapter 3

Healing the Sick as a Messianic Activity

3.1 Introduction

Apart from Matthew 1 and Matt 22:41–46, Jesus is addressed as the Son of David in a series of episodes, which are almost exclusively related to Jesus' therapeutic activity. The origin and function of this remarkable connection between Jesus' messianic identity and his healing miracles cannot be easily explained in view of an almost universally accepted axiom that the Davidic Messiah was not expected to be a miracle worker.[1] It is usually assumed that this link represents an early Christian development, which cannot be traced back to Jewish documents.[2] The accuracy of the former cannot be disputed. There are indeed no known pre-Christian texts that make the link between the Davidic Messiah and the miracles of healing. The accuracy of the latter, however, must be seriously questioned. The assumption that the concept of the Son of David who heals represents a development that is far removed from the Jewish framework stands in a considerable tension with the thoroughly Jewish character of Matthew's Gospel and its overall tendency to present Jesus' life as a fulfillment of Scripture. Despite several attempts to advance the thesis that

---

[1] There is a broad consensus among contemporary biblical scholars that "there is not one pre-70 Jewish writing that depicts the Messiah as one who will come and heal the sick or give sight to the blind" (Charlesworth, "Solomon and Jesus," 150).

[2] F. Hahn, for example, claims that in these texts "the earthly work of Jesus is interpreted in the light of His compassion with men and the outreach of His loving assistance. To what extent a specifically Christian interpretation is here imposed on the 'Son of David' theory, is seen when it is realized that the messianic king of Judaism was not expected to be a doer of miraculous deeds" (*The Titles of Jesus in Christology: Their History in Early Christianity*, trans. H. Knight and G. Ogg [London: Lutterworth Press, 1969], 253–254). With a similar understanding, C. Burger criticizes J. M. Gibbs' attempt to trace the Matthean texts back to their Jewish roots. Gibbs claims that in the miracle stories Jesus is addressed "as the Messianic King of David's line, with power to judge and to dispense mercy" ("Purpose and Pattern in Matthew's Use of the Title 'Son of David'," 449). In Burger's view, Gibbs "übersieht, dass die christliche Interpretation des Prädikates 'Davidssohn' bei Matthäus schon weit vom jüdischen Bild des davidischen Königs abgeführt hat" (*Jesus als Davidssohn*, 90). According to Burger, this is a Christian development that has been influenced by the Hellenistic concept of "divine man" (ibid., 44, 169).

the author of the First Gospel was a Gentile,[3] many features of the text, such as its predominantly Jewish style, language, and theology speak in favor of the notion that the Gospel was written by a Jewish Christian who wanted to provide a sustained argument for Jesus' messiahship that can be both intelligible and convincing for his predominantly Jewish Christian audience.[4] Given this assumption, it is reasonable to expect that Matthew's link between the Davidic Messiah and healing the sick would have to be constructed in such a way to make sense within the categories that characterized the world view of the first-century Jews.

This chapter represents a search for this "sense making" link between the Messiah of the Davidic line and the concept of healing. After an overview of the Matthean passages that make a positive connection between Jesus' identity as the Son of David and his healing activity, two major solutions to this problem will be presented and critically evaluated. The first proposal claims that Matthew's presentation of the Son of David who heals originates in the traditions about Solomon as exorcist. The second proposal claims that Matthew's portrayal of the Son of David who heals originates in the traditions about the prophetic Messiah as a miracle worker. In both cases we are dealing with traditions in which the link between a certain type of figure (Solomon or a prophet like Moses) and the miracles of healing has already been established. The critical assessment of these proposals will be based on the assumption that we can speak about the appropriation of a certain tradition only under the condition that its main motifs can be recognized in the text under consideration. After demonstrating that both solutions fail to pass this test, the chapter will end with a new proposal that seeks to find a "sense making" link

---

[3]K. Clark, "The Gentile Bias of Matthew," *JBL* 66 (1947): 165–172; Strecker, *Der Weg der Gerechtigkeit*, 76; W. Trilling, *Das wahre Israel: Studien zur Theologie des Matthäus-Evangeliums*, SANT 10 (München: Kösel, 1964), 215; S. van Tillborg, *The Jewish Leaders in Matthew* (Leiden: Brill, 1972), 171–172; Frankemölle, *Jahwebund und Kirche Christi*, 200.

[4]Luz, *Matthew 1–7*, 80–82; A. M. Leske, "Isaiah and Matthew: The Prophetic Influence in the First Gospel," in *Jesus and the Suffering Servant: Isaiah 53 and Christian Origins,* ed. W. H. Bellinger and W. R. Farmer (Harrisburg: Trinity Press International, 1998), 152–155; B. D. Ehrman, *The New Testament: A Historical Introduction to the Early Christian Writings* (New York: Oxford University Press, 1997), 79–84; M. Hengel ("Zur matthäischen Bergpredigt und ihrem jüdischen Hintergrund," in *Judaica, Hellenistica et Christiana: Kleine Schriften II*, WUNT 109 [Tübingen: Mohr Siebeck, 1999], 238) believes that Matthew "freilich der palästinisch-jüdischen (und judenchristlichen) Tradition noch nähersteht als sein aus Cilicien stammender 'Kollege' Paulus." P. Stuhlmacher (*Biblische Theologie des Neuen Testament*, vol. 2 [Göttingen: Vandenhoeck & Ruprecht, 1999], 151) claims that the Gospel of Matthew is "das gewichtigste judenchristliche Buch des Neuen Testaments neben dem Hebräerbrief." For a refutation of the thesis about Matthew's supposed ignorance of the Jewish traditions, such as a distinction between the Pharisees and Sadducees (16:12; 22:23) or *parallelismus membrorumn* (21:5–7), see Luz, *Matthew 1–7*, 79–80.

between the Messiah of the Davidic line and the concept of healing in Matthew's midrashic interpretation of Scripture.

3.2 The Son of David Passages in Matthew's Narrative

3.2.1 The Healing of the Two Blind Men

The episode about the healing of two blind men appears almost at the end of the composition of chapters 8–9 where Matthew predominantly recounts Jesus' deeds.[5] The precise nature of the structure and theology of Matt 8–9 is far from being a settled issue.[6] Nevertheless, in view of the mutual

---

[5]Following the Sermon on the Mount in chapters 5–7, chapters 8–9 present Jesus as the miracle worker. The terms "Messiah of the Word" as a designation for the former and "Messiah of Deed" as a designation for the latter, originally proposed by J. Schniewind (*Das Evangelium nach Matthäus*, 36, 106), are accepted by many scholars; cf. the comment by H. J. Held, "Matthew as Interpreter of the Miracle Stories," in *Tradition and Interpretation in Matthew*, ed. G. Bornkamm, G. Barth, and H. J. Held, trans. P. Scott (London: SCM Press, 1963], 246: "His [Matthew's] collection of the miraculous deeds of Jesus thus has a Christological function. The evangelist presents Jesus at the beginning of his Gospel not only as the Messiah of the word (in the Sermon on the Mount) but also as the Messiah of deed (by his miraculous deeds)." Even though these labels are not inappropriate, one should be aware that chapters 8–9 represent not only a collection of miracles, but include also other incidents, such as the inquiry of the so-called "Would-be Followers" of Jesus about the meaning of discipleship (8:18–22), the calling of Matthew (9:9–13), and the question of the disciples of John about fasting (9:14–17).

[6]For a discussion see Held, "Matthew as Interpreter," pp. 246–299; W. G. Thompson, "Reflections on the Composition of Matt 8:1–9:34," *CBQ* 33 (1971): 365–388; B. F. Dewes, "The Composition of Matthew 8–9," *SEAJT* 12 (1972): 92–101; C. Burger, "Jesu Taten nach Matthäus 8 und 9," *ZTK* 70 (1973): 272–287; J. D. Kingsbury, "Observations on the 'Miracle Chapters' of Matthew 8–9," *CBQ* 40 (1978): 559–573; B. Gerhardsson, *The Mighty Acts of Jesus According to Matthew*, Scripta Minora Regiae Societatis Humaniorum Litterarum Lundensis 1978/79:5 (Lund: CWK Gleerup, 1979), 39–40; J. Moiser, "The Structure of Matthew 8–9: A Suggestion," *ZNW* 76 (1985): 117–118; U. Luz, "Die Wundergeschichten von Matt 8–9," in *Tradition and Interpretation in the New Testament*, ed. G. F. Hawthorne and O. Betz, FS E. E. Ellis (Grand Rapids, Michigan: William B. Eerdmans, 1987), 149–165. The first and probably the best known analysis of Matthew's miracle stories from the perspective of redaction criticism was done by H. J. Held. He treats chapters 8–9 as a composition made up of three groups of miracles, each of them with a distinct theme. According to this view, the theme of the first group (8:2–17) is the Servant of God Christology, the theme of the second group (8:18–9:17) is the confession that "the Christ of the miracle stories is the Lord of his congregation," and the theme of the last section (9:18–31) is faith. The healing of the dumb demoniac described in 9:32–34 is treated as a conclusion of the whole composition, which puts it into a Christological framework ("Matthew as Interpreter," 247–248). Thompson ("Reflections on the Composition of Matt 8:1–9:34," 365–388) not only accepts Held's division of chapters 8–9, but also similarly defines the thematic threads which unify each of the three blocks: the person of Jesus as the theme for the first part, discipleship as the theme of the second, and faith as the theme of the third. On the other side, Burger

interconnectedness of various pericopes within the entire composition[7] and the impossibility of dividing it into separate subsections on the principle of their thematic unity,[8] it seems that it can be treated as a unified whole. It is a coherent cycle of miracles within a common and discernible narrative framework and a new geographical location.[9]

Towards the end of this cycle, Matthew narrates in 9:27–31 how two blind men follow Jesus crying aloud, ἐλέησον ἡμᾶς, υἱὸς Δαυίδ. Jesus' response, however, is delayed until they enter the house.[10] A short dialogue follows, in which the blind confirm their faith in Jesus' miraculous power, after which the actual miracles take place. The whole episode is concluded with Jesus' request for secrecy.

This short episode, which is most likely Matthew's own composition,[11] is silent in regard to the question of why two blind men suddenly approach Jesus

---

("Jesu Taten nach Matthäus 8 und 9," 284–287) and Kingsbury ("Observations on the 'Miracle Chapters' of Matt 8–9," 562) divide the whole composition not into three, but four sections. Burger disagrees with Held not only in regard to composition but also in regard to the main theme, which is, in his opinion, ecclesiology, i.e. "die Gründungslegende der christlichen Kirche" ("Jesu Taten nach Matthäus 8 und 9," 287). For a critique of the proposals which attempt to define the theme(s) of chapters 8–9 without taking enough care for the narrative dimension of the whole composition, see Luz, "Die Wundergeschichten von Matt 8–9," 149–152.

[7]See the analysis of Matthew's compositional technique by Thompson, "Reflections on the Composition of Matt 8:1–9:34," 365–388.

[8]Cf. Luz, "Die Wundergeschichten von Matt 8–9," 151.

[9]All miracles in chapters 8–9 are situated in relation to Capernaum. Matthew's redactional technique provided the coherent setting for all the events reported. The cleansing of the leper occurs on the way to the city after the Sermon on the Mount (8:8a), and the dialogue with the centurion happens in the city itself (8:5a), as well as the healing of Peter's mother-in-law and the miracles on the same evening (8:14–17). After the short excursion to the land of the Gadarenes (8:18, 23, 28) Jesus returns to Capernaum (9:1), which remains the setting for all the events reported in chapter 9.

[10]Given the fact that in all previously narrated healings in chapters 8–9 Jesus always reacted at once, it is a bit strange that this does not happen also here. Held ("Matthew as Interpreter," 280–281) treats this feature of Matt 9:27–31 as a difficulty which an active faith has to overcome in order to achieve its goal, which he also discovers in other healing stories. In listing various obstacles which faith has to overcome, he mentions the crowd, the religious barriers between Jews and Gentiles, the hopelessness of the case, the petitioner's own unbelief and the hesitance of Jesus to respond. He notes that the last cause occurs only in the healing of two blind men in Matt 9:27–31 and the daughter of the Canaanite woman in Matt 15:21–28.

[11]Since Matt 9:27–31 resembles the healing of two other blind men just before Jesus enters Jerusalem, narrated in Matt 20:29–34, it is often called its "doublet." Both occurrences are apparently based on Mark 10:46–52. There are several similarities between Matt 9:27–31 and Mark 10:46–52: the motif of the healing of the blind, their cry for mercy which includes the address "Son of David," the fact that healing does not take place immediately, and Jesus' reference to the faith of the blind. A direct verbal link between 9:27–31 and Mark 10:46–52 is the unique combination of κράζειν καὶ λέγειν which in the whole New Testament can be found only in Matt 9:27 and Mark 10:47. Because of the similarities in the content, but only a

in their search for help by calling him the Son of David. In previous instances in chapters 8–9, people in need asked Jesus for help either by calling him κύριε[12] or by avoiding any direct address.[13] Yet the fact that a quite unanticipated identification of Jesus as the Son of David by two invalids in 9:27 is not accompanied by any explanatory note leaves the impression that the Davidic title somehow sums up the experience of Jesus as a healer in the preceding episodes. This strategic significance of the healing of the two blind men within the whole miracle cycle in chapters 8–9 has been generally recognized. By such arrangement, the entire cycle in chapters 8–9 has been placed into the Davidic framework.[14] On the other hand, even though the Davidic title appears as an outcome of the preceding episodes, within the framework of the happening itself described in Matt 9:27–31 the recognition of Jesus as the Son of David precedes the actual experience of healing. Jesus is beseeched for mercy exactly in his capacity as the Son of David.

3.2.2 The Healing of the Blind and Dumb Demoniac

The next episode that contains a reference to the Son of David is found in chapter 12, which is usually regarded as a clearly structured composition.[15] Even though there is no consensus concerning the nature of this structure, it is generally assumed that v. 22 marks the beginning of a new section.[16]

Matt 12:22–24 is an introduction to and a cause of the Beelzebul controversy. The text echoes Matt 9:32–34, an account which directly follows the healing of the two blind men reported in 9:27–31. Matt 12:22–24 is a report of the healing of a blind and dumb demoniac, followed by a question

---

few direct verbal agreements, "it seems probable that the Markan episode has served Matthew as the inspiration for 9:27–31" (Davies and Allison, *Matthew,* vol. 2, 133).

[12]Prior to Matt 9:27–31, this address appears only in chapter 8 (vv. 2, 6, 8, and 25).

[13]Cf. Matt 9:2–8, 18–26. The address υἱὲ τοῦ θεοῦ by two Gadarene demoniacs is not a human response.

[14]Cf. Verseput, "The 'Son of God' Title," 534.

[15]Matthew appears to have composed this chapter from the Markan material (Mark 1:23–3:12; 3:22–35; 8:11–12) and Q (Luke 6:43–45; 11:14–15, 19–23, 29–32).

[16]P. F. Ellis (*Matthew: His Mind and His Message* [Collegeville: Liturgical Press, 1974], 54) sees chapter 12 closely connected to chapter 11 with which it forms an a b a' pattern (a: 11:2–27, b:11:28–12:21, a': 12:22–50). R. H. Gundry (*Matthew,* 220–250) divides chapter 12 into four sections: 12:1–21, 22–27, 28–45, 46–50. Davies and Allison (*Matthew,* vol. 2, 233–234) divide the chapter into two sections (vv. 1–21 and 22–50), and in each they discover a similar triadic structure, parallel to chapter 11. In their view, in the first section of chapter 12, vv. 1–8 and 9–14 deal with the issue of unbelief/rejection, whereas the theme of vv. 15–21 is invitation/acceptance. They see the same thematic division in the second section of chapter 12, vv. 22–37 and 38–45 dealing with unbelief/rejection and vv. 46–50 dealing with invitation/acceptance. U. Luz (*Matthew 8–20: A Commentary,* ed. H. Koester, trans. J. E. Crouch, Hermeneia [Minneapolis: Fortress Press, 2001], 177) also sees the structure of chapter 12 as parallel to chapter 11, but divides the chapter itself into four sections: vv. 1–21, 22–37, 38–45, and 46–50.

from the crowd that has witnessed this miracle: μήτι οὗτός ἐστιν ὁ υἱὸς Δαυίδ? The Pharisees immediately react to it by accusing Jesus of casting out demons by Beelzebul.

A similar accusation that Jesus casts out demons by the help of Beelzebul can be found in the Markan material (Mark 3:22), but it is not preceded by the story about exorcism. On the other hand, Luke 11:14–15 contains the same combination as Matthew – exorcism followed by the accusation that Jesus casts out demons by Beelzebul. Regardless of the reconstruction of the redactional history of the text,[17] it should be pointed out that only the Matthean version expands the description of the demoniac by including the notion that he was also blind (τυφλὸς), and consequently, that after the healing he was able not only to speak (λαλεῖν) but also to see (βλέπειν). The verb ἐκβάλλω, which appears in Matt 9:32–34 and Luke 11:14, has been replaced with θεραπεύω. Finally, only the version in Matt 12:22–24 clarifies the nature of the amazement of the crowd through the addition of the puzzling question, "This man cannot be the Son of David, can he?" (μήτι οὗτός ἐστιν ὁ υἱὸς Δαυίδ;).

It is somewhat unclear whether μήτι in the question of the people implies a positive or negative reply. According to the rules of Greek grammar, μήτι is used in questions when a negative answer is expected.[18] On the other hand, the fact that Matthew contrasts the question of the crowd with the negative reaction of the Pharisees suggests that a positive answer is expected.[19] If one would try to do justice to both options, the question of the crowd should be understood as an inquiring statement with a certain measure of uncertainty.[20]

The accusation of the Pharisees that Jesus casts out demons by Beelzebul is introduced with the comment, "But when the Pharisees heard it, they said . . ." (οἱ δὲ Φαρισαῖοι ἀκούσαντες εἶπον). This aorist participle ἀκούσαντες clearly indicates that the question of the crowd is the source of the conflict and not the miracle itself.[21]

---

[17]Many interpreters assume that Matthew connected Mark 3:22–30 with the Q-material preserved in Luke 11:14–23, but basically followed the Q order; cf. Burger, *Jesus als Davidssohn,* 77; Luz, *Matthew 8–20,* 199; Davies and Allison, *Matthew,* vol. 2, 332. Since, however, the story of the dumb demoniac in Matt 9:32–34 is closer to Luke 11:14–15 than the version in Matt 12:22–24, some exegetes believe that Matthew first produced 9:32–34 by redacting the Q material, and then created 12:22–24 by redacting his own version in chapter 9; cf. Burger, *Jesus als Davidssohn,* 77.

[18]Cf. Blass and Debrunner, *A Greek Grammar of the New Testament,* 220 §427.

[19]Cf. Loader, "Son of David, Blindness, Possession, and Duality in Matthew," 573; Strecker, *Der Weg der Gerechtigkeit,* 118.

[20]A. Suhl calls it a "fragende Vermutung" ("Der Davidssohn im Matthäus-Evangelium," 72); cf. also Strecker, *Der Weg der Gerechtigkeit,* 118; Burger, *Jesus als Davidssohn,* 79.

[21]Cf. Zahn, *Das Evangelium des Matthäus,* 454 n.71; Hummel, *Auseinandersetzung zwischen Kirche und Judentum im Matthäusevangelium,* 123; Verseput, "The 'Son of God' Title," 535.

3.2.3 The Healing of the Daughter of the Canaanite Woman

Matt 15:21–28 belongs to a larger section composed only from the material found in Mark.[22] In contrast to his practice elsewhere, Matthew neither changed Markan sequential order nor organized the material into thematic blocks. The account about the Canaanite (Syrophoenician) woman can be found only in Matt 15:21–28 and Mark 7:24–31. Matthew's version, however, significantly differs from Mark's. One of its peculiarities is its greater length, which does not conform to Matthew's practice in other miracle stories. A closer scrutiny, however, reveals that the shortening of the narrative section typical of Matthew has been done here too, but the dialogue has been expanded.[23] The effect is that the distance between the reader and the events of the story becomes hardly noticeable. The dramatic encounter between Jesus and the foreign woman occurs almost before his/her eyes.

In contrast to Mark who describes the petition of the woman as a request to cast the demon out of her daughter (ἵνα τὸ δαιμόνιον ἐκβάλῃ ἐκ τῆς θυγατρὸς αὐτῆς – Mark 7:26), Matthew presents it as her personal cry for help, "Have mercy on me, O Lord, Son of David" (ἐλέησόν με, κύριε υἱὸς Δαυίδ – Matt 15:22). In this way, the request for an act of exorcism has been replaced by the plea for mercy from the Son of David. Consequently, at the end of the episode, Matthew omits the Markan reference to the exorcism from Jesus' concluding words (ἐξελήλυθεν ἐκ τῆς θυγατρός σου τὸ δαιμόνιον) and adds instead a praise of the woman's great faith (μεγάλη σου ἡ πίστις· γενηθήτω σοι ὡς θέλεις). Finally, instead of the Markan concluding comment about the successfully accomplished exorcism (εὗρεν τὸ παιδίον βεβλημένον ἐπὶ τὴν κλίνην καὶ τὸ δαιμόνιον ἐξεληλυθός), Matthew speaks about the instant healing: ἰάθη ἡ θυγάτηρ αὐτῆς ἀπὸ τῆς ὥρας ἐκείνης. Due to these alterations, an exorcistic account becomes a story of a more general healing.

The geographical setting of Jesus' encounter with the Canaanite woman is the district of Tyre and Sidon where Jesus withdrew after the controversy with the Pharisees over the issue of purification (Matt 15:1–20). Although there is no information regarding the specific locale of the event, it seems that it occurred in a public place. All the characters in the story relate to Jesus, and

---

[22]Compare Matt 13:53–16:20 with Mark 6:1–8:30.

[23]For this tendency of Matthew's redaction, see Held, "Matthew as the Interpreter," 233–237. According to Held's now famous analysis of Matthew's redaction of miracle stories, the following applies to most of them: (a) the recession of descriptions and the predominance of formal expressions, especially at the beginning and the end, (b) omission of all secondary people and secondary actions, and (c) the increasing meaning of the conversation between the suppliant and Jesus. S. Byrskog points out that "the abbreviation of the episodal comments effects a focalization on the Jesus-saying, which is sometimes placed in a dialogue with other characters" (*Jesus the Only Teacher: Didactic Authority and Transmission in Ancient Israel, Ancient Judaism and the Matthean Community*, ConBNT 24 [Stockholm: Almqvist & Wiksell International, 1994], 375).

Matthew presents the whole event as a composition of four small scenes, each beginning with an initiative by one of the characters around Jesus, and ending with Jesus' reaction.[24] In the first scene, the Canaanite woman comes to Jesus asking for mercy because her daughter is possessed by a demon. Jesus, however, does not answer a word. In the second scene, the embarrassed disciples beg Jesus to send her away, but Jesus replies to them that he is sent only to the lost sheep of the house of Israel. In the third scene, the woman kneels before Jesus, imploring again, "Lord, help me." Jesus, however, responds by saying that it is not fair to take the children's bread and throw it to the dogs. In the fourth scene, the woman rejoins Jesus by pointing out that even the dogs eat the crumbs that fall from their master's table. Finally, Jesus gives up and emphatically declares, "O woman, great is your faith! Be it done for you as you desire." The episode ends with a brief report about the actual miracle.

Since Matthew organized and expanded the traditional material in such a way that every initiative of a character is coupled with Jesus' response, the causal coherence of events within the plotted story is strengthened. Within the broader context, however, the structure of Matt 15:21–28 creates a high level of tension. The behavior of Jesus does not coincide with the general trait of his character – compassion. On the other hand, Matthew takes pains to show that there is a specific reason for Jesus' initial attitude, which does not effect his basic disposition toward those who come to him in expectancy of mercy.

3.2.4 The Healing of Two Other Blind Men

Starting with the Matthean characteristic formula that concludes each of the five great discourses in his Gospel, καὶ ἐγένετο ὅτε ἐτέλεσεν ὁ Ἰησοῦς τοὺς λόγους τούτους, Matt 19:1 marks the beginning of a new subsection within the Gospel of Matthew. It also introduces a new geographical setting: Jesus definitively leaves Galilee and enters the region of Judea beyond the Jordan. Chapters 19 and 20 describe events that take place on his journey to Jerusalem.[25]

Matt 20:29–34, similar to Mark 10:46–52, is placed directly before Jesus' entry into Jerusalem. However, in contrast to Mark who speaks about a blind beggar named Bartimaeus, Matthew, similar to the episode narrated in 9:27–31, talks about two blind men without indicating their names. Numerous novelistic details are removed, with the consequence that the story becomes somewhat colorless. Among the most significant alterations is Matthew's reformulation of the cry for help of the two blind men (20:30c). The reference

---

[24]Cf. Davies and Allison, *Matthew*, vol. 2, 541.

[25]Cf. Matthew's comments about Jesus' movement toward Jerusalem: Matt 20:17 (καὶ ἀναβαίνων ὁ Ἰησοῦς εἰς Ἰεροσόλυμα), 20:18 (ἰδοὺ ἀναβαίνομεν εἰς Ἰεροσόλυμα), and 20:29 (καὶ ἐκπορευομένων αὐτῶν ἀπὸ Ἰεριχώ).

to the name Ἰησοῦς is deleted and only the address "Son of David" retained, with the vocative υἱὲ Δαυὶδ (Mark 10:47) being rephrased into the vocative nominative υἱὸς Δαυὶδ (Matt 20:30).[26] Matthew also inverts the word order in the petition, with the result that in Matthew, in contrast to Mark, the petition for mercy comes first, followed by the title Son of David. The second cry is identical to the first, except that it includes the vocative κύριε.[27] Finally, it should be noted that instead of letting Jesus refer to the faith of the blind like Mark 10:52 (ἡ πίστις σου σέσωκέν σε), Matthew, in a manner of an omniscient narrator, informs the reader about Jesus' feelings (σπλαγχνισθεὶς δὲ ὁ Ἰησοῦς) and describes the act of healing.

The structure of the episode is relatively simple. The characters in the story are Jesus, the disciples (not explicitly mentioned, but most probably included into αὐτῶν in v. 29a), the crowd, and two blind men. The entire affair can be divided into two scenes, each beginning with the cry of the blind, "Have mercy on us, Son of David!" After their first cry, the crowd reacts, trying to make them silent. There is no information about Jesus' reaction at this point. However, after the cry has been repeated, Jesus stops, calls them, and asks what their petition is. Their answer, "Lord, let our eyes be opened," moves Jesus by pity, and he responds by healing them. The causal connection of events reported coincides with their temporal sequence. The only event which creates tension is the behavior of the crowd. The author does not try to either interpret or motivate it. Jesus' behavior, on the other hand, is in complete agreement with the general picture the reader gained of him by reading Matthew's narrative.

3.2.5 The Triumphant Entry and Healing the Sick in the Temple

The entire description of Jesus' entry into Jerusalem is in Matthew, in contrast to Mark, presented as a single episode. Events which occurred on two different days in Mark now constitute two different scenes of a single episode in Matthew's Gospel. Matthew achieves this by joining the cleansing of the Temple directly to Jesus' entry into Jerusalem.[28] Matthew strengthens the

---

[26]According to Blass and Debrunner, *A Greek Grammar of the New Testament,* 81–82 §147 (3), this is a semitized vocative nominative.

[27]Whether the first cry of the two blind men includes the address is far from certain. It is preserved in 𝔓[45vid], C, W, *f*[1] but absent in א, D, Θ, *f*[13]. B. M. Metzger admits "that it can be argued that the shortest reading (ἐλέησον ἡμᾶς, υἱὸς Δαυίδ) is original and all other readings are scribal expansions" (*Textual Commentary on the Greek New Testament: A Companion Volume to the United Bible Societies' Greek New Testament,* 3rd ed. [London: United Bible Societies, 1971], 24), but ponders that it is more likely that the later copyist shortened the original in an attempt to accommodate it to the earlier account about the healing of the two blind men in chapter 9.

[28]The story of cursing the fig tree (Mark 12:12–14) thus no longer divides the two events as in Mark, but is reported after the cleansing of the Temple as an event which occurred at the beginning of the following day when Jesus returned to the Temple for the second time.

unity of 21:1–17 by filling the gap between the two separate incidents with a small transitional scene (vv. 10–11) and by drawing a parallel between the cry of children in the Temple and the cry of the crowd which follows Jesus into Jerusalem (vv. 9 and 15).

Jesus' entry into Jerusalem is composed of two sub-scenes, the first depicting the preparation for the entry (vv. 1–7), and the second focusing on the entry itself (vv. 8–11). The most interesting feature of Matthew's account of the preparation for the entry is his addition of a donkey (ὄνος) to the colt (πῶλος) mentioned in Mark 11:2, 4, 5, 7 and Luke 19:30, 33, 35.[29] It is likely that Matthew added the second animal in order to show that Jesus literally fulfilled the prophecy from Zech 9:9,[30] which he also added to the account of Jesus' entry to Jerusalem (vv. 4–5).[31] The quotation itself is a mixture of two scriptural texts. The first line of the citation of Zech 9:9 ("Rejoice greatly, O Daughter Zion! Shout aloud, O daughter Jerusalem!") is replaced with a

---

[29]There is no indication in either Mark or Luke that the animal referred to is a donkey. W. Bauer ("The 'Colt' of Palm Sunday," *JBL* 72 [1953]: 220–229) even argues that the absolute use of πῶλος suggests a horse.

[30]Other explanations are also possible. Thus A. Frenz ("Mt. XXI 5.7," *NovT* 13 [1971]: 259–260) defends the historical accuracy of Matthew's version by insisting that it corresponds to a normal everyday life. He believes that both the ὄνος and the foal are viewed as a unity. Jesus actually rode only on the donkey, but she would not have gone willingly without her foal. A similar view is held by R. H. Gundry, except that he thinks that the "unbroken young donkey was ridden and the mother was led closely alongside the younger animal" (*The Use of the Old Testament*, 199). B. Lindars (*New Testament Apologetic: The Doctrinal Significance of the Old Testament Quotations* [London: SCM Press, 1961], 114) thinks that Matthew deduced the presence of the mother donkey from the unriddenness of the colt (Mark 11:2). K. Stendahl (*The School of St. Matthew*, 200) believes that "Matthew knew a tradition, which spoke about two asses." S. V. McCasland ("Matthew Twists the Scriptures," *JBL* 80 [1961]: 143–148) claims that the two donkeys result from Matthew's misunderstanding of Zech 9:9. J. P. Meier (*The Vision of Matthew: Christ, Church and Morality in the First Gospel*, Theological Inquiries [New York: Paulist Press, 1979], 19–23) uses the same interpretation to argue that the author of Matthew's Gospel must have been a Gentile who was not familiar with *parallelismus membrorum* in Hebrew poetry, because no Jew would have made such a mistake. However, rather than accusing Matthew of misunderstanding the *parallelismus membrorum*, it seems preferable to explain Matthew's understanding of the text as an application of midrashic exegesis, according to which an unusual, or abnormal construction of the biblical text is used to discover its hidden reference to contemporary events. M. Hengel ("Zur matthäischen Bergpredigt und ihrem jüdischen Hintergrund," 234–237) highlights various parallels from the rabbinic and other Jewish writings, which show that Jewish interpreters could completely disregard synonymous *paralelismus membrorum* if this served the goal they wanted to achieve. Hengel concludes that Matthew's procedure closely resembles the *pesher* method which, without regard to synonymous parallelisms, applied biblical prophecies to the present and the future of the sect (ibid., 237).

[31]In view of the fact that John's version of Jesus' entry into Jerusalem (John 12:14–15) also includes the quotation from Zech 9:9 indicates that in some early Christian circles this story became firmly associated with Zechariah's prophecy.

phrase that comes from Isa 62:11 ("Say to the daughter of Zion") through a *gezerâ šawâ* technique.[32] In this way, Matthew adjusted the text of the citation to the narrative framework of Matt 21:1–11. Jerusalem does not applaud to Jesus, but must be told that the royal figure is coming.[33]

Matthew's description of the actual entry into Jerusalem is characterized by several peculiarities. By substituting the Markan expression οἱ πολλοί (Mark 11:8) with ὁ δὲ πλεῖστος ὄχλος (Matt 21:8), and by adding the designation οἱ δὲ ὄχλοι to the Markan material in the next verse (Matt 21:9), Matthew clearly excludes the disciples from the masses who spread their garments on the road and cry.[34] Also, in the presentation of the shout of the crowd, Matthew replaces Mark 11:10a ("Blessed is the kingdom of our father David that is coming") with "Hosanna to the Son of David!" There is no doubt, however, that Matthew, like Mark, understands this phrase as a royal designation, especially in light of his citation of Zech 9:9 that speaks about the coming king. It is therefore somewhat surprising that only in Matthew do we find a short exchange between the citizens of Jerusalem and the accompanying crowds, in which the latter explain the identity of Jesus to the former by saying that "this is the prophet Jesus (ὁ προφήτης Ἰησοῦς) from Nazareth" (v. 11).

The short scene that follows the cleansing of the Temple described in Matt 21:14–16 is absent from the other Synoptics, and it is very likely that it represents a Matthean composition.[35] After the various merchants and money-changers disappear from the Temple, the blind and the lame enter it and Jesus heals them.[36] The children in the Temple respond to the act of healing with the jubilation ὡσαννὰ τῷ υἱῷ Δαυίδ. The indignation of the chief priests and the scribes is presented by Matthew as a reaction to both the healing of the sick and the praise of children, but their question indicates that the conflict itself

---

[32]The text of the quotation is closer to the MT than to the LXX. Notably, the LXX does not have the key word ὄνος. The only point at which the Matthean text form is not a literal equivalent of the MT is in the use of the singular ὑποζύγιον for the plural אתנות. Also, in contrast to the Hebrew text, Matthew understands ὄνος as feminine while the same word in the MT means he-ass. This is the reason why R. Gundry (*The Use of the Old Testament*, 197–199) argues that ὄνος in the narrative should not be equated with ὄνος in the quotation.

[33]Cf. Lohmeyer, *Das Evangelium des Matthäus*, 296; N. Lohfink, "Der Messiaskönig und seine Armen kommen zum Zion: Beobachtungen zu Matt 21,1–17," in *Studien zum Matthäusevangelium*, ed. L. Schenke, FS W. Pesch (Stuttgart: Verlag Katholisches Bibelwerk, 1988), 188–189; Burger, *Jesus als Davidssohn*, 83–84.

[34]The redaction of Luke, in contrast to Matthew, limited the rejoicing group only to the circle of disciples (Luke 19:37).

[35]Cf. Luz, *Matthäus*, vol. 3, 179.

[36]N. Lohfink emphasizes that "diese sorgfältige Komposition zeigt, dass der Herauswurf der einen und das Eintreten und Geheiltwerden der anderen wie zwei Seiten einer und derselbe Sache erscheinen sollen" ("Der Messiaskönig," 192). U. Luz (*Matthäus*, vol. 3, 188) notes that the novelty of this episode lies not in the coming but the healing of the blind and the lame in the Temple.

has nothing to do with the former. The provocation comes from the latter, i.e. the praise of Jesus as the Son of David. Their question directed to Jesus demands his opinion concerning this public acclamation of his identity as the Son of David. Jesus responds with a counter question which reminds his opponents of the text of Ps 8:3: ἐκ στόματος νηπίων καὶ θηλαζόντων κατηρτίσω αἶνον. This citation does not belong to the group of the so-called formula-quotations, because there is no introductory formula. The quotation itself, however, follows the LXX completely, even in its peculiar translation of αἶνον ("praise") for עֹז ("strength").[37]

3.2.6 The Summary of Results

In all but one (Matt 20:29–34) of the texts considered above, the references to the Son of David are the result of Matthew's redaction. In each individual case, the designation "Son of David" is used in an absolute sense. It is never accompanied by another clarifying denotation.[38] Since the mere usage of the designation "Son of David" always suffices to point to its referent, it functions as a title. In this study, the term "title" is used as a semantic designation that has a clearly defined reference.[39] If a certain term has more than one reference, it cannot be called a "title."[40] In that sense, titles share many similarities with proper names, even though they do not necessarily refer to persons who actually exist (or have existed in the past), but can also refer to certain expected figures, such as the Messiah, who are not yet identified in the real world.[41] Because of this feature, they are closer to the so-called "descriptive names" whose reference is explicitly fixed by a definite description.[42]

---

[37]K. Stendahl notes that "it is just in a quotation from the Psalter that the most literal agreements between the NT and the LXX appear" (*The School of St. Matthew*, 134).

[38]J. D. Kingsbury (*Matthew: Structure, Christology, Kingdom*, 103–113) has demonstrated that κύριος does not function as a fixed Christological title in Matthew. It only expresses Jesus' superiority.

[39]In his ABD article on the names of God in the Old Testament, M. Rose offers a similar definition of the term "name." "The 'name' is a 'distinguishing mark' . . . . A 'distinguishing mark' makes it possible to differentiate, to structure, and to order. In this respect 'to name' or 'to designate' belongs to the ordering of creation" (M. Rose, "Names of God in the OT," in *ABD* 4, ed. D. N. Freedman [New York: Doubleday, 1992], 1002).

[40]It is somewhat surprising how rare are the definitions of the term "title." F. Hahn, for example, never defines this concept despite the name of his book *The Titles of Jesus in Christology*. In his book *The Names of Jesus* (London: Macmillan, 1954), V. Taylor speaks about the "names and titles of Jesus" without ever explaining the difference between the two. Moreover, his book is a mixture of personal names, common names, and Christological titles in a narrow sense, which only adds to the confusion.

[41]Rose notes that "the 'distinguishing mark' (name) is not quite identical with what is designated; this little difference allows one to think and to hope that the name will endure. This hope also indicates an aspect of the salutary significance of the name: it juxtaposes the experience of human transience with hope of durability" ("Names of God in the OT," 1002)

[42]Cf. G. Evans, "Reference and Contingency," *The Monist* 62 (1979): 161–184.

Notwithstanding the particularities of each individual episode in Matthew's narrative, they contain several persisting motifs that can be discerned. In three occasions (Matt 9:27–31, 15:21–28, and 20:29–34), whose common feature is that certain individuals need healing, the identification of Jesus as the Son of David precedes the actual miracle. Even more, it seems that he is appealed to heal exactly in his capacity as the Son of David. In each particular case, he is approached with an almost identical cry for mercy: ἐλέησον ἡμᾶς/με, υἱὸς Δαυίδ (Matt 9:27; 15:22; 20:30, 31). This word order is peculiar to the Gospel of Matthew. Both Mark (10:47, 48) and Luke (18:38, 39) have the address first and then the petition for mercy (υἱε Δαυίδ, ἐλέησον με). The fact that apart from these cases the cry ἐλέησον can be found only in Matt 17:15 allows the conclusion that Matthew puts the plea for mercy almost exclusively into the mouth of those individuals who address Jesus as the Son of David. Each time they also address him as κύριος,[43] which indicates that they ascribe him "the superior status . . . in a general manner."[44] They believe that Jesus can and is willing to help them. However, they always meet obstacles "either to reach him or to induce him to heal,"[45] which hinder the straight fulfillment of their wishes, but their faith gives them power to persist.[46] It is somewhat surprising that the Canaanite woman, being a non-Jew, appeals to Jesus by calling him the Son of David. Her dialogue with Jesus clearly demonstrates that her gesture needs to be explained, even argued for.[47] Finally, none of the individual healings is accompanied by an explicit scriptural quotation or a controversy concerning the application of the Davidic title to Jesus.[48]

In other two episodes, Matt 12:22–24 and Matt 21:14–17, the identification of Jesus as the Son of David takes place after the miracle. In both instances it

---

[43]Κύριε is inserted between the cry for mercy and the address υἱὸς Δαυίδ in Matt 15:22 and 20:31. Even though κύριε is not part of the address in Matt 9:27, it occurs in the very next sentence that the blind men utter in 9:28.

[44]Byrskog, *Jesus the Only Teacher*, 277.

[45]Kingsbury, "The Title 'Son of David'," 599.

[46]Although there is no explicit reference to faith in chapter 20, the link between the persistence of the petitioners for mercy from the Son of David in chapters 9 and 15 and their faith has been so firmly established that it does not have to be repeated here again.

[47]In Matthew's Gospel, this episode is an exceptional case which, taken in isolation, does not resolve the complex relationship between Israel and Gentiles. The tension between Matthew's particularism and universalism will not be solved before the end of the narrative, when in 28:16–20 Jesus sends his disciples to all the nations; cf. Davies and Allison, *Matthew*, vol. 2, 543–544. The argument of the Canaanite woman serves as an anticipation of and a preparation for the final extension of Jesus' ministry at the end of the Gospel, as does 8:5–13 (esp. v. 11).

[48]Matt 9:27–31 is no exception in that regard. The objection of Pharisees in 9:34 is the reaction to the marvel of the crowds caused by the healing of a dumb demoniac narrated in 9:32–33, and not to the use of the title "Son of David" by the blind men in the previous episode.

is done by bystanders, not the person/s who has/have been healed. The recognition of Jesus appears here as a direct consequence of the observation of a miraculous act. Also, in both cases Matthew reports the protestation of Jewish leaders. In Matt 12:24, the Pharisees directly react to the question of the crowd in regard to Jesus' identification with the Son of David by replying: "It is only by Beelzebul, the prince of demons, that this man casts out demons." In Matt 21:15, the chief priests and the scribes become indignant when they hear the praise of Jesus as the Son of David by the children in the Temple.[49] Thus it appears that only the public application of the title "Son of David" to Jesus provokes the objection of Jesus' opponents, whereas their reaction to its individual usage is not reported.

There are, however, certain differences that should not be overlooked. In chapter 21, the children in the Temple unequivocally recognize Jesus as the Son of David on the basis of his healing of the blind and the lame. The crowds in chapter 12, however, are to a certain extent ambivalent in regard to the question whether the one who has just healed the blind and dumb demoniac should be recognized as the Son of David or not. This kind of attitude is consistent with the overall thrust of Matthew's narrative, which depicts the crowd in a constant uncertainty in regard to Jesus' true identity. This group of characters often expresses divergent feelings. To Jesus' teaching the crowds usually respond with astonishment (Matt 7:28; 22:33). The response to Jesus' miracles, however, shows greater diversity: at times it is a mixture of fear and glorification of God (Matt 9:8), marvel (Matt 9:33), amazement (Matt 12:23), or pure praise (Matt 15:31).[50] The role of the crowd at Jesus' entry into Jerusalem is also significant. Their jubilation is similar to the cry at the royal procession. However, their answer to the question of the inhabitants of Jerusalem indicates that they regard Jesus merely as a prophetic figure.[51] The fact that through Matthew's redaction of the Markan material the disciples are clearly dissociated from the shouting crowd indicates that the crowd's understanding of Jesus as the Son of David is, although not completely false, still a misunderstanding of his messianic role.

Thus the case of the crowds stands in certain tension, if not in contrast to four blind beggars, one pagan woman, and a group of children who unequivocally identify Jesus as the Son of David. Their common characteristic, perceptively noticed by Jack D. Kingsbury, is that they belong

---

[49]This observation was first made by Suhl, "Der Davidssohn in Matthäus-Evangelium," 70.

[50]It is not surprising that two major contributions to the Son of David theme in Matthew are focused on the role of the crowds in relation to the Davidic title; see Gibbs, "Purpose and Pattern in Matthew's Use of the Title 'Son of David'" 446–464, and Suhl, "Der Davidssohn im Matthäus-Evengelium," 69–75.

[51]U. Luz (*Matthäus*, vol. 3, 184) notes that the answer of the crowd leaves open the question whether they have in mind the eschatological prophet like Moses (cf. Deut 18:15), or an ordinary prophet.

to "no-accounts" in Jewish society.[52] In these isolated cases, Matthew quite clearly establishes a positive relationship between Jesus' miracles and his identity, regardless of which comes first, the identification, or the miracle.

3.3 The Relevance of Jesus' Miracles for His Messianic Identity

3.3.1 The Ambiguity of Jesus' Miracles

Throughout his narrative, Matthew shows that Jesus' miracles bring mixed results. Often they provoke amazement, sometimes faith, but also hostility and opposition. And yet, Matthew consistently shows that Jesus' identity cannot be decided upon apart from his deeds. The question of John the Baptist, reported in Matt 11:2, is one of the clearest examples in this regard. John has heard about Jesus' miracles but is uncertain how to interpret them. He is tortured by the question: "Are you he who is to come, or shall we look for another?" By adding the phrase τὰ ἔργα τοῦ Χριστοῦ to the Q material,[53] Matthew created a tension between his own comment that Jesus' acts indeed are the messianic deeds and the apparent inability of his characters, here John, to interpret them messianically. Also, it is equally important to note that Jesus refuses to offer any direct answer to the question about his identity, but instead points back to his own actions (πορευθέντες ἀπαγγείλατε Ἰωάννῃ ἃ ἀκούετε καὶ βλέπετε – Matt 11:4). The whole episode resembles a closed circle where everything begins and ends with Jesus works.

Other characters in Matthew's narrative also have difficulties with perceiving Jesus' true identity. The ambivalent role of the crowds has been already mentioned above. A closer analysis of their comprehension of Jesus' identity only confirms this impression. Matt 9:33 contains the first of several direct speeches attributed to the crowds in Matthew's narrative: οὐδέποτε ἐφάνη οὕτως ἐν τῷ Ἰσραήλ. The next direct discourse attributed to the crowds appears in Matt 12:23 (μήτι οὗτός ἐστιν ὁ υἱὸς Δαυίδ), which undoubtedly shows crowds' growing interest in the person of Jesus. People from Galilee, Judea, and beyond Jordan even continue to follow Jesus on his way toward Jerusalem. Matthew vividly describes the evolution of certain expectations around Jesus, which culminate at his entry into Jerusalem but end up in a completely reversed attitude at his arrest (Matt 26:55) and the trial before Pilate (Matt 27:20–23).

In contrast to the crowds, Jewish leaders are united in their hostile reaction to Jesus from the very beginning of his ministry. It is, however, important to

---

[52]Kingsbury, "The Title 'Son of David'," 598–599.
[53]Cf. Luke 7:18.

note that they do not deny Jesus' miracles, but only their interpretation.[54] In Matt 9:34, the Pharisees react to the opinion of the crowd concerning the meaning of the miracle they witnessed. Similarly, in Matt 12:24 they respond to the crowd's supposition that the one who healed the blind and dumb demoniac might be the Son of David. Finally, even though in 21:15 Matthew presents the indignation of the chief priests and the scribes as a reaction to both the healing of the sick and the praise of the children, their question indicates that the conflict itself has nothing to do with the healing. The provocation comes from the second event, i.e. the praise of Jesus as the Son of David.

Within this broader context of mixed, even negative feelings, the positive identification of Jesus as the Son of David by a few troubled individuals and the group of children in the Temple comes somewhat as a surprise. Yet, within the context of manifold reactions to Jesus' miracles, each identification of Jesus, even the correct one, sounds somewhat ambiguous. This raises the question about the counteracting parameters that provide the conditions for the incontestable affirmation of Jesus' messianic identity. In other words, it is significant to discern the factors, which in the final analysis justify Matthew's truth claim that those who identified Jesus as the Son of David on the basis of his healing miracles indeed were right.[55] Before we turn to this question, however, it is important to discuss the obstacles which, in Matthew's presentation, hinder or even prevent the correct understanding of a visual event or a spoken word.

3.3.2 The Hindrances of the Proper Understanding of Jesus' Miracles

In Matt 13:13, the Matthean Jesus justifies his method of speaking in parables to the crowds "because seeing they do not see, and hearing they do not hear, nor do they understand" (ὅτι βλέποντες οὐ βλέπουσιν καὶ ἀκούοντες οὐκ ἀκούσιν οὐδὲ συνίουσιν). Notably, Jesus' explanation starts with the reference to seeing, which most likely goes back to Jesus' miracles narrated in previous chapters, since no immediate visual event is reported in chapter 13. Jesus' comment echoes a well attested scriptural tradition that a certain act might not

---

[54]Davies and Allison (*Matthew*, vol. 2, 140) note that "the burning issue . . . is not what Jesus did but what his deeds mean."

[55]This aspect of Matthew's narrative has been often neglected. Thus, for example, B. Gerhardsson notes that "it is part of the character of the mighty acts as much as that of the marvels and signs and the portents in the biblical tradition that they are ambiguous. They can be given a positive interpretation: behind them stands God; this man has been sent by him. Or they can be given a negative interpretation: behind them stand false gods, demons, the spirits of lies and deception; this man is a false prophet leading the people astray" (*The Mighty Acts of Jesus,* 18). It is important to add, however, that Matthew takes pains to delimit this ambiguity on the level of the narrative so that the reader is never in doubt which interpretation is correct.

be properly understood because of human limitations and inability to perceive the visual, even acoustic experience.[56] Thus, for example, in Deut 29:1 Moses addresses the people by confirming the optical character of the exodus event they have witnessed: "You have seen all that the Lord did before your eyes" (אתם ראיתם את כל־אשר עשה יהוה לעיניכם [MT]; ὑμεῖς ἑωράκατε πάντα ὅσα ἐποίησεν κύριος [LXX]). However, this experience has not generated comprehension. The reason for this deficiency of understanding is given in Deut 29:3: "But to this day the Lord has not given you a mind to understand, or eyes to see, or ears to hear" (ולא־נתן יהוה לכם לב לדעת ועינים לראות ואזנים לשמע [MT]; καὶ οὐκ ἔδωκεν κύριος ὁ θεὸς ὑμῖν καρδίαν εἰδέναι καὶ ὀφθαλμοὺς βλέπειν καὶ ὦτα ἀκούειν [LXX]).

In Matthew's narrative, Jesus' miracles receive diverse interpretations not only because some characters do not have the appropriate scriptural knowledge, but also because of their human limitations. The very act of seeing, or even hearing, fails to achieve its goal because of the crowds' inability to properly interpret what they see and hear. In Matt 13:10–17, Jesus uses the language of seeing and hearing that is similar to Deut 29:1–4, but which is interpreted here in light of the prophecy from Isa 6:9: "You shall indeed hear but never understand, and you shall indeed see but never perceive" (ἀκοῇ ἀκούσετε καὶ οὐ μὴ συνῆτε καὶ βλέποντες βλέψετε καὶ οὐ μὴ ἴδητε). The reason for this lack of understanding is the dullness of their heart (ἐπαχύνθη γὰρ ἡ καρδία τοῦ λαοῦ τούτου), heaviness of their ears (τοῖς ὠσὶν αὐτῶν βαρέως ἤκουσαν), and closedness of their eyes (τοὺς ὀφθαλμοὺς αὐτῶν ἐκάμμυσαν).

On the other hand, Jewish leaders possess the scriptural knowledge, which should enable them to properly interpret Jesus' words and deeds, including his miracles, but they do not do so because of their spiritual blindness. This metaphor is especially prominent in chapter 23, where Jesus accuses the Pharisees of being the "blind guides" (ὁδηγοὶ τυφλοί – vv. 16 and 24), "blind fools" (μωροὶ καὶ τυφλοί – v. 17), and "blind men" (τυφλοί – v. 19). The metaphor of blindness reinforces the plausibility of Matthew's story, because it would have otherwise remained enigmatic to the Christian reader why Jesus' career, which in Matthew's narrative represents a complete fulfillment of Scripture, has eventually created the conflict with the Jewish leaders whose scriptural knowledge was generally affirmed.

In contrast to both groups, the disciples are those who understand. They have eyes that see and ears that hear (ὑμῶν δὲ μακάριοι οἱ ὀφθαλμοὶ ὅτι καὶ τὰ ὦτα ὑμῶν ὅτι ἀκούουσιν – Matt 13:16). They are the only group of characters in the Matthean narrative who can give an affirmative answer to

---

[56]Cf. W. J. Bittner, *Jesu Zeichen im Johannesevangelium: Die Messias-Erkenntnis im Johannesevangelium vor ihrem jüdischen Hintergrund*, WUNT II/26 (Tübingen: J. C. B. Mohr [Paul Siebeck], 1987, 76–79.

Jesus' question in Matt 13:51: "Have you understood all this?" (Συνήκατε ταῦτα πάντα; λέγουσιν αὐτῷ, Ναί). It has often been pointed out that the disciples in Matthew represent the church for which he writes his Gospel. They are, to use Ulrich Luz's term, "transparent" for the followers of Jesus in subsequent times.[57] Yet, it is significant to note that in Matthew's presentation, their comprehension of Jesus' messianic identity is after all God's work, which overcomes human limitations of understanding. The clearest example can be found in Matt 16:16–17. After Peter confesses Jesus as the Messiah, the Son of the living God (Σὺ εἶ ὁ Χριστὸς ὁ υἱὸς τοῦ θεοῦ τοῦ ζῶντος), Jesus replies: "Blessed are you, Simon Bar-Jona! For flesh and blood has not revealed (ἀπεκάλυψεν) this to you, but my Father who is in heaven."

There are, however, other passages in Matthew's Gospel which contain the same idea, most notably in the segment of the texts which refer to Jesus as the Son of David. The short scene in the Temple described in Matt 21:14–17 is unique not only because it represents the only miracle Jesus performed in Jerusalem, but also because it represents the only instance of Jesus' response to the identification of his person as the Son of David. To be sure, he replies to the objection raised by the chief priests and the scribes when they heard the praise of children ὡσαννὰ τῷ υἱῷ Δαυίδ, but his response in verse 16 shows that he affirms children's words and identifies them as a praise which comes from God and which is to God. He expresses his agreement with their jubilation by quoting Ps 8:3 LXX, a text which contains three important aspects. The acclamation of Jesus as the Son of David is recognized as the "perfect praise"; this praise is presented as the result of God's initiative; and babes (νήπιοι) are identified as means through which the act of praising takes place.

The only other passage in Matthew's Gospel where the word νήπιοι also appears is Matt 11:25. In his prayer, Jesus thanks his father, the lord of heaven and earth, that he has hidden these things (ἔκρυψας ταῦτα) from the wise and understanding and revealed them to babes (ἀπεκάλυψας αὐτὰ νηπίοις). A comparison between both texts reveals several substantial similarities. Both of them represent Jesus' sayings. In both cases Jesus speaks about divine initiative, and in both cases νήπιοι are the receivers of God's gift, defined in Matt 21:16 as the perfect praise and in Matt 11:25 as the revelation of "these things" (ταῦτα/αὐτά). It has been shown above that the perfect praise in Matt 21:16 refers to Jesus' identity as the Son of David. In the case of Matt 11:25, although it is not immediately clear what is the antecedent of ταῦτα / αὐτά, the only plausible candidate is τὰ ἔργα τοῦ Χριστοῦ (Matt 11:2, 19). This interpretation is supported by the fact that the preceding pericope, Matt 11:20–24, refers to Jesus' mighty deeds which were not understood by the Galilean

---

[57]U. Luz, "Die Jünger im Matthäusevangelium," *ZNW* 62 (1971): 141–171.

cities.[58] The content of divine revelation, however, is not the mighty deeds as such because they can be easily seen, heard, and experienced (Matt 11:4, 20), but their correct understanding.

Furthermore, Matt 11:25–27 demonstrates that Jesus stands in an intimate relationship with God whom he addresses as Father. This interconnectedness between Jesus' divine sonship, his messiahship, and the idea of divine revelation is also present in Peter's confession in Matt 16:16. It cannot be a coincidence that throughout the entire Gospel of Matthew, the noun πάτερ and the verb ἀποκαλύψω occur together only in Matt 11:25, 27 and 16:16.[59]

The concealment of this spiritual insight from the outsiders is another intertextual echo between Matt 21:16 and Matt 11:25. In the latter, Jesus explains that the wise and understanding are those for whom the truth remains hidden, whereas his words in Matt 21:16 imply that his dialogue partners, the chief priests and the scribes, do not comprehend what the children do. Moreover, Matthew's narrative reinforces Jesus' positive attitude toward children. In Matt 18:1–4, Jesus declares a child a model of true greatness. In Matt 19:14, Jesus says that a child should be an example for those who want to enter the kingdom of heaven. Children thus emerge as a group of apparently insignificant characters in Matthew's story who are acknowledged by Jesus as possessing a special insight that many of the other characters are lacking.

It is therefore not accidental that the title "Son of David" appears almost exclusively in the context of the healing of blindness. It has been often pointed out that physical blindness in Matthew symbolizes spiritual blindness.[60] The identification of Jesus as the Son of David seems to be based on a special spiritual insight which is hidden from those who are spiritually blind, but which has been revealed to the weak and humble, i.e. to those who are "marginal" in terms of their status in society.

3.3.3 Search for the Proper Context of Jesus' Miracles

As much as the previous conclusion holds true for the characters within the plot of Matthew's story, its purpose is not to suggest that the spiritual understanding is reserved only for a few privileged individuals. After all, the ambiguity of Jesus' miracles and the inability of certain characters to perceive Jesus' true identity exists only on the level of the story. These features disappear at the level of the narrative, where Matthew wants to convince the reader beyond any reasonable doubt that Jesus is indeed the Son of David, the

---

[58]Cf. Davies and Allison, *Matthew*, vol. 2, 276–277; Verseput, "The 'Son of God' Title," 555 n.66.

[59]In addition to 11:25, 27 and 16:16, the verb ἀποκαλύπτω is used only in 10:26, but in a more general sense than in the other three instances.

[60]Cf. Gibbs, "Purpose and Pattern in Matthew's Use of the Title 'Son of David'," 451–452; Suhl, "Der Davidssohn im Matthäus-Evangelium," 80; Kingsbury, "The Title 'Son of David'," 600–601; Loader, "Son of David, Blindness, Possession, and Duality in Matthew," 570–585.

royal messianic figure who in that capacity acts as a healer of his people. Matthew achieves this goal by creating a clearly defined context that removes the polyvalence of the events he narrates. This inference is based on the insights from modern linguistics, which show that an isolated semantic unit is potentially equivocal. In a specific context, however, this ambiguity disappears through the semantic "filtering" of possible meanings.[61]

The question thus becomes: What is the context in which Matthew's presentation of the Davidic Messiah who heals the sick makes sense? There is no doubt that Matthew links together two different concepts which have not been associated as such in the pre-Christian writings. Nonetheless, he expects his readers to "see" and "understand" the logic of this process, which, even when not completely apparent to an outsider, provides a sound explanation to an insider. Given the Jewish character of Matthew's Gospel, an answer to this question will be sought within the parameters set up by the Jewish texts and traditions with which Matthew and his audience might have been familiar.

3.4 Solomon as Exorcist

3.4.1 Introduction

One way of explaining Matthew's link of Jesus' identity as the Son of David to the miracles of healing is to relate it to certain traditions about Solomon who acts as a great exorcist. This celebration of Solomon was popular in many circles in early Judaism. The interpretation attracted a significant scholarly attention after the initial publication of Loren Fisher's article "Can This Be the Son of David?"[62] in which he examined a number of Aramaic incantation bowls that mention Solomon, the Son of David, and his ability to exorcise demons. Fisher found the strongest support for his view in Matt 12:22–24, because the question μήτι οὗτός ἐστιν ὁ υἱὸς Δαυίδ could be understood as a reaction of the crowds to an act of exorcism, but subsequent publications have demonstrated that other passages, especially those in which Jesus is addressed with the plea ἐλέησον ἡμᾶς/με υἱὸς Δαυίδ, also offer some material that can be investigated in light of the traditions about Solomon.

---

[61]J. Lyons (*Language, Meaning, and Context* [London: Fontana, 1981], 75) insists that "no word can be fully understood independently of other words that are related to it and delimit its sense. Looked at from a semantic point of view, the lexical structure of a language – the structure of its vocabulary – is best regarded as a large and intricate network of sense-relations: it is like a huge, multidimensional spider's web, in which each strand is one such relation and each knot in the web is a different lexeme." See also F. Francois, "Kontext und Situation," in *Linguistik: Ein Handbuch*, ed. A. Martinet, trans. I. Rehbein and S. Stelzer (Stuttgart: J. B. Metzler, 1973), 42–48.

[62]Fisher, "Can This Be the Son of David?" 82–97.

A few years after Fisher, Evald Lövestam broadened the scope of Jewish literature and examined the *Testament of Solomon* and some fragments of the Dead Sea Scrolls Psalms.[63] Klaus Berger's article, published shortly afterwards, focused on the same early Jewish documents, but claimed that the wisdom traditions about Solomon, which also ascribe him the authority over demons, represent the most appropriate background of the New Testament references to the Son of David.[64] In a most thorough examination of these hypotheses, which was published a year later, Denis C. Duling offered a reconstruction of a trajectory of the traditions about Solomon.[65] In his view, a convergence or conflict between the Solomonic traditions and the royal messianic traditions could have occurred either in pre-Christian Judaism or in Christianity. Recently James H. Charlesworth investigated the pre-Markan tradition of Mark 10:47[66] and argued that Jesus was hailed as the Messiah neither in the historical nor in the literary (Markan) setting of the Bartimaeus episode, but as "a healer, after the order of Solomon."[67]

3.4.2 Solomon as Exorcist in Jewish Literature

The *locus classicus* of the tradition about Solomon who is able to control demons can be found in Josephus' *Antiquities* 8.2.5.

> Now so great was the prudence and wisdom which God granted Solomon that he surpassed the ancients, and even the Egyptians, who are said to excel all men in understanding, were not only, when compared with him, a little inferior but proved to fall far short of the king in sagacity . . . . There was no form of nature with which he was not acquainted or which he passed over without examining, but he studied them all philosophically and revealed the most complete knowledge of their several properties. And God granted him knowledge of the art used against demons for the benefit and healing of men. He also composed incantations by which illnesses are relieved, and left behind forms of exorcisms with which those possessed by demons drive them out, never to return.

After these introductory remarks about Solomon himself, Josephus goes on to describe how Solomon's knowledge was applied in the first century.

> And this kind of cure is of very great power among us to this day, for I have seen a certain Eleazar, a countryman of mine, in the presence of Vespasian, his sons, tribunes and a number of other soldiers, free men possessed by demons,

---

[63]Lövestam, "Jésus Fils de David chez les Synoptiques," 97–109.

[64]Berger, "Die königlichen Messiastraditionen des Neuen Testaments," 1–44.

[65]Duling, "Solomon, Exorcism, and the Son of David," 235–252; idem, "The Therapeutic Son of David," 392–410.

[66]Charlesworth, "Solomon and Jesus," 125–151.

[67]Ibid., 147.

and this was the manner of the cure: he put to the nose of the possessed man a ring which had under its seal one of the roots prescribed by Solomon, and then, as the man smelled it, drew out the demon through his nostrils, and, when the man at once fell down, adjured the demon never to come back into him, speaking Solomon's name and reciting the incantations which he had composed. Then, wishing to convince the bystanders and prove to them that he had this power, Eleazar placed a cup or foot-basin full of water a little way off and commanded the demon, as it went out of the man, to overturn it and make known to the spectators that he had left the man. And when this was done, the understanding and wisdom of Solomon were clearly revealed, on account of which we have been induced to speak of these things, in order that all men may know the greatness of his nature and how God favoured him, and that no one under the sun may be ignorant of the king's surpassing virtue of every kind.[68]

Josephus understands Solomon's ability to exorcise demons as an art (τὴν κατὰ τῶν δαιμόνων τέχνην), whose purpose is the benefit and healing of human beings (εἰς ὠφέλειαν καὶ θεραπείαν τοῖς ἀνθρώποις). Its ultimate source is understanding and wisdom that Solomon received from God (ὁ θεὸς παρέσχε Σολομῶνι φρόνησιν καὶ σοφίαν), which greatly exceeded any other form of human knowledge and wisdom. The crucial element in Josephus' account, however, is the remark that Solomon left behind certain forms of exorcisms (τρόπους ἐξορκώσεων) that were known to some individuals who were able to apply them in practice. The tradition is thus handed over through the transmission of a special type of cure (αὔτη . . . ἡ θεραπεία), whose three essential elements are a ring under whose seal was one of the roots prescribed by Solomon, the mention of Solomon's name, and a recitation of the incantations which he composed.

The scriptural foundation of this tradition can be found in 1 Kgs 5:9–14, which declares in verse 10 that Solomon's wisdom (חכמה [MT], ἡ φρόνησις [LXX]) surpassed the wisdom of all the people of the East and all the wisdom of Egypt. Duling has convincingly demonstrated that this literary tradition about Solomon continued in Prov 1:1, Cant 1:1, Eccl 1:1, 12, 16–18, and Wis 8:10–11; 9:7–8, 12.[69] *Wisdom of Solomon* additionally expands the motif of Solomon's wisdom to include the encyclopedic knowledge of the universe (Wis 7:16–20), including the knowledge of healing arts: the violent force of spirits (πνευμάτων βίας), the species of plants (διαφορὰς φυτῶν), and the powers of roots (δυνάμεις ῥιζῶν). A common view is that the first provides the background of Josephus' description of Solomon's power over evil

---

[68]Trans. H. S. J. Thackeray and R. Marcus, *Josephus in Nine Volumes*, vol. 5: *Jewish Antiquities, Books V–VIII*, LCL (Cambridge: Harvard University Press; London: William Heinemann, 1958), 593–597.

[69]Duling, "Solomon, Exorcism, and the Son of David," 237.

spirits,[70] even though the anarthrous noun πνεύματα does not necessarily denote demons, but rather winds, breaths, or spirits.[71] The other two expressions refer to the botanical knowledge of plants and roots which can be used for healing. The continuation of this tradition can be found in Josephus' account of the use of a root prescribed by Solomon (ῥίζαν ἐξ ὧ ὑπέδειξε Σολομών) in the exorcistic procedure that he witnessed.[72]

According to Josephus' account about various Jewish sects in the first century C.E., the Essenes were especially interested in treatment of diseases, and for this purpose made "investigations into medicinal roots and the properties of stones."[73] Philo also confirms that the *Therapeutai* "profess a healing art better than that current in towns which cures only bodies, while theirs treats also souls oppressed by grievous and well-nigh intolerable diseases."[74] Their interest in exorcistic techniques is attested in 1QapGen 20.16–21, 28–29 which presents Abraham as an exorcist,[75] 4Q242 (4QPrNab) which mentions an unknown Jewish exorcist,[76] and 11Q5 (11QPs^a) 27.10 which ascribes to David songs for making music over the stricken (הפגועים). 11Q11 (11QPsAp^a) contains a liturgy for healing the stricken,[77] which might

---

[70]Cf. C. C. McCown, *The Testament of Solomon* (Leipzig: J. C. Hinrich, 1922), 91; R. H. Charles, *The Apocrypha and Pseudepigrapha of the Old Testament in English: With Introductions and Critical and Explanatory Notes to the Several Books* (Oxford: Clarendon Press, 1913), 546; Duling, "Solomon, Exorcism, and the Son of David," 239.

[71]Cf. L. P. Hogan, *Healing in the Second Tempel Period*, NTOA 21 (Göttingen: Vandenhoeck & Ruprecht, 1992), 52.

[72]*Ant.* 8.2.5. Another similarity is that both Josephus and the author of *Wisdom* interpret Solomon's knowledge of healing arts as God's gift, which justifies their use. Cf. *1 En.* 7–9, which present the knowledge of roots, plants, and astronomy as the forbidden knowledge that has been revealed by the fallen angels.

[73]*J.W.* 2.8.6.

[74]*Contempl.* 1.1.

[75]The exorcism is performed through laying on of hands and a prayer, which is an unusual practice because it is neither found in the Hebrew Scripture nor in the rabbinic literature; cf. D. Flusser, "Healing Through the Laying on of Hands in a Dead Sea Scroll," *IEJ* 7 (1957): 107. It is also uncertain whether the text contains the reading ויתוך ("will depart from you") or תרך ("expel" or "cast out").

[76]On the basis of the similarities between the Prayer of Nabonidus and Daniel 4, the term גזר, which is commonly translated as "exorcist" after the initial proposal by G. Furlani ("Aram. Gazrin = scongiurotori," in *Anti della accademia nationale et filogiche*, Serie Ottava IV [1948]: 177–196), is usually taken as a reference to Daniel; see Hogan, *Healing in the Second Tempel Period*, 154.

[77]Published first by J. P. M. van der Ploeg, "Le Psaume XCI dans une Recension de Qumran," *RB* 72 (1965): 210–217; see also his essay "Un petit rouleau de psaumes apocryphes (11QPsAp^a)," in *Tradition und Glaube: Das frühe Christentum in seiner Umwelt*, ed. G. Jeremias, H.-W. Kuhn, and H. Stegemann, FS K. G. Kuhn (Göttingen: Vandenhoeck & Ruprecht, 1971), 128–139. For a critical edition of the text see J. A. Sanders, "A Liturgy for Healing the Stricken (11QPsAp^a)" in *The Dead Sea Scrolls: Hebrew, Aramaic, and Greek Texts with English Translations*, vol. 4A: *Pseudepigraphic and Non-Masoretic Psalms and*

be one of the compositions referred to in 11Q5.[78] Among the four psalms comprised in this scroll is also Psalm 91, which is known in rabbinic literature as the "song for the stricken" (*y. Šabb.* 6:2), "song referring to evil demons" (*b. Šeb.* 15b), and "song for demons" (*y. 'Erub.* 10:26c).[79] The psalm, which is partially preserved in column 1, contains the evidence that Solomon was also known at Qumran. The name Solomon (שלומה) appears in line 2, followed by the reference to the spirits and demons ([הר]וחות והשדים) in line 3.

One of the most intriguing references for our present investigation is found in *Liber Antiquitatum Biblicarum,* a document from the first century pseudonymously attributed to Philo. Chapter 60 contains the song, which David played for Saul in order to exorcise the evil spirit from him. It ends with the promise to David that he will have a descendant who will subdue the evil spirit: "But let the new womb from which I was born rebuke you, from which after a time one born from my loins will rule over you" (*Arguet autem te metra nova unde natus sum, de qua nascetur post tempus de lateribus meis qui vos domabit.*)[80] This cryptic formulation is interpreted either as a reference to Jesus,[81] the royal Messiah,[82] or Solomon.[83] In favor of the messianic interpretation are certain linguistic similarities with 2 Sam 7:11 (LXX), Ps 132:11 (LXX), and *T. Levi* 18:12,[84] but the evidence is not sufficiently compelling for such a claim. The promise of David's descendant can be equally well applied to Solomon, whereas *T. Levi* 18 is a hymn to a new priest and not to the royal Messiah.[85] In view of the widespread tradition about

---

Prayers, ed. J. H. Charlesworth and H. W. L. Rietz (Tübingen: J. C. B. Mohr [Paul Siebeck], 1997), 216–233.

[78]Cf. Hogan, *Healing in the Second Tempel Period*, 162.

[79]Cf. M. Jastrow, *A Dictionary of the Targumim, the Talmud, Babli and Yerushalmi, and the Midrashic Literature* (New York: Jastrow Publishers, 1967), 1135; J. A. Sanders, *Psalms Scroll of Qumran Cave 11 (11QPs^a)*, DJD 4 (Oxford: Clarendon, 1965), 93; J. P. M. van der Ploeg, "Un petit rouleau de psaumes apocryphes (11QPsAp^a)," 128–129.

[80]*L.A.B.* 60.3.

[81]J. Klausner, *The Messianic Idea in Israel: From Its Beginning to the Completion of the Mishnah,* trans. W. F. Stinespring (New York: Macmillan, 1955), 367 n.7.

[82]P. Riessler, *Altjüdisches Schrifttum ausserhalb der Bibel, übersetzt und erläutert,* 2nd ed. (Darmstadt: Wissenschaftliche Buchgesellschaft, 1966), 1318; M. Philonenko, "Remarques sur un hymne essénien de caractère gnostique," *Sem* 11 (1961): 52; Berger, "Königliche Messiastraditionen," 8.

[83]M. R. James, "Citharismus regis David contra daemonum Saulis," in *Apocrypha Anecdota,* TS 2/3 (Cambridge: University Press, 1893), 81; McCown *The Testament of Solomon,* 91; Charlesworth, "Solomon and Jesus," 141.

[84]Cf. Duling, "Solomon, Exorcism, and the Son of David," 240.

[85]K. Berger, after initially declaring that it remains open whether this text refers to Solomon or to the future descendant of David ("Königliche Messiastraditionen," 6), claims two pages later that *L.A.B.* 60.3 contains an open messianic formulation. His comment that this text speaks about the future birth of a Son of David is equally misleading, because the term "Son of David" does not appear as such. Thus D. J. Harrington notes that "it is unlikely that

Solomon's ability to subdue demons, it is more likely that *L.A.B.* 60.3 alludes to Solomon as exorcist.[86]

In contrast to the documents mentioned above, which come either from the first century B.C.E. or the first century C.E., the *Testament of Solomon* has been exposed to a number of recensions, which hinder a more precise determination of its date. It is usually assumed that it could have been written sometime between the second and the fourth century C.E.[87] This document contains a folktale about Solomon who builds the Temple in Jerusalem. Since, however, his building project was hindered by a demon, he prays to God for help, which he receives in the form of a magic seal-ring that gives him the authority over demons. He knows their names and questions them regarding their activities, including those which cause illness. He is able to seal them with the ring and force them to obey him. This syncretistic document which combines various beliefs about astrology, demonology, magic, and medicine is, as Duling notes, "an important response to basic human problems: the presence of human frailty, sickness, and potential death."[88]

The term "Son of David" appears several times in the text. In some manuscripts, the phrase ὁ Σολομῶν υἱὸς Δαυείδ can be found in the Greek title, prologue, and a first few verses.[89] As a form of address, however, it appears only twice. In most of the manuscripts, the archangel Michael addressees Solomon in 1:7 as Σολομῶν υἱὸς Δαυείδ, whereas MS H contains also a similar address in 20:1, here in the form of a plea of an old man who is tortured by his son: βασιλεῦ Σολομῶν υἱὸς Δαυείδ, ἐλέησόν με. The similarity of the latter with the form of address found in the New Testament cannot be overlooked. The question, however, which must be answered first is whether we have here an independent tradition, or a secondary development influenced by Christianity. Berger assigned great importance to the form of address found in *T. Sol.* 20:1 and argued that it represents an independent formulation that is free from any synoptic influence.[90] Yet in view of several obvious Christian interpolations in MS P,[91] the appearance of the formulation which resembles the synoptic cry in a single manuscript cannot be taken as a strong evidence for

---

this is a reference to the future Messiah (or Jesus), given the lack of interest in such a figure throughout Ps-Philo" ("Pseudo-Philo: A New Translation and Introduction," in *The Old Testament Pseudepigrapha,* ed. J. H. Charlesworth, vol. 2 [New York: Doubleday, 1985], 373 n.60e).

[86]Ibid.

[87]D. C. Duling, "Testament of Solomon: A New Translation and Introduction," in *OTP* 1, ed. J. H. Charlesworth, (Garden City, NY: Doubleday, 1985), 940–943.

[88]Ibid., 944.

[89]This formulation appears in the title of MSS P Q I; MS L and recension C; Prologue 1:1; recension C 12:1; 13:12; MS D 1:1; MS E 11:1.

[90]Berger, "Königliche Messiastraditionen," 7.

[91]Cf. two references to the crucifixion of Jesus in *T. Sol.* 12:3 and 15:10–12.

an independent tradition.[92] Moreover, the cry for help in *T. Sol.* 20:1 does not come from a person tortured by a demon, as Berger assumes,[93] but from an old man who accused his son of mistreating him and appealed to Solomon for justice, not exorcism.

The evidence for the traditions about Solomon who acts as an exorcist is also found in Aramaic magical texts.[94] They represent incantations for expelling demons from people and their dwellings, written around 600 C.E. on the inside of magical bowls. However, even though they are quite late, they contain certain traditions about Solomon similar to those that we observed in earlier texts. At least eighteen bowls contain the phrase "King Solomon, Son of David," and twelve to thirteen mention his seal-ring. Bellow is the selection of a few representative examples:

> Charmed and sealed is all evil that is in the body of Mihr-hormizd b.M. (8) and in his house (and) his wife and his sons and his daughters and his cattle and his property and in all his dwelling, by the signet of Ariôn son of Zand and by the seal of King Solomon son of David, (9) by which were sealed the Oppressors and the Latbê . . .[95]

> This amulet is designated for the salvation, for the guarding, and for the sealing of the house of Parruk the son of 'Araznish (and) all his dwelling. This is the seal-ring of King Solomon the son of (2) David, the luck of which no one has mastered – By 'HS – and before which no one is standing . . .[96]

> . . . (4) they, their houses, their children, and their possessions are sealed with the seal-ring of 'El Shaddai, blessed be He, and with the seal-ring of King (5) Solomon the son of David, who worked spells on male demons and female liliths . . .[97]

---

[92]Cf. Duling, "Solomon, Exorcism, and the Son of David," 243.

[93]Berger, "Königliche Messiastraditionen," 7.

[94]For a full treatment of this literature see J. A. Montgomery, *Aramaic Incantation Texts from Nippur* (Philadelphia: The University Museum, 1913); C. H. Gordon, *Adventures in the Nearest East* (London: Pnoenix House, 1957); E. M. Yamauchi, "Aramaic Magic Bowls," *JAOS* 85 (1965): 511–523; and C. D. Isbell, *Corpus of the Aramaic Incantation Bowls,* SBLDS 17 (Missoula, Mont.: Scholars Press, 1975). The references to Solomon, especially to the magical power of his ring, can also be found in rabbinic literature (*b.Git.* 68a) and the hellenistic magical papyri; see Papyrus No. IV in K. Preisendanz, *Papyri Graecae Magicae: Die griechischen Zauberpapyri,* ed. A. Henrichs, vol. 1 (Stuttgart: Teubner, 1973–1974), 102–104; English translation: *The Greek Magical Papyri in Translation,* ed. H. D. Betz, trans. W. C. Grese (Chicago: University of Chicago Press, 1986), 55–56.

[95]Montgomery No. 34 (Montgomery, *Aramaic Incantation Texts,* 232).

[96]Isbell No. 47 (Isbell, *Corpus of the Aramaic Incantation Bowls,* 108–109) = Gordon A (C. H. Gordon, "Aramaic Magical Bowls in the Istanbul and Baghdad Museums," *ArOr* 6 [1934]: 322).

[97]Isbell No. 48 (Isbell, *Corpus of the Aramaic Incantation Bowls,* 110–111) = Gordon B (Gordon, "Aramaic Magical Bowls," 319–334).

Sealed and dou[bly-se]aled is the house of Zidin Shabor the son of 'Elisheba, with seventy knots, (2) with seventy bonds, with seventy seals . . . with the seal-ring of Gabriel (4) the mighty angel, the Prince of Fire, with the seal-ring of 'Aspanadas-Diwa, the jinee of King Solomon the son of David, and the seal-ring of King Solomon the son of David . . .[98]

More examples could be given, but they contain similar material. They regularly refer to the "King Solomon, Son of David" (דשלמוה/דשלימון מלכא בר דויד), his "seal-ring," or his "seal." In contrast to Josephus, Aramaic incantation bowls contain no information about what is under the seal-ring.

The survey of the material that refers to Solomon's power over demons indicates the presence of several typical elements. The most common motif is the presence of a demon and Solomon's ability to force it to leave the person/dwelling it inhabits. Solomon's name is regularly mentioned in this context,[99] whereas the term "Son of David" appears only in the *Testament of Solomon* and the Aramaic magical texts.[100] The material from the first century on usually contains the references to his seal-ring, an object used in exorcistic techniques for sealing the demon(s). This motif presupposes the transferability of Solomon's power to another person(s). The clearest evidence is found in *Ant.* 8.2.5 and the *Testament of Solomon,* but other texts which mention the seal-ring of Solomon imply this as well. Josephus speaks about forms of exorcism left by Solomon, and mentions the ring, which had under its seal one of the roots prescribed by Solomon. Also, in *T. Sol.* 15:14, Solomon declares that he writes his testament to the sons of Israel "so that (they) might know the powers of the demons and their forms, as well as the names of the angels by which they are thwarted."[101]

3.4.3 Solomon as Exorcist and the Gospel of Matthew

If we assume for a moment a titular usage of the term "Son of David" in the Jewish texts considered above,[102] which is by no means certain, it would be possible to explain Matthew's association of the title "Son of David" and

---

[98]Isbell No. 50 (Isbell, *Corpus of the Aramaic Incantation Bowls,* 114–115) = Gordon E (Gordon, "Aramaic Magical Bowls," 466–474).

[99]The exception is *L.A.B.* 60.3.

[100]D. Duling refers to this as a "subsidiary part" of the trajectory of Solomon-as-exorcist. ("Solomon, Exorcism, and the Son of David," 249)

[101]Cf. the conclusion of the *Testament of Solomon* in MSS H N: "(8) And I wrote this, my testament, to the Jews and bequeathed it to them as a remembrance of my end. Let my testament be guarded for you as a great mystery against the unclean spirits so that you know the devices of the evil demons and the powers of the holy angels; because a great Lord Sabaoth, the God of Israel, prevails, and he made subject to me all the demons, by whom was given to me a seal of an eternal testament." (*OTP* 1, 987 n.f.)

[102]Fisher "Can This Be The Son Of David?" 89–90; Berger, "Die königliche Messiastraditionen," 3–9; Charlesworth, "Solomon and Jesus," 138.

Jesus' healing miracles in two different ways. One solution would be to maintain that the crowds in chapter 12 and various individuals in other occasions identify Jesus not as the Messiah but as *Solomon redivivus*. This interpretation, however, cannot be sustained in view of the fact that in the narrative framework of Jesus' miraculous healings Matthew clearly shows that he understands the term "Son of David" as a messianic title.

A second option would be to argue that the Matthean Jesus is indeed identified as the Davidic Messiah, but that this identification comes from the tradition originally associated with Solomon. Matthew's Gospel in that case either presupposes (at the pre-Matthean level) or itself accomplishes the merging of two distinct traditions.[103] The main weakness of this solution is that Matthew's presentation of Jesus' healing activity lacks all the essential elements found in the traditions about Solomon. There is no direct confrontation of Jesus and a demon, no seal-ring, no secret knowledge of how to exorcise demons, no reference to Solomon's name, and no technical language associated with exorcisms.

Moreover, it seems that Matthew deliberately wished to dissociate Jesus' miraculous healings from the exorcistic connotations. It cannot be accidental that in the only two episodes where Jesus is asked to heal a person possessed by a demon in his capacity as the Son of David, Matt 12:22–24[104] and 15:21–28,[105] the verb ἐκβάλλω has been omitted from the Markan material and replaced either with the verb θεραπεύω (Matt 12:22)[106] or with the plea for mercy (Matt 15:22). Also, in Matt 15:28, two Markan references to the actual exit of a demon from the girl[107] have been replaced first with Jesus' praise of her mother's faith and then with the report about the momentous healing.

These changes do not represent isolated cases, but fit the pattern found elsewhere in Matthew. In the two almost identical summaries which bracket the material in chapters 5–9, Matt 4:23 and 9:35, Matthew replaced τὰ δαιμόνια ἐκβάλλων from Mark 1:39 with θεραπεύων πᾶσαν νόσον καὶ πᾶσαν μαλακίαν ἐν τῷ λαῷ. Thus in contrast to the Markan Jesus whose main

---

[103]Cf. Fisher's proposal that the question of the crowd in Matt 12:23 probably refers to the Messiah, but that "in the original tradition" this was a reference to Solomon ("Can This Be the Son of David?" 89).

[104]Matt 12:22 mentions a blind and dumb demoniac (δαιμονιζόμενος τυφλὸς καὶ κωφός).

[105]Matt 15:22 speaks about the Syrophoenician woman's daughter being severely possessed by a demon (ἡ θυγάτηρ μου κακῶς δαιμονίζεται).

[106]Fisher's comment that here "we first have the report of the exorcism" ("Can This Be the Son of David?" 89) is therefore not entirely correct.

[107]Cf. ἐξελήλυθεν ἐκ τῆς θυγατρός σου τὸ δαιμόνιον (Mark 7:29) and δαιμόνιον ἐξεληλυθός (Mark 7:30). Note also Matthew's omission of the reference to the unclean spirit (πνεῦμα ἀκάθαρτον) from Mark 7:25, which is consistently done throughout the narrative. Matthew omitted ten out of eleven references to the unclean spirit from the Markan material (the only exception is Matt 10:1).

activity is preaching in the synagogues and casting out demons, the main activity of the Matthean Jesus is threefold: teaching in the synagogues, preaching the gospel of the Kingdom, and healing every disease and every infirmity among the people. Moreover, even though Matt 4:24 mentions demoniacs (δαιμονιζόμενοι), they belong to a more general category (those afflicted with various diseases and pains) whom Jesus healed (ἐθεράπευσεν). Thus the Matthean Jesus heals the possessed in the same way that he heals other illnesses among the people.[108]

The form-critical distinction between demonological aetiologies of illness and the techniques of healing which use exorcism, introduced by Gerd Theissen, can be especially helpful here.[109] In the former, the demon causes the disease, while in the latter, the demon inhabits the victim. Accordingly, "the healer deals with the effects of the demon's action, the exorcist with its presence."[110] Due to Matthew's redaction the exorcistic *topoi* are hardly recognizable. Neither in Matt 12:22–24 nor in Matt 15:21–28 does Jesus confront the demon as a personified opponent. Rather, the emphasis is shifted from the possession toward the illness caused by a demon.[111]

These observations about Matthew's editorial activity support the conclusion that his Gospel neither presupposes nor accomplishes the converging of the traditions about Solomon as exorcist and the Davidic Messiah. Rather, Matthew creates a context in which Jesus' healing miracles

---

[108]This is the reason why D. C. Duling proposes that "the more broadly based or inclusive nature of Jesus' healing in Matthew may be designated with the term 'therapeutic'" ("The Therapeutic Son of David," 398). Cf. also J. A. Comber, "The Verb *therapeuô* in Matthew's Gospel," *JBL* 97 (1978): 431–434. This conclusion is reached on the basis of Matthew's summaries and the details of his redaction (Matthew changed his Markan source in 14:14; 17:16; 19:2, modified Q in 8:7; 10:1; 12:22; 17:18; and added the verb θεραπεύω in 4:23, 24; 9:35; 15:30; 21:14), and it neither depends on nor is undermined by the observation that Matthew's Gospel still contains several reports of Jesus' exorcisms (8:28–34; 9:32–34; 17:14–21). For a full treatment of these texts see D. Trunk, *Der Messianische Heiler: Eine redaktions- und religionsgeschichtliche Studie zu den Exorzismen im Matthäusevangelium*, HBS 3 (Freiburg/Basel/Wien: Herder, 1994).

[109]G. Theissen, *The Miracle Stories of the Early Christian Tradition*, ed. J. Riches, trans. F. McDonagh (Philadelphia: Fortress, 1983), 86.

[110]Ibid. Theissen further explains that "the mere absence of demonological motifs is not a distinctive feature of healings as opposed to exorcisms; what is distinctive is that the motifs of conflict are replaced by images of the transmission of a healing power, images which doubtless bring us closer to the dawn of medicine than to the powerful words of exorcism" (ibid., 90). This, however, does not mean that there is a clear-cut distinction between healings and exorcisms, because the latter can be also used for the purpose of healing. Josephus, *Ant.* 8.2.5 and the *Testament of Solomon* (especially chapter 18) clearly demonstrate this. Cf. Charlesworth's comment that "it is thus conceivable – indeed probable – that Solomon was considered to be not only an exorcist but also a healer" ("Solomon and Jesus," 140).

[111]Cf. Trunk, *Der Messianische Heiler,* 61, 143.

function as the messianic deeds and not as the acts of the miracle worker after the order of Solomon.

Early Jewish texts considered above demonstrate that in early Judaism these two traditions were never really associated.[112] First of all, in the passages that contain the references to the Son of David, the latter function as grammatical appositions. They offer additional information about Solomon – about his origin[113] – and are never used as titles. In none of the texts do we find the term "Son of David" used in an absolute sense, but always as a qualifier of the reference to Solomon.[114] In both documents which contain the term "Son of David," the *Testament of Solomon* and the collection of Aramaic incantation bowls, we merely find the combination "[the] King Solomon, [the] Son of David."[115] It is quite possible that this was a linguistic protection against an eventual confusion which might have occurred if the term "Son of David" had been used in an absolute sense to denote *Solomon redivivus*, alongside the absolute use of the same designation for the Davidic Messiah attested in *Pss. Sol.* 17:21 and the rabbinic literature.

Furthermore, the term "Son of David" is always applied to the historical Solomon, and not to a person who possesses the knowledge of Solomon and uses it in practice. When Josephus reports about the exorcism to which he witnessed, he refers to the main actor by his personal name, Eleazar. Solomon's name is mentioned only in the description of the healing process in which it performed a certain function, not otherwise. It is therefore very questionable whether we can speak about *Solomon redivivus*,[116] even less about the titular use of the term "Son of David" in this sense. The ability to heal by exorcising demons with the help of certain techniques left over from Solomon does not qualify a person to bear the title "Son of David." Or the

---

[112] *L.A.B.* 60.3 does not offer any decisive evidence in that regard. Berger's conjecture that Psalm 72 offered the opportunity for the combination of the messianic expectations with the description of Solomon ("Königliche Messiastraditionen," 8) remains unsupported by the evidence that this has ever been done.

[113] Duling calls this "a casual reference to descent" ("Solomon, Exorcism, and the Son of David," 249).

[114] The same applies to the Old Testament. Fisher's comments about the use of this "title" in the Old Testament are therefore misleading, even though he acknowledges that this term regularly refers to Solomon ("Can This Be the Son of David?" 90). The additional evidence from the Siegel-inscription found in A. Delatte, *Anecdota atheniensia,* I (Paris: É. Champion, 1927), 605, No. 17 (Ἰωὴλ βοήθει ἰδοὺ Σολομών, υἱὸς Δαυίδ, δράκοντος γλῶσσαν ἔχων, βασιλέως ἐγκέφαλον) only confirms the above conclusion.

[115] Cf. a similar non-titular usage of the designation "Son of David" in Matt 1:20: Ἰωσὴφ υἱὸς Δαυίδ.

[116] The terminology which appears in the secondary literature lacks clarity in that regard. Fisher, for example, sometimes speaks about someone healing in the name of Solomon, and at other times about Solomon impersonated ("Can This Be the Son of David?" 91).

opposite, to call someone "Son of David" does not necessarily imply that this person is able to exorcise demons in the manner of Solomon.

On the other hand, the Jewish texts demonstrate the connection between certain types of exorcisms and the traditions about Solomon's great wisdom, knowledge of nature, and authority over demons. It is thus quite possible that Jesus' massive exorcistic activity could have given rise to certain associations with Solomon, which, as Charlesworth has argued, might have been prominent even in some Christian circles.[117] Matthew's addition of the title to the episode which directly leads into the Beelzebul controversy probably supports this conjecture. As the dialogue following the question of the crowds in Matt 12:23 demonstrates, Jesus' exorcistic activity provides the framework of the dispute. The assumption of the Pharisees that Jesus exorcises demons is not questioned by any participant in the controversy, not even by Jesus. Jewish leaders take for granted that the healing of the blind and dumb demoniac is an act of exorcism (ἐκβάλλει τὰ δαιμόνια – Matt 12:24), and Jesus' reply does not question this presumption (εἰ ἐγὼ . . . ἐκβάλλω τὰ δαιμόνια – 12:27, 28). The disputable issue is by whose help he performs exorcisms. Jesus persuasively demonstrates that the Beelzebul accusation does not make sense (Matt 12:25–27). Rather, he exorcises by the Spirit of God, and this is taken as a proof that the Kingdom of God has arrived.

Matthew's formulation of Jesus' answer deserves further consideration. Whereas Luke speaks about the finger of God (ἐν δακτύλῳ θεοῦ), the Matthean Jesus exorcises by the Spirit of God (ἐν πνεύματι θεοῦ). The latter is a rare expression, found in none of the Gospels except in the Gospel of Matthew. Apart from Matt 12:28, it occurs also in the baptismal scene described in Matt 3:16, followed by an account of the divine voice which acknowledges Jesus' divine sonship in a clear allusion to Ps 2:7.[118] The royal framework is reinforced through the reference to the πνεῦμα τοῦ θεοῦ, which in one of the most frequently quoted messianic texts in early Judaism, Isa 11:1–9, represents the first quality of the future deliverer, mentioned right after the description of his Davidic origin.

The reference to the Spirit of God in Matt 12:28 thus reveals that the accusation that Jesus exorcises demons with the help of Beelzebul represents for Matthew a denial of his messiahship.[119] The protasis of the conditional clause with which Jesus replies to his accusers (εἰ δὲ ἐν πνεύματι θεοῦ ἐγὼ ἐκβάλλω τὰ δαιμόνια) implies that the claim which has been denied is in fact that Jesus exorcises demons by the Spirit of God, and that this represents an

---

[117]Charlesworth, "Solomon and Jesus," 125–151.

[118]Cf. Juel, *Messianic Exegesis,* 79–80.

[119]D. Trunk perceptively notes that "die Heilungstaten Jesu . . . wurden von dem pharisäischen Gegnern gerade gegen die Messianität Jesu angespielt. Der Streit um die Interpretation der Exorzismen gewinnt so eine paradigmatische Bedeutung für den Streit um den Messias Israels, den 'Sohn Davids'" (*Der Messianische Heiler,* 92).

activity which he performs in his capacity as the Davidic Messiah.[120] Matthew's editorial reshaping of the introductory episode into an act of healing devoid of exorcistic elements shows the way he wanted his readers to understand it – as a messianic healing. Only in this way does the Pharisaic reaction to the question of the crowd in Matt 12:23 make sense.[121]

Whether these features of the text echo the actual dispute of the Matthean community with Pharisaic Judaism and eventually some Christian circles, who claimed that Jesus is only the Son of David after the order of Solomon, but not the Davidic Messiah, cannot be established with any certainty. The assertion that Matthew takes over from Q that "something greater than Solomon is here" (καὶ ἰδοὺ πλεῖον Σολομῶνος ὧδε – Matt 12:42), followed by a passage about

---

[120]Duling ("The Therapeutic Son of David," 402) suggests that the question of the crowd leads to a view "that Jesus as therapeutic Son of David can also exorcize by the Spirit of God." The reference to the Spirit of God, however, is not an addition to Matthew's portrayal of the Son of David, but its crucial element which gives it its messianic flavor. The baptismal scene presented in Matt 3:13–17 and the fulfillment quotation that precedes the Beelzebul controversy (Matt 12:17–21) indicate that Jesus' receipt of the Spirit is understood by Matthew as the messianic anointing. It should be noted, however, that the logic of Matthew's argument in vv. 27–28 is rather obscure. F. W. Beare, for example, claims that these verses are "wholly lacking in logic" (*The Gospel according to Matthew. A Commentary* [Oxford: Basil Blackwell, 1981], 278–279). For a good overview of various interpretative attempts see Davies and Allison, *Matthew*, vol. 2, 339–341. Jesus' question in v. 27 (καὶ εἰ ἐγὼ ἐν Βεελζεβοὺλ ἐκβάλλω τὰ δαιμόνια, οἱ υἱοὶ ὑμῶν ἐν τίνι ἐκβάλλουσιν) suggests that two similar activities must have similar causes. Thus, if the Pharisees believe that their "sons" exorcise demons with God's help, they must grant the same source to Jesus. V. 28 takes this conclusion as a premise of the next step in the argument. The assumption that Jesus exorcises demons by the Spirit of God leads to the conclusion that this indicates the presence of the kingdom of God. The status and significance of the exorcisms of the members or sympathizers of the Pharisaic sect, however, remain unclear. It would appear that they too should prove the presence of the kingdom. Matthew, however, seems to draw a tacit distinction between the two. Only Jesus is explicitly said to be the bearer of the Spirit of God, which for Matthew represents a unique and incontestable messianic quality.

[121]Fisher calls the accusation of the Pharisees "foolishness" because the Aramaic magical texts demonstrate that "it is always by using the power of the good gods or the power of the magician that evil demons are overcome" ("Can This Be the Son of David?" 91). However, this illogical accusation makes sense in the Matthean framework, because it is functionally transformed into a denial of Jesus' possession of the Spirit of God. Jesus' emphatic conclusion in Matt 12:31–32 that every sin and blasphemy will be forgiven to humans except the blasphemy against the Spirit (ἡ δὲ τοῦ πνεύματος βλασφημία) only confirms this reconstruction. In Mark 3:30, a similar saying is supplemented by an explanation because of its loose tie to the Beelzebul controversy: "because they said, he has an unclean spirit" (ὅτι ἔλεγον, πνεῦμα ἀκάθαρτον ἔχει). In Matthew 12, however, such an accusation has not been made. Rather, Jesus' opponents deny that he has the Spirit of God. In Luke 12:10, the logion about blasphemy against the Holy Spirit is completely detached from the Beelzebul controversy.

the return of the unclean spirit,[122] might strengthen the plausibility of this historical reconstruction.[123] In such a context, Matthew's "Son of David" Christology could have functioned, as Duling suggests, as "a way of neutralizing any popular Solomon-as-exorcist tradition, if Matthew knew about it."[124]

3.5 The Eschatological Prophet

3.5.1 Introduction

Another solution to the question of why Matthew linked Jesus' messianic identity to his healing miracles would be to claim that Matthew either failed to distinguish or intentionally combined the functions of the Son of David and the expected eschatological prophet. According to Deut 18:15, 18 and 34:10–12, the expected "prophet like Moses" was to be a teacher certified by miracles.[125] It is conceivable that Matthew combined these two originally distinct eschatological figures. Even though this hypothesis has not attracted any significant scholarly attention in the studies which deal with the title "Son of David," the Mosaic typology is a well-known and widely accepted notion in the Matthean studies in general.[126]

The difficulty that this proposal immediately encounters is that we hardly have any direct reference to this figure in the pre-Christian literature,[127] which raises the question whether this was a viable focus of Jewish expectations at

---

[122]Taken in isolation or in a different context (cf. Luke 11:29–36), this phrase does not necessarily imply Solomon's exorcistic ability, but can be taken as a mere reference to his wisdom.

[123]Duling's suggestion that Matt 12:42 might imply that "the healing Son of David supersedes the exorcistic Son of David" ("Solomon, Exorcism, and the Son of David," 251) is certainly correct, but requires further clarification in regard to the conceptual framework of the formulation "the healing Son of David." The intelligibility of the latter is provided by the messianic framework which Matthew creates.

[124]Duling, "The Therapeutic Son of David," 409.

[125]Cf. D. L. Tiede, *The Charismatic Figure as Miracle Worker*, SBLDS 1 (Missoula, Mont.: Scholars Press, 1972), 102–113, who points out that Deut 34:10–12 shows that "although the Deuteronomist refuses to let miraculous performances to be the sole criterion for authenticating a prophet like Moses (cf. Deut 13:1–5, 18:9–22), it is clear that the signs and wonders are essential for authenticating the special presence of God with the prophet like Moses."

[126]Cf. D. C. Allison, *The New Moses: A Matthean Typology* (Minneapolis: Fortress Press, 1993).

[127]J. J. Collins calls him "a shadowy figure" (*The Scepter and the Star*, 116). For a detailed investigation of the expectation of the prophet like Moses, see H. M. Teeple, *The Mosaic Eschatological Prophet*, SBLMS 10 (Philadelphia: Society of Biblical Literature, 1957).

all.[128] The exception is the Samaritan Taheb, but besides the Samaritan Pentateuch we have no other Samaritan sources that antedate the 2nd century C.E. which could testify to this tradition.[129]

Two relatively recent contributions demonstrate the ongoing scholarly dissension in regard to the significance of this figure in first-century Palestine. Thus Richard A. Horsley contends that the absence of the prophet like Moses in the rabbinic literature indicates that this kind of expectation was something marginal,[130] whereas David M. Frankfurter claims that "there is considerable evidence that a popular folklore of the Mosaic prophet and his signs played a large part in Palestinian Jewish belief."[131] A short review of the available evidence is therefore in order. My interest at this point is the expectation of the prophet like Moses, and not of another prophetic figure called Elijah that has its scriptural basis in Mal 3:1 (which refers to the messenger who will prepare the way before the Lord) and Mal 4:5 (which speaks about the prophet Elijah who will appear before the great and terrible day of the Lord).[132]

3.5.2 The Eschatological Prophet in Jewish Literature

The scriptural basis of the expectation of the prophet like Moses can be found in Deut 18:15 (נביא מקרבך מאחיך כמני יקים לך יהוה אלהיך אליו תשמעון; προφήτην ἐκ τῶν ἀδελφῶν σου ὡς ἐμὲ ἀναστήσει σοι κύριος ὁ θεός σου αὐτοῦ ἀκούσεσθε [LXX]) and Deut 18:18 (נביא אקים להם מקרב אחיהם כמוך ונתתי דברי בפיו ודבר אליהם את כל־אשר אצונו; προφήτην ἀναστήσω αὐτοῖς ἐκ τῶν ἀδελφῶν αὐτῶν ὥσπερ σὲ καὶ δώσω τὸ ῥῆμά μου ἐν τῷ στόματι αὐτοῦ καὶ λαλήσει αὐτοῖς καθότι ἂν ἐντείλωμαι αὐτῷ [LXX]). However, nowhere else in Israel's Scripture can we find a definite evidence of this hope. According to 1 Macc 4:46, there was an expectation of a "prophet" (προφήτης). He is called a "trustworthy prophet" (προφήτης πιστός) in 1 Macc 14:41,[133] but neither

---

[128]For a review of the debate concerning the extension of the expectations of the prophet like Moses in Judaism, see J. Jeremias, "Μωυσῆς," in *TDNT* 4 (1967), 858 n.125.

[129]Cf. F. Dexinger, "Reflections on the Relationship between Qumran and Samaritan Messianology," in *Qumran-Messianism: Studies on the Messianic Expectations in the Dead Sea Scrolls*, ed. J. H. Charlesworth, H. Lichtenberger, and G. S. Oegema (Tübingen: Mohr Siebeck, 1998), 83–99.

[130]R. A. Horsley, "'Like One of the Prophets of Old': Two Types of Popular Prophets at the Time of Jesus," *CBQ* 47 (1985): 441–443.

[131]D. M. Frankfurter, "The Origin of the Miracle-List Tradition and Its Medium of Circulation," in *SBL 1990 Seminar Papers,* ed. D. J. Lull, SBL Seminar Papers Series 29 (Atlanta: Scholars Press, 1990), 349.

[132]It is quite apparent that Matthew's Gospel presupposes such a belief. Thus Matt 17:13 ("Then the disciples understood that he was speaking to them of John the Baptist") is Matthew's addition to Mark's account of the dialogue between Jesus and his disciples about the coming of Elijah that should precede the appearance of the Messiah (Mark 9:9–13), which clearly demonstrates that for Matthew, John the Baptist is the expected prophet Elijah.

[133]Cf. Ps. 74:9, which contains a lament that there is no longer any prophet.

reference makes a connection between this figure and Moses or identifies him as the Messiah.

The evidence from the Dead Sea Scrolls is equally sparse. 1QS 9.11 contains the phrase "until the coming of the prophet and the Messiahs of Aaron and Israel" (עד בוא נביא ומשיחי אהרון וישראל). This clause, however, not only distinguishes the expected prophet from the priestly and royal Messiahs, but it also fails to ascribe him any messianic quality.[134] CD MS A 6.7 identifies מחוקק, which can mean either "ruler," "rod," or "lawgiver," with the interpreter of the Law (דורש התורה), who is then in CD MS A 7.18 identified as the "star" prophesied in Numbers 24:17. On the basis of these two references from the *Damascus Document*, and the fact that 4Q175 (4QTest) lines 5–8 contain the citation of Deut 18:18–19 followed by the quotation of Num 24:15–17, Naftali Wieder argued that the Interpreter of the Law is the "prophet like Moses."[135] This conclusion, however, fails to convince, because it rests on a dubious methodology of harmonizing divergent Qumran texts. Also, despite the fact that the *Testimonia* show that Deut 18:18 was understood as an eschatological prophecy,[136] this document is only a collection of proof-texts, which do not link Deut 18:18–19 to any known Qumran figure.[137] Finally, דורש התורה in 4Q174 frgs. 1–2 and 21 line 11 is clearly distinguished from the messianic figure called the "Branch of David" (דויד צמח).

On the other hand, despite the fact that we do not have a strong evidence for the expectation of the eschatological prophet like Moses in early Jewish writings, there are indications that the prophetic and royal figures did sometimes become fused in early Judaism. Wayne A. Meeks has collected extensive evidence for a royal Mosaic prophet figure as a background of the

---

[134]It is certainly true that "these figures . . . are closely related to one another as far as their eschatological function is concerned," (Dexinger, "Reflections on the Relationship between Qumran and Samaritan Messianology," 90), but it should not be forgotten that the term "Messiah" is reserved merely for the priestly and royal figures. Only to the extent that the prophet accompanies the priestly and royal Messiahs we can speak about his "messianic" function. For a defense of the latter see F. García Martínez and J. T. Barrera, *The People of the Dead Sea Scrolls: Their Writings, Beliefs and Practices* (Leiden: Brill, 1995), 186.

[135]N. Wieder, "The 'Law-Interpreter' of the Sect of the Dead Sea Scrolls: The Second Moses," *JJS* 4 (1953): 158–175.

[136]For the study of the relationship between 1QS 9.11 and 4Q175 lines 5–8 see A. S. van der Woude, *Die messianische Vorstellungen der Gemeinde von Qumrân*, SSN 3 (Assen: Van Gorcum, 1957), 83, 186.

[137]Cf. Tiede, *The Charismatic Figure as Miracle Worker*, 192.

apparent fusion of the two in John 6:14–15,[138] even though he did not see this royal figure as a Davidic Messiah.[139]

3.5.3 The Eschatological Prophet and the Gospel of Matthew

Dale C. Allison has shown that Matthew extensively used the Moses typology alongside the royal Davidic motifs and argued for the presence of this typology throughout Matthew's narrative.[140] Furthermore, Matthew's characters on several occasions identify Jesus as a prophetic figure. Thus it cannot be denied that οἱ ὄχλοι, whenever they express any definite opinion about the question of who Jesus is,[141] always identify him as a prophet. In Matt 16:13–14, this has been presented as part of the report of the disciples, while in Matt 21:9–11, this prophetic expectation is directly linked to the concept of the Son of David. The crowd who has just hailed Jesus as the Son of David at his entry into Jerusalem introduces him in verse 11 as the prophet (ὁ προφήτης) to the citizens of Jerusalem, thus identifying the two. It seems that for the mob the two titles are viewed as synonymous.

Taken by itself, this evidence strongly supports the idea that Matthew has fused the functions of the Davidic Messiah and the eschatological prophet. The difficulty, however, comes from the fact that the opinions of certain characters in the narrative do not have to represent the opinion of the author. Caution is needed especially in the case of the crowd, because even though Matthew does not deny that they are interested in Jesus, he gives certain hints to the reader which show that they in fact never come to the correct understanding of Jesus' true identity. Thus in Matt 13:11 Jesus sharply differentiates the disciples who understand the mysteries of heaven from the crowd who does not. The latter are those who seeing do not see and hearing do not hear nor comprehend (βλέποντες οὐ βλέπουσιν καὶ ἀκούοντες οὐκ ἀκούουσιν οὐδὲ συνίουσιν – Matt 13:13). In Matt 16:13–20, Matthew sharply distinguishes Peter's confession of Jesus' messiahship from the opinion of the people. Only the latter receives the confirmation of Jesus, not the former. In light of this observation, it is quite significant that due to Matthew's redaction in 21:8–9, the ambiguity of Mark 11:8–9 has been clarified and the disciples clearly excluded from the shouting crowd who acclaims Jesus as the Son of David at his entry into Jerusalem and later identify him as the prophet.[142] It is therefore

---

[138]W. A. Meeks, *The Prophet-King: Moses Traditions and the Johannine Christology*, NovTSup 14 (Leiden: E. J. Brill, 1967), 100–285.

[139]Meeks' claim is that John 7:40 implies that John distinguishes the figures of the Prophet and the Messiah (*The Prophet-King*, 25–26).

[140]Allison, *The New Moses: A Matthean Typology*.

[141]Matt 12:23, being a question, does not belong to this category.

[142]Cf. Suhl, "Der Davidssohn im Matthäus-Evangelium," 70 and Kingsbury, "The title 'Son of David'," 592. The redaction of Luke, in contrast to Matthew, limits the rejoicing group only to the circle of disciples (Luke 19:37).

fair to say that even though Matthew presents the attitude of the crowd up to Jesus' entry into Jerusalem as generally positive, he offers enough evidence for the suspicion that their understanding of Jesus, although not completely false, is still a misunderstanding of his messianic role.

Another, even more significant objection against the assumption that Matthew has fused the functions of the eschatological prophet and the royal Davidic Messiah comes from the fact that Jesus' miracles in Matthew, as elsewhere in the Synoptics, are never called "signs." In this tradition, the word σημεῖον is never applied to Jesus' miraculous deeds. The reason for this "taboo"[143] is probably to be found in the understanding of the word σημεῖον in the sense of a legitimating sign. Jesus is thus consistently presented as refusing to authenticate himself by any sign.[144] The exact nature of this refusal, however, requires a more precise definition of the role of signs in the prophetic tradition.

3.5.4 Sign as a validation of a prophetic claim

In his investigation of Jesus' miracles as the messianic signs in the Gospel of John, Wolfgang J. Bittner offered a detailed and compelling analysis of the role of a sign in the process of getting knowledge.[145] He has demonstrated that in the Old Testament, אות regularly denotes a subject matter of sensual, visual perception. Its role is to provide knowledge for the purpose of gaining assurance about certain events, persons, or processes. In general, signs can serve various purposes, such as providing proof or confirming a certain claim, certifying protection, provoking faith, or eliciting remembrance.[146] In all these cases, the LXX consistently translates אות with σημεῖον.

In the prophetic tradition, a sign has a special role of validating the prophetic claim. The true prophet is recognized by his ability to announce the occurrence of a certain event, which then really takes place.[147] The act of announcement is a context-creating activity in which a certain event is assigned an unequivocal role that transforms it into a sign.[148] The "sign" which authenticates the prophetic claim can but does not have to be a miracle. For a person who knows the context, the sign is an incontestable confirmation of the claim that has been made. In other words, what matters is that it is predicted in advance and then followed by the actual occurrence of the event. The miraculous element consists not in the miraculous nature of a sign, but in the

---

[143]Gerhardsson, *The Mighty Acts of Jesus*, 13.

[144]Ibid., 14.

[145]Bittner, *Jesu Zeichen*, 17–87.

[146]Ibid., 22–24; cf. also H. Gunkel, *Genesis*, 8th ed. (Göttingen: Vandenhoeck & Ruprecht, 1969), 150.

[147]Cf. 1 Samuel 10.

[148]In Bittner's words, "Die Eindeutigkeit liegt an seinem 'Kontext,' in den es durch die vorangehende Vereinbarung gestellt ist" (*Jesu Zeichen*, 76).

miraculous nature of the knowledge of its materialization.[149] The law about false prophets in Deut 13:1–2 expressly confirms that the sequence – the announcement followed by the advent of that which has been foretold – inherently belongs to the nature of a sign: "If a prophet or a dreamer appears among you and promises you a sign or a wonder (אוֹת אוֹ מוֹפֵת; σημεῖον ἢ τέρας [LXX]), and the sign or the wonder declared by him takes place (וּבָא הָאוֹת וְהַמּוֹפֵת אֲשֶׁר־דִּבֶּר; καὶ ἔλθῃ τὸ σημεῖον ἢ τὸ τέρας ὃ ἐλάλησεν [LXX]) . . ." The possibility that such a person might lead people astray is taken as a real danger exactly because the announcement of a sign followed by its appearance will be understood by the audience as the authentication of the prophetic claim.

This basic structure can be found in various Old Testament passages, such as Isa 7:10–16 or Exod 10:1–2. The latter explicitly calls the plagues that were announced to Pharaoh by Moses and Aaron אוֹתֹת (τὰ σημεῖα [LXX]). Similarly, Deut 34:10–11 declares that Moses was the prophet in Israel whom nobody ever surpassed "for all the signs and wonders (לְכָל־הָאֹתֹת וְהַמּוֹפְתִים; ἐν πᾶσι τοῖς σημείοις καὶ τέρασιν [LXX]) that the Lord sent him to perform in the land of Egypt."

An association of Moses and the signs that he performed can be also found in apocryphal and pseudepigraphical literature. Thus according to Sir 45:3, "by his [Moses'] words he brought signs (σημεῖα) swiftly to pass and He glorified him in the presence of the king." Psuedo-Philo's *Liber Antiquitatum Biblicarum* contains several passages which refer either to Moses' signs and wonders (*signa et prodigia* – L.A.B. 9.7) or simply signs (*L.A.B.* 9.10).

Josephus has a similar understanding of the role of a sign (σημεῖον), which can but does not have to be a wonder/miracle (τέρας).[150] When referring to Moses, Josephus speaks only about σημεῖα, and not τέρατα, presumably in an attempt to dissociate him from any magic and sorcery. The signs that Moses performs confirm his sending as a divine sending.[151]

Josephus' writings also contain several accounts about the first-century pseudo-prophets, which additionally confirm the nature of sign discussed

---

[149]Ibid., 25.

[150]Cf. Josephus, *Ant.* 1.20.2. Jacob should deem his victory over an angel of God a sign (σημεῖον) of great blessings to come.

[151]During the burning bush encounter, God encourages Moses to use signs to convince all the people (καὶ σημείοις πρὸς τὸ πιστεύεσθαι παρὰ πᾶσι χρῆσθαι) that he is sent by God (*Ant.* 2.12.3). In the next paragraph, Josephus adds that Moses found these signs at his service not on that occasion only but always when he needed them (Μωυσεῖ μέντοι τὰ σημεῖα ταῦτα οὐ τότε μόνον, διὰ παντὸς δε ὁπότε δεηθείη συνετύγχανεν) (*Ant.* 2.12.4); cf. also *Ant.* 2.13.2–3. For a comparison between the miracles in Josephus, rabbinic writings, and the Gospel of John see O. Betz, "Das Problem des Wunders bei Flavius Josephus im Vergleich zum Wunderproblem bei den Rabbinen und im Johannesevangelium," in *Josephus-Studien: Untersuchungen zu Josephus, dem antiken Judentum und dem Neuen Testament,* ed. O. Betz, K. Haacker, and M. Hengel (Göttingen: Vandenhoeck & Ruprecht, 1974), 23–44.

above. *Ant.* 18.4.1 offers a report about the Samaritan who led an armed band toward Mount Gerizim during Pilate's procuratorship. According to Josephus, he promised his followers that he would show them the sacred vessels buried there. The whole undertaking was, however, interrupted by Pilate who either killed the participants, or took them as prisoners.[152]

Josephus' account about Theudas (*Ant.* 20.5.1) is similar. He claimed to be a prophet (προφήτης) and that at his command the river would divide and provide an easy passage for his followers. Josephus' comment is that he deceived (ἠπάτησεν) many with these promises.[153]

According to *Ant.* 20.8.6, a certain Egyptian also claimed to be a prophet (προφήτης), and convinced the people to follow him to the Mount of Olives by promising them that he would show them there that the walls of Jerusalem would fall at his command. In the same passage Josephus also mentions "impostors and deceivers" (οἱ δὲ γόητες καὶ ἀπατεῶντες ἄνθρωποι) who persuaded the crowd to follow them by promising them clear "marvels and signs" (τέρατα καὶ σημεῖα).[154] Also, *J.W.* 6.5.2 contains a report about a

---

[152]"The Samaritan nation too was not exempt from disturbance. For a man who made light of mendacity and in all his designs catered to the mob, rallied them, bidding them go in a body with him to Mount Gerizim, which in their belief is the most sacred of mountains. He assured them that on their arrival he would show them the sacred vessels which were buried there, where Moses had deposited them. His hearers, viewing this tale as plausible, appeared in arms. They posted themselves in a certain village named Tirathana, and, as they planned to climb the mountain in a great multitude, they welcomed to their ranks the new arrivals who kept coming. But before they could ascend, Pilate blocked their projected route up the mountain with a detachment of cavalry and heavy-armed infantry, who in an encounter with the firstcomers in the village slew some in a pitched battle and put the others to flight. Many prisoners were taken, of whom Pilate put to death the principal leaders and those who were most influential among the fugitives." (*Ant.* 18.4.1; trans. L. H. Feldmann, *Josephus in Nine Volumes*, vol. 9: *Jewish Antiquities, Books XVIII–XX*, LCL, 61–63)

[153]"During the period when Fadus was procurator of Judaea, a certain impostor named Theudas persuaded the majority of the masses to take up their possessions and to follow him to the Jordan River. He stated that he was a prophet and that at his command the river would be parted and would provide them an easy passage. With this talk he deceived many. Fadus, however, did not permit them to reap the fruit of their folly, but sent against them a squadron of cavalry. These fell upon them unexpectedly, slew many of them and took many prisoners. Theudas himself was captured, whereupon they cut off his head and brought it to Jererusalem. These, then, are the events that befell the Jews during the time that Cuspius Fadus was procurator." (*Ant.* 20.5.1; ibid., 441–443)

[154]"Moreover, impostors and deceivers called upon the mob to follow them into the desert. For they said that they would show them unmistakable marvels and signs that would be wrought in harmony with God's design. Many were, in fact, persuaded and paid the penalty of their folly; for they were brought before Felix and he punished them. At this time there came to Jerusalem from Egypt a man who declared that he was a prophet and advised the masses of the common people to go out with him to the mountain called the Mount of Olives, which lies opposite the city at a distance of five furlongs. For he asserted that he wished to demonstrate from there that at his command Jerusalem's walls would fall down, through which he promised

certain "false prophet" (ψευδοπροφήτης) who promised "the signs of deliverance" (τὰ σημεῖα τῆς σωτηρίας) to the people. Josephus adds that he was one of many prophets who deceived the people who were in despair and thus susceptible to quick persuasions.[155]

The reliability of these reports has often been questioned. However, even though they are not unbiased accounts, they demonstrate a persistent structure that can be found whenever a prophetic claim is made. A certain event is promised to happen, and only its actual occurrence can confirm the trustworthiness of a prophet. The fact that these announcements have not been followed by their realization demonstrates that the claimants were false prophets.[156]

A differentiation between sign and miracle is also found in the rabbinic literature. There are accounts about wonders performed by certain rabbis or charismatic figures, but they are almost never called "signs."[157] The latter appears only in the situation when someone claims to speak prophetically. Thus *b. Sanh.* 98a contains a dialogue between Rabbi Yose ben Kisma and his disciples, in which they ask him, "When will the son of David come?" His answer is, "I am afraid that you will ask me for a sign [as proof of what I say]." His disciples first assure him that they will not demand a sign from him, but change their mind after he gives his answer. After the demand for a sign is repeated, Rabbi Yose ben Kisma replies, "'If so, the water in the Banyas cave will turn to blood.' And it turned to blood."[158] The reason that the sign was

---

to provide them an entrance into the city. When Felix heard of this he ordered his soldiers to take up their arms. Setting out from Jerusalem with a large force of cavalry and infantry, he fell upon the Egyptian and his followers, slaying four hundred of them and taking two hundred prisoners. The Egyptian himself escaped from the battle and disappeared." (*Ant.* 20.8.6; ibid., 479–481)

[155]"They owed their destruction to a false prophet, who had on that day proclaimed to the people in the city that God commanded them to go up to the temple court, to receive there the tokens [signs] of their deliverance. Numerous prophets, indeed, were at this period suborned by the tyrants to delude the people, by bidding them await help from God, in order that desertions might be checked and that those who were above fear and precaution might be encouraged by hope. In adversity man is quickly persuaded; but when the deceiver actually pictures release from prevailing horrors, then the sufferer wholly abandons himself to expectations." (*J.W.* 6.5.2; trans. H. S. J. Thackeray, *Josephus in Nine Volumes*, vol. 3: *The Jewish War, Book IV–VII*, LCL, 459)

[156]Cf. Bittner, *Jesu Zeichen*, 35.

[157]Cf. M. Becker, *Wunder und Wundertäter im frührabbinischen Judentum: Studien zum Phänomen und seiner Überlieferung im Horizont von Magie und Dämonismus*, WUNT II/144 (Tübingen: Mohr Siebeck, 2002), 200-201. Becker explains this phenomenon by pointing out that "gerade das Hohenpriestertum und die Tora bzw. die göttliche Vorsehung [werden] den häufig zweifelhaften 'Wunderzeichen' und Prophetien vorgeordnet" (ibid., 201).

[158]For the Hebrew text, English translation, and the commentary by Rabbi Adin Steinsaltz see *The Talmud: The Steinsaltz Edition*, vol 21: *Tractate Sanhedrin*, part 7 (New York: Random House, 1999), 20.

eventually demanded is that it was needed to confirm the trustworthiness of the prophecy about the time of the appearance of the Messiah.

We can now return to Matthew's Gospel and Jesus' refusal to produce a sign. This tradition is preserved in Matt 12:38–39 and 16:1–4. In the former, in contrast to Mark who reports that Jesus was asked to produce a sign from heaven (σημεῖον ἀπὸ τοῦ οὐρανοῦ – Mark 8:11), Matthew speaks only about a sign (σημεῖον). This alteration indicates that in this case the demand was not to produce a miraculous sign, but a sign which is announced in advance and then followed by its materialization – a legitimating sign by which a prophet demonstrates his call.[159] Matt 16:1–4, on the other hand, preserves the Markan "sign from heaven," which is demanded, similar to Mark, right after the feeding of four thousand. In this case, the allusion to the prophet like Moses seems to be reinforced by a request for the miraculous sign. Nevertheless, the reference to τὸ σημεῖον Ἰωνᾶ τοῦ προφήτου as the only sign that will be given suggests that in each case a prophetic sign is meant. It has the same structure: an announcement that must be followed by the actual occurrence of the event, which in this case is Jesus' resurrection. A demand for a sign thus clearly demonstrates that Jesus' miracles were perceived as prophetic signs neither by him nor by his audience. He is not asked to do more miracles, but to effectuate an act of a different kind, which will have the character of a sign.[160]

One reason for this strong denial of the sign character of Jesus' miracles might be found in Deut 13:1–5 and 18:9–14, which present a counter-type of a prophet like Moses who also performs "signs and wonders" but leads people astray. Josephus' reports about the first-century pseudo-prophets confirm the thesis of David L. Tiede that "any figure who was presented or proclaimed himself as the 'prophet like Moses' on the basis of the performance of miracles would have been immediately open to the criticism of his opponents that he was 'leading people astray'."[161] A very similar understanding can be found in Jesus' eschatological speech, which warns the disciples that false messiahs and false prophets will appear whose main activity will be to show great signs and wonders (σημεῖα μεγάλα καὶ τέρατα) in order to lead the elect astray (Matt 24:24).

On the other hand, despite the potential danger inherent in the claim that the miracles are prophetic signs, Tiede is certainly right that "it appears that it would have been almost impossible for a Jew of the Hellenistic period to conceive an image of Moses which did not include the aspect of miracle

---

[159]Cf. O. Linton, "The Demand for a Sign from Heaven (Mark 8,11–12 and Parallels)," *ST* 19 (1965): 112–129; Gerhardsson, *The Mighty Acts of Jesus*, 13–14.

[160]Allison (*The New Moses: A Matthean Typology*, 235) is therefore inaccurate when he says that "Jesus has, on previous occasions, preformed stupendous signs and wonders, and he will do so again. But all his marvelous works have availed and will avail not, for the unbelief of his opponents cannot be undone."

[161]Tiede, *The Charismatic Figure as Miracle Worker*, 180.

working."[162] Matthew's unwillingness to present Jesus' miracles as the prophetic signs thus appears as a strong evidence against the supposition that he has fused the functions of the royal Messiah and the prophet like Moses in the passages which link Jesus' healing miracles to his messianic identity.[163]

3.6 Jesus' Healings in Light of the Summaries of His Public Activity

3.6.1 Introduction

If the traditions about Solomon as exorcist and the prophet like Moses do not create the background of Matthew's portrayal of Jesus as the Son of David who acts as a healer of the sick, we are still faced with the problem of the intelligibility of this unusual connection. Why should Matthew's Jewish Christian readers understand Jesus' healing miracles as the acts which confirm that he is the Davidic Messiah? I propose to start with Matthew's own narrative strategies that create the context in which the individual episodes where Jesus is addressed as the Son of David are recounted. It can be noticed that at various points in the narrative, the narrator interrupts the narration and makes several interpretative comments that should help the reader, not the characters in the plotted story, understand the events that are narrated.[164] They generally have the form of summaries of Jesus' public activity.

3.6.2 Summarizing Accounts of Jesus' Ministry

According to two almost identical summaries in Matt 4:23 and 9:35, Jesus' ministry in Israel consisted of teaching, preaching the kingdom, and healing every disease and infirmity among the people. Their structural importance is that they bracket the material in chapters 5–9 and function as an *inclusio* of this segment of Matthew's narrative. In contrast to Mark,[165] Matthew does not report any miracle before his first summary in 4:23. He also adds verse 24, in which he describes Jesus' fame as being spread throughout the whole of Syria, so that all those who were sick came to him to be healed. Matthew lists various diseases and specifies among them particularly demoniacs, epileptics,

---

[162]Ibid.

[163]This conclusion is not a denial of a Moses typology in Matthew's narrative, but only a denial of this particular function of Jesus' miracles. This conclusion is supported by the research of D. C. Allison, who otherwise strongly argues for the Moses typology in Matthew's Gospel, but has to admit, after examining the miracle collection in chapters 8–9, "I here doubt the presence of a Moses typology" (*The New Moses: A Matthean Typology*, 213).

[164]Cf. the explicit appeal to the reader in Matt 24:15//Mark 13:14, "let the reader understand" (ὁ ἀναγινώσκων νοείτω).

[165]The healing of the man with an unclean spirit (Mark 1:21–28) is reported before the first summary in Mark 1:32–34.

and paralytics. By carefully redacting the Markan *Vorlage* (Mark 1:39), Matthew completely omits any mention of Jesus' exorcistic activity and speaks instead about his healings in a more general sense. He also expands the concluding summary in 9:35 by adding verse 36 in which he informs the audience that Jesus had compassion towards the harassed and helpless crowd.

The summary in Matt 8:16–17 follows the first three healing miracles narrated in chapter 8. The summary proper appears in verse 16, which relates that many (πολλούς) possessed with demons were brought to Jesus, and that he healed all (πάντας) who were sick. This is followed by the comment in verse 17 that "this was to fulfill what was spoken by the prophet Isaiah" and a quotation of Isa 53:4a.

The summary in Matt 11:2–6 differs from other summaries because it is not the narrator but Jesus himself who makes it.[166] John the Baptist, who is in prison, sends his disciples to inquire of Jesus whether or not he is "the coming One" (ὁ ἐρχόμενος). Jesus answers by enumerating various groups of sick and unfortunate who have been recovered from their afflictions: the blind receive their sight, the lame walk, lepers are cleansed, the deaf hear, the dead are raised up, and the poor have good news preached to them. Even though these clauses are not direct scriptural quotations, they echo various texts from the Book of Isaiah, such as Isa 26:19, 29:18, 35:5–6, and 61:1.

The summary itself in Matt 12:15–21 is quite short. Matthew reports that after Jesus withdrew from the Pharisaic hostility, many (πολλοί) followed him, and he healed them all (πάντας).[167] Jesus' request for secrecy follows, accompanied by the narrator's comment that "this was to fulfill what was spoken by the prophet Isaiah" and the lengthy citation of Isa 42:1–4.

The summary in Matt 14:13–14 also appears within the report of Jesus' withdrawal. The crowd follows him, which elicits Jesus' compassion so that he heals their sick. The significance of the latter becomes especially apparent when viewed in light of Matthew's redaction. By replacing the Markan clause καὶ ἤρξατο διδάσκειν αὐτοὺς πολλά (Mark 6:34c) with καὶ ἐθεράπευσεν τοὺς ἀρρώστους αὐτῶν (Matt 14:14c), Matthew connects Jesus' compassion not with his teaching, but with his healing.

The summary in Matt 15:29–31 is preceded by the story of the healing of the Canaanite woman's daughter. Matthew reports that after Jesus went up on the mountain, a great crowd came to him, bringing the lame, the maimed, the blind, the dumb, and many others, and he healed them. Similar to Matt 11:5, this text emphasizes the regained health of these groups: the dumb speak, the

---

[166]B. Gerhardsson (*The Mighty Acts of Jesus,* 30) proposes the term "quasi-summary" for this passage, "quasi" because it is a saying of Jesus from the form-critical point of view, and "summary" because it contains a summarizing statement concerning Jesus' ministry as a whole.

[167]Cf. Matt 8:16.

maimed are made whole, the lame walk, and the blind see. The references to the lame, the maimed, the blind, and the dumb echo Isa 35:5–6, which describes the recovered constitution of precisely these four groups of the afflicted.[168]

The last summary of this kind can be found in Matt 19:1–2. Matthew reports that after Jesus left Galilee and entered Judea, the large crowd followed him and he healed them there.

Even such a brief survey allows several important conclusions. Despite the fact that according to Matt 4:23 and 9:35, healing every disease and infirmity among the people appears alongside teaching and preaching, the remaining summaries refer only to Jesus' therapeutic activity. In many of them Matthew stresses a broader and more general scope of Jesus' healings. Instead of Mark's "many," the Matthean Jesus regularly heals "all" the sick. Moreover, he heals all kinds of sicknesses. Jesus looks like an extraordinary physician who is able to cure every kind of infirmity. Moreover, he is compassionate toward the crowd, especially to those who suffer. The most striking feature of these summaries, however, is that they do not merely describe what Jesus does and how he feels, but in two cases (Matt 8:16–17 and Matt 12:15–21), they contain distinct comments of the narrator which explain to the reader the necessity and meaning of Jesus' cures. In both instances, Jesus' healings are presented as a direct fulfillment of Scripture. In two other cases (Matt 11:2–6 and Matt 15:29–31), the summaries are formulated in such a way that the reader is reminded, though in an allusive way, of certain prophecies about future blessings from the Book of Isaiah.

Jesus' individual healings, including those in which he is either addressed or recognized as the Son of David, are thus wrapped in the web of Matthew's editorial comments which provide guidance for their proper understanding. This insight prompts me to propose a thesis for the rest of this study: The force of Matthew's argumentation in its role of a context-building activity, which annuls the polyvalence of Jesus' miracles, comes from its scriptural basis.

Matthew's attempt to present Jesus' life as the fulfillment of Scripture is evident throughout his Gospel but is especially reinforced through the typical introductory formula, "This was to fulfill what was spoken by the prophet." In the case of Jesus' healing miracles, however, the appeal to Scripture has an additional function, which seems to come from the nature of the messianic claim.[169] Unfortunately, apart from the New Testament writings, we do not have any other evidence from the first century about the way a messianic pretender would have warranted such a claim. There is, however, one passage in the Babylonian Talmud, which despite its later date might shed some light on this question. It is found in *b. Sanh.* 93b and has a form of a legend about

---

[168]Cf. Duling, "The Therapeutic Son of David," 402.

[169]Cf. Bittner, *Jesu Zeichen*, 37–38.

Bar Kokhba who has apparently made a claim to be the Messiah. The text is especially significant because in contrast to the Jewish texts which describe the expected messianic figure whose coming still lies in the future, *b. Sanh.* 93b deals with the problem of proving the messianic claim of an actual historical person. Since the rabbis have to prove the messianic and not the prophetic sending, they do not require Bar Kokhba to produce a sign.[170] Rather, they compare his abilities with the description of the Messiah in Isa 11:2–3. According to Rava, the meaning of the statement, "And his delight shall be in the fear of the Lord; and he shall not judge after the sight of his eyes, neither decide after the hearing of his ears," is that "the Messiah will be able to smell the parties appearing before him and judge between them," arrived at through a play of words on והריחו ("his delight" – Isa 11:3) and הריח ("smell"). Since the Messiah, according to Isa 11:3, "shall not judge after the sight of his eyes, neither decide after the hearing of his ears," he must judge through his sense of smell. The possession of the Spirit, which enables him to make the correct judgment without examining the witness but by merely smelling him/her, should authenticate his messianic claim. However, when the rabbis saw that Bar Koziba ("Son of the lie," a pejorative name given to Bar Kosiba), who claimed to be the Messiah "could not smell and judge, they killed him."[171]

This legendary story,[172] despite significantly postdating early Christian writings (not only by its literary form, but also by its content) nonetheless indicates the specific nature of the messianic claim, which can be proven only on the scriptural basis. New Testament documents unanimously confirm this conclusion. The argument for Jesus' messiahship is always a scriptural argument. Donald Juel notes that the "first believers were Jews, for whom conversation with the Sacred Scriptures was the primary mode of theological reflection."[173] To provide the scriptural argument for Jesus' messiahship,

---

[170]In the rabbinic literature, the "signs of the Messiah" (אתות המשיח) always refer to the eschatological signs which announce the nearness or the coming of the Messiah, and not to the signs which he was supposed to perform and authenticate his claim; cf. Bittner, *Jesu Zeichen*, 38 n.32, and Strack-Billerbeck, *Kommentar*, vol. 4 part 2, 977–1015.

[171]For the Hebrew text, English translation, and the commentary by Rabbi Adin Steinsaltz see *The Talmud: The Steinsaltz Edition*, vol 20: *Tractate Sanhedrin*, part 6 (New York: Random House, 1999), 126–127.

[172]P. Schäfer calls it "eine rein literarische Komposition ohne jeden historischen Wert" (*Der Bar Kokhba-Aufstand: Studien zum zweiten jüdischen Krieg gegen Rom*, TSAJ 1 [Tübingen: J. C. B. Mohr, 1981], 58). Schäfer disagrees with the common opinion that this is an early text that betrays the knowledge of the rabbis of the failure of Bar Kokhba's revolt. In his view, this passage is a 4th century composition that projects the messianic predicates articulated by Rabbi Akiba back to Simeon bar Kosiba (cf. *y. Ta'an.* 68d). Schäfer, however, overlooks the fact that both rabbinic and Christian sources offer substantial evidence that the leader of the Second Jewish Revolt was widely known as Bar Kokhba, which is a messianic title.

[173]Juel, *Messianic Exegesis*, 8.

however, required a creative use of scriptural traditions, because Jesus' career differed significantly from the descriptions found in scriptural passages that were interpreted messianically in early Jewish writings. As much as no "one expected the Messiah to suffer for sins" and "to rise from the dead,"[174] no one expected the Messiah to perform healing miracles. This difficulty, however, was not irresolvable. Like their Jewish contemporaries, early Christian exegetes, were not bound to the literary meaning of the text. Midrashic interpretation was a common practice in the ancient world. In the talmudic legend mentioned above, the rabbis made a word–play on the term that appears in Scripture and arrived at a conclusion that differs from the plain meaning of the text.

It should not be therefore surprising to see that Matthew quotes or alludes to the scriptural passages from the Book of Isaiah that do not belong to the "classic" texts which informed the messianic expectations in the first century. If my hypothesis is correct, it is to be expected to find various interpretative techniques that Matthew used to argue that Jesus' healings not merely fulfill scriptural predictions in general but represent messianic acts in particular. This is the topic of the next chapter, which will examine the nature of Matthew's scriptural argumentation and its impact on the understanding of the role of Jesus' healing miracles in the comprehension of his messianic identity.

3.6.3 Conclusions

We have seen that healing miracles in which Jesus is called the Son of David fall into roughly two categories. On the one side are stories about certain individuals who approach Jesus in their search for help by addressing him with this title. On the other side are stories in which Jesus is either recognized or acclaimed as the Son of David on the basis of the healing(s) he has just performed. In both cases, however, the connection between this title and Jesus' activity is strong but never explicated. The difficulty comes from the fact that Jesus' miracles have ambiguous nature which provoke all sorts of reactions from the characters in the plotted story. Yet, on the level of the narrative Matthew makes it sufficiently clear that only certain interpretations are correct and that others are not. For him, the messianic title "Son of David" is the most appropriate response to Jesus within the context of his therapeutic ministry.

In search for the rationale of this association between the title and the conduct of Jesus as the Messiah, I have examined two possible explanations, which find the origin of this link in a certain type of miracle-working figure in Judaism. In the first case, the solution is seen in certain traditions about Solomon, the son of David, who has the ability to exorcise demons. A closer scrutiny of the available texts has shown, however, that Matthew, even if he might have been fairly familiar with such popular expectations, takes pains not

---

[174]Ibid., 13.

to associate Jesus with but to dissociate him from these traditions. Jesus never directly confronts a demon, does not possess a secret knowledge of exorcisms, does not have a seal-ring, and is addressed as the "Son of David" in an absolute and thus titular sense. The second solution, likewise, sees the origin of Matthew's portrayal of Jesus as the Son of David in the tradition about another type of a miracle-worker – the eschatological prophet like Moses. The attractiveness of this hypothesis is obvious – in this tradition miracles prove the identity and the sending of the miracle-worker. As much as this feature can be recognized in the way Matthew narrates his story about Jesus, the miracles in his Gospel do not function as legitimating prophetic signs. They are never announced in advance and thus given the proper context of interpretation that is typical for prophetic signs. It is not surprising then to see that various characters understand them differently.

In the last section of this chapter, I have explored the only context that Matthew gives to Jesus' miracles – the narrative context that provides a literary setting that delimits their interpretation where the reader is concerned. Within this context, the most explicit feature is Matthew's attempt to provide a scriptural basis for Jesus' healings, which seems to belong to the very nature of a messianic claim. This chapter thus ends with a hypothesis that still needs to be proven through a detailed analysis of Matthew's scriptural argument for Jesus' messiahship.

Chapter 4

Scriptural Basis of Jesus' Messianic Healings

4.1 Introduction

Matthew presents two different types of scriptural argument regarding the relevance of Jesus' healings for the comprehension of his messiahship. On the one hand, he explicitly claims that Jesus' healing miracles represent the fulfillment of Scripture. In both passages which contain this assertion, Matt 8:16–17 and 12:15–21, scriptural quotations are introduced with the well-known Matthean fulfillment formula. In both cases, the citations are taken from Deutero-Isaiah, and in both cases they belong to the so-called servant passages. It will be argued below that Matthew understands them as messianic texts and uses them for the purpose of demonstrating that there is a direct link between Jesus' healings and his messiahship.

On the other hand, Matthew presents an implicit scriptural proof of the miracles of healing as messianic deeds. Matt 11:2–6, which makes this claim, contains an elaborate argument that consists of several mutually interwoven layers. In this case, the link between Jesus' healing activity and his identity is not made directly and requires the uncovering of the complex tradition history of each step that appears in the argument. The question of John the Baptist betrays the influence of the tradition based on Hab 2:3 about the delay of the end-time, which in some Jewish texts takes the form of the delay of the coming of the Messiah. Jesus' answer is appropriately formulated as a set of recognizable biblical allusions, which function as "the signs of the times." Only by perceiving the exceptional nature of the present and identifying it as *the* messianic time, the person of the Messiah could be recognized and his miracles appropriately called the messianic deeds. The chapter will include an examination of various early Jewish texts that describe the eschatological blessings that are comparable to Jesus' answer to John the Baptist. A special attention will be given to 4Q521 (4QMessAp), which is remarkably similar to Matt 11:2–6 (and its parallel in Luke 7:18–23), in order to determine to what extent it can be used for illuminating the meaning and function of the Matthean passage.

4.2 Jesus' Healings as the Explicit Fulfillment of Scripture

4.2.1 The Use of Isa 53:4a in Matt 8:16–17

The summary in Matt 8:16–17 follows the Sermon on the Mount and the first three healing miracles described in chapters 8–9. Like Mark 1:32–34, Matthew speaks about Jesus' exorcisms and healings, but in a reversed order. Instead of having healings first and exorcisms second, he mentions the casting of the spirits out of those who were possessed with demons first and the more general healings second. Moreover, Matthew's text inverts Markan "many" and "all." Mark 1:32–34 mentions that all (πάντας) who were sick or possessed were brought to Jesus and that he healed many (πολλούς) of those who were ill, and cast out many (πολλά) demons. Matt 8:16 reverses this by saying that many (πολλούς) possessed with demons were brought to Jesus, and that he healed all (πάντας) who were sick.

As a result, the emphasis falls on Jesus' healings, which is reinforced by the quotation of Isa 53:4a, which Matthew added to the summary. The changes Matthew made to the Markan material can be partially explained by the need to create the appropriate introduction to and the link with the citation of Isa 53:4a.[1] The latter belongs to the so-called formula quotations, which is introduced here with the clause "This was to fulfill what was spoken by the prophet Isaiah" (ὅπως πληρωθῇ τὸ ῥηθὲν διὰ Ἡσαΐου τοῦ προφήτου λέγοντος – Matt 8:17a). The quotation of Isa 53:4a is appropriate here because it does not follow the spiritualized interpretation of the LXX (found also later in the text of Isaiah Targum), but stands closer to the Hebrew text which refers to physical illness.[2] A comparison of Matthew's rendering of the quotation with the LXX, Aquila (Symmachus), MT, and Isaiah Targum can be illuminating not only regarding the text form he used, but also regarding his theological interests.

---

[1] This applies primarily to the interchange between healings and exorcisms, as noted by Lindars, *New Testament Apologetic*, 153. Matthew's tendency to replace Markan "many" with "all" has to be explained on other grounds, because it is not conditioned by the quotation of Isa 53:4a.

[2] K. Stendahl, (*The School of St. Matthew*, 95–127) argued that Matthew's formula quotations employ a special citation technique, which is different from the quotations that have parallels in other synoptic Gospels. In Stendahl's view, this method can be called a "targumizing procedure," because it demonstrates great freedom in adapting the Old Testament text to the desired purpose. For a critique see Gundry, *The Use of the Old Testament*, 155–159, who claims that a mixed text-form of Scriptural citations can be found in all groups of synoptic quotations and should not be limited to Matthean formula quotations only. Gundry's critique, however, does not undermine the suitability of the term "targumizing" for this type of technique of quoting Scripture.

Matt 8:17	Isa 53:4a LXX	Aquila (Symmachus)
αὐτὸς τὰς ἀσθενείας	οὗτος τὰς ἁμαρτίας	ὄντως αὐτὸς[3] τὰς νόσους
ἡμῶν ἔλαβεν καὶ	ἡμῶν φέρει καὶ	ἡμῶν ἀνέλαβεν καὶ
τὰς νόσους ἐβάστασεν	περὶ ἡμῶν ὀδυνᾶται	τοὺς πολέμους (Symm. πόνους)
		ἡμῶν ὑπέμεινεν

Isa 53:4a MT   *Tg. Isa.* 53:4a

אכן חלינו הוא נשא ומכאבינו סבלם   בכן על חובנא הוא יבעי ועויתנא בדיליה ישתבקן

The pronoun αὐτός, with which the quotation in Matthew begins, stands closer
to the Hebrew pronoun הוא than the Septuagint's translation οὗτος. Matthew's
quotation does not contain the word ἁμαρτία found in the LXX, but uses the
word ἀσθένεια which is closer to the Hebrew חלי,[4] as well as to the Greek
noun νόσος found in Aquila's translation, which also follows the Hebrew text.[5]
Thus the phrase τὰς ἀσθενείας ἡμῶν can be understood as a literal translation
of חלינו.[6] Further, Aquila and Symmachus show that Matthew's use of the verb
λαμβάνω to translate נשא is equally valid as the verb φέρω found in the LXX.[7]
The noun νόσος in the second part of Matthew's quotation differs from Aquila
(πόλεμος) and Symmachus (πόνος), but it stands closer to the MT than the
LXX which contains the prepositional phrase περὶ ἡμῶν.[8] Finally, the verb
βαστάζω is attested neither in the LXX nor in Aquila and Summachus. The
difficulty here is that the implied meaning of the verb βαστάζω in Matthew's
context is that of removal, which is apparently not the sense of סבל, since the
latter does not mean "to take away," but to "bear."[9] However, Aquila's
translation of סבל with βαστάζω in Isa 53:11 shows that this is a possible
rendering of this verb.[10]

Matthew's citation thus does not have any exact parallel in other Greek
versions, although its meaning comes close to the text of Aquila. It is very

---

[3]Symmachus puts αὐτός after ἡμῶν.

[4]The LXX translates חלה with ἀσθενεῖν in Judg 16:7, 11, 17; Hos 11:6; Ezek 34:4; Dan
8:27.

[5]Aquila's translation is generally characterized by rigid literal rendering of Hebrew words
into Greek, even if this sometimes results in non-Greek constructions. See H. Hegermann,
Jesaja 53 in Hexapla, Targum und Peschitta, BFCT II/56 (Gütersloh: C. Bertelsmann Verlag,
1954).

[6]Gundry, *The Use of the Old Testament,* 109.

[7]The LXX translates נשא with λαμβάνω in Isa 40:24; 41:16; 57:13.

[8]The LXX never translates מכאב with νόσος.

[9]G. A. Deissmann, *Bible Studies: Contributions chiefly from Papyri and Inscriptions to the
History of the Language, the Literature, and the Religion of Hellenistic Judaism and Primitive
Christianity*, trans. A. Grieve (Edinburgh: T.&T. Clark, 1901), 102–103.

[10]Gundry, *The Use of the Old Testament,* 111, adds that the connotation of burden-bearing
of the verb סבל does not oppose the idea of removal implied in βαστάζω.

likely that it represents Matthew's own rendering of the Hebrew text of Isa 53:4a.[11] It is noteworthy that Matthew left out that part of the citation that speaks about the suffering of the servant of Yahweh. This means that Matthew interprets the prophecy not as atonement for sin, but as the taking away of literal sickness. This impression is reinforced through the usage of both nouns, ἀσθένεια and νόσος, which appear together only in Matthew's translation. The term νόσος connects this citation directly to the surrounding summaries in Matt 4:23–24 and 9:35. The servant of Yahweh as Matthew presents him in 8:17 is not a sick person[12] who voluntarily accepts the substitutionary suffering as in Isaiah 53, but a mighty healer who frees the sick from their illnesses.

The question of why and at which stage of tradition the image of the servant of Yahweh was applied to Jesus is a long debated and still unsettled issue.[13] In the past, the dominant approach was that either Jesus himself understood his mission in terms of the atoning death of the servant of Yahweh or that this has been done by his followers at the earliest stages of early Christian tradition.[14]

---

[11]A. Schlatter (*Der Evangelist Matthäus*, 282–283) has shown that the vocabulary of the citation corresponds to Matthew's phraseology. He has argued that ἀσθένεια, despite being a *hapax legomenon*, is not such a strange term in view of the fact that ἀσθενεῖν and ἀσθενής belong to Matthew's vocabulary (Matt 10:8; 25:36, 39). Further, λαβεῖν with the meaning "to take away" can be found in Matt 5:40 and 15:26; νόσος appears in Matt 4:23, 24; 9:35; 10:1; βαστάζειν with the meaning "to bring away" is used also in Matt 3:11. K. Stendahl (*The School of St. Matthew*, 107), H. J. Held ("Matthew as Interpreter of the Miracle Stories," 259), R. H. Gundry (*The Use of the Old Testament*, 109–111), and W. Rothfuchs (*Die Erfüllungszitate des Matthäus-Evengeliums*, 73–74) also agree that the citation is Matthew's own translation of the Hebrew text.

[12]R. H. Gundry claims that "the Matthaean context requires removal only from the sick to Jesus, but not a subsequent taking away" (*The Use of the Old Testament*, 111). M. Hooker (*Jesus and the Servant: The Influence of the Servant Concept of Deutero-Isaiah in the New Testament* [London: SPCK, 1959], 83), however, aptly notes that "the words are applied only in a very loose sense to Jesus: for while he cured those who suffered, he did not transfer their ailments to himself." See also D. Hill, "Son and Servant: An Essay on Matthean Christology," *JSNT* 6 (1980): 9. B. Lindars (*New Testament Apologetic*, 154) underscores the necessity of understanding the meaning of the verbs in the quoted verse as "take away," but accuses Matthew of falsifying "the intention of the original context," which "does not mean that Jesus cured diseases, but that he bore them himself." In Lindars' view, "the proper Christian understanding of this verse is the atoning efficacy of the passion." For the critique of Lindars' approach see the discussion that follows.

[13]For the most recent debate about the significance of Isaiah 53 for Christian origins see two collections of essays: *Jesus and the Suffering Servant: Isaiah 53 and Christian Origins*, ed. W. H. Bellinger and W. R. Farmer (Harrisburg: Trinity Press International, 1998), and *Der leidende Gottesknecht: Jesaja 53 und seine Wirkungsgeschichte mit einer Bibliographie zu Jes 53*, ed. B. Janowski and P. Stuhlmacher, FAT 14 (Tübingen: J. C. B. Mohr [Paul Siebeck], 1996).

[14]V. Taylor, *The Gospel according to St. Mark* (London: Macmillan, 1959), 378; Lindars, *New Testament Apologetic*, 77–88; J. Jeremias, "παῖς θεοῦ," in *TDNT* 5 (1967), 677–717. The most recent defenses of this position are offered by W. R. Farmer, "Reflections on Isaiah

This view has been most systematically challenged by Morna Hooker in her book *Jesus and the Servant*. She questioned the methodology on which the assumption of the significance of the suffering servant for Jesus' career relies, most vehemently espoused by C. H. Dodd, who claimed that early Christians quoted scriptural passages with the entire context in view.[15] Hooker agreed with Henry J. Cadbury, who argued that the atomistic use of Scripture equally characterized early Christian interpreters as their Jewish contemporaries.[16] In her analysis of relevant texts, Hooker demonstrated both the scarcity of the actual quotations from the Isaianic servant passages and the dependence of the recognition and interpretation of various allusions on the *apriori* assumption about the existence of the concept of the "Suffering Servant" in early Judaism.[17]

Donald Juel collected additional evidence about the diversity of interpretations of Isaiah's servant poems in early Jewish literature, which confirms Hooker's main claim that there was nothing like a uniformly defined concept of the "Servant," even less the "Suffering Servant" in the first century.[18] Thus, the LXX understands Yahweh's servant as a collective term, which refers to Israel and Jacob,[19] Jesus Ben Sirach applies it either to the righteous one[20] or to Elijah,[21] whereas the Babylonian Talmud applies the

---

53 and Christian Origins," in *Jesus and the Suffering Servant*, ed. Bellinger and Farmer, 260–280, and P. Stuhlmacher, "Jes 53 in den Evangelien und in der Apostelgeschichte," in *Der leidende Gottesknecht*, ed. Janowski and Stuhlmacher, 93–105.

[15]C. H. Dodd, *According to the Scriptures: The Substructure of New Testament Theology* (London: Nisbet, 1952), 88–96.

[16]H. J. Cadbury, "The Titles of Jesus in Acts," in *The Beginnings of Christianity*, part 1: *The Acts of the Apostles*, ed. F. J. F. Jackson and K. Lake, vol. 5: *Additional Notes to the Commentary*, ed. K. Lake and H. J. Cadbury (London: Macmillan, 1933), 369–370.

[17]For a succinct summary of Hooker's conclusions, see *Jesus and the Servant*, 147–163.

[18]Juel, *Messianic Exegesis*, 121–127. Juel also notes that "'Servant of God,' whether in Greek or Hebrew, is never treated as a title like Christ. It does not appear in Jewish literature in statements like, 'So and so is the servant of the Lord.'" (ibid., 124)

[19]Isa 42:1 LXX ('Ιακωβ ὁ παῖς μου ἀντιλήμψομαι αὐτοῦ Ἰσραηλ ὁ ἐκλεκτός μου προσεδέξατο αὐτὸν ἡ ψυχή μου ἔδωκα τὸ πνεῦμά μου ἐπ' αὐτόν κρίσιν τοῖς ἔθνεσιν ἐξοίσει). Israel is identified as Yahweh's servant also in *Pss. Sol.* 17:21 (ἰδέ, κύριε, καὶ ἀνάστησον αὐτοῖς τὸν βασιλέα αὐτῶν, υἱὸν Δαυιδ, εἰς τὸν καιρόν ὃν ἴδες σύ, ὁ θεός, τοῦ βασιλεῦσαι ἐπὶ Ἰσραηλ παῖδά σου).

[20]Sir 11:12–13 (ἔστιν νωθρὸς προσδεόμενος ἀντιλήμψεως ὑστερῶν ἰσχύι καὶ πτωχεία περισσεύει καὶ οἱ ὀφθαλμοὶ κυρίου ἐπέβλεψαν αὐτῷ εἰς ἀγαθά καὶ ἀνώρθωσεν αὐτὸν ἐκ ταπεινώσεως αὐτοῦ καὶ ἀνύψωσεν κεφαλὴν αὐτοῦ καὶ ἀπεθαύμασαν ἐπ' αὐτῷ πολλοί); cf. Isa 52:15 (οὕτως θαυμάσονται ἔθνη πολλὰ ἐπ' αὐτῷ). Wis 2:13 (ἐπαγγέλλεται γνῶσιν ἔχειν θεοῦ καὶ παῖδα κυρίου ἑαυτὸν ὀνομάζει) also applies the servant imagery to the righteous one.

[21]Sir 48:9–10 (ὁ ἀναλημφθεὶς ἐν λαίλαπι πυρὸς ἐν ἅρματι ἵππων πυρίνων ὁ καταγραφεὶς ἐν ἐλεγμοῖς εἰς καιροὺς κοπάσαι ὀργὴν πρὸ θυμοῦ ἐπιστρέψαι καρδίαν πατρὸς πρὸς υἱὸν καὶ καταστῆσαι φυλὰς Ἰακωβ); cf. Isa 49:6 (καὶ εἶπέν μοι μέγα σοί

servant imagery to Moses.[22] Only the Isaiah Targum consistently interprets Isa 52:13–53:12 as a reference to the Messiah. This is, however, achieved through a drastic reinterpretation of the Hebrew text, which removes every allusion to suffering from the messianic figure and transfers it either to his enemies or to Israel. Verse 4, for example, presents the Messiah in the intercessory role – he shall pray on behalf of Israel's transgressions, which will be pardoned for his sake.[23] Juel concludes that the messianic interpretation of Isaianic servant passages was one possible, but certainly not the only, way in which these poems could have been read.[24]

The citation of Isa 53:4a in Matt 8:17 shows that the application of a verse from Isaiah 53 did not have to be associated with the idea of redemptive suffering.[25] Isa 53:4a was quoted, and for that purpose translated by Matthew, in order to prove that Jesus' healings represent the fulfillment of Scripture. The way this purpose has been achieved demonstrates the early Christian

---

ἐστιν τοῦ κληθῆναί σε παῖδά μου τοῦ στῆσαι τὰς φυλὰς Ἰακωβ καὶ τὴν διασπορὰν τοῦ Ἰσραηλ ἐπιστρέψαι)

[22] b. Soṭah 14a.

[23] For the interpretation of Isaiah 53 in the Isaiah Targum, see Hegermann, *Jesaja 53 in Hexapla, Targum und Peschitta*; P. Seidelin, "Der 'Ebed Jahwe' und die Messiasgestalt im Jesajatargum," *ZNW* 35 (1936): 194–231; J. Ådna, "Der Gottesknecht als triumphierender und interzessorischer Messias. Die Rezeption von Jes 53 im Targum Jonathan untersucht mit besonderer Berücksichtigung des Messiasbildes," in *Der leidende Gottesknecht*, ed. Janowski and Stuhlmacher, 129–158.

[24] Juel, *Messianic Exegesis*, 126. Juel's conclusion still holds even when additional evidence from the post-biblical period is considered. For a detailed analysis of the tradition-history of Isaiah 53 in pre-Christian literature, see M. Hengel, "Zur Wirkungsgeschichte von Jes 53 in vorchristlicher Zeit," in *Der leidende Gottesknecht*, ed. Janowski and Stuhlmacher, 49–91. Hengel upholds the conclusion that in view of early Jewish atomistic use of Scripture "wir dürfen daher keine einheitliche, auf dem 4. Gottesknechtslied gründende Gesamtdeutung eines Kollektivs oder einer Einzelgestalt erwarten" (ibid., 52). His examination of relevant passages has shown that the interpretations of Isaiah 53 were exceedingly diverse. In his assessment, the strongest influence had the exaltation motif from Isa 53:12, especially in the collective sense applied to true Israel or the righteous ones, as seen in Daniel 11 and 12, Wisdom 2 and 5, and probably 4Q491. The same motif of exaltation, now applied to an individual and combined with Dan 7:13 and Isaiah 11, appears *1 Enoch*. 1QIsa[a] and 4Q540/541 probably contain allusions to Isaiah 53 in reference to the eschatological High Priest. Even though Hengel does not want to exclude the possibility that in pre-Christian Judaism some circles might have expected "leidende und sühnende eschatologisch-messianische Gestalten," he has to admit that on the basis of the extant evidence available at present, "das Motiv des stellvertretenden Sühnetods tritt in den vorchristlichen Texten durchweg mehr oder weniger zurück." (ibid., 91)

[25] Hooker draws from this the following conclusion: "For if the very quotations which would, used in certain contexts, make abundantly evident the identification of Jesus with the Servant who by his suffering expiates the sins of others are instead used only of his work in other spheres, then this is strong evidence that such an identification was never made, either by Jesus or by his earliest followers." (*Jesus and the Servant*, 83)

atomistic use of Scripture. Matt 8:17 quotes only the first half of Isa 53:4, and this in a very literal sense established through the verbal, even forced translation of the Hebrew text. It is therefore difficult to sustain Lindars' claim that "it is not enough . . . to see it merely as scriptural justification for the miracles, for it comes from a chapter which describes the suffering of the Servant himself. The fundamental issue is that Jesus' own sufferings are redemptive."[26] Such a conclusion is untenable, because the quoted text omits any reference to suffering and contains only that part of Isa 53:4 which is able to provide the scriptural basis for Jesus' healings.

To stop here, however, would be insufficient. What remains to be answered is the question about the reason for the selection of this and not another scriptural passage. As Juel has noted, "Christians did not search the whole of the Scripture for passages that struck them as parallels to Jesus' career or as possible foreshadowings. There was more logic and order in their movement through the Bible."[27] Juel's thesis is that the confession that Jesus is the Messiah provided the basis for the application of various servant passages to Jesus, because God calls the Messiah "my servant" (עבדי) in several Old Testament texts which were traditionally interpreted as messianic in postbiblical Judaism, such as Zech 3:8 (עבדי צמח) and Ps 89:39–40 (משיחך – עבדך).[28] The Targum Isaiah demonstrates that the messianic interpretation of servant songs was a feasible rendering, among several other alternatives, such as Israel, Elijah, Moses, etc.[29] It is, however, important to recognize that in each case, there was an already established scriptural link between that particular figure and the expression "my (if this is Yahweh's oracle) / your (if Yahweh is the addressee) servant." This further means that the application of servant imagery to a certain figure was not arbitrary, but guaranteed by scriptural evidence.

In the case of Jesus, the most plausible explanation can be found in his previous identification as the Messiah.[30] This assumption finds a firm confirmation in Matthew's narrative. Jesus is identified as the Messiah of the

---

[26]Lindars, *New Testament Apologetic,* 86; cf. also Stuhlmacher, "Jes 53 in den Evangelien und in der Apostelgeschichte," 101–102. Stuhlmacher's attempt to read the quotation of Isa 53:4a in Matt 8:17 through the lenses of Matthew's quotation of Isa 42:1–4 in Matt 12:17–21 and, by implication, within the framework of the servant's redemptive suffering, presupposes Dodd's methodology of scriptural quotations. The analysis of the quotation itself, however, strengthens the assumption of an atomistic exegesis, which in this instance showed no interest in a link between Jesus' healings and his approaching suffering.

[27]Juel, *Messianic Exegesis,* 130.

[28]Juel, *Messianic Exegesis,* 131. Cf. also *2 Bar.* 70:10 which contains the designation "my Servant, the Anointed One."

[29]This diversity of actual interpretations of servant passages demonstrates that we cannot speak about "a Messianic intention behind the Servant passages" and "a recognition of that intention from the beginning," as R. H. Gundry claims in *The Use of the Old Testament,* 230.

[30]Juel, *Messianic Exegesis,* 131.

Davidic line already at the beginning of the Gospel. Moreover, the quotation of Isa 53:4a in Matt 8:17 does not offer any alternative formulation of Jesus' identity. The term παῖς does not appear in the text that is quoted, which, in view of the fact that the existence of the figure called "Servant" in the time when Matthew wrote his Gospel cannot be demonstrated, excludes the possibility that this citation could have induced his readers to identify Jesus as the "Servant." Since at the end of the miracle cycle in Matthew 8–9 Jesus is addressed by the two blind men with the messianic title "Son of David," the quotation of Isa 53:4a can be understood as the preliminary hint which Matthew offers to his readers concerning the messianic significance of Jesus' healings.

This inference finds support in the possibility that Matthew's choice of Isa 53:4a and its wording, especially the use of the term ἀσθενεία, might have been influenced by the imagery of *Pss. Sol.* 17:38–40.[31] The latter describes the expected Son of David as a caring shepherd, who will not let any of his flock weaken (οὐκ ἀφήσει ἀσθενῆσαι ἐν αὐτοῖς – v. 40c). He himself is a mighty person (ἰσχυρὸς ἐν ἔργοις αὐτοῦ – v. 40a) who will not weaken (καὶ οὐκ ἀσθενήσει – v. 38b). This image of the Davidic Messiah has been modeled after the description of the ideal Davidic king in Ezek 34:23–24. He is presented as a benevolent shepherd who is directly contrasted to the shepherds of Israel sharply criticized in Ezek 34:2–4. The latter metaphorically describes the people of Israel as weak, sick, injured, and lost. The LXX translates the first two participles of the verb חלה (הנחלות and החולה) that appear in Ezek 34:4 with ἠσθενηκός and κακῶς ἔχον.[32] A similar comparison of the people to the scattered sheep because of the lack of proper leadership can be found in Zech 10:2c. The LXX reinforces the metaphor of healing by translating יענו with ἐκακώθησαν and by rephrasing the reason for affliction כי־אין רעה ("for there was no shepherd") into διότι οὐκ ἦν ἴασις ("because there was no healing").

Matthew's use of similar language, i.e. his choice of ἀσθενεία as a translation of חלינו in a quotation whose purpose is to give scriptural justification of healing the sick (τοὺς κακῶς ἔχοντας), betrays the influence of the same tradition which likens the people to the injured sheep and the future king of the Davidic line to an ideal shepherd. The basis for an association of the metaphor of a shepherd, which has been applied to the expected king of the Davidic line, with the concept of the servant, which emerges behind Matthew's messianic reading of Isa 53:4a, can be found in Ezek 34:23, which links all three terms together: "I will set up over them one shepherd, my

---

[31] I am not speaking about literary dependence, but the influence of ideas and imageries.

[32] F. Martin, "The Image of Shepherd in the Gospel of Saint Matthew," *ScEs* 27 (1975): 275, notes that "the whole tone of Ez 34 already prepares the way for seeing the shepherd as a healer."

servant David, and he will shepherd them" (והקמתי עליהם רעה אחד ורעה אחד
את עבדי דויד [MT]; καὶ ἀναστήσω ἐπ' αὐτοὺς ποιμένα ἕνα καὶ ποιμανεῖ
αὐτούς τὸν δοῦλόν μου Δαυιδ [LXX].

Matthew's Gospel shows that that the author knew about this traditional metaphor for a Davidic king. Matt 2:6 quotes 2 Sam 5:2,[33] which contains God's promise to David that he will shepherd his people Israel (σὺ ποιμανεῖς τὸν λαόν μου τὸν Ἰσραηλ). In Matthew, this promise is directly applied to the expected Messiah of the Davidic line (ὅστις ποιμανεῖ τὸν λαόν μου τὸν Ἰσραήλ). Further, Matt 9:36, which likens the people to the sheep without a shepherd (ὡσεὶ πρόβατα μὴ ἔχοντα ποιμένα), functions as an explanatory comment of Jesus' ministry of teaching, preaching, and healing (Matt 9:35). In Matt 15:24, this metaphor appears in the context which explicitly associates the Son of David and healing. Jesus replies to the Canaanite woman who asks for help that he is sent only to the lost sheep of the house of Israel (οὐκ ἀπεστάλην εἰ μὴ εἰς τὰ πρόβατα τὰ ἀπολωλότα οἴκου Ἰσραήλ).[34] The last passage indicates that for Matthew, Jesus' ministry of healing belongs to his duty as a shepherd of his people. The basis for this inference is provided by Ezek 34:4, where the task of searching the lost (ὁ ἀπολωλός) appears alongside the task of strengthening the weak and healing the sick. The fact that this and similar passages in Jewish literature always contain metaphorical descriptions does not undermine this reconstruction, because Matthew, similar to his contemporaries, betrays the tendency to interpret the text literally if this suits his purpose,[35] without worrying about its intended meaning. In this way he "concretizes this OT metaphor,"[36] which enables him to apply it directly to Jesus' ministry of healing.

It is therefore not surprising that Matthew found Isa 53:4a to be an appropriate scriptural passage that can be directly applied to Jesus' healing activity. Ezek 34:23–24 shows that texts such as Isa 53:4a could have been interpreted as messianic predictions not only because of a potential link between the expected Davidic king and the servant of Yahweh, but also because of an eventual association of both figures with the concept of the shepherd who cares for and cures his flock.

---

[33]Matt 2:6 conflates Mic 5:1 and 2 Sam 5:2.

[34]Cf. a similar command given to the disciples in Matt 10:6.

[35]Matthew's ability to "oscillate" between the literal and metaphorical meaning of certain concepts has been already noted in chapter 3 of this study with reference to the healing of the blindness. Other examples include the quotation of Isaiah 6:9–10 in Matt 13:14–15, where the verb ἰάσομαι preserves its metaphorical sense, and Matt 9:12, where both ἰατρός and κακῶς ἔχοντες are used as metaphors.

[36]Martin, "The Image of Shepherd in the Gospel of Saint Matthew," 277.

4.2.2 The Use of Isa 42:1–4 in Matt 12:15–21

The summary itself is very brief, most probably devised through the process of ponderous shortening and rephrasing of Mark's summary in Mark 3:7–12. Matt 12:15 reports that after Jesus' withdrawal, which was motivated by his knowledge of the murderous plot of the Pharisees to destroy him (ὁ δὲ Ἰησοῦς γνούς), many followed him (καὶ ἠκολούθησαν αὐτῷ [ὄχλοι] πολλοί) and he healed them all (καὶ ἐθεράπευσεν αὐτοὺς πάντας). In contrast to Mark 3:7–12, Matthew's text does not contain the reference to the unclean spirits. Consequently, Jesus' order not to make him known (καὶ ἐπετίμησεν αὐτοῖς ἵνα μὴ φανερὸν αὐτὸν ποιήσωσιν – Matt 12:16) is not given to the unclean spirits as in Mark, but to the sick persons who were healed. Matthew linked this command for silence directly to the quotation of Isa 42:1–4 with the purpose of showing that this is another fulfillment of Old Testament prophecy.

Two objections regarding the propriety of the quotation to its present context are usually raised at this point. The first relates to the explicit tie between the quotation and the narrative. Some interpreters have argued that Matthew preserved the Markan command for silence only because he needed a link to the Old Testament quotation.[37] Moreover, even this link seems to fulfill its purpose poorly, because the connection of the quotation to the preceding command appears to be problematic. In Matt 12:16, the command for silence is given to those who were healed, whereas Matt 12:19, the only part of the citation that is explicitly connected to the context, speaks about a peaceful ministry of the servant, which can be applied only to the silence of Jesus.[38] The second objection relates to the entire text of the quotation. It has been often pointed out that the citation hardly illuminates or is illuminated by its immediate Matthean context in chapter 12.[39] Rather, it seems to refer to the broader scope of Matthew's Christology by giving scriptural foundation to various aspects of Jesus' ministry.[40] Since both objections challenge the

---

[37]Cf. Luz, *Matthew 8–20*, 191. R. T. France, however, proposes a dialectical relationship: "On the one hand the removal of the quotation would allow the narrative to flow on with little apparent interruption, while on the other hand the narrative in most cases seems to have little point once that quotation is removed" (*Matthew: Evangelist and Teacher* [Exeter: The Paternoster Press, 1989], 180).

[38]Luz, *Matthew 8–20*, 191.

[39]B. Lindars even claims that "the resulting text owes nothing to its present context" (*New Testament Apologetic*, 145 n.1).

[40]One can find the entire spectrum of diverse opinions regarding the purpose of the quotation of Isa 42:1–4 in Matt 12:18–21, such as that Matthew wanted to emphasize the humility and lowliness of Jesus (G. Barth, "Matthew's Understanding of the Law," in *Tradition and Interpretation in Matthew*, ed. G. Bornkamm, G. Barth, and H. J. Held, trans. P. Scott [London: SCM Press, 1963], 128), his proclamation to the Gentiles (Walker, *Die Heilsgeschichte im ersten Evangelium*, 78), or more broadly, that this as is a miniature of Matthew's Christology which should not be limited to one aspect only (Loader, "Son of David, Blindness, Possession, and Duality in Matthew," 576–577; Luz, *Matthew 8–20*, 190–196).

relatedness of the quotation to Matthew's reference to Jesus' healings, they
will be addressed in the analysis that follows.

4.2.2.1 The Secrecy Motif

The assumption of the purely formal role of the command for silence is based
on the common opinion evolved after the impressive analysis of William
Wrede on the messianic secret in the Gospels,[41] that this motif plays an
important role only in the Gospel of Mark. Wrede was convinced that the
secrecy motives in Matthew and Luke "are not simply to be thought of as the
expression of their own views, for the very good reason that for the most part
they merely reproduce and rearrange material they have taken over [from
Mark]."[42] Consequently, Wrede declared that "the idea of the messianic secret
no longer has the importance for Matthew that it has for Mark."[43]

Wrede's conclusion is certainly justified in regard to the most important
aspect of the messianic secret in the Gospel of Mark, which is Jesus' command
for silence to the demons concerning his identity as the Son of God. Matthew
indeed does not have any story in which a demon recognizes Jesus and is
silenced. Yet it should be noticed that Matthew retains all Markan commands
for silence which relate to Jesus' healing ministry.[44] The command to the
cleansed leper to keep silent (Mark 1:43–44) is preserved in the parallel
account in Matthew (Matt 8:4), and a similar charge to the bystanders who saw
the healing of Jairus' daughter (Mark 5:43) is transposed to the account of the
healing of the blind who recognize Jesus as the Son of David (Matt 9:30).[45] In
view of the fact, attested otherwise, that Matthew is usually a very careful
redactor of the received tradition, it is difficult to imagine that he had not
preserved these commands for silence purposely.

The reason for secrecy in Matthew begins to emerge in chapter 12. Both
previous commands for silence were given to individuals, not the crowd. Matt
12:16 is the first and only request for secrecy given to the group of people,
which, in contrast to the ambiguous formulations of the two previous
requests,[46] here clearly refers to Jesus' identity (καὶ ἐπετίμησεν αὐτοῖς ἵνα μὴ

---

[41]W. Wrede, *Das Messiasgeheimnis in den Evangelien: Zugleich ein Beitrag zum
Verständnis des Markusevangeliums* (Göttingen: Vandenhoeck & Ruprecht, 1901); English
translation: *The Messianic Secret*, trans. J. C. G. Greig (Cambridge/London: James Clarke,
1971).

[42]Wrede, *The Messianic Secret*, 152.

[43]Ibid., 154.

[44]Mark 7:36 and 8:26 do not appear in Matthew because he did not include these episodes
into his narrative.

[45]The vocabulary of this command partly comes from Mark 1:43–44 (ἐνεβριμήθη αὐτοῖς
and ὁρᾶτε), but the phrase μηδεὶς γινωσκέτω links Matt 9:30 firmly to Mark 5:43.

[46]The formulations ὅρα μηδενὶ εἴπῃς (Matt 8:4) and ὁρᾶτε μηδεὶς γινωσκέτω (Matt
9:30) seem to refer to "keeping secret the fact of his [Jesus] healing activity" (D. J. Verseput,

φανερὸν αὐτὸν ποιήσωσιν).[47] Its purpose is to prevent an untimely public recognition of Jesus as the Messiah, which, in Matthew's presentation, logically follows from his healing ministry, and which, in turn, regularly provokes a hostile reaction of Jesus' opponents. This structure can be easily discerned in the scene that immediately follows (Matt 12:22–24). Jesus' healing of a blind and dumb demoniac provokes a public speculation regarding his identity as a Son of David, to which the Pharisees instantly object by accusing Jesus of being in league with Beelzebul.

This inference is reinforced by Matt 16:20, which, unlike the commands for silence considered above, does not appear in the context of Jesus' healings. The charge for silence is taken from Mark 8:30, but Matthew reformulates a slightly indefinite expression περὶ αὐτοῦ found in Mark into an unmistakable messianic reference ὅτι αὐτός ἐστιν ὁ χριστός.[48] The following verse (Matt 16:21), however, introduces into the narrative a new phase of development – Jesus' suffering and death in Jerusalem. Before that, Jesus tried to avoid an open conflict with the Jewish leaders and often withdrew from their murderous hostility. This motif of withdrawal is often supplemented by Jesus' various requests for silence.[49] Matt 16:20 concludes this section of the narrative by

---

The Rejection of the Humble Messianic King: A Study of the Composition of Matthew 11–12, EHS.T 291 [Frankfurt am Main: Peter Lang, 1986], 192–193).

[47]Cf. a similar usage of ποιήσας φανερὸν τὸν ἐξευρηκότα in Josephus, *Ant.* 3.4.2. The critique of J. H. Neyrey ("The Thematic Use of Isaiah 42,1–4 in Matthew 12," *Bib* 63 [1982]: 468) that "if secrecy is even a minor Matthean motif in 12,15–16 (and hence in 12,19a), it is contradicted by the very context of this passage in which miracles are intentionally public, not private" misses the point, because Jesus does not request the secrecy of his healings, but of his identity.

[48]This phrase which echoes and, in fact, replaces Peter's words σὺ εἶ ὁ χριστὸς ὁ υἱὸς τοῦ θεοῦ τοῦ ζῶντος in Matt 16:16, clearly shows that for Matthew both ὁ χριστός and ὁ υἱὸς τοῦ θεοῦ are messianic references, as has been argued in chapter 2.

[49]D. Good ("The Verb ΑΝΑΧΩΡΕΩ in Matthew's Gospel," *NT* 32 [1990]: 1–12) analyzed the motif of Jesus' withdrawal in the Gospel of Matthew and came to the conclusion that it is a prominent theme in response to hostility in fulfillment of prophecy. Thus in Matt 2:12–15, first the magi and then Joseph withdraw from Herod. In Matt 2:22–23, Joseph withdraws again to Nazareth in order to get away from Archelaus. Both times Matthew interprets these withdrawals as the fulfillment of prophecy. In Matt 4:12–18, Jesus withdraws to Galilee after hearing about John's imprisonment, and Matthew again interprets this as the fulfillment of prophecy. In Matt 12:15–21, Jesus withdraws because of the opposition of the Pharisees, and this serves as the fulfillment of another prophecy. The next withdrawal is presented in Matt 14:12–14 as Jesus' reaction to John's execution, but this time an explicit motif of the fulfillment of prophecy is missing. Good proposes that the feeding miracle serve as an implicit fulfillment motif. The last occurrence of Jesus' withdrawal is found in Matt 15:21–28, presented again as a reaction to the hostility of the Pharisees. An explicit fulfillment motif is missing again, but Good suggests that the healing of the Canaanite woman's child fulfills the prophecy quoted in Matt 12:18, 21. Because of the lack of the explicit fulfillment motifs in the last two instances, N. Elliott ("The Silence of the Messiah: The Function of 'Messianic Secret' Motifs across the Synoptics," in *SBL 1993 Seminar Papers*, ed. E. H. Lovering, SBL Seminar

putting it into the framework of the messianic secret. From now on Jesus will not evade the public confession of his messiahship, which will finally lead him to the cross.[50]

In light of these observations, Matthew's additional command for secrecy to the people whom he healed (Matt 12:16) no longer appears as a contingent component with a merely formal function of connecting the quotation of Isa 42:1–4 to the narrative. Rather, it emerges as an essential constituent of Matthew's portrayal of Jesus as the Messiah, which is reinforced by the explicit association of Jesus' withdrawal from the Pharisaic opposition and his request for secrecy.

4.2.2.2 The Relatedness of the Quotation to the Context

A reply to the second objection, i.e. that the citation of Isa 42:1–4 hardly befits its Matthean context, requires a prior, though brief, examination of the text itself. Matt 12:18–21 contains the longest citation in Matthew's Gospel, which represents neither the quotation of the MT nor the LXX, even though it contains the elements from both. C. H. Dodd noted that "at almost every point where it is possible to substitute a different verb or noun, the substitution is made."[51] This is usually explained either by assuming a certain pre-Matthean history of the text[52] or by ascribing it to the interpretative work of the author of the Gospel himself.[53] Donald Verseput aptly notes that any decision in that regard depends on one's view of the extent the quotation is assimilated to the context.[54] In an anticipation of the results of the following analysis of the Matthean form of the citation, which will seek to demonstrate a close correspondence between the quotation and its context, all alterations from the MT and the LXX will be ascribed to the evangelist himself. A columnar presentation of the Matthean version of the quotation, the MT, and the LXX, followed by the targumic rendering of Isa 42:1–4, has the purpose of fostering the comparison.

Papers Series 32 [Atlanta: Scholars Press, 1993], 604–633) corrects Good's scheme by proposing the connection of the motif of withdrawal with "the elements of opposition" and "manifestation of Jesus as messiah in *the narrative* [italics his]" (ibid., 614).

[50]The fact that there is an additional request for secrecy after Matt 16:20, found in Matt 17:19, does not undermine the above conclusion. This command does not refer to Jesus' messianic identity but to the vision (τὸ ὅραμα) that Peter, James, and John had witnessed. Also, in contrast to previous charges, this one is given with a time restriction – until the Son of Man is raised from the dead.

[51] Dodd, *According to the Scriptures*, 89.

[52]According to B. Lindars (*The New Testament Apologetic*, 147) the text had been previously used in the church for apologetic purposes. K. Stendahl (*The School of St. Matthew*, 107–115) ascribes it to the work of the Matthean School.

[53]Barth, "Matthew's Understanding of the Law," 125; Hill, "Son and Servant," 9.

[54]Verseput, *The Rejection of the Humble Messianic King,* 194.

Matt 12:18–21	Isa 42:1–4 LXX	Isa 42:1–4 MT
ἰδοὺ ὁ παῖς μου	Ἰακωβ ὁ παῖς μου	הן עבדי
ὃν ᾑρέτισα,	ἀντιλήμψομαι αὐτοῦ,	אתמך־בו
ὁ ἀγαπητός μου	Ἰσραηλ ὁ ἐκλεκτός μου	בחירי
εἰς ὃν εὐδόκησεν ἡ ψυχή μου.	προσεδέξατο αὐτὸν ἡ ψυχή μου.	רצתה נפשי
θήσω τὸ πνεῦμά μου ἐπ' αὐτόν,	ἔδωκα τὸ πνεῦμά μου ἐπ' αὐτόν,	נתתי רוחי עליו
καὶ κρίσιν τοῖς ἔθνεσιν ἀπαγγελεῖ.	κρίσιν τοῖς ἔθνεσιν ἐξοίσει.	משפט לגוים יוציא
οὐκ ἐρίσει οὐδὲ κραυγάσει,	οὐ κεκράξεται οὐδὲ ἀνήσει	לא יצעק ולא ישא
οὐδὲ ἀκούσει τις ἐν ταῖς	οὐδὲ ἀκουσθήσεται ἔξω	ולא־ישמיע בחוץ
πλατείαις	ἡ φωνὴ αὐτοῦ.	קולו
τὴν φωνὴν αὐτοῦ.	κάλαμον τεθλασμένον	קנה רצוץ
κάλαμον συντετριμμένον	οὐ συντρίψει	לא ישבור
οὐ κατεάξει	καὶ λίνον καπνιζόμενον	ופשתה כהה
καὶ λίνον τυφόμενον	οὐ σβέσει,	לא יכבנה
οὐ σβέσει,	ἀλλὰ εἰς ἀλήθειαν ἐξοίσει	לאמת יוציא
ἕως ἂν ἐκβάλῃ εἰς νῖκος	κρίσιν.	משפט
τὴν κρίσιν.	ἀναλάμψει	לא יכהה
	καὶ οὐ θραυσθήσεται	ולא ירוץ
	ἕως ἂν θῇ	עד־ישים
	ἐπὶ τῆς γῆς κρίσιν	בארץ משפט
καὶ τῷ ὀνόματι αὐτοῦ	καὶ ἐπὶ τῷ ὀνόματι αὐτοῦ	ולתורתו
ἔθνη ἐλπιοῦσιν.	ἔθνη ἐλπιοῦσιν	איים ייחילו

Tg. Isa. 42:1–4

הא עבדי אקרבניה בחירי דאתרעי ביה מימרי אתין רוח קודשי עלוהי דיניל עממין יגלי
לא יצוח ולא יכלי ולא ירים בברא קליה
ענותניא דכקני רעיע לא יתבר וחשיכיא דכבוצין עמי לא יטפי לקושטיה יפיק דינא
לא יהלי ולא ילאי עד דיתקין בארעא דינא ולאוריתיה נגוון יכתרון

Matt 12:18 introduces the servant with the particle ἰδοὺ, which resembles הן better than the LXX.[55] The use of ὁ παῖς μου is not surprising, as the translations of the LXX and Theodotion demonstrate. However, since an equally suitable translation could have been δοῦλος,[56] Matthew's choice of παῖς should be understood as deliberate.[57] Unlike the LXX, which inserts Jacob and Israel into the text in order to ascertain the collective interpretation of the servant of Yahweh, Matthew applies this text to Jesus only.

---

[55] Ἰδοὺ appears also in the translations of Theodotion, Aquila, and Symmachus.
[56] Cf. the translations of Aquila and Symmachus.
[57] Stendahl, *The School of St. Matthew,* 109; Rothfuchs, *Die Erfüllungszitate des Matthäus-Evengeliums,* 73.

The choice of αἱρετίζω as a translation of חמך is unique to Matthew because it does not appear in any of the existing versions of Isa 42:1. It emphasizes the idea of divine election rather than protection.[58] Even if one would agree with the suggestion of Robert H. Gundry that αἱρετίζω still belongs to the range of possible meanings of חמך ("take hold of to acquire," "bring or adopt to oneself"),[59] it is more likely that it anticipates ὁ ἐκλεκτός from the LXX and thus בחירי in the MT,[60] in order to make room for ὁ ἀγαπητός from the heavenly voice at Jesus' baptism and transfiguration.[61] This further means that ὁ ἀγαπητός μου should not be understood as a rendering of בחירי,[62] but as a term that has its origin in the Christian tradition of Jesus' baptism. The similarity between Matt 12:18 and the Matthean version of the baptismal tradition is strengthened through Matthew's reformulation of the divine voice in the baptismal scene from a private revelation into a public introduction (Matt 3:17).[63] On the other hand, even though the LXX translates רצתה with προσεδέξατο αὐτὸν, Matthew's choice of the phrase εἰς ὃν εὐδόκησεν should not be interpreted as an assimilation to ἐν ᾧ εὐδόκησα from the heavenly voice at the baptism (Matt 3:17), because Theodotion and Symmachus demonstrate that this was a common translation of רצתה.[64]

The rest of the quotation of Isa 42:1 generally agrees with the LXX, with the exception of the verbs θήσω and ἀπαγγελεῖ. The dominant opinion is that both verbs stand closer to the targumic text than to the MT.[65] It is often argued that Matthew's choice of the verb (τίθημι) and the tense (future) is more suitable for the Aramaic אתין than the Hebrew perfect נתתי. Similarly, the verb ἀπαγγελεῖ in the sense of promulgation appears to be closer to the Aramaic יגלי than to the Hebrew יוציא.[66] However, the influence of the Targum is

---

[58]Verseput, *The Rejection of the Humble Messianic King*, 195.

[59]Gundry, *The Use of the Old Testament*, 112. Gundry also calls attention to the Targum's translation אקרבניה ("I will bring him near").

[60]αἱρετίζω is the usual translation of the LXX for בחר; cf. Hag 2:23 where ἡρέτισα translates בך בחרתי.

[61]Cf. Stendahl, *The School of St. Matthew*, 110; Rothfuchs, *Die Erfüllungszitate des Matthäus-Evengeliums*, 73; Gundry, *The Use of the Old Testament*, 112; Verseput, *The Rejection of the Humble Messianic King*, 196. B. Lindars, on the other hand, despite considering the possibility that ἀγαπητός might have come from the baptismal narrative, prefers to see it as a legitimate translation of בחירי, "because the idea of choice has already been included in the verb" (*New Testament Apologetic*, 147).

[62]All of the existing Greek versions have ὁ ἐκλεκτός μου.

[63]Verseput, *The Rejection of the Humble Messianic King*, 196.

[64]An example of such assimilation can be found on Codex Bezae and *f*[1], but this reading can hardly be considered original. The combination of εὐδοκεῖν and the accusative often appears in the LXX.

[65]Stendahl, *The School of St. Matthew*, 111; Gundry, *The Use of the Old Testament*, 113.

[66]Gundry, *The Use of the Old Testament*, 113.

probably exaggerated.[67] In several instances, such as Exod 12:7; 26:35; 29:12; Num 11:25, 29; 2 Chr 32:6, the LXX uses (ἐπι)τίθημι for נתן. Also, in Isa 48:20, the LXX translates יצא with the verb ἀναγγέλειν. These examples demonstrate that in both cases Matthew's rendering was within acceptable limits of the range of meanings of these verbs. The use of the future tense most likely represents an adjustment to the tense of יוציא and the subsequent verbs which appear in the quotation. In this way, the reception of the Spirit has been firmly linked to the tasks that the servant is expected to perform.[68]

Matt 12:19 contains a series of three verbs, all of which are in the negative form, like the MT and the LXX, but none of which completely conforms to the Hebrew text and the LXX. This discrepancy is especially obvious in the case of the first verb ἐρίσει, which has been often regarded as a derivation from the OT Peshitta, rather than the translation of the Hebrew יצעק.[69] There is no need, however, for such an explanation, because the range of meaning of צעק also includes a forensic sense of verbal disputation, such as "to shout/cry out complainingly" in order to obtain one's rights.[70] The examples for the latter can be found in 2 Kgs 8:3, 5; 6:26; Exod 22:22, and Sir 8:2. As the targumic rendering יכלי demonstrates, the second verb κραυγάσει similarly belongs to the range of meaning of the Hebrew נשא.[71] The third verb ἀκούσει represents

---

[67]Cf. Rothfuchs, *Die Erfüllungszitate des Matthäus-Evengeliums*, 73; Verseput, *The Rejection of the Humble Messianic King,* 197.

[68]Verseput, *The Rejection of the Humble Messianic King,* 197.

[69]This interpretation, originally proposed by E. Nestle ("Matthew xii.19 – Isaiah xlii.2," *ExpTim* 20 [1908/1909]: 92–93) was refuted by W. C. Allen in the same issue of *Expository Times* (*ExpTim* 20 [1908/1909]: 140–141). This thesis about the dependence of ἐρίσει on Syriac versions has been accepted by both K. Stendahl (*The School of St. Matthew,* 111–112) and B. Lindars (*New Testament Apologetic* 148). They argue that Matthew's translation comes from the root ריב which appears in the Syriac Peshitta with the meaning "cry aloud," but which in Western Aramaic and Hebrew means "contend," "strive," or "plead." According to Stendahl, this is Matthew's conscious choice that has been made in order to conform the quotation to its present context. Lindars, however, believes that this is a mistranslation and claims that the process of adaptation was completed before the quotation was incorporated into the Gospel. In his view, the text originally referred to the patient and silent suffering of Jesus, but when it was incorporated into Matthew's context, the active form of ἀκούσει τις ἐν and the concrete phrase ἐν ταῖς πλατείαις were used to give the impression of the quiet nature of Jesus' ministry. Lindars' proposal, however, remains a mere conjecture.

[70]This thesis was first proposed by B. Gärtner ("The Habakkuk Commentary [DSH] and the Gospel of Matthew," *ST* 8 [1955]: 20–21) and then followed by R. Gundry (*The Use of the Old Testament,* 113), W. Rothfuchs (*Die Erfüllungszitate des Matthäus-Evengeliums,* 74), and D. J. Verseput (*The Rejection of the Humble Messianic King,* 198–199).

[71]Matthew's translation presupposes קול as an addition to the Hebrew. Cf. P. A. H. de Boer, *Second-Isaiah's Message,* OTS 11 (Leiden: E. J. Brill, 1956), 45; J. Morgenstern, "The Suffering Servant – A New Solution," *VT* 11 (1961): 301. The verb κραυγάζω does not otherwise appear in Matthew's Gospel.

the least difficulty, because its active form is closer to the Hiph'il ישמיע found in the MT than the passive translation of the LXX.[72]

The phrase ἐν ταῖς πλατείαις appears only in Matthew, but again, it falls within the range of meaning of בחוץ. Thus in several occasions, such as Ps 17:43, Isa 15:3, Ezek 7:19, 26:11, 28:23, the LXX translates the plural חוצות with πλατεῖα. Finally, the accusative τὴν φωνήν better renders קולו as the object of the verb, than the nominative of the LXX. Thus even though Matt 12:19 differs from the LXX significantly, it still represents a recognizable translation of the Hebrew text. Since, however, the choice of certain verbs and phrases cannot be explained on the basis of the most common rendering of the MT, it is most likely that it has been motivated by the demands of the context in which the citation appears, as the discussion below will seek to demonstrate.

Matt 12:20 contains an abbreviated form of Isaiah's text. After quoting the first two clauses from Isa 42:3, Matthew apparently jumps to Isa 42:4b. Apart from this contraction, Matthew's text, despite deviating from the LXX, does not significantly depart from the sense of the MT. Thus both pairs of adjectives συντετριμμένον and τυφόμενον (Matthew), and τεθλασμένον and καπνιζόμενον (the LXX) translate the Hebrew text equally well.[73] The variants found in Theodotion (στιππύον ἀμαυρόν) and Aquila and Symmachus (λίνον ἀμαυρόν) testify to the diversity of feasible translations of the MT at this point. Matthew's choice of κατεάξει ("break off") seems to be even closer to the Hebrew ישבור than συντρίψει ("smash, crush") found in the LXX.[74] The second verb (σβέσει) appears also in the LXX and is attested in all other Greek translations.

The omitted section from Isaiah refers to the servant's strength and courageousness, which apparently was not Matthew's concern at this point. As a result, the concluding phrase (ἕως ἂν ἐκβάλῃ εἰς νῖκος τὴν κρίσιν) has been directly linked to the description of the servant's gentle behavior. The origin of the latter, however, is somewhat uncertain because it can be derived directly from neither the MT nor the LXX of Isa 42:3–4. The prepositional phrase ἕως ἂν suggests that the text must have been based on the clause עד־ישים בארץ משפט from Isa 42:4b, but the expression εἰς νῖκος seems to resemble the form of לאמת from Isa 42:3c, which has been apparently omitted in Matthew's quotation. The dominant opinion is that εἰς νῖκος stems from לנצח found in Hab 1:4.[75] The latter contains the phrase ולא־יצא לנצח משפט, which can be

---

[72]Gundry, *The Use of the Old Testament,* 114.

[73]Barth, "Matthew's Understanding of the Law," 127; Gundry, *The Use of the Old Testament,* 114; Verseput, *The Rejection of the Humble Messianic King,* 200.

[74]Cf. Gundry, *The Use of the Old Testament,* 114.

[75]This thesis has been originally proposed by A. Rahlfs, "Über Theodotion-Lesarten im Neuen Testament und Aquila-Lesarten bei Justin," *ZNW* 20 (1921): 186–189, and then followed by Stendahl, *The School of St. Matthew,* 113–114; Gundry, *The Use of the Old*

linked to Isa 42:3c because both clauses contain the verb יצא and the noun משפט. The reconstruction is based on the observation that in several occasions, such as 2 Sam 2:26, Amos 1:11, 8:7, Jer 3:5, and Lam 5:20, the LXX translates the term לנצח with εἰς νῖκος, whereas Aquila does it regularly.[76] Accordingly, Matthew must have arrived at his translation through a conflation of Isa 42:3c and 4b and association of the former with Hab 1:4.

This conclusion has been challenged by Jan de Waard[77] who examined Matthew's quotation in light of 1QHᵃ (1QHymnsᵃ) 12(=4).25,[78] which contains the following clause: ותוצא לנצח משפטם. De Waard argued that the latter represents a quotation of Isa 42:3 and not Hab 1:4 because, firstly, the Habakkuk text is in the negative whereas 1QHᵃ 12.25 is in the affirmative, secondly, both Isa 42:3 and 1QHᵃ 12.25 have Hiph'il imperfect, whereas Hab 1:4 contains Qal imperfect, and thirdly, the author of *Hodayot* prefers the text of Deutero-Isaiah. Consequently, לנצח in 1QHᵃ 12.25 should be understood as a variant for לאמת in Isa 42:3 MT. This further means that Matthew's clause ἕως ἂν ἐκβάλῃ εἰς νῖκος τὴν κρίσιν represents a free rendering of Isa 42:3c (יוציא משפט לאמת) that is comparable to the one found in 1QHᵃ 12.25. Only the introductory phrase ἕως ἂν was taken from Isa 42:4b which begins with אד. This interpretation also better explains the origin of the verb ἐκβάλλειν, which is more suitable as a translation of יצא than of שים.[79]

After so many discrepancies between Matthew's text and the LXX that have been noted in Matt 12:18–20, the concluding clause in Matt 12:21 comes as a surprise.[80] It is suddenly almost in complete accord with the LXX, which for its part departs from the MT significantly. Thus only Matthew and the

---

Testament, 114–115; Lindars, *The New Testament Apologetic*, 149; J. Grindel, "Matthew 12:18–21," *CBQ* 29 (1967): 113–115.

[76]Cf. Rahlfs, "Über Theodotion-Lesarten im Neuen Testament," 186–189. Unfortunately, Aquila's translation of Hab 1:4 is missing. 1 Cor 15:54, which quotes Isa 25:8, also follows Aquila and translates לנצח with εἰς νῖκος.

[77]J. de Waard, *A Comparative Study of the Old Testament Text in the Dead Sea Scrolls and in the New Testament*, STDJ 4 (Leiden: Brill, 1965), 68–70.

[78]De Waard used the old numbering of columns (given in parenthesis) proposed by E. L. Sukenik, *The Dead Sea Scrolls of the Hebrew University* (Jerusalem: Magnes, 1955). The numbering adopted here is based on the reconstruction offered by É. Puech, "Quelques aspects de la restauration du Rouleau des Hymnes (1QH)," *JJS* 39 (1988): 38–55, and used by García Martínez, F. and E. J.C. Tigchelaar, ed. *The Dead Sea Scrolls Study Edition*. 2 vols. Leiden/ Boston: Brill; Grand Rapids: Eerdmans, 2000.

[79]Cf. 2 Chr 23:14; 29:5, 16; Ezra 10:3, where the LXX translates הוציא with ἐκβάλλειν. J. Grindel ("Matthew 12,18–21,"113) points out that this is not a typical translation of the LXX for יצא. It is also significant that the LXX never translates שים with ἐκβάλλειν.

[80]This unexpected agreement with the LXX induced some scholars, such as B. W. Bacon (*Studies in Matthew* [New York: H. Holt, 1930], 475), J. Jeremias, ("Ἀμνὸς τοῦ θεοῦ – παῖς θεοῦ," *ZNW* 34 [1935]: 119–120), and G. D. Kilpatrick (*The Origins of the Gospel according to St. Matthew*, 94) to argue that this verse is an interpolation. However, the external evidence (the omission of the verse in minuscule 33) for this hypothesis is weak.

LXX render ולחורתו with τῷ ὀνόματι, whereas all other Greek versions correctly translate the Hebrew with τῷ νόμῳ. Matthew's choice of ἔθνη for איים also conforms to the LXX, which otherwise translates this Hebrew word this way only here and in Isa 41:5. The only difference between Matthew and the LXX is that the former contains the classical Greek construction, dative + ἐλπίζω, whereas the latter uses the preposition ἐπί. Some scholars have argued that this discrepancy speaks in favor of two independent traditions, with the underlying Hebrew text which was different from the one preserved in the MT.[81] This hypothesis, which assumes that the original text contained the noun שם, is considerably weakened by the observation that a confusion between ὄνομα and νόμος was a typical scribal error in the LXX.[82] It is therefore more plausible to assume that in 12:21 Matthew chose to follow the LXX than to speculate that he had a different Hebrew text.

The occasional departures of Matthew's text from the MT and the LXX seem to be motivated by his desire to conform the scriptural text to the career of Jesus. Such a conclusion can be readily made on the basis of the introductory clause in Matt 12:17, which explicitly claims that both Jesus' healings and the request for silence represent the fulfillment of Scripture. Yet, it has been often pointed out that the citation is unnecessarily long because it contains the material which goes beyond the requirements of its immediate context. It appears that only verses 19–20b can be explicitly tied to the narrative, whereas both the beginning (Matt 12:18) and the closing (Matt 12:20c–21) seem to refer to a broader scope of Jesus' ministry. In the following, I will seek to demonstrate that the entire quotation has the purpose of showing that Jesus' healings belong to the domain of Jesus' messianic chores and as such fulfill the Scripture. The presumably "superfluous" additions at the beginning and the end have the task of putting the quotation into the messianic framework, which firmly ties some features of the traditional Jewish expectations of the Davidic Messiah with the Matthean narrative.

(a) κάλαμον συντετριμμένον οὐ κατεάξει καὶ λίνον τυφόμενον οὐ σβέσει (Matt 12:20a)

I will start with the most obvious link between the quotation and the narrative. The main assertion of Matt 12:20a is that the servant "will not break a bruised reed or quench a smoldering wick." In contrast to the rest of the quotation, the meaning of this verse is metaphorical.[83] It is generally recognized that it refers

---

[81] J. Ziegler, *Untersuchungen zur Septuaginta des Buches Isaias*, ATA 12/3 (Münster: Aschendorff, 1934), 141; Gundry, *The Use of the Old Testament*, 115; Rothfuchs, *Die Erfüllungszitate des Matthäus-Evengeliums*, 76–77.

[82] See LXX Ps 118:165; 2 Chr 6:16; Exod 16:4.

[83] Cf. the Isaiah Targum, which clarifies the metaphor by turning it into an explicit comparison: "The poor who are like a bruised reed he will not break, and the needy who are

to Jesus' healings because they are mentioned in the most immediate context of the citation (Matt 12:15).[84] Also, Matthew's description of the crowds in 9:36 as harassed and helpless (ἐσκυλμένοι καὶ ἐριμμένοι)[85] fits well with the idea of powerlessness of the recipients mentioned in Matt 12:20a. The former is found in the follow-up of the summary of Jesus' activity in Matt 9:35, which echoes the programmatic summary in Matt 4:23 and thus concludes the cycle of Jesus' words and deeds in chapters 5–9. In view of the diversity of the material in these chapters and the summaries themselves, it would be certainly incorrect to limit the description of the helplessness of the crowds to the sick only.[86] Matt 9:36 likens them to the sheep without a shepherd, which undoubtedly refers to a more comprehensive experience of lostness that includes both physical and spiritual dimensions.

And yet, Jesus' compassionate response (ἐσπλαγχνίσθη περὶ αὐτῶν), which in Matt 9:36 appears as a direct outcome of his perception of the crowds as harassed and helpless, is in Matthew's Gospel regularly presented as Jesus' reaction to the physical suffering of the people. Thus Matt 14:13–14,[87] which betrays the same interest in Jesus' compassion, explicitly links the latter to Jesus' healing activity. More significantly, this is achieved only through Matthew's redaction of the Markan material, i.e. through his replacement of the clause "and he began to teach them many things" (καὶ ἤρξατο διδάσκειν αὐτοὺς πολλά – Mark 6:34b) with "and he healed their sick" (καὶ ἐθεράπευσεν τοὺς ἀρρώστους αὐτῶν – Matt 14:14b).[88] In this way Matthew connected Jesus' compassion not with his teaching, as Mark, but with his healings. In Matt 20:34, Jesus' compassion is provoked by the sight of the two

---

like a dimly burning wick he will not quench" (עֲנַוְתָנִיָּא דְּכְנֵי רְעִיעַ לָא יְתַבַּר וַחֲשִׁיכַיָּא דִכְבוּצִין עֲמִי לָא יַטְפֵי).

[84]Trilling, *Das wahre Israel*, 103, 126; Lohmeyer, *Das Evangelium des Matthäus*, 187; Barth, "Matthew's Understanding of the Law," 128; Neyrey, "The Thematic Use," 470; Verseput, *The Rejection of the Humble Messianic King*, 200.

[85]This description is Matthew's own addition to the material found in Mark 6:34.

[86]This point is emphasized by G. Barth ("Matthew's Understanding of the Law," 128), who links Matt 12:20 not only to the description of the crowds in Matt 9:36, but also to 11:28 (οἱ κοπιῶντες καὶ πεφορτισμένοι). Barth finds support for this inference in the concluding statement of Matt 12:20 (ἕως ἂν ἐκβάλῃ εἰς νῖκος τὴν κρίσιν), which indicates that the first part of v. 20 should not be limited to the sick only, but must include Jesus' entire ministry which will be brought to victory. A similar argument is presented by D. Hill ("Son and Servant," 12) who also notes the concluding statement in Matt 12:20 and suggests that the preceding metaphor should be broadened to include not only those who are sick but also the weak, the lost, and the broken.

[87]This is another summary of Jesus' activity based on Mark 6:34.

[88]Another example of Matthew's replacement of Markan reference to teaching with the reference to healing can be found in Matt 19:2. A comparison with Mark 10:1, its Markan source, reveals that instead of the clause "and again, as his custom was, he taught them (καὶ ὡς εἰώθει πάλιν ἐδίδασκεν αὐτούς), Matthew wrote "and he healed them there" (καὶ ἐθεράπευσεν αὐτοὺς ἐκεῖ).

blind men, who beseech him for mercy in his capacity as the Son of David. In this case, the text relates the verbs σπλαγχνίζομαι and ἐλεέω.[89] The latter also regularly appears in the context of human suffering and misery. It is therefore safe to assume that the two metaphorical clauses in Matt 12:20a refer primarily, though not exclusively, to Jesus' compassionate behavior to the sick and suffering.

(b) ἕως ἂν ἐκβάλῃ εἰς νῖκος τὴν κρίσιν (Matt 12:20b)

The concluding statement in Matt 12:20 is directly related to the first two assertions in the same verse. It speaks about the final victory of κρίσις, which also sets up the time limit of the activities described previously. The meaning of κρίσις, however, is far from being clear. It can denote either judgment or justice, and a decision in this regard depends on one's view of the role of this concept in v. 18d (καὶ κρίσιν τοῖς ἔθνεσιν ἀπαγγελεῖ), which is part of the citation itself, as well as its meaning in the Matthean narrative. The interpretation that is usually favored is that κρίσις refers to the final judgment alluded to throughout chapter 12, especially in verse 36 (ἡμέρα κρίσεως).[90] This approach juxtaposes the statements in verses 18d and 20b and reads the meaning of κρίσις from the former into the latter. It remains unclear, however, how to relate this understanding to the first part of verse 20a, which, according to the scholarly consensus, refers to Jesus' gentle behavior towards the sick and needy. Why would the final judgment function as a time constraint of Jesus' engagement on behalf of the unfortunate, and what is the sense of the claim that it will be brought to victory? Since this relationship between the elements in the quoted verse was brought about by Matthew's targumized rendering of Isa 42:3–4, this aspect of the citation must be accounted for in any attempt to clarify its meaning in Matthew's narrative.

The first part of Matt 12:20 suggests that in all likelihood the term κρίσις here refers to the justice which intervenes on behalf of the weak, despised, and the helpless, i.e. those whose rights need to be protected.[91] Ps 72 presents this obligation as a royal task. The duty of the king is to judge the poor with justice (κρίνειν ... τοὺς πτωχούς σου ἐν κρίσει – Ps 71:2 LXX), to defend their cause (κρινεῖ τοὺς πτωχοὺς τοῦ λαοῦ – Ps 71:4a LXX), and to give deliverance to

---

[89]Cf. also a similar relatedness of both verbs in the parable of the unforgiving servant (Matt 18:21–34), which contains another reference to σπλαγχνίζομαι, though not applied to Jesus. The last occurrence of this verb can be found in Matt 15:32, which introduces the miracle of the feeding of the four thousand. Even though in this particular case Jesus' compassion is not directed toward the sick, but those who are hungry, it is still a reaction to physical and not spiritual affliction.

[90]F. Hahn, *Das Verständnis der Mission im Neuen Testament*, WMANT 13 (Neukirchen-Vluyn: Neukirchener Verlag, 1963), 109–110; Verseput, *The Rejection of the Humble Messianic King*, 201.

[91]Cf. Hill, "Son and Servant," 12.

the needy (σώσει τοὺς υἱοὺς τῶν πενήτων – Ps 71:4b LXX).[92] It is true that Psalm 72 speaks about the protection of the poor and not the healing of the sick. Yet it can be shown that Matthew ties this category of people directly to those who need physical healing. In Matt 11:5, they together comprise the group of the recipients of Jesus' messianic deeds: the blind (τυφλοί), the lame (χωλοί), lepers (λεπροί), the deaf (κωφοί), the dead (νεκροί), and the poor (πτωχοί). It can be therefore said that the sick and suffering, who appear to comprise the primary reference of the metaphors in Matt 12:20a, belong to all those who need help and protection,[93] until the justice ultimately prevails and this protection is no longer needed.[94] For Matthew, this is the royal task, which Jesus as the kingly Messiah faithfully fulfills in his career.

(c) οὐκ ἐρίσει οὐδὲ κραυγάσει, οὐδὲ ἀκούσει τις ἐν ταῖς πλατείαις τὴν φωνὴν αὐτοῦ (Matt 12:19)

This clause is commonly understood as referring to the quiet nature of Jesus' ministry, exemplified either in the silence that was required from the cured (Matt 12:16)[95] or in Jesus' withdrawal from the Jewish leaders and his refusal to engage in controversy and polemic (Matt 12:15a).[96] The latter has been especially emphasized by Krister Stendahl who found support for his view in the forensic nature of the verb ἐρίζειν ("to shout complainingly," "to shout to obtain one's rights"), which hardly favors the idea of silence.[97] We have seen, however, that in Matthew the latter functions as an outcome of the former. Jesus requires secrecy of his identity in order to avoid the controversy about it. The continuation of the narrative in chapter 12 after the quotation of Isa 42:1–4 does not contradict this demand but rather exemplifies what happens if the silence is not maintained.

---

[92]Cf. also Ps 72:12–14 (71:12–14 LXX).

[93]Cf. the targumic reading of Isa 42:3, which likens the poor to a bruised reed, and the needy to a dimly burning wick.

[94]In favor of this view speaks the verbal link between the verb ἐκβάλλειν in Matt 12:20b and 12:24–28, where it refers to casting out demons. Cf. W. Grundmann, *Das Evangelium nach Matthäus* (Berlin: Evangelische Verlagsanstatt, 1968), 326, and Neyrey, "The Thematic Use," 466–467.

[95]Wrede, *The Messianic Secret,* 156; Cullmann, *The Christology of the New Testament,* 69.

[96]Barth, "Matthew's Understanding of the Law," 127; Hooker, *Jesus and the Servant,* 84; P. Bonnard, *L'Évangile selon Saint Matthieu,* 3rd ed., CNT (Genève: Labor et Fides, 1992), 178; Trunk, *Der Messianische Heiler,* 191. Many interpreters stress the cumulative effect of the command for silence and Jesus' withdrawal from controversy, which leaves the impression of the unobtrusive, quiet character of Jesus' behavior. Cf. Zahn, *Das Evangelium des Matthäus,* 451–452; Strecker, *Der Weg der Gerechtigkeit,* 70; Trilling, *Das wahre Israel,* 126; Gerhardsson, *The Mighty Acts of Jesus,* 24.

[97]Stendahl, *The School of St. Matthew,* 111. D. J. Verseput clarified this further by pointing out that "the translator is thus drawing out the picture of one who does not take action against those who wrong him" (*The Rejection of the Humble Messianic King,* 198).

It can be also noticed that this statement apparently contradicts the speaking character of the servant's mission, which creates a tension between the servant's restraint in acquiring his own rights and his active engagement in announcing judgment to the nations.[98] This tension which exists in the quotation itself, however, nicely concurs with Jesus' own behavior. In some occasions Matthew presents him as withdrawing from the Pharisees' murderous hostility, whereas in others as being actively engaged in the polemics with them.

(d) ἰδοὺ ὁ παῖς μου ὃν ᾑρέτισα, ὁ ἀγαπητός μου εἰς ὃν εὐδόκησεν ἡ ψυχή μου (Matt 12:18a)

In contrast to verses 19 and 20, which are generally recognized to refer to the introductory episode, i.e. to the report about Jesus' withdrawal, his healing the sick, and his request for secrecy, the first verse of the quotation seems to be completely unrelated to these issues. In view of great economy which Matthew shows otherwise when quoting Scripture,[99] there is no reason to suppose that he included the opening verse only because it preceded the passage he really wanted to quote. Isa 42:1 appears at the beginning of the citation because it has the task of qualifying the term ὁ παῖς μου by giving it an unmistakable messianic connotation. This is achieved through the introduction of the term ἀγαπητός from the baptismal tradition and linking it firmly to the term παῖς. In this way, the servant is identified from the outset as the beloved son, whom God confirmed as the Messiah at his baptism.[100]

This reconstruction seriously questions the common assumption that the baptismal story "has been written up around Isa 42:1."[101] This hypothesis, originally proposed by Joachim Jeremias,[102] claims the priority of servant over royal messianic categories in the *Bat Qol* at Jesus' baptism. It is not necessary to repeat some of the difficulties in explaining the transition from the servant to the messianic imagery, which have been mentioned in the preceding section. The examination of the text of the quotation of Isa 42:1 strengthens this critique because it indicates that this citation is not presupposed by but rather

---

[98] Cf. Neyrey, "The Thematic Use," 463–465.

[99] See, for example, the omission of the second half of Isa 53:4 in Matt 8:17.

[100] O. L. Cope (*Matthew: A Scribe Trained for the Kingdom of Heaven*, CBQMS 5 [Washington: The Catholic Biblical Association of America, 1976], 36) makes a similar claim by suggesting that "it is strongly to be suspected that Matthew has reshaped the opening lines to agree closely with the voice at the baptism in order to have the reader recall the messiahship of Jesus." Later, however, he links the term παῖς, which in his view can mean either servant or son, to Matt 12:46–50, where Jesus declares that those who do the will of his father are his brothers, sisters, and mothers (ibid., 49–50). The difficulty here is that the term παῖς does not lead into the concept of the son without the mediating force of the baptismal tradition, in which the latter functions as a messianic designation.

[101] Lindars, *New Testament Apologetic*, 146.

[102] Jeremias, "παῖς θεοῦ," 701–702.

presupposes the divine voice at Jesus' baptism. Especially the term ἀγαπητός cannot be explained on the basis of the textual history of Isa 42:1, but its origin must be looked for elsewhere,[103] presumably in the texts which were either recognized as or associated with the royal messianic traditions.

Ps 2:7 is the most likely candidate for the former, because it contains the declaration of the divine sonship of the anointed king. Despite the fact that there is no definite evidence that this psalm was interpreted messianically in pre-Christian Judaism,[104] it was often used by early Christian interpreters in their attempts to demonstrate that Jesus is the expected Messiah.[105] The earliest version of the first part of the *Bat Qol* found in Mark 1:11b (σὺ εἶ ὁ υἱός μου) strongly resembles the language of Ps 2:7 LXX (υἱός μου εἶ σύ). Moreover, the noun υἱός in the baptismal voice cannot be explained as a derivation of the original παῖς.[106] Finally, the targumic rendering of this psalm, "Beloved (חביב) as a son to his father you are to me," shows that Ps 2:7 could have been the source even for the term ἀγαπητός,[107] especially in view of the fact that the meaning of the latter as "the only son" is more suitable to the concept of υἱός than παῖς.[108] Another text which could have provided the language for the term ἀγαπητός is Gen 22:2, 12, 16, where Isaac is called Abraham's beloved son. Even though Genesis 22 was not a recognized messianic text in early Judaism, it played an important role in early Christian interpretation of Jesus' messiahship,[109] and could have been used, along with Ps 2:7, as a source of language in the baptismal tradition.[110]

Krister Stendahl has presented an additional argument for the priority of servant imagery in Jesus' baptism by claiming that the voice from heaven represents the (modified) citation of Isa 42:1 because the confirmation that

---

[103]M. Hooker (*Jesus and the Servant*, 70–71) made a detailed list of the Old Testament passages where the LXX uses the term ἀγαπητός. With the exception of Ps 67:12 and Isa 26:17, which seem to presuppose the Hebrew text that differs from the MT, ἀγαπητός appears as the translation of the following Hebrew terms: (1) יחיד (Gen 22:2, 12, 16; Amos 8:10; Jer 6:26; Judg 11:34; Zech 12:10), (2) ידיד (Pss 44:1 [45:1]; 59:7 [60:5]; 83:2 [84:1]; 107:7 [108:6]; 126:2 [127:2]; Isa 5:1, and (3) יקיר (Jer 38:20 [31:20]).

[104]See section 2.2.2.2.

[105]See section 2.2.2.3.

[106]Juel, *Messianic Exegesis*, 79.

[107]Suggested by Gundry, *The Use of the Old Testament*, 30, 112.

[108]M. Hooker (*Jesus and the Servant*, 71) noticed that all uses of the term ἀγαπητός in the LXX which translate יחיד and יקיר (Gen 22:2, 12, 16; Amos 8:10; Jer 6:26; Judg 11:34; Zech 12:10; Jer 38:20 [31:20]) refer to an only son (or daughter), and concluded that "it is almost identical in meaning with μονογενής." In her view, "this suggests that the origin of the word is to be found in the Old Testament concept of the only Son, rather than in that of the Servant."

[109]Gal 3:13–22; Rom 8:32.

[110]Juel, *Messianic Exegesis*, 79–80, 85–88; see also G. Vermes, "Redemption and Genesis xxii: The Binding of Isaac and the Sacrifice of Jesus," in *Scripture and Tradition in Judaism*, 2nd ed. (Leiden: E. J. Brill, 1973), 193–227; N. A. Dahl, "The Atonement: An Adequate Reward for the Akedah?" in *The Crucified Messiah*, 146–160.

follows is implied though not quoted.[111] In his view, only "such an interpretation makes the 'quotation' suitable as a proof-text about the spirit descending upon the Messiah."[112] There is no need to repeat the critique of this approach to the New Testament scriptural quotations. In this particular case, however, one should add that Isa 42:1 does not speak about the Spirit descending upon the Messiah, but upon the servant of Yahweh. Without a convincing explanation of the link between the two, the former statement remains dubious. Additionally, Stendahl overlooked the crucial role of the Spirit in Isa 11:1–2, a text which was, unlike Isa 42:1–2, generally considered messianic in early Jewish literature. The descent of the Spirit upon Jesus was understood from the beginning as the messianic anointing, which was primarily interpreted with the help of royal messianic categories. This is especially clear in the Gospel of Matthew, where the unusual expression [τὸ] πνεῦμα [τοῦ] θεοῦ (Matt 3:16) demonstrates that the author understood the descent of the Spirit in light of Isa 11:2.

In the reconstruction proposed here, the conflation of Ps 2:7 with Isa 42:1 in the account of Jesus' baptism represents the second stage in the interpretative tradition, after the baptism has been understood as the messianic anointing with the Spirit. Both texts were linked together not only because of the potential association of the Messiah and the servant of Yahweh in general, but also because of the reference to the Spirit in particular.

(e) θήσω τὸ πνεῦμά μου ἐπ' αὐτόν (Matt 12:18b)

The endowment with the Spirit is in Matthew's rendering of Isa 42:1 closely tied to the accomplishment of the activities enumerated in the rest of the quotation. Apart from the last clause in Matt 12:18c, which still remains to be clarified, the analysis so far has shown that all other duties are either directly or indirectly related to the cure of the sick. This relationship between the structural elements of the citation can be also detected in its narrative setting. In chapter 12, the possession of the Spirit is directly linked to Jesus' ability to heal, i.e. to the question by whose power and authority he performs the cures and, with this, to the question of his messianic identity.[113] Matt 12:28

---

[111]Stendahl acknowledges his indebtedness to the methodology of J. Jeremias in *The School of St. Matthew*, 110 n.1.

[112]Ibid.

[113]O. L. Cope (*Matthew,* 36) argued that the entire chapter 12 has been organized around the quotation of Isa 42:1–4. Even though some of his conclusions fail to convince, his main claim certainly holds true: "From the miracle story which introduced the debate to the closing sentence . . . the Beelzebul controversy in Matthew has shown a consistent, highly organized argument which has been constructed as support for the claim that the line in the Isaiah citation 'I will pour out my spirit upon him' applies to Jesus" (ibid., 39–40).

indicates that the endowment with the Spirit functions as the hermeneutical key of Jesus' miracles, which ultimately verifies his messiahship.[114]

(f) καὶ κρίσιν τοῖς ἔθνεσιν ἀπαγγελεῖ (Matt 12:18c)

This statement shows that the servant will be actively engaged in announcing κρίσις to the Gentiles.[115] The main question here is whether this term connotes judgment in the sense of divine denunciation of the nations along the lines of Matt 25:31–46 or not.[116] Since the noun ἔθνη appears twice in this quotation, here and in the concluding verse 21, and in view of the fact that the latter speaks about the hope of the nations, the term κρίσις appears to have a positive function, denoting justice rather than judgment.[117] This is especially evident in Matt 12:41–42, which describes the final resolution of the conflict between "this generation" on the one side and the "men of Nineveh" and "the queen of the South" on the other, which will take place ἐν τῇ κρίσει. This conflict, however, is not of a general nature,[118] but is more specifically defined within the context of chapter 12 as the conflict about Jesus' messianic identity. The controversy between Jesus and the Pharisees begins after the latter deny that Jesus is the Son of David. This denial takes the form of an accusation that Jesus casts out demons by the help of Beelzebul (Matt 12:22–24). Jesus' reply begins in verse 25 and ends in verses 36–37 with the reference to the Day of Judgment (ἐν ἡμέρᾳ κρίσεως), not having been interrupted by any additional comment by his adversaries. It represents therefore in its entirety an answer to the initial question. Jesus' second reference to judgment (Matt 12:41–42) follows up the Pharisaic demand for a sign, which also belongs to the same realm of the polemic about Jesus' messianic identity. Thus in both cases, the

---

[114]O. L. Cope has aptly summarized the logic of Matthew's argument: "Why should Jesus' exorcisms mean anything other than Pharisaic exorcisms? The answer lies in an assumption which does not appear in the argument. It is the contention that Jesus is the Messiah and activity on his part done by the power of the Holy Spirit would prove it, because this is promised to the Messiah in Isa 42:2, 'I will pour out my Spirit upon him.' In other words, if the Pharisees' charge is wrong, then the people's response is right and Jesus is the Son of David, and the Kingdom is dawning in the deeds of Jesus" (ibid., 38).

[115]J. H. Neyrey ("The Thematic Use," 462) argues that Matt 12:41–42 shows that the Gentiles listened to God's messengers but the Jews did not. He thus contrasts Gentile acceptance with Jewish rejection. Also vv. 46–50 should be, in his view, formally linked to Matt 12:18d because they broaden Jesus' family to include everyone who does God's will. Differently O. L. Cope (*Matthew*, 45), who links these verses to God's proclamation that Jesus is his son.

[116]Cf. McNeile, *The Gospel According to St. Matthew*, 172; Verseput, *The Rejection of the Humble Messianic King*, 197; Davies and Allison, *Matthew*, vol. 2, 325.

[117]Cf. Gundry, *Matthew*, 229.

[118]J. H. Neyrey's comment that "the hearers (Jew and Gentile) are confronted with God's word and must make a decision, a judgment in belief or unbelief," ("The Thematic Use," 462) is too indefinite.

Day of Judgment brings the final resolution of the polemical question of who Jesus is. Its outcome will be the ultimate vindication of the Gentiles and the condemnation of their Jewish counterparts.[119]

(g) καὶ τῷ ὀνόματι αὐτοῦ ἔθνη ἐλπιοῦσιν (Matt 12:21)

The citation ends in a thoroughly positive tone by asserting that the Gentiles will hope in "his name."[120] The latter is sometimes taken as a recognizable link with the context. Thus Jerome H. Neyrey points out that even though there is no reference to ὄνομα αὐτοῦ in chapter 12, it contains many Christological titles. Thus, Jesus is proclaimed as the Son of Man in 12:8, 40, the servant in 12:18, the Son of David in 12:23, the greater one in 12:6, 41, 42, and by virtue of the citation of Isa 42:1 at Jesus' baptism, also the Son of God.[121] Neyrey's proposal to look for a "name" of Jesus in the narrative context certainly deserves attention. Some of his suggestions, however, fail to convince because they do not represent the titles in the proper sense. Thus the term "Son of Man" is not a confession of Jesus' identity, but his self-designation. Similarly, none of the "greater than" descriptions can be properly called Jesus' names. Also, the term "my servant" in the citation itself remains an empty designation since there is no evidence that we can speak about a discernible concept of the "Servant" in the first century. We are thus left with only two titles from Neyrey's list, the Son of David and, through the mediating force of baptismal tradition, the Son of God. In this context, both of them refer to Jesus' messiahship.

The reference to the hope of the Gentiles appears to serve a similar purpose, especially in view of the postulation that Matthew's decision to follow the LXX in Mat 12:21 might have been motivated by a desire to make an allusion to Isa 11:10b (ἐπ' αὐτῷ ἔθνη ἐλπιοῦσιν; אליו גוים ידרשו [MT]),[122] which is linked to the promise of David's descendant who will rule the nations. The relationship of the Gentiles to the expected Davidic Messiah is especially elaborated in *Pss. Sol.* 17. This psalm on the one hand portrays the Gentiles as the foreign intruders from whom Jerusalem should be purged (καθάρισον Ἰερουσαλὴμ ἀπὸ ἐθνῶν – *Pss. Sol.* 17:22b) and who will eventually serve under the yoke of the Son of David (καὶ ἕξει λαοὺς ἐθνῶν δουλεύειν αὐτῷ ὑπὸ τόν ζυγὸν αὐτοῦ – *Pss. Sol.* 17:30). On the other hand, their relationship to the future Davidic ruler is utterly positive. They will come from the ends of the

---

[119]Cf. also Matt 10:15; 11:22, 24.

[120]An interpretation which assumes that Matt 12:18d refers to the proclamation of the divine verdict to the Gentiles has the task of explaining the apparent tension between this verse and Matt 12:21. D. Verseput, for example, softens the idea of judgment through the notion of mercy: "His victorious accomplishment of the divine decision would result in bringing them an expectation of mercy" (*The Rejection of the Humble Messianic King*, 202).

[121]Neyrey, "The Thematic Use," 465.

[122]Cf. Rom 15:12.

earth to see his glory (ἔρχεσθαι ἔθνη ἀπ' ἄκρου τῆς γῆς ἰδεῖν τὴν δόξαν αὐτοῦ – *Pss. Sol.* 17:31), and he will be a righteous king over them (καὶ αὐτὸς βασιλεὺς δίκαιος . . . ἐπ' αὐτούς – *Pss. Sol.* 17:32). They will thus participate in the blessings of the messianic time initially promised only to Israel.[123]

Matthew's narrative itself offers support for the conclusion that the reference to the Gentiles who will hope in "his name," which concludes Matthew's quotation of Isa 42:1–4, should be understood as a final reminder that the entire citation refers to the Messiah. As already noted above, Matt 12:41–42 refers to the ultimate resolution of the polemical question whether Jesus is the Messiah or not, which will put the Gentiles in a far better position than the unbelieving Jews. Additionally, even though there is not much evidence that Matthew was interested in the question of the mission to the Gentiles,[124] he intentionally added a Gentile woman to a few who were able to recognize Jesus as the Son of David. The episode in Matt 15:21–28 demonstrates that a foreign woman, despite being initially rejected in her plea for help, put her hope in the Davidic Messiah, expecting from him mercy along the lines of *Pss. Sol.* 17:34b (καὶ ἐλεήσει πάντα τὰ ἔθνη), and was not disappointed.

We can thus conclude that Matt 12:15–21 contains a skillfully constructed argument with a demonstrable scriptural proof that Jesus' healings properly belong to the realm of his messianic duties. The text of the quotation has been adapted to the double task it aims to achieve – to be applicable to Jesus' career on the one hand, and to be perceived as the messianic text on the other.

---

[123]There is also a notable similarity between the presentation of God's mercy to Israel which will characterize the messianic time (17:45; 18:5, 9), and the promise that the Messiah will be compassionate to all the nations (καὶ ἐλεήσει πάντα τὰ ἔθνη – *Pss. Sol.* 17:34b).

[124]Cf. Jesus' command to his disciples not to go anywhere among the Gentiles, but only to the lost sheep of the house of Israel (Matt 10:5–6). There are, however, other passages which either present the Gentile characters in a more positive light than their Jewish counterparts or betray the universal character of Matthew's Gospel: the mention of the four foreign women in Matthew's genealogy (Matt 1:1–17), the coming of the wise men from the East to visit the infant Messiah (Matt 2:1–12), the reference to the Galilee of the Gentiles (Matt 4:15), the healing of the servant of a Gentile centurion (Matt 8:5–13), and finally the great commission to the disciples to go and preach the gospel to all nations (Matt 28:16–20). For a discussion of this aspect of Matthew's narrative, see R. T. France, "The Formula-Quotations of Matthew 2 and the Problem of Communication," *NTS* 27 (1980/1981): 237–240; idem, "Exegesis in Practice: Two Samples," in *New Testament Interpretation: Essays on Principles and Methods*, ed. I. H. Marshall (Exeter: Paternoster, 1977), 253–264; D. R. A. Hare and D. J. Harrington, "'Make Disciples of all the Gentiles' (Mt 28:19)," *CBQ* 37 (1975): 359–369; Trilling, *Das wahre Israel*, 26–28; B. J. Hubbard, *The Matthean Redaction of a Primitive Apostolic Commissioning: An Exegesis of Matthew 28:16–20*, SBLDS 19 (Missoula: Scholars Press, 1974), 84–87; J. P. Meier, "Nations or Gentiles in Matthew 28:19?" *CBQ* 39 (1977): 94–102; Gundry, *Matthew*, 595–596; S. Brown, "The Matthean Community and the Gentile Mission," *NovT* 22 (1980): 193–221; L. Gaston, "The Messiah of Israel as Teacher of the Gentiles: The Setting of Matthew's Christology," *Int* 29 (1975): 24–40.

4.3 Jesus' Healings as the Messianic Deeds

4.3.1 Jesus' Dialogue with the Disciples of John the Baptist

The significance of Matt 11:2–6 lies in its unique classification of Jesus' miracles as the deeds of the Messiah (τὰ ἔργα τοῦ χριστοῦ). This is the only text that establishes a direct relationship between the healing miracles and Jesus' messianic identity by qualifying the former as his messianic "works." Apart from this succinct designation which appears in the introduction to the main scene, the text consists of a question of John the Baptist communicated through his disciples to which Jesus answers in an indirect way by enumerating the wonders which are currently taking place.

This summary, however, differs from other summaries in Matthew's Gospel in two significant ways. Formally speaking, this is not a summary of the narrator, but of Jesus himself. More significantly, there is no formula quotation attached to it because this is neither a direct quotation of an Old Testament text, nor a passage to which an explicit quotation is appended. Rather, the summary itself represents a conflation of several Old Testament passages and it will be shown below that its argumentative force lies precisely in its ability to evoke the memory of these texts. The parallel to Matt 11:2–6 can be found in Luke 7:18–23, which indicates that this tradition comes from Q. Matthew narrates how John the Baptist, who has been already imprisoned (Matt 4:13), heard of the deeds of the Messiah (τὰ ἔργα τοῦ χριστοῦ), and sent his disciples to ask Jesus whether he was "the Coming One" (ὁ ἐρχόμενος) or they should wait for another.

Matthew's account about the meeting between Jesus and the disciples of John is characteristically brief when compared with the parallel account in Luke. In contrast to the latter, Matthew does not mention that Jesus was performing miracles of healing and exorcism at the time of the encounter with John's disciples. For this reason Jesus' answer to his visitors, which begins with, "Go and tell John what you hear and see" (πορευθέντες ἀπαγγείλατε Ἰωάννῃ ἃ ἀκούετε καὶ βλέπετε – 11:4), clearly refers back to chapters 5–9. This impression is strengthened by Matthew's reversal of order of ἃ ἀκούετε καὶ βλέπετε, in contrast to Luke who has ἃ εἴδετε καὶ ἠκούσατε (Luke 7:22). The list first mentions five different types of Jesus' miracles, all of which are exemplified in Matt 8–9. The healing of the blind is described in Matt 9:27–31, the healing of the lame in Matt 9:2–8, the cleansing of the leper in Matt 8:1–4, the healing of the deaf in Matt 9:32–34, and the raising of the dead in Matt 9:18–26. Finally, the preaching of the good news has its counterpart in the Sermon on the Mount. There is little doubt that the interpretation of the intriguing phrase τὰ ἔργα τοῦ χριστοῦ, which Matthew added to the Q material, depends on the understanding of the question of John the Baptist and the answer Jesus gave him. To these issues we now turn.

4.3.2 The Question (Matt 11:3)

The question "Are you he who is to come or should we wait for another?" (σὺ εἶ ὁ ἐρχόμενος ἢ ἕτερον προσδοκῶμεν) expresses a genuine bewilderment of John and demonstrates his inability to relate the reports about Jesus' miracles and the question of Jesus' messianic identity.[125] As such it stands in a definite tension to the phrase τὰ ἔργα τοῦ χριστοῦ, which correlates the two in a most direct manner. John's question confirms the general impression from early Jewish literature the miracles were not the messianic signs. They were not able to authenticate the messianic claim in any clear fashion because the Messiah was not expected to be a wonder-worker. Yet on the other hand, the question demonstrates that the miracles could have given rise to the query of one's eventual messianic identity. The text presupposes a certain correlation between the two, but this relationship remains ambiguous and unspecified.

In Matthew, the term ὁ ἐρχόμενος is a messianic designation. Even if its usage in Matt 3:11 (ὁ δὲ ὀπίσω μου ἐρχόμενος ἰσχυρότερός μού ἐστιν) might be ambiguous,[126] its appearance in Matt 21:9 (ὡσαννὰ τῷ υἱῷ Δαυίδ. εὐλογημένος ὁ ἐρχόμενος ἐν ὀνόματι κυρίου)[127] clearly demonstrates that it refers to the royal Messiah of the Davidic line. John the Baptist thus appears to be asking whether Jesus is the expected Davidic Messiah or not. However, this impression is only partly correct, because the second part of the question indicates that the alternative is not to simply dismiss the hope that Jesus is the Messiah, even though this is implied, but to wait for another (ἢ ἕτερον προσδοκῶμεν).

August Strobel has cogently shown that this alternative reflects a dilemma that has been created by the experience of the delay of the expected end-time events, whose scriptural basis can be found in Hab 2:3.[128] This text offers an assurance to the reader that even if the end seems to be delayed, he/she should wait for it: "For there is still a vision for the appointed time; it speaks of the

---

[125]It is not surprising that John's question represented an embarrassment for the church. With the exception of Tertullian, who believed that the Spirit was taken from John (*Adv. Marc.* 18), most of the church Fathers declared that the question was asked for John's disciples' sake. See *The Ante-Nicene Fathers*, vol. 3, 375 n. 15. A. Strobel (*Untersuchungen zum eschatologischen Verzögerungsproblem*, NovTSup 2 [Leiden/Köln: E. J. Brill, 1961], 267–272) argued that the embarrassment created by John's question speaks in favor of its historicity. John's question also creates a breach in the plot of Matthew's narrative, because Matt 3:11–17 gives the impression that he knew who Jesus was.

[126]For a succinct discussion of various possibilities see Davies and Allison, *Matthew*, vol. 1, 312–314.

[127]The same phrase (εὐλογημένος ὁ ἐρχόμενος ἐν ὀνόματι κυρίου) occurs again in Matt 23:39.

[128]Strobel, *Untersuchungen zum eschatologischen Verzögerungsproblem*, 265–277. Other candidates are various references to the eschatological coming of God (Isa 40:10, Zech 14:5) or his representative (Ps 118:26, Mal 3:1–2), but none of them contains the reference(s) to the possibility of waiting.

end, and does not lie. If it seems to tarry, wait for it; it will surely come, it will not delay" (כי עוד חזון למועד ויפח לקץ ולא יכזב אם־יתמהמה חכה־לו כי־בא יבא לא יאחר [MT]; διότι ἔτι ὅρασις εἰς καιρὸν καὶ ἀνατελεῖ εἰς πέρας καὶ οὐκ εἰς κενόν ἐὰν ὑστερήσῃ ὑπόμεινον αὐτόν ὅτι ἐρχόμενος ἥξει καὶ οὐ μὴ χρονίσῃ [LXX]).

Matthew's text is especially close to Aquila's translation of Hab 2:3b: ἐὰν [δὲ] μελλήσῃ, προσδέχου αὐτόν, ὅτι ἐρχόμενος ἥξει καὶ οὐ βραδυνεῖ. This suggests that John's question should be interpreted within the parameters set up by this scriptural text and its subsequent messianic interpretation.[129]

One of the clearest references to Hab 2:3 can be found in 1QpHab 7.5–14, which divides this verse into two parts. Hab 2:3a is quoted in lines 5–6 followed by a commentary in lines 7–8. Hab 2:3b is quoted in lines 9–10 followed by a commentary in lines 10–14. The entire section is preceded by the well-known reference to the Righteous Teacher, to whom God made known all the mysteries of the words of his servants the prophets (כול רזי דברי עבדיו הנבאים).[130] The pesher on Hab 2:3a relates the prophecy concerning the appointed time and the assurance that "it will not deceive" (ולוא יכזב)[131] to the prolongation of the last end-time (יארוך[132] הקץ האחרון).[133] This additional qualification of the term קץ has the purpose of clarifying that it refers to the eschatological time.[134] Since the verb in question is either Qal imperfect (יארוך) or Hiph'il imperfect (יאריך) from ארך,[135] it can be translated either as "will be prolonged"[136] or "will be delayed in coming."[137] The latter implies that God is the subject who causes the prolongation of the coming of the end-time. This conclusion is confirmed in the pesher on the second half of Hab 2:3.

---

[129]For a comprehensive analysis of all passages found in early Jewish and Christian literature which betray the influence of Hab 2:3, see ibid., 7–170. For our purposes here, however, only those which can be related to Matt 11:3 and its messianic outlook are relevant.

[130]1QpHab 7.5.

[131]1QpHab 7.6.

[132]Instead of Qal imperfect it is possible to read Hiph'il imperfect יאריך, as proposed by Y. Ratzaby, "Remarks Concerning the Distinction Between Waw and Yodh in the Habakkuk Scroll," JQR 41 (1950–51): 157; see, however, the objection by E. Qimron, The Hebrew of the Dead Sea Scrolls, HSS 29 (Atlanta: Scholars Press, 1986), 311.112.

[133]1QpHab 7.7.

[134]Cf. W. H. Brownlee, The Midrash Pesher of Habakkuk, SBLMS 24 (Missoula: Scholars Press, 1979), 115.

[135]Ibid.; M. P. Horgan, Pesharim: Qumran Interpretations of Biblical Books, CBQMS 8 (Washington, D.C.: The Catholic Biblical Association of America, 1979), 38.

[136]Horgan, Pesharim, 16.

[137]S. Talmon, "Notes on the Habakkuk Scroll," VT 1 (1951): 35. A. Strobel (Untersuchungen zum eschatologischen Verzögerungsproblem, 10–11, 161–170) similarly argues that the last phrase from Hab 2:3, ולוא יאחר, which appears in 1QpHab 7.9–10, can be parsed either as Pi'el imperfect ("be late" but also "cause to be late" = "delay") or Pu'al imperfect ("being delayed").

The problem that the men of truth (אנשי האמת)[138] might encounter "when the last end-time is drawn out for them" (בהמשך עליהם הקץ האחרון)[139] is solved by claiming that "all of God's end-times will come according to their fixed order, as he decreed for them in the mysteries of his prudence" (כול קיציﹶﹶ[140] אל יבואו לתכונם כאשר חקק להם ברזי ערמתו).[141] The solution to the apparent delay of the end-time events is found in the affirmation of God's predetermined design of all affairs on the one side, and human inability to penetrate it on the other. In this way, the reality of the delay is denied and it is treated as a mere, indeed erroneous human impression that is contrasted to the firm belief that everything is going to take place in the time that has been predestined by the divine decree.

The interpretation of Hab 2:3 in 1QpHab 7.5–14 thus appears to have a double aim: to warn from an uncontrolled enthusiastic expectation of the near end, and to encourage faith in the coming of the promised future salvation.[142] Yet, since the text neither mentions nor hints at any role of the Messiah in this scenario, it would be incorrect to say that the Habakkuk Pesher interprets Hab 2:3 messianically.[143] It does, however, demonstrate the application of this

---

[138] 1QpHab 7.10.

[139] 1QpHab 7.12.

[140] קיציﹶ is the plural construct of קץ, spelled in an unusual way with the first י representing a short i-vowel; cf. Horgan, *Pesharim*, 39.

[141] 1QpHab 7.13–14.

[142] Cf. Strobel, *Untersuchungen zum eschatologischen Verzögerungsproblem*, 9. According to S. Talmon, the Qumran covenanters initially expected the advent of the future eon "at a tangibly near juncture in history," but later transposed their expectation "to a not anymore datable juncture in history" ("Types of Messianic Expectation at the Turn of the Era," in *King, Cult and Calendar in Ancient Israel* [Jerusalem: Magnes Press; Leiden: Brill, 1986], 215) See also H.-W. Kuhn, *Enderwartung und gegenwärtiges Heil: Untersuchungen zu den Gemeindeliedern von Qumran mit einem Anhang über Eschatologie und Gegenwart in der Verkündigung Jesu*, SUNT 4 (Göttingen: Vandenhoeck & Ruprecht, 1966).

[143] So Strobel, *Untersuchungen zum eschatologischen Verzögerungsproblem*, 9. He believes that "die Unterscheidung von messianischem und eschatologischem Zeitalter kann gegen den Tatbestand der Naherwartung der Sekte nicht ins Feld geführt werden, weil beide zusammengehören und eine unteilbare Hoffnung bilden." It remains unclear, however, in which sense Strobel uses the terms "messianic" and "eschatological." It seems that he applies the former to the near-end expectation and the latter to the future-end expectation. Thereby he completely neglects the question of the presence/absence of the Messiah. Since methodologically we cannot label a certain text "messianic" if it does not contain a reference to the Messiah, it will be incorrect to claim that 1QpHab 7.5–14 interprets Hab 2:3 messianically. J. H. Charlesworth repeatedly called attention to the diversity of Qumran messianic expectations. In his essay "Challenging the *Consensus Communis* Regarding Qumran Messianism (1QS, 4QS MSS)" in *Qumran-Messianism: Studies on the Messianic Expectations in the Dead Sea Scrolls*, ed. J. H. Charlesworth, H. Lichtenberger, and G. S. Oegema [Tübingen: Mohr Siebeck, 1999], 120–134), Charlesworth points out that some documents, such as the *War Scroll*, demonstrate that "the idea that God alone will resolve all the problems in the cosmos, and will not depend on any messiah or archangel was popular at

biblical text to the end-time events and to the experience of their eventual delay.

The targumic reading of Hab 2:3 betrays a similar conviction to the one found in 1QpHab 7.13 that the end has been predetermined by God, and affirms that despite the reader's impression of a delay, the end will occur when the time set up by the divine decree comes: "For the prophecy is ready for a time and the end (קצא) is fixed, nor shall it fail; if there is delay (ארכא)[144] in the matter wait for it, for it shall come in its time and shall not be deferred (ולא יתעכב)."

The messianic interpretation of this biblical passage can be found in the rabbinic literature, which treats the question of the delay of the coming of the Messiah to a greater length. *b. Sanh.* 97a contains a passage in which the rabbis discuss the time of the appearance of the Son of David. The periodization of time into the seven year cycles, at the end of which the Son of David will appear, is questioned by Rav Yosef, who remarks, "Surely many Sabbatical cycles were like that, and he [the Son of David] did not come!"[145] The explicit quotation of Hab 2:3 and its subsequent discussion appears in *b. Sanh.* 97b. On the basis of this scriptural text Rabbi Natan argues that any calculation of the end should be given up. The text then addresses the problem of the delay of the coming of the Messiah, which is articulated by Rabbi Shamuel bar Nahmani, who spoke in the name of Rabbi Yohanan: "May those who calculate the end (קיצין) swell up, for they said: Since the designated time came, and he did not come, he will no longer come."[146] The solution to this problem is found in the idea of waiting, for which Hab 2:3 offers scriptural justification. Thus Rabbi Shamuel continues: "Rather, wait for him, as it is stated, 'Though it tarry, wait for it.'"[147]

One important aspect of the rabbinic treatment of the delay of the coming of the Messiah is the discussion of the reason(s) for his apparent delay. In *b. Sanh.* 97b, the puzzling question takes the form: "And since we are waiting, and He [God] waits, who is preventing (מי מעכב) [him]?"[148] Two

---

Qumran in the first century B.C.E." (ibid., 125). He concludes that "messianism at Qumran may never have been the most dominant theological concern," because "the Qumran messianic belief is conspicuously absent in many major Qumran works, especially the *Hodayoth*, the *War Scroll* (cf. 1QM 11.7), and the *Qumran Pseudepigraphic Psalms, Daily Prayers*, and all the Pesharim" (ibid., 133).

[144]Cf. the interpretation of Hab 2:3a in 1QpHab 7.7 which begins with פשרו אשר יארוך הקץ האחרון.

[145]For the Hebrew text, English translation, and the commentary by Rabbi Adin Steinsaltz see *The Talmud: The Steinsaltz Edition*, vol 21: *Tractate Sanhedrin*, part 7 (New York: Random House, 1999), 4.

[146]Ibid., 11.

[147]Ibid.

[148]Ibid. A. Strobel (*Untersuchungen zum eschatologischen Verzögerungsproblem*, 20) notes that מעכב takes the role of יאחר because the Jewish-Aramaic verb עכב ("delay") was in

fundamentally different answers have been offered. The first sees the reason for the delay in the deficiencies of the people who do not appear worthy of it,[149] whereas the second affirms the sovereignty of God and his divine decree,[150] even though there was an awareness of the incongruity between the two.[151] The former view is also found in *Pesiq. Rab.* 34, which contains the claim that behind an ostensible delay of the appearance of the Messiah stands God's mysterious design: "And all the good things that I intend to bestow upon you are on account of the Messiah who has been kept in confinement all these years."[152]

Certain passages from first-century apocalyptic literature demonstrate that we are dealing here with a very old tradition. In *4 Ezra* 12:32, the lion which appears in Ezra's fifth vision is deciphered as the reference to the Davidic Messiah: "This is the Messiah whom the Most High has kept until the end of days (*his est unctus, quem reservavit Altissimus in finem*), who will arise from the posterity of David." A similar notion about the Messiah who has been kept in secrecy by God until the coming of the appointed time for his appearance is found in *4 Ezra* 13:26–27: "As for your seeing a man come up from the heart

---

this time much more common than Pi'el or Pu'al of אחר. This change can be already noted in the targumic rendering of Hab 2:3, which replaces לא יאחר with ולא יתעכב (see above). For the evidence see Jastrow, *A Dictionary of the Targumim, The Talmud Babli und Yerushalmi and the Midrashic Literature,* vol. 1, part 2, 1077b. 1078a.

[149]"[A Sage] of the School of Eliyahu taught: 'The world will exist for six thousand years: Two thousand years of chaos, two thousand years of Torah, two thousand years of the days of the Messiah. But because of our transgressions which were many [the Messiah did not come at the end of the fourth millennium], what came out came out [i.e. those years which have already passed have already passed]." (*b. Sanh.* 97a–97b, *The Talmud: The Steinsaltz Edition,* vol 21: *Tractate Sanhedrin,* part 7, 8; the comments in the square brackets are by Rabbi Adin Steinsaltz; see also *y. Ta'an.* 1:1)

[150]"The [divine] quality of justice is preventing [him]. And since the [divine] quality of justice is preventing [him], why are we waiting? To receive reward, as it is stated: 'Happy are all they that wait for him.'" (*b. Sanh.* 97b; ibid., 11)

[151]"Rabbi Yehoshua ben Levi raised the [following] contradiction [between two parts of the same verse dealing with the promise of redemption (Isaiah 60:22): 'I the Lord will hasten it in its time']. The verse states [that redemption will come] 'in its time,' [implying that redemption will only come at its predetermined time. And] that [same] verse states [that] 'I will hasten it' [implying that redemption might come before that time! Rabbi Yehoshua ben Levi explained:] If [Israel] merits [it through repentance and good deeds, God will fulfill the promise,] 'I will hasten it,' [and bring redemption before its appointed time. But] if [Israel] does not merit [it, God will only bring redemption] 'in its time.'" (*b. Sanh.* 98a; ibid., 18) These two positions have been intensively discussed among the rabbis for at least three centuries; see J.-J. Brierre-Narbonne, *Exégèse talmudique des prophéties messianiques* (Paris: Librairie Orientaliste Paul Geuthner, 1934), 48.

[152]Transl. by W. G. Braude, *Pesikta Rabbati,* vol. 2, YJS 18 (New Haven and London: Yale University Press, 1968).

of the sea,[153] this is he whom the Most High has been keeping for many ages (*ipse est quem conservat Altissimus multis temporibus*)." The claim that it will be possible to see the Messiah only in the time designated for his advent is finally underscored in *4 Ezra* 13:52, which asserts that "just as no one can explore or know what is in the depths of the sea, so no one on earth can see my Son or those who are with him, except in the time of his day (*sic non poterit quisquam super terram videre filium meum vel eos, qui cum eo sunt nisi in tempore diei*).

A distinction between the period of the hiddenness of the Messiah and the time of his visible appearance is also apparent in the *Similitudes of Enoch*. According to *1 En.* 48:6b, the messianic figure, who is in this passage called the "Son of Man" (48:2) and the "Elect One" (48:6a),[154] "was concealed in the presence of (the Lord of the Spirits) prior to the creation of the world, and for eternity." This idea is elaborated even more in 62:7: "For the Son of Man was concealed from the beginning, and the Most High One preserved him in the presence of his power; then he revealed him to the holy and the elect ones."

These passages show that already in the first century one stream of the tradition that goes back to Hab 2:3[155] reinterpreted the eventual delay of the

---

[153]*4 Ezra* 13:32 identifies the man coming up from the sea as "my Son," who has been identified as the Messiah in *4 Ezra* 7:28–29. Thus even though in *4 Ezra* 13:3–14:9 (commonly classified as the third messianic section in the book) the author does not employ the word "Messiah," the messianic connotation of the term "my Son" is unmistakable in view of the literary unity of the book as a whole. See Stone, *Features of the Eschatology of IV Ezra*, 11–17; E. Breech, "These Fragments I have Stoned Against my Ruins: The Form and Function of *4 Ezra*," *JBL* 92 [1973]: 267–274; E. P. Sanders, *Paul and Palestinian Judaism: A Comparison of Patterns of Religion* (Philadelphia: Fortress Press; London: SCM Press, 1977), 418; Charlesworth, "The Concept of the Messiah in the Pseudepigrapha," 205.

[154]In *1 En.* 48:10, the Son of Man and the Elect One are equated with the Messiah, whereas in *1 En.* 53:6, the Righteous One and the Elect One are applied to the same person. In view of such a close relationship between the titles and the similarity of functions attributed to them, it is accurate to conclude "that the Elect One, the righteous One, the Messiah, and the Son of Man are different titles for the same messianic and eschatological figure." (Charlesworth, "From Jewish Messianology to Christian Christology," 240)

[155]The question concerning an apparent delay of the promised blessings of the new age dominates Ezra's first vision (cf. *4 Ezra* 4:33–34). The possibility that human sinfulness could cause the delay is taken into account. Thus in *4 Ezra* 4:39, Ezra asks: "And it is perhaps on account of us that the time of threshing is delayed for the righteous (*prohibeatur iustorum area*) – on account of the sins of those who dwell on earth." Uriel's reply, however, dismisses this possibility by claiming that the time of the end does not depend on human repentance. It is firmly set up by God and can be neither delayed nor hurried, similar as the pregnant woman after nine months can no longer keep (*retinere*) the child in her womb (*4 Ezra* 4:40–42). The deterministic view of *4 Ezra* is comparable to that of Qumran sectarians because it assumes the times that are "weighed and divided, fixed in advance," even though, as M. E. Stone notes, it is not carried down to the level of human nature (Stone, *Fourth Ezra*, 93). These issues are similarly treated in *2 Baruch*. Baruch's prayer in 21:25 ("And now, show your glory soon and do not postpone that which was promised by you") betrays that an eventual delay of the end-

end-time events as the delay of the advent of the Messiah. Various phrases which express the duration of time, such as "until the end of days" (*4 Ezra* 12:32) or "for many ages" (*4 Ezra* 13:27), and the verbs which denote keeping and preservation (*4 Ezra* 12:32; 13:27; *1 En.* 62:7) link these texts to the subject matter of Hab 2:3.[156] Thereby, similar to the Habakkuk Pesher, the reasons for this seeming delay are ascribed to God and his predetermined design of the end-time events. With this, the objectivity of the delay is *de facto* denied (because in reality there is no delay at all), and the entire problem is attributed to the human inability to perceive the actual events and the lack of patience to wait.

The question of John the Baptist thus appears in a new light. It betrays the puzzlement caused by an apparent delay of the expected time of salvation that is so clearly articulated in Hab 2:3, a passage to which John's question appears to be linguistically related. In that sense, it possesses a discernible temporal aspect, which refers to human (in)capability to recognize either the appearance or the nearness of the end-time. It is thus not accidental that John's question offers an alternative to wait for another (ἢ ἕτερον προσδοκῶμεν). Yet, it also emulates the narrowing down of this issue to the question of the delay of the Messiah, like the apocalyptic circles behind the *Similitudes of Enoch*, *4 Ezra*, and *2 Baruch*. The effect of this is twofold. On the one side, the end-time has been qualified as the messianic time. On the other side, the temporal aspect has been supplemented, or rather replaced by a personal aspect. John's question in fact does not refer to the recognition of the messianic time, but to the recognition of the Messiah himself, as the emphatic pronoun σύ and the terms ὁ ἐρχόμενος and ἕτερον clearly indicate.[157]

4.3.3 The Answer (Matt 11:5–6)

Jesus does not answer the question of John the Baptist with a simple "Yes" or "No," but with a recapitulation of the events that are currently taking place. With this, the answer consciously neglects the personal aspect of the query and responds only to its implied temporal component. The reasons for this treatment of John's question and the inner logic of Jesus' reply are far from

---

time events has been considered. Nevertheless, the general position in regard to "the course of times" (*2 Bar.* 14:1) is that "they will come and will not tarry" (*2 Bar.* 20:6), a claim that is comparable to the one in 1QpHab 7.13 that all of God's end-times will come according to their fixed order.

[156]This link was first noted by A. Strobel who criticized the previous research on this topic, especially the work of E. Sjöberg (*Der verborgene Menschensohn in den Evangelien* [Lund: C. W. K. Gleerup, 1955], 41–98), because "die Nähe zur eschatologischen Verzögerungsterminologie (s. die 'langen' Zeiten') wird allgemein nicht gewürdigt" (*Untersuchungen zum eschatologischen Verzögerungsproblem*, 25).

[157]A. Strobel (*Untersuchungen zum eschatologischen Verzögerungsproblem*, 273) neglects this aspect and deals only with the temporal side of the question.

being obvious.[158] Before dealing with these issues, however, a brief examination of the textual form of Jesus' answer is in order. It consists of a series of six clauses, all of which allude to various passages from the Book of Isaiah. Below is an overview of the texts in question.

Matt 11:5	Isaiah LXX		Isaiah MT
τυφλοὶ ἀναβλέπουσιν	Isa 29:18	ὀφθαλμοὶ τυφλῶν βλέψονται	עיני עורים תראינה
	Isa 35:5	τότε ἀνοιχθήσονται	אז תפקחנה
		ὀφθαλμοὶ τυφλῶν	עיני עורים
	Isa 61:1	τυφλοῖς ἀνάβλεψιν	ולאסורים פקח־קוח
χωλοὶ περιπατοῦσιν	Isa 35:6	τότε ἁλεῖται ὡς ἔλαφος	אז ידלג כאיל
		ὁ χωλός	פסח
λεπροὶ καθαρίζονται			
κωφοὶ ἀκούουσιν	Isa 29:18	καὶ ἀκούσονται	ושמעו
		ἐν τῇ ἡμέρᾳ ἐκείνῃ κωφοὶ	ביום־ההוא החרשים
	Isa 35:5	ὦτα κωφῶν ἀκούσονται	ואזני חרשים תפתחנה
νεκροὶ ἐγείρονται	Isa 26:19	ἀναστήσονται οἱ νεκροί	יחיו מתיך
		καὶ ἐγερθήσονται	נבלתי יקומון הקיצו
		οἱ ἐν τοῖς μνημείοις	
πτωχοὶ			
εὐαγγελίζονται	Isa 61:1	εὐαγγελίσασθαι πτωχοῖς	לבשר ענוים

It is immediately apparent that none of the passages from Isaiah are directly quoted. Nevertheless, the texts from Isaiah share with Matt 11:5 certain formal elements. They are lists[159] which contain promises for the future given to certain groups of people. Both Matt 11:5 and the Isianic passages use the identical nouns for them (τυφλοί, ξωλοί, κωφοί, νεκροί, πτωχοί), only the cases differ depending on the grammatical structure of the sentence. All the lists in Isaiah contain the verbs in the future tense,[160] whereas in Matt 11:5 the verbs are in the present tense. It is therefore fair to conclude that Jesus' reply alludes to various Isaianic texts by combining several motifs that appear in them, with the purpose of showing that the promises given in the past are now being

---

[158]W. Grimm aptly asks: "Inwiefern ist die Täuferfrage nach dem 'Kommenden' eigentlich beantwortet?" (*Weil ich dich liebe: Die Verkündigung Jesu und Deuterojesaja*, ANTJ 1 [Bern: Herbert Lang; Frankfurt: Peter Lang, 1976], 125)

[159]The only exception is Isa 26:19.

[160]The only exception is Isa 61:1, because this passage contains the commission and not the promise. However, since this commission refers to the future work of the speaker, it is comparable to other lists considered above.

fulfilled.[161] Giving sight to the blind and preaching good news to the poor are already associated in Isa 61:1 LXX.[162] The blind, the lame, and the deaf are linked together in Isa 35:5–6, whereas Isa 29:18 correlates only the references to the blind and the deaf. Thus four out of six groups that appear in Jesus' answer (the blind, the lame, the deaf, and the poor) have been already variously associated in Isa 29:18 (the blind and the deaf), 35:5–6 (the blind, the lame, and the deaf), and 61:1 (the blind and the poor). Only two of them hang somehow in the air. The cleansing of the lepers is not mentioned in Isaiah at all, while the raising of the dead appears only in Isa 26:19, which does not link it to any of the other motifs.

The fact that Jesus' answer apparently describes the state of affairs that is already known to John without directly responding to his query raises the question about its intrinsic logic. The key to this enigma is often found in the allusive character of Jesus' answer. It is formulated in such a way as to evoke memory of the texts from Isaiah that envision the future salvation in terms of the recovery of health of the sick and preaching good news to the poor. Thus Davies and Allison suggest that it "supplies a hermeneutical suggestion,"[163] whose purpose is to put Jesus' deeds into the proper scriptural framework. Similarly, Strobel contends that Jesus replies to the scripture-based question of John the Baptist with a scripture-based answer.[164]

Since the allusive character of Jesus' answer can be hardly denied, it is very likely that the salvation oracles from Isaiah, especially Isa 35:5–6 and 61:1, form the background of Matt 11:5. The difficulty, however, comes from the subsequent and often undemonstrated assumption that these Isaianic texts refer to the blessings of the messianic time. Thus Davies and Allison assert that

---

[161]K. Stendahl (*The School of St. Matthew*, 91) compares the allusive character of Matt 11:5 to the way Isa 6:9–10 is referred to in Matt 13:13. A comprehensive list of the passages to which Matt 11:5 alludes can be found in Grimm, *Weil ich dich liebe*, 124–126. However, his inclusion of Isa 42:18 in the list of texts to which Matt 11:5 alludes cannot be justified, because this is not a promise for the future, but a metaphorical command for the present.

[162]The LXX, Symmachus and Theodotian replace the reference to the freedom for the captives found in the MT (פקח־קוח ולאסורים – a metaphorical reference to the opening [of eyes] of those who are bound in the sense of freeing them from a dark prison) with the reference to giving the literal sight to the blind. The reason for this might have been that the verb פקח otherwise regularly refers to opening of eyes or ears. Also, the equation between opening of eyes and liberation from prison is already made in Isa 42:7. The LXX apparently understands פקח as a noun by translating it by ἀνάβλεψις, and then translates the preceding word ולאסורים by τυφλοῖς. The Targum Isaiah intensifies the captivity aspect through an additional emphasis of the role of light: "to those who are bound, 'Be revealed / come forth to light.'" The quotation of Isa 61:1 in Luke 4:18 shows that the translation of the LXX was better applicable to Jesus' career and for this reason readily adopted in Christian circles.

[163]Davies and Allison, *Matthew*, vol. 2, 243.

[164]A. Strobel notes that "wie besonders bei rabbinischen Streit- und Schulgesprächen üblich, steht der schriftgebundenen Frage die schriftgebundene Antwort gegenüber" (*Untersuchungen zum eschatologischen Verzögerungsproblem*, 273).

"Jesus is the Coming One of John's preaching, the Messiah of prophecy who, through his proclamation to the poor and his miraculous and compassionate deeds, brings to fulfillment the messianic oracles uttered so long ago by Isaiah the prophet."[165] Similarly, Strobel also treats these texts as "messianic."[166] The methodological problem with this approach is that these passages do not contain any reference to a figure that can be properly called "the Messiah." Isa 26:19, 29:18, and 35:5–6 describe the blessings of the future age, but they are nowhere associated with the coming of the Messiah. Isa 61:1 is the only text that refers to the actions of an individual, but even though this person is the herald of good news who is anointed by the Spirit of the Lord, he is not called "the Messiah".

On the other hand, Matthew's editorial phrase τὰ ἔργα τοῦ χριστοῦ shows that he understood these texts messianically.[167] This interpretation implies two prior inferences that Matthew's argument presupposes, which have to be clarified. On the one hand, Matthew apparently regards Jesus' miracles and preaching good news to the poor as the signs of the impending messianic kingdom. It can be shown that some of Matthew's contemporaries, though not many, shared similar expectations. In this sense, it appears that Matthew understood Jesus' answer as a direct reply to the implied temporal aspect of John's question. On the other hand, Matthew links the signs of the messianic time to the person of the Messiah by interpreting them as his own deeds. With this, Matthew as the narrator, not Jesus himself, replies to the personal aspect of John's question. Even though this inference cannot be traced back to any known view of the Messiah preserved in early Jewish literature, it could have been arrived at through the midrashic interpretation of scriptural passages from

---

[165]Davies and Allison, *Matthew*, vol. 2, 242.

[166]"Die Botschaft an den Täufer stellt in der vorliegenden Gestalt eine einfache poetische Form gebrachte Sammlung von 'messianischen' Jesaja-Sprüchen dar" (Strobel, *Untersuchungen zum eschatologischen Verzögerungsproblem*, 274). In Strobel's view, Isa 61:1 is the "tragende klassische Belegstelle der messianischen Erlösungszeit" (ibid.).

[167]Whether this can be also said for Jesus himself (either the Jesus of history if the authenticity of the saying is granted, or the Jesus of the Q material if the reconstruction stops at this point) depends on one's view of the tradition history of the text. Thus on the basis of the similarity between Jesus' answer and the Qumran fragment 4Q521, C. A. Evans claims that "4Q521 significantly supports the traditional view that Jesus did indeed see himself as Israel's Messiah" ("Jesus and the Dead Sea Scrolls from Qumran Cave 4," in *Eschatology, Messianism, and the Dead Sea Scrolls*, ed. C. A. Evans and P. Flint, SDSSRL 1 [Grand Rapids, Michigan: William B. Eerdmans, 1997], 97). Similarly, E. P. Meadors offers an argument for the implicit Christology of Q. He believes that both 4Q521 and the tradition history of Isa 61:1–3 show that "Jesus' association with Isa 61:1–3 in Q in all likelihood signals something special, indeed something unique – dare we say something eschatological – about the person and work of Jesus himself" ("The 'Messianic' Implications of the Q Material," *JBL* 118 [1999]: 259).

Isaiah to which Jesus' answer alludes. An attempt to reconstruct the logic of this process will be presented below.

4.3.3.1 The Temporal Aspect of the Answer

Many interpreters take for granted that "the healing of all illnesses was expected in the messianic end-time."[168] The most serious challenge to this assumption was presented by Hans Kvalbein, who reviewed all the evidence provided in Strack-Billerbeck's commentary[169] and concluded that these "texts speak quite generally about a coming time of salvation without illness, pain and distress. The salvation is described in collective terms referring to the people as a whole. God himself is the redeemer. The Messiah has no function as healer or physician in these texts, and they do not even mention healing miracles."[170] Kvalbein's conclusion, if correct, would have significant impact on the subject matter of this study. A reexamination of the evidence from the early Jewish writings is therefore in order. Special attention will be given to the question of the relationship between the end-time blessings and the Messiah.

Jubilees 23:26–30

> And in those days, children will begin to search the law, and to search the commandments and to return to the way of righteousness. And the days will begin to increase and grow longer among those sons of men, generation by generation, and year by year, until their days approach a thousand years, and to a greater number of years than days. And there (will be) no old men and none who is full of days, because all of them will be infants and children. And all of their days they will be complete and live in peace and rejoicing and there will be no Satan and no evil (one) who will destroy, because all of their days will be days of blessing and healing. And then the Lord will heal his servants, and

---

[168]Strack-Billerbeck, *Kommentar*, vol. 1, 593 [translation mine]. Cf. Schniewind, *Das Evangelium nach Matthäus*, 139–140; Hagner, *Matthew 1–13*, 301; Luz, *Matthew 8–20*, 134; A. Richardson, *The Miracle-Stories of the Gospels* (London: SCM Press, 1941), 43; J. Becker, *Jesus von Nazaret* (Berlin/New York: Walter de Gruyter, 1996), 220; Bittner, *Jesu Zeichen im Johannesevangelium*, 136. A more specific claim that "der Messias seinem Volk Israel alle jene Güter widerbringen werde, die durch Adams Fall verloren gegangen waren; dazu gehörte natürlich auch die Beseitigung von Krankheit und Tod" (Strack-Billerbeck, *Kommentar*, vol. 1, 593) has been universally rejected.

[169]H. Kvalbein, "The Wonders of the End-Time: Metaphoric Language in 4Q521 and the Interpretation of Matthew 11.5 par." *JSP* 18 (1998): 101–106. Even before the appearance of Kvalbain's article, some interpreters raised objections against the view advocated by Strack and Billerbeck, but they were not accompanied by such a detailed analysis of the relevant passages. For example, E. P. Sanders (*Jesus and Judaism* [Philadelphia: Fortress Press, 1985], 163) made merely a general comment that "subsequent Jewish literature does not indicate that Jews habitually looked for miracles as a sign of the coming end."

[170]Kvalbein, "The Wonders of the End-Time," 101–102.

they will rise up and see great peace. And they will drive out their enemies,
and the righteous ones will see and give praise, and rejoice forever and ever
with joy.[171]

The future age of salvation is here described as a time of peace, spiritual
renewal, increase of life expectations, disappearance of aged populace, and
healing. Kvalbein appropriately notes that the context "points to a life in this
world and not to a life after death or after a resurrection of the dead."[172] His
conclusion, however, that "no individual miracles of healing are mentioned"[173]
is true only to the extent that the text does not speak about specific diseases or
afflicted individuals that are going to be healed. Yet the assertion that "the
Lord will heal his servants" suggests individual healings, especially in view of
the context which presumes a gradual and not a sudden change of life
conditions. The text does not mention any messianic figure and ascribes all the
improvements concerning the length and quality of life to God.

1 Enoch 96:3

But you, who have experienced pain, fear not, for there shall be a healing
medicine for you, a bright light shall enlighten you, and a voice of rest you
shall hear from heaven.[174]

In this passage, a healing medicine is promised to those who have previously
suffered. Since, however, there is no indication that this suffering comes from
physical illnesses,[175] it is certainly more appropriate to understand the
reference to healing metaphorically.[176]

4 Ezra 7:120–126

And what good is it that an everlasting hope has been promised us, but we
have miserably failed? Or that safe and healthful habitations have been
reserved for us, but we have lived wickedly? Or that the glory of the Most
High will defend those who have led a pure life, but we have walked in the
most wicked ways? Or that a paradise shall be revealed, whose fruit remains
unspoiled and in which are abundance and healing, but we shall not enter it,

---

[171]*OTP* 2, 101–102.

[172]Kvalbein, "The Wonders of the End-Time," 103.

[173]Ibid.

[174]*OTP* 1, 76.

[175]Cf. the contrasting passage in *1 En.* 95:4, which asserts that the sinners will have no
remedy.

[176]Two additional passages from *1 Enoch* are mentioned in Strack-Billerbeck's
commentary, *1 En.* 5:8 and *1 En.* 25:5–7 (the reading in manuscripts B and C), but even
though they refer to prolonged life expectations due to the disappearance of ailments, they do
not mention healings as a recovery of health by those who were previously ill; cf. Kvalbein,
"The Wonders of the End-Time," 103.

because we have lived in unseemly places? Or that the faces of those who practiced self-control shall shine more than the stars, but our faces shall be blacker than darkness? For while we lived and committed iniquity we did not consider what we should suffer after death.[177]

This section which describes life in a paradise where fruit is abundant and grants healing evidently refers to a life after death. The text, however, does not presume that in the afterlife, people will still suffer from maladies and thus need to regain health. *4 Ezra* 8:51–53 confirms this inference by specifying that illness will be banished from paradise. Kvalbein's assessment that "in this life of resurrection, healing from sickness and pain has no function"[178] is quite accurate.

2 Baruch 73:1–3, 6–7

And it will happen that after he [the Anointed One] has brought down everything which is in the world, and has sat down in eternal peace on the throne of the kingdom, then joy will be revealed and rest will appear. And then health will descend in dew, and illness will vanish, and fear and tribulation and lamentation will pass away from among men, and joy will encompass the earth. And nobody will again die untimely, nor will any adversity take place suddenly . . . And the wild beasts will come from the wood and serve men, and the asps and dragons will come out of their holes to subject themselves to a child. And women will no longer have pain when they bear, nor will they be tormented when they yield fruits of their womb.[179]

The messianic reign is presented in this text as a paradise *redivivus*, characterized by the absence of illness, fear, tribulation, premature death, and childbirth pains. Like Isa 11:6–9, this vision of the future includes an expectation of a nonviolent behavior of wild animals. Yet, this is not a description of the afterlife but of life on earth.[180] Even though the expected blessings are not envisioned to take place through the agency of the Messiah, they characterize the time of his reign. The dew of health and other "marvels," however, seem to have a permanent character since they will not have to be repeated on a daily basis. The text even adds that illness will disappear. The conclusion that the text "does not necessarily imply healing miracles or individual healings"[181] is undoubtedly accurate.

---

[177]*OTP* 1, 541.
[178]Kvalbein, "The Wonders of the End-Time," 104.
[179]*OTP* 1, 645.
[180]Kvalbein, "The Wonders of the End-Time," 105.
[181]Ibid.

2 Baruch 29:3, 6–7; 30:1

> And it will happen that when all that which should come to pass in these parts
> has been accomplished, the Anointed One will begin to be revealed . . . And
> those who are hungry will enjoy themselves and they will, moreover, see
> marvels every day. For winds will go out in front of me every morning to bring
> the fragrance of aromatic fruits and clouds at the end of the day to distill the
> dew of health . . . And it will happen after these things when the time of the
> appearance of the Anointed One has been fulfilled and he returns with glory,
> that then all who sleep in hope of him will rise.[182]

The concluding statement of this paragraph indicates that this is a description
of the messianic time before the resurrection of the dead. It is characterized by
constant marvels, including the dew of health. The miraculous aspect of the
latter is reinforced through its daily reoccurrence, which suggests that the
universal health is not yet achieved. There is no doubt that these miracles of
healing are not expected to take place through the agency of the Messiah but
through a divine intervention into the laws of nature.[183] Yet it is important to
recognize that they accompany the revelation of the Messiah. They begin to
take place when the Anointed One begins to be revealed. Although the text
does not clarify the nature of this relationship, it allows for several
conclusions. First, both the miracles and the revelation of the Messiah are the
result of divine initiative. Second, there is a direct link between the wonders
and the messianic time. The marvels verify that "the time of the appearance of
the Anointed One" (*2 Bar.* 30:1) is taking place. Third, the recognition of the
messianic time points to the presence of the Messiah and thus participates,
though in an unspecified way, in the revelation of his person.

Two additional documents, one roughly contemporaneous with *2 Baruch*
(the end of the first century C.E.), and the other written more than a century
earlier, depict a similar relationship between God's marvelous acts, the time of
the Messiah, and the revelation of his identity, even though they do not contain
explicit references to healings. The first reference is found in *4 Ezra* 7:26–29:

> For behold, the time will come, when the signs which I have foretold to you
> will come to pass; the city which now is not seen shall appear, and the land
> which now is hidden shall be disclosed. And everyone who has been delivered
> from the evils that I have foretold shall see my wonders. For my son the
> Messiah shall be revealed with those who are with him, and those who remain
> shall rejoice four hundred years.[184]

---

[182]*OTP* 1, 630–631.

[183]Kvalbein notices the similarity with the exodus wonders, especially the manna in the
desert ("The Wonders of the End-Time," 105).

[184]*OTP* 1, 537.

Even though this selection does not specify the nature of eschatological wonders, it presents them as observable events that will take place simultaneously with the revelation of the Messiah. This constellation of events suggests that the end-time wonders contribute, albeit in a mysterious way, to the messianic revelation.

The second reference can be found in chapters 17 and 18 of the *Psalms of Solomon*. They assert that the time of the Messiah's appearance has been decided upon by the divine decree and is known only to God. Thus the prayer for the Davidic Messiah begins in 17:21 with an expression of confidence that God is in control: "See, Lord, and raise up for them their king, the son of David, to rule over your servant Israel in the time known to you, O God (εἰς τὸν καιρόν ὃν ἴδες σύ, ὁ θεός)." Similarly, 18:5 conveys a wish that "may God cleanse Israel for the day of mercy in blessing, for the appointed day when his Messiah will reign (εἰς ἡμέραν ἐκλογῆς ἐν ἀνάξει χριστοῦ αὐτοῦ)." What should be noted, however, is that despite the impenetrability of God's verdict, when the messianic time begins humans will be able to perceive the wonderful state of affairs that is going to take place on God's initiative. Thus *Pss. Sol.* 17:44 declares that "blessed are those born in those days to see the good things of Israel which God will bring to pass" (μακάριοι οἱ γενόμενοι ἐν ταῖς ἡμέραις ἐκείναις ἰδεῖν τὰ ἀγαθὰ Ἰσραηλ ... ἃ ποιήσει ὁ θεός). *Pss. Sol.* 18:6 repeats almost verbatim that "blessed are those born in those days, to see the good things of the Lord which he will do for the coming generation" (μακάριοι οἱ γενόμενοι ἐν ταῖς ἡμέραις ἐκείναις ἰδεῖν τὰ ἀγαθὰ κυρίου ἃ ποιήσει γενεᾷ τῇ ἐρχομένῃ). The similarity of these declarations and the texts considered above lies not in the content of "the good things," because they clearly do not refer to an improvement of health and life expectancy, but to political and social conditions. Rather, the similarity lies in the observation that God's wonderful acts confirm the advent of the messianic time and foster human perception of its arrival.

The texts reviewed above show that the expectations regarding the improvement of health in the future were far too diverse to allow a general conclusion "that we have no evidence at all for the assumption that the Jews in the Hellenistic and Early Roman period expected healing miracles for individual Israelites in the time of salvation."[185] We have seen that *Jub.* 23:26–30 and *2 Bar.* 29:3, 6–7 speak about the improvement of health of people in the time of salvation, which is envisioned in both texts to take place in this world and not in the afterlife. Moreover, *2 Bar.* 29:6–7 explicitly calls these events "marvels." The texts that link the betterment of health (*2 Bar.* 29:3, 6–7; 30:1) or a complete disappearance of illness (*2 Bar.* 73:1–3, 6–7) to the appearance of the Anointed One, present these blessings as the characteristics of the messianic time and ascribe them completely to God's sovereignty.

---

[185]Kvalbein, "The Wonders of the End-Time," 106.

Finally, *2 Bar.* 29:3, 6–7; 30:1 suggest that the miracles of healing and other marvels play a role in the revelation of the Messiah. Nevertheless, it must be acknowledged that none of the texts elaborate in any detail the idea of health improvement by providing a more specific information about the types of diseases or of the afflicted individuals that are going to be cured.

This conclusion must be now reconsidered in light of the evidence from 4Q521, a document from Qumran that was first published in 1992 under the name "Une apocalypse messianique,"[186] even though it represents, by its genre, an eschatological psalm.[187] Fragment 2, column 2 (supplied by fragment 4) contains the text which describes the end-time salvation in terms of healing of the blind, resurrection of the dead, and preaching good news to the poor. The Messiah is explicitly mentioned at the beginning, but the redemptive acts are entirely ascribed to God. Émile Puech originally described this document as "an exhortation based on the blessings or chastisements which God will bring about through, or in the days of, his Messiah."[188] The subsequent discussion, however, focused only on the first part of Puech's formulation ("which God will bring about through . . . his Messiah"). Controversial issues

---

[186]É. Puech, "Une apocalypse messianique (4Q521)," *RevQ* 15 (1992): 475–519 (plates 1–3, pp. 520–522); idem, *La croyance des Esséniens en la vie future: Immortalité, résurrection, vie éternelle? Histoire d'une croyance dans le Judaïsme ancien*, vol. 2, EtB.NS 22 (Paris: Lecoffre/Gabalda, 1993), 627–692. J. Starcky described this document already in 1956 ("Le travail d'édition des fragments manuscrits de Qumrân," *RB* 63 [1956]: 66). Puech's publication was preceded only by a publication of a photograph and English translation of one fragment by R. H. Eisenman ("A Messianic Vision," *BAR* 17.6 [1991]: 65). The first English translations of the document were offered by G. Vermes, "Qumran Forum Miscellanea I," *JJS* 43 (1992): 303–305, and R. H. Eisenman and M. O. Wise, *The Dead Sea Scrolls Uncovered: The First Complete Translation and Interpretation of 50 Key Documents Withheld for Over 35 Years* (Shaftesbury/Rockport/Brisbane: Element, 1992): 17–23. For a complete transcription and translation of all the fragments see É. Puech, *Qumrân Grotte 4*, vol. 18, DJD 25 (Oxford: Clarendon Press, 1998), 1–38; and pls. I–III. In addition to "Messianic Apocalypse," 4Q521 was sometimes called "On Resurrection" (E. Tov, "The Unpublished Qumran Texts from Caves 4 and 11," *JJS* 43 [1992]: 126) or "The Messiah of Heaven and Earth" (Eisenman and Wise, *The Dead Sea Scrolls Uncovered*, 19).

[187]Cf. K.-W. Niebuhr, "4Q521, 2 II – Ein Eschatologischer Psalm," in *Mogilany 1995: Papers on the Dead Sea Scrolls Offered in Memory of Aleksy Klawek*, ed. Z. J. Kapera (Kraków: The Enigma Press, 1996), 151–168; R. Bergmeier, "Beobachtungen zu 4Q521 f2, II, 1–13," *ZDMG* 145 (1995): 41; J. J. Collins, "A Herald of Good Tidings: Isaiah 61:1–3 and its Actualization in the Dead Sea Scrolls," in *The Quest for Context and Meaning: Studies in Biblical Intertextuality*, ed. C. A. Evans and S. Talmon, FS J. A. Sanders, BIS 28 (Leiden: Brill, 1997), 234; Zimmermann, *Messianische Texte aus Qumran*, 347. For Puech's defense of the designation "apocalypse," see his essay, "Some Remarks on 4Q246 and 4Q521 and Qumran Messianism," in *The Provo International Conference on the Dead Sea Scrolls: Technological Innovations, New Texts, and Reformulated Issues*, ed. D. W. Parry and E. Ulrich, STDJ 30 (Leiden: Brill, 1999), 551–552. Puech's designation will be used in this study for the sake of convenience.

[188]Puech, "Une apocalypse messianique (4Q521)," 514 [translation mine].

included the question whether God performs the end-time miracles through the agency of the Messiah, and if so, whether the messianic figure should be understood primarily in royal, prophetic, or priestly categories. A startling similarity between this text and Jesus' answer to the Baptist's question in Matt 11:5 and Luke 7:22 only intensified scholarly interest in these questions.[189] The second part of Puech's formulation ("which God will bring about . . . in the days of his Messiah") was, until now, largely neglected. In the following, I will try to demonstrate that, similarly to the Jewish documents considered above, the text of 4Q521 emphasizes the temporal aspect of the expected miracles by presenting them as the signs of the messianic time rather than being interested in the manner or agency of their actual execution.

4.3.3.2 A Messianic Apocalypse (4Q521)

According to Puech, 4Q521 was most likely written in the first quarter of the first century B.C.E.[190] A more precise dating of its composition is impossible, because the document is a copy and not the original.[191] It consists of 16 fragments. The largest and best preserved is fragment 2. A transcription and translation of its second column (supplied with the text from fragment 4) is as follows.

---

[189]Cf. J. J. Collins, "The Works of the Messiah," *DSD* 1 (1994): 98–112; idem, *The Scepter and the Star*, 117–123; idem, "A Herald of Good Tidings," 225–240; M. Becker, "4Q521 und die Gesalbten," *RevQ* 18 (1997): 73–96; K.-W Niebuhr, "Die Werke des eschatologischen Freudenboten (4Q521 und die Jesusüberlieferung)," in *The Scriptures in the Gospels*, ed. C. M. Tuckett, BETL 131 (Leuven: University Press, 1997), 637–646; Kvalbein, "The Wonders of the End-Time," 87–110.

[190]This dating is based on the paleographical examination of the script; cf. Puech, DJD 25, p. 5.

[191]For the argument that the original was written by the members of the Essene community in the second half of the second century B.C.E., see Puech, *La croyance*, 664–669; idem, "Some Remarks on 4Q246 and 4Q521," 552. Puech bases his conclusion on the following observations: the Tetragrammaton is suppressed in the quotations of Ps 146 and replaced by אדני, medial letters appear in the final positions, the relative -ש is used alongside אשר, etc. Puech's dating of the document is based on the appearance of the terms such as חסידים, צדיקים,ענוים, and קדושים, and certain similarities in vocabulary with *Hodayot* and other Qumran documents. Other interpreters are more cautious. J. J. Collins ("The Works of the Messiah," 106) notices the absence of the typical sectarian terminology and the presence of certain ideas such as the resurrection, which are rarely found in the sectarian literature. In his view, this document was probably not composed at Qumran. R. Bergmeier ("Beobachtungen zu 4Q521 f2, II, 1–13," 44–45) contends that 4Q521 does not contain the typical features of Qumran theology, but of other early Jewish psalms. J. Zimmermann (*Messianische Texte aus Qumran*, 348, 387) calls attention to the differences in language, orthography, and content and believes that 4Q521 might have been composed in "protoessenischen chasidischen Kreisen" (*ibid.*, 388). He, however, adds an important qualification. Even if 4Q521 might not be a Qumran composition, its reception by the Qumran Community allows at least a conclusion that its eschatological ideas were close enough to the eschatological expectations of the group itself.

Frgs. 2, Col. 2 and 4[192]

כי הש[מ]ים והארץ ישמעו למשיחו 1

[וכל א]שר בם לוא יסוג ממצות קדושים 2

התאמצו מבקשי אדני בעבדתו *vacat* 3

הלוא בזאת תמצאו את אדני כל המיחלים בלבם 4

כי אדני חסידים יבקר וצדיקים בשם יקרא 5

ועל ענוים רוחו תרחף ואמונים יחליף בכחו 6

כֹּי יכבד את חסידים על כסא מלכות עד 7

מתיר אסורים פוקח עורים זוקף כפֹ[ופים] 8

ולֹ[ע]לֹם אדבק [במ]יֹחלים ובחסדו יֹן 9

ופרֹ[י] מעש[ה]טֹוֹב לאיש לוא יתאחר 10

ונכ/בֹודות שלוא היו יעשה אדני כאשר ד[בר] 11

כֹּי ירפא חללים ומתים יחיה ענוים יבשר 12

ו[דלי]ֹם יֹשֹבֹ[י]ע [נֹ]תֹושים ינהל ורעבֹים יעשֹר 13

ונבֹ[ן] °[ ] וכלם כֹּקֹדֹ[ושים] 14

וא[15

Translation:

1 [. . . for hea]ven and earth will listen to his Messiah,

2 [and] no[ne w]ho is in them will turn away[193] from the commandments of holy ones.

3 You who are seeking the Lord, strengthen yourselves in his service. (VACAT)

4 Is it not in this that you will find the Lord, all who hope in their hearts?

5 For the Lord will seek out the devout and call the righteous ones by name,

6 and his spirit will hover over the poor ones, and he will renew the faithful ones by his might.

7 For he will glorify the devout ones on the throne of an eternal kingdom,

8 freeing captives, giving sight to the blind ones, (and) raising up those who are bo[wed down].

9 For[e]ver I will cling [to those who] hope, and in his mercy y[. . .]

10 And the fru[it of a] good [wor]k will not be delayed for anyone,

11 and the glorious things that have not taken place the Lord will do as he s[aid],

12 for he will heal the wounded and give life to the dead, he will preach good news to the poor ones

---

[192]Text and restoration by Puech, DJD 25, p. 10.

[193]The translation follows the modification proposed by Puech, "Some Remarks on 4Q246 and 4Q521," 553.

13   and [sat]isfy the [weak] ones, he will lead those who have been cast out
      and enrich the hungry ones,
14   and *nb*[. . .]° and all, like the hol[y ones . . .]
15   and '[. . .]

The opening line asserts that "[hea]ven and earth will listen to his Messiah (or,
his Anointed)."[194] The structure of this clause presupposes a distinction
between the grammatical subject (heaven and earth) and the logical subject
(God's Anointed[195]), whom heaven and earth will obey.[196] Since the second

---

[194]למשיחו can be read either as singular (לִמְשִׁיחוֹ) or defective plural (לִמְשִׁיחָו). In general,
defective plural ending, i.e. ו- instead of יו-, is attested in Qumran writings, but it is far less
frequent than the full ending. Thus, plural understanding of למשיחו is possible even though
statistically not very likely. Since a compelling decision cannot be based on probabilities, other
factors, such as content and context must be taken into account; cf. Zimmermann,
Messianische Texte aus Qumran, 386. It is questionable whether the plural משיחיה in 4Q521
frg. 8 line 9 can help here, because it has the feminine plural ending, whereas למשיחו has the
masculine ending, which, according to Qumran orthography, can have two forms; cf. Puech,
"Some Remarks on 4Q246 and 4Q521," 557. M. Becker ("4Q521 und die Gesalbten," 78)
insists that למשיחו must be plural because משיחיה in 4Q521 frg. 8 line 9 is clearly plural, and
there is no reason to suppose a conceptual change in a single document. But, as Puech notes,
"it is difficult to use these examples [i.e. the plural משיחיה in frg. 8 line 9 and the partially
preserved form [ ]משיח in frg. 9 line 3] far from the columns under investigation and may be in
another context" ("Some Remarks on 4Q246 and 4Q521," 557). The explanation proposed by
F. García Martínez ("Messianic Hopes in the Qumran Writings," in *The People of the Dead
Sea Scrolls: Their Writings, Beliefs, and Practices*, ed. F. García Martínez and J. Trebolle
Barrerra [Leiden: Brill, 1995], 168) that למשיחו must be singular because the parallel
expressions in line 6 with pronominal suffixes, רוחו and בכחו, are also in singular, cannot be
sustained because lines 1 and 6 cannot be brought in any direct relationship; cf. Puech, "Some
Remarks on 4Q246 and 4Q521," 556–557; Becker, "4Q521 und die Gesalbten," 76. It is
difficult to make an informed decision here, because the fragmentary nature of the text does
not allow much certainty. If Isa 61:1 can be taken as a hermeneutical key of this passage, then
singular seems to be more appropriate than plural.

[195]Since אדני is either the main object or subject of the claims that follow after line 2, there
is little doubt that the third person pronominal suffix in למשיחו refers to God.

[196]The verb שמע could mean either "listen" or "obey." Zimmermann (*Messianische Texte
aus Qumran*, 349) argues that "obey" is more appropriate here, because it better corresponds
to the parallel phrase "not turning away from the commandments" in line 2. The idea of haven
and earth listening to/obeying the Messiah is not attested in the extant Jewish writings.
According to some interpreters, this is an allusion to Isa 1:2a, although this text represents an
invitation to listen to God; cf. Puech, "Une apocalypse messianique," 487; Bergmeier,
"Beobachtungen zu 4Q521 f2, II, 1–13," 39; Becker, "4Q521 und die Gesalbten," 84;
Zimmermann, *Messianische Texte aus Qumran*, 348. Other candidates are Deut 32:1, where
Moses asks heaven and earth to listen to his words (Puech, "Une apocalypse messianique,"
487; Becker, "4Q521 und die Gesalbten," 84; Zimmermann, *Messianische Texte aus Qumran*,
348), Psalm 2, which speaks about the universal reign of God's Anointed (Bergmeier,
"Beobachtungen zu 4Q521 f2, II, 1–13," 39, 43), and Sir 48:3, which narrates Elijah's famous
command to the heavens (Collins, *The Scepter and the Star*, 120).

line might function as a parallel to the first, some interpreters have proposed to understand משיחו as plural in order to match the plural קדושים.[197] Such an inference, however, is far from being certain, because *parallelismus membrorum* does not require an exact correspondence, even less synonymous meaning, of each individual element.[198] Moreover, parallelism between the first two lines is an assumption that still needs to be proven.[199] In an anticipation of the analysis that follows, which will seek to demonstrate the similarity between 4Q521 frg. 2 col. 2 and the end-time messianic visions found in the Jewish documents examined above, משיחו will be understood here as singular. If so, the first two lines portray an eschatological harmony of cosmic proportions, which is expressed through a complete subservience of heaven and earth to God's Anointed and a universal obedience to God's commandments.

In the rest of the fragment, משיחו is not mentioned. Moreover, the actions listed in lines 5–8, such as renewing the faithful ones by his might (ואמונים יחליף בכחו), glorifying the pious on the throne of an eternal kingdom (יכבד את חסידים על כסא מלכות עד), releasing captives (מתיר אסורים), giving sight to the blind (פוקח עורים), and raising up those who are bowed down (זוקף כפ[ו]פים), are all ascribed to the Lord.[200] The same applies to the second list of eschatological promises found in lines 11–13, which assert that "he [the Lord] will heal the wounded" (ירפא חללים), "give life to the dead" (ומתים יחיה), "preach good news to the poor" (ענוים יבשר), "[sat]isfy the [weak]" (ו[דלי]ם

---

[197]Cf. Niebuhr, "4Q521, 2 II – Ein Eschatologischer Psalm," 153; idem, "Die Werke des eschatologischen Freudenboten," 638; H. Stegemann, *Die Essener, Qumran, Johannes der Täufer und Jesus: Ein Sachbuch* (Freiburg: Herder, 1994), 49–51. Following the same reasoning, i.e. drawing the consequences from the *parallelismus membrorum* between the first two lines, R. Bergmeier ("Beobachtungen zu 4Q521 f2, II, 1–13," 39) makes the opposite conclusion and claims that קדושים in line 2 should be understood as singular.

[198]For example, there is no exact correspondence of individual terms in two parallel clauses found in *Pss. Sol.* 11:1: "Sound in Zion the trumpet to summon the saints. Proclaim in Jerusalem the voice of him who brings good tidings" (σαλπίσατε ἐν Σιων ἐν σάλπιγγι σημασίας ἁγίων, κηρύξατε ἐν Ἰερουσαλημ φωνὴν εὐαγγελιζομένου). *Pss. Sol.* 17:43c offers another interesting example, which compares the words of the Messiah to the words of the Holy Ones: οἱ λόγοι αὐτοῦ ὡς λόγοι ἁγίων. Concerning the terms משיחו and קדושים in 4Q521 frg. 2 2.1–2, Zimmermann (*Messianische Texte aus Qumran*, 349–351) understands the former as a reference to a human figure and the latter to the angels.

[199]Puech ("Some Remarks on 4Q246 and 4Q521," 555) sees lines 2 and 3 as parallel. Under this assumption, קדושים would correspond to מבקשי אדני, with no implications on משיחו in line 1.

[200]The divine name is not presented by the Tetragammaton, but by אדני. These lines contain many expressions from Ps 146:5–8; line 8 quotes verbatim Ps 146:7b–8a–b with the omission of יהוה. The subject of these actions is אדני from line 5.

[יש[יע]), "lead those who have been cast out" (נחושים ינהל), and "enrich the hungry" (ורעבים יעשר).[201]

Even though the grammatical subject of these clauses is God (אדני), the role and character of God's Anointed mentioned in line 1 can still be investigated.[202] The most common argument used to support the claim that God will perform these actions through the agency of his Messiah is based on the exegetical finding that nowhere else is God ever said to preach the good news to the poor. This is the task of a herald or messenger.[203] This can further mean, by implication, that other actions must also be performed through human agency. John J. Collins thus argues that despite the fact that God is the grammatical subject of line 12, God cannot be the immediate logical subject but requires an agent.[204] Since, however, no other human figure is mentioned in the text except the Messiah, he must be the one who will actually execute these deeds on God's behalf.[205]

Regarding the character of the Messiah who will act as God's executor, proposals have been made that he is either a royal, prophetic, or priestly figure. The initial argument for a Davidic Messiah was based on an erroneous transcription and translation of the document, which presumes that the grammatical subject of lines 12–13 is the Messiah.[206] In this reading, the

---

[201]In contrast to the first list, the second list of future blessings does not contain any direct scriptural quotation, even though it is introduced with a formula at the end of line 11: "the Lord will do as he s[aid]" (יעשה אדני כאשר ד[בר]). The actions described in lines 12 and 13 allude to several biblical passages, such as Deut 32:39a, Isa 26:19; 61:1, and Ps 146:7a–b.

[202]These studies presuppose an internal coherence between lines 1–2(3) and the rest of the column. If however, a new psalm begins in line 3, as suggested by R. Bergmeier ("Beobachtungen zu 4Q521 f2, II, 1–13," 43), such an inquiry would lose its main basis. Consequently, attempts have been made to demonstrate the unity of the column. J. J. Collins ("A Herald of Good Tidings," 235) argues that the internal cohesion is provided by a string of allusion to Psalm 146 in lines 1–9. Puech ("Some Remarks on 4Q246 and 4Q521," 554), however, points out that "the quotation of Psalm 146:7b–8a in line 8 does not authorize seeing a pseudoquotation of Psalm 146:6 in lines 1–2." It seems to me that the unity of the passage is provided by its relatedness to Isa 61:1, a text which speaks of the anointing of a messenger who is called to bring good news to the poor, which is enumerated among the eschatological blessings in line 12.

[203]Cf. Collins, "The Works of the Messiah," 100.

[204]Ibid.; idem, "A Herald of Good Tidings," 235–236. For a critique see Bergmeier, "Beobachtungen zu 4Q521 f2, II, 1–13," 236; Puech, "Some Remarks on 4Q246 and 4Q521," 558.

[205]This is not a denial of God's ultimate sovereignty because, as Collins notes, "works performed through an agent would, of course, be nonetheless the works of God" ("A Herald of Good Tidings," 235).

[206]Eisenman and Wise incorrectly transcribed the first part of line 11 as ונכ/ב\ורות שלוא היו מעשה אדני, which they translated as "And as for the wonders that are not the work of the Lord." This translation suggests that the Messiah is the implied grammatical subject of lines 12–13. Some of the first interpretations of 4Q521 presume this transcription and translation; cf. M. O. Wise and J. D. Tabor, "The Messiah at Qumran," *BAR* 18.6 (1992): 60–65; J. D.

Messiah in 4Q521 was seen as a direct precursor of the Christian understanding of Jesus as the Messiah.[207] It is, however, equally possible to understand משיחו as a royal figure on the basis of a more reliable reading of the text, as Puech himself proposes. For him, 4Q521 is another Qumran document that must be seen within a relatively stable framework of Qumran messianism, which is, in his view, dominated by a belief in two Messiahs – priestly and royal. He finds additional support for the concept of the kingly Messiah in the word "[his] scepter" (שבט[ו]) which appears in frg. 2 3.6.[208] However, the reading[209] and translation[210] of this word are uncertain. Moreover, the extant text of the third column does not contain any direct reference to a messianic figure.

John J. Collins has presented the most elaborate argument for a prophetic Messiah.[211] In his view, the Messiah mentioned in line 1 "most probably serves as God's agent in raising the dead."[212] Since, however, the Jewish writings do not attribute raising the dead to the royal Messiah, "the messianic activity envisaged in this text is appropriate to an eschatological prophet rather than to a king."[213] The strength of the argument that Collins presents depends on a twofold evidence – that the resurrection of the dead is never attributed to the royal Messiah and that the term "Messiah/Anointed" in the Dead Sea

---

Tabor and M. O Wise, "4Q521 'On Resurrection' and the Synoptic Gospel Tradition: A Preliminary Study," *JSP* 10 (1992): 149–162; reprinted in *Qumran Questions*, ed. J. H. Charlesworth, BibSem 36 (Sheffield: Sheffield Academic Press, 1995), 151–163 (subsequent page references are from this publication); O. Betz and R. Riesner, *Jesus, Qumran and the Vatikan: Clarifications*, trans. J. Bowden (New York: Crossroad, 1994), 90–93; P. Stuhlmacher, *Wie treibt man Biblische Theologie*, BThSt 24 (Neukirchen-Vluyn: Neukirchener Verlag, 1995), 32.

[207]Thus, for example, Wise and Tabor assert that "our Qumran text, 4Q521, is, astonishingly, quite close to this Christian concept of the messiah [i.e. the messiah who is David's descendant and who is God's cosmic agent]. Our text speaks not only of a single messianic figure ('[the hea]vens and the earth will obey His Messiah, [the sea and all th]at is in them'), but it also describes him in extremely exalted terms, quite like the Christian view of Jesus as a cosmic agent" ("The Messiah at Qumran," 60); see also Tabor and Wise, "4Q521 'On Resurrection'," 151–163.

[208]Puech, "Une apocalypse messianique (4Q521)," 497; cf. DJD 25 (1998), 18–19.

[209]It if questionable whether the second letter should be read as ב or ט. Moreover, the third letter is hardly visible. Cf. F. García Martínez, "Messianische Erwartungen in den Qumranschriften," in *Jahrbuch für Biblische Theologie*, vol. 8: *Der Messias* (Neukirchen: Neukirchener Verlag, 1993), 183, and Collins, "The Works of the Messiah," 103.

[210]שבט can be also translated as "tribe." Cf. Collins, "The Works of the Messiah," 103.

[211]Collins, "The Works of the Messiah," 98–112; idem, *The Scepter and the Star*, 117–123; idem, "A Herald of Good Tidings," 225–240. Collins' view has been accepted and further developed by Zimmermann, *Messianische Texte aus Qumran*, 382–385. In contrast to Collins, Zimmermann allows for an eventual fusion of royal, priestly, and prophetic features, even though he believes that in 4Q521 the latter stand in the foreground.

[212]Collins, "The Works of the Messiah," 98.

[213]Ibid., 99.

Scrolls can refer to a prophet. The former can be easily demonstrated. Even though certain early Jewish documents, such as *2 Baruch*[214] and *4 Ezra*,[215] as well as some rabbinic writings[216] associate the resurrection with the messianic age,[217] they do not attribute the agency of this event to the Davidic Messiah. It is, however, more difficult to show that the prophetic anointing in the Dead Sea Scrolls has messianic implications. Even though Isaiah 61:1, which forms the background of 4Q521 frg. 2 2.12, is also alluded to in 11Q13,[218] "the anointed of the spir[it]" ([ח]משיח הרו[ח]) mentioned in 11Q13 2.18 is not necessarily, as Collins argues, "a prophetic figure."[219] Rather, as the quotation of Dan 9:25, which most likely followed the introductory clause "about whom Dan[iel] said" (אשר אמר דנ[יאל]), indicates, he is "a leader/ruler/prince" (נגיד). Even though CD MS A 2.12 contains the expression משיחי רוח קדשו, a highly atomistic character of Qumran documents hinders a straightforward transfer of prophetic characteristics from this text to 11Q13 2.18. Moreover, the references to the prophets as "anointed ones" in CD MS A 2.12, 6.1, and 1QM 11.7 are in plural, not singular. In view of these objections, an identification of משיחו in 4Q521 as a prophetic Messiah can only be tentative.[220]

---

[214]*2 Bar.* 30:2 describes the events following the earthly career of the Messiah and claims that when he returns in glory "all who have died and set their hopes on him will rise again."

[215]*4 Ezra* 7:29–32 speaks about the death of the Messiah followed by the resurrection which occurs after seven days of primeval silence.

[216]J. J. Collins objects that in the book *Messiah in Context: Israel's History and Destiny in Formative Judaism* (Philadelphia: Fortress, 1984), 86–98, J. Neusner only "claims that there was a 'prevalent notion that the Messiah would raise the dead' but cites no evidence in support of this view" ("The Works of the Messiah," 101 n.12). This critique is probably too severe because Neusner does offer several examples in support of his claim. They, however, merely demonstrate the association between the Davidic Messiah and the time of his appearance but not his agency in the resurrection: "It was like what someone says, 'Until the dead will live!' . . . 'until David's son will come'" (*y. Qid.* 4:1 II/I); "It is the land in which the dead will first come to life in the time of the Messiah" (*y. Ket.* 12:3 VIII H).

[217]It should be noted that these documents, including 4Q521, speak about the resurrection in the most literal sense. Kvalbein's thesis that the end-time wonders described in 4Q521 are metaphorical and not literal descriptions of the future ("The Wonders of the End-Time," 87–110) is therefore untenable. For a critique, see Zimmermann, *Messianische Texte aus Qumran*, 364.

[218]M. P. Miller, "The Function of Isa 61:1–2 in 11Q Melchizedek," *JBL* 88 (1969): 467–469, has shown that in 11Q13, "Isa 61:1–2, unlike the other Scripture citations, is not quoted as text, but in each case forms an integral part of the interpretative comment" (ibid., 469).

[219]Collins, "The Works of the Messiah," 101.

[220]My critique of Collins' argument is limited to his thesis that the agent of God's glorious acts is the messianic eschatological prophet. I am not denying the possibility that he might be "a prophet after the manner of Elijah" ("A Herald of Good Tidings," 235). Collins presents quite a strong argument for the Elijah-typology in 4Q521 ("The Works of the Messiah, 101–106; "A Herald of Good Tidings," 235–236). Thus it cannot be denied that "Elijah's command of the heavens was legendary" ("A Herald of Good Tidings," 235) (cf. 1 Kgs 17:1, Sirach 48:3), or that Elijah is traditionally associated with raising the dead. What is lacking is the

The notion of a priestly Messiah tries to avoid some of the aforementioned difficulties. Underscoring the fact that anointing was not a characteristic of Israel's prophets,[221] but only of kings and priests, Karl-Wilhelm Niebuhr concentrates on the latter and comes to the conclusion that 4Q521 emphasizes the eschatological authority of priesthood.[222] Yet, even though there are many biblical[223] and non-biblical[224] references to priestly anointing, the critique of John J. Collins that "Niebuhr is unable to cite a single case where either term [i.e. anointed or holy] is used substantively as a noun with clear reference to priests in plural"[225] is certainly accurate. Another venue is taken by Puech, who takes Isa 61:1 as an interpretative key to 4Q521 and argues that the former represents "the speech of the (new) priests to his brethren the priests, and the assembly."[226] Accordingly, he ascribes the "I" of line 9 to the High Priest addressing the members of his community. However, even under the assumption that Isa 61:1 in its original context might have contained a speech of a priestly figure, which is far from being certain, its rich history of interpretation in the post-biblical writings shows that this text could be used for various purposes regardless of its original meaning.[227] An argument based on the sense of the biblical passage in its original setting needs to be strengthened by additional evidence in order to be convincing.

We can thus conclude that interpretations which aim to clearly define the role and character of God's Messiah in line 1 by seeing him as God's agent in bringing about the end-time blessings remain highly speculative. The text neither clarifies the relationship between God and his Anointed nor gives any specific information about his identity.

---

evidence that such a figure can be called "the Anointed." A conjecture on the basis of 4Q521 is in itself inconclusive.

[221]God's command to Elijah to anoint Elisha in 1 Kgs 19:16 is the only biblical reference to prophetic anointing. Puech ("Some Remarks on 4Q246 and 4Q521," 556) regards this instance as an error which was made because of the parallelism with God's commandment to anoint the king. Accordingly, CD MS A 2.12; 6.1, and QM 11.7 contain, in his view, figurative, not literal, descriptions of the prophets.

[222]Cf. Niebuhr, "4Q521, 2 II – Ein eschatologischer Psalm," 151–168; idem, "Die Werke des eschatologischen Freudenboten," 637–646. In Niebuhr's view, the first two lines in 4Q521 frg. 2, col 2 create a synonymous *parallelismus membrorum*. Since למשיחו corresponds to קדושים, Niebuhr interprets the former as a reference to the priests, arguing that holiness is a most common priestly characteristic. For a critique, see Zimmermann, *Messianische Texte aus Qumran*, 381.

[223]The examples include Exod 28:41; 29:7; 30:30–31; 40:14–15; Lev 4:3, 5, 16; 7:36; 8:12; 21:10; Num 3:3; 35:25; Sir 45:15, etc.

[224]1QM 9.6–9; 4Q375 2.9; 4Q376 1.1; 1QS 9.11.

[225]Collins, "A Herald of Good Tidings," 236.

[226]Puech, "Some Remarks on 4Q246 and 4Q521," 557.

[227]See section 4.3.3.3.

4Q521 shares several important features with other Jewish documents that speak about the eschatological blessings. First, the uniqueness of the events that are going to happen in the future is strongly emphasized. Thus, for example, *4 Ezra* 7:27 speaks about "wonders" (*mirabilia*), *Pss. Sol.* 17:44 and 18:6 about "the good things" (τὰ ἀγαθά), and 4Q521 frg. 2 2.11 about "the glorious things that have not taken place" (ונכ/ב\דות שלוא היו). Second, these marvels are the result of divine, not human activity. In *4 Ezra*, a divine voice calls them "my wonders" (*mirabilia mea*), *Pss. Sol.* 17:44 explicitly says that it is God who will bring to pass the good fortunes of Israel (ἃ ποιήσει ὁ θεός), whereas 4Q521 frg. 2 2.11 asserts that the glorious things that have not taken place "the Lord will do" (יעשה אדני). Finally, these wonderful events could sometimes testify or point to the presence of the Messiah. The relationship between the two, however, is never fully explicated. *2 Bar.* 29 and *4 Ezra* 7 speak about the "revelation" of the Messiah, *Pss. Sol.* 17 and 18 see him as God's agent in executing at least some of the future blessings, whereas 4Q521 assigns him high authority in a very general sense (heaven and earth will obey him) but does not specify his exact role when these events begin to take place.

In contrast to the Jewish texts which are only thematically related to 4Q521, the Q passage preserved in Matt 11:2–6 and Luke 7:18–23 contains the closest known parallel to this document, because both texts go beyond their common scriptural basis in Isa 61:1 by adding the reference to the resurrection of the dead in front of the reference to preaching good news to the poor.[228] A direct dependence of the Q material on 4Q521, however, cannot be established. It is more likely that both texts go back to a common tradition.[229] The comparison between the two passages was initially based on the inference that in 4Q521, God acts through the agency of the Messiah. As a result, the temporal component that is otherwise quite dominant in both texts has gone largely ignored.[230]

As already indicated above, Jesus does not answer the question of John the Baptist with a simple affirmation or denial, but with a recapitulation of the

---

[228]Thus, according to Collins, "The Works of the Messiah," 107, the "parallel between 4Q521 and the Saying Source is intriguing since both go beyond Isaiah 61 in referring to the raising of the dead." See also Tabor and Wise, "4Q521 'On Resurrection'," 162–163.

[229]This explanation of the relationship between the Q and 4Q521 is now accepted by many interpreters; cf. Collins, "The Works of the Messiah." 107; G. Brooke, "Luke-Acts and the Qumran Scrolls: The Case of MMT," in *Luke's Literary Achievement: Collected Essays*, ed. C. M. Tuckett, JSNTSup 116 (Sheffield: Academic Press, 1995), 75–76; K. Berger, *Qumran und Jesus: Wahrheit unter Verschluss?* (Stuttgart: Quell, 1993), 100; F. Neirynck, "Q 6,20b–21; 7,22 and Isaiah 61," in *The Scriptures in the Gospels*, ed. C. M. Tuckett, BETL 131 (Leuven: University Press, 1997), 58.

[230]This does not mean that this aspect was completely overlooked. Neirynck, for example, proposes that "in defining the genre of the logion itself, the parallel in 4Q521 can be helpful as an example of the *topos* of a description of the time of salvation" ("Q 6,20b–21; 7,22 and Isaiah 61," 62).

events that are currently taking place. With this, the answer consciously neglects the personal aspect of the inquiry and responds only to its implied temporal component. By alluding to the salvation oracles from Isaiah, especially Isa 35:5–6 and 61:1, Jesus enumerates the end-time blessings, some of which[231] are in 4Q521 explicitly associated with the appearance of the Messiah. His answer thus points to the observable signs of the messianic time, and not to the person of the Messiah.[232] In this way, Jesus makes a somewhat vague link between his miracles and his messianic identity. This ambiguity is clearly reflected in the concluding sentence, "And blessed is he who takes no offense at me" (καὶ μακάριός ἐστιν ὃς ἐὰν μὴ σκανδαλισθῇ ἐν ἐμοί [Matt 11:6; Luke 7:23]).

The redactional activity of Matthew and Luke shows that both evangelists tried to remove this indefiniteness. Matthew refers to Jesus' miracles as "the deeds of the Messiah" (τὰ ἔργα τοῦ χριστοῦ), whereas Luke adds that Jesus himself was curing many diseases at the time of the encounter with John's disciples. It is easy to understand their apologetic interest. They wanted to demonstrate that a historical person, Jesus of Nazareth, was indeed the expected Messiah.

However, neither the Qumran covenanters who copied and preserved 4Q521 in their library, nor the original author(s) of this document, had such an interest. If line 10, which claims that "the fru[it of a] good [wor]k will not be delayed for anyone" can serve as an indicator of their concern, they wanted to be assured that the end-time blessings, understood as a reward for their service of the Lord, will certainly take place. The need for such a reassurance might have come from the experience of the delay of the eschatological recompense.

---

[231]Giving sight to the blind, raising the dead, and preaching good news to the poor.

[232]H. Frankemölle believes that this feature of the Q-text speaks in favor of its high age: "Nicht ein 'Ich-bin-es' ist Zielpunkt der Aussage, vielmehr die messianische Praxis . . . . Endzeitliches Heil Gottes bricht an, dahinter tritt auch der Bote Jesus zurück. Vielleicht könnte gerade diese implizite Christologie ein Zeichen für ein hohes Alter für das hinter dem Text liegende Verständnis sein" ("Jesus als deuterojesajanischer Freudenbote? Zur Rezeption von Jes 52,7 und 61,1 im Neuen Testament, durch Jesus und in den Targumim," in *Vom Urchristentum zu Jesus*, ed. H. Frankemölle and K. Kertelge, FS J. Gnilka [Freiburg: Herder, 1989], 53). J. J. Collins also points out that "insofar as Isaiah 61 and the texts that allude to it emphasize the exchatological liberation rather than the person of the messenger, they provide a paradigm of messianic action that would seem to fit well the career of the historical Jesus as it is described in the Synoptics" ("A Herald of Good Tidings," 239–240). At the end of his monumental study of miracles and miracle workers in rabbinic Judaism, M. Becker compares Jesus' and rabbinic miracles and concludes that the main difference between them is the eschatological character of the former; see Becker, *Wunder und Wundertäter im frührabbinischen Judentum*, 417–442. Becker reaches a conclusion that is very similar to the one proposed above: "Die 'Wunder' fungieren dabei als Zeichen der universalen, kosmischen Wende, eines eschatologischen Dramas . . . sie sind sichtbare Zeichen der hereinbrechenden Gottesherrschaft" (ibid., 442).

The encouragement given in line 3 to those who are seeking the Lord to strengthen themselves in his service, is in fact a call for a patient endurance, as the phrase המיחלים בלבם ("those who hope/wait in their hearts") in line 4 clearly indicates.[233] This reconstruction of the *Sitz im Leben* of 4Q521 frg. 2 col. 2 is supported by the linguistic and thematic relatedness of the phrase לוא יתאחר in line 10 to Hab 2:3 (לא יאחר). In both instances we have the negative particle followed by the imperfect of the verb אחר,[234] and in both instances the phrases refer to the future (eschatological) events.[235] This similarity suggests that the subsequent lines in 4Q521, which enumerate various "glorious things that have not taken place" but which "the Lord will do as he said," might have performed a similar function as Jesus' answer to the implied temporal component in the question of John the Baptist. They point to the eschatological blessings which, according to the author of the document, have scriptural basis because he introduces them with the clause כאשר ד[בר]. The main difference between 4Q521 and Q is that the former expects these events to occur in the future, whereas the latter maintains that they are already taking place in the present.

4.3.3.3 The Personal Aspect of the Answer

By adding the phrase τὰ ἔργα τοῦ χριστοῦ to the introduction of the dialogue between Jesus and John's disciples, Matthew eliminates the ambiguity between the signs of the messianic time and the person of the Messiah, which characterizes the traditional material. With this, he goes beyond the literal meaning of scriptural texts to which Jesus' answer alludes. And yet, it can be shown that the connection that he makes between the miraculous events that are taking place and the person who does them comes from the midrashic interpretation of Isa 61:1, the text which apparently envelops various allusions to Isaianic salvation oracles in Jesus' answer.[236]

The list in Matthew 11:5 starts with τυφλοὶ ἀναβλέπουσιν, a clause which echoes Isa 29:18, Isa 35:5, and Isa 61:1 LXX. The parallel with the latter, however, is most obvious[237] because of the choice of the noun τυφλοί[238] and

---

[233]Cf. Zimmermann, *Messianische Texte aus Qumran*, 347, 353.

[234]The main difference is Pi'el in Hab 2:3 and Hitpa'el in 4Q521.

[235]The similarity between 4Q521 frg. 2 2.10 and Hab 2:3 has been already noticed by J. Zimmermann (*Messianische Texte aus Qumran*, 361), who cautiously concludes: "Es könnte sich um eine Bekräftigung dafür handeln, dass Gott das verheissene Heil gewiss und ohne Verzögerung eintreffen lassen wird."

[236]J. M. Robinson notes that the first and last items on the list stand "in chiastic order" and ponders that the healings in-between might have been "perhaps triggered by an intervening phrase in Isa 61:1: ἰάσασθαι" ("The Sayings Gospel Q," in *The Four Gospels 1992*, ed. F. Van Segbroeck *et al.* FS F. Neirynck, BETL 100 [Leuven, 1992], 363–364).

[237]Cf. J. S. Kloppenborg, *The Formation of Q* (Philadelphia: Fortress, 1987), 108 n.24; Strobel, *Untersuchungen zum eschatologischen Verzögerungsproblem*, 274. K. Stendahl (*The School of St. Matthew*, 91) regards Matt 11:5 as an allusion to Isa 61:1, because in his view

the verb ἀναβλέπουσιν.[239] Similarly, the concluding clause πτωχοὶ εὐαγγελίζονται most clearly alludes to εὐαγγελίσασθαι πτωχοῖς in Isa 61:1. Moreover, Isa 61:1 is the only text among scriptural passages whose memory Jesus' answer might have induced, which ascribes these actions to an individual, who emphatically declares at the beginning, "The Spirit of the Lord Yahweh is upon me because Yahweh anointed me" (πνεῦμα κυρίου ἐπ' ἐμέ οὗ εἵνεκεν ἔχρισέν με [LXX]; רוח אדני יהוה עלי יען משח יהוה אתי [MT]). It is thus easily conceivable that for Matthew – who in chapter 3 already presented Jesus' baptism as the anointing with the Spirit – the introductory line of Isa 61:1 was most applicable to Jesus' career.

Such an understanding of Isaiah 61 is attested in early Christian writings,[240] especially in the Gospel of Luke, which makes Isa 61:1–2 the content of Jesus' inaugural sermon at Nazareth (Luke 4:16–21). However, in contrast to Luke who interprets this text in light of Elija – Elisha traditions, Matthew understands Isa 61:1 as a messianic text. For him, Jesus' baptism represents the messianic anointing. Matthew is the only evangelist who uses the unusual formulation [τὸ] πνεῦμα [τοῦ] θεοῦ (Matthew 3:16), in a clear allusion to Isa 11:2 (πνεῦμα τοῦ θεοῦ [LXX]; רוח יהוה [MT]). The fact that Isa 61:1 contains a similar expression (πνεῦμα κυρίου [LXX]; רוח אדני יהוה [MT])[241] enables an easy association between these two texts. The evidence that Matthew has in fact done so can be seen in his conclusion that the one who has been anointed with the Spirit is the Anointed one, χριστός, which by the time Matthew wrote his Gospel functioned as a well-known *terminus technicus* for the Messiah, especially in Christian circles. Hence, Jesus' works must be the "works of the Messiah" (τὰ ἔργα τοῦ Χριστοῦ).

"this is in fact the only text of those in question where ἀναβλέπειν is used to express the healing of the blind." R. Gundry, however, sees Matt 11:5 primarily as an allusion to Isa 35:4, 6 (*The Use of the Old Testament*, 79–80, 207), even though he also examines its link to Isa 61:1. C. M. Tuckett (*Q and the History of Early Christianity: Studies on Q* [Edinburgh: T.&T. Clark, 1996], 129 n.77) also believes that "the reference to the 'blind seeing' could derive from Isa 35:5 rather than Isa 61 LXX."

[238]τυφλοῖς (Isa 61:1), ὀφθαλμοὶ τυφλῶν (Isa 29:18 and 35:5).

[239]ἀνάβλεψιν (Isa 61:1), βλέψονται (Isa 29:18), ἀνοιχθήσονται (Isa 35:5).

[240]It is usually assumed that Isaiah 61 influenced, at some stage, the shape of the Beatitudes (Luke 6:20b–23; Matthew 5:3–12), especially the subject of πτωχοί in the first beatitude. Many scholars especially acknowledge the formative influence of Isa 61:1–2 on Matt 5:3–4; cf. J. Dupont, "Introduction aux Béatitudes," *NRTh* 108 (1976): 100; Neirynck, "Q 6,20b–21; 7,22 and Isaiah 61," 29–45; M. Hengel, "Zur matthäischen Bergpredigt und ihrem jüdischen Hintergrund," 243–247.

[241]The closeness between the two texts is especially obvious in Hebrew, which, as we have seen, Matthew knew well. The LXX translates both God's ineffable name and honorary name with only one designation, κύριος.

Before the publication of 4Q521, one could have easily concluded that a messianic interpretation of Isa 61:1 was a uniquely Christian development.[242] In the Hebrew Bible, Isa 61:1–3 could be understood as a midrash on the servant songs in Deutero-Isaiah, especially Isa 42:1–4, 7[243] even though form-critically it represents a prophetic call.[244] It is clearly understood in the latter sense in the Targum Isaiah, which introduces 61:1 with the clause, "The prophet said" (אמר נביא), thus indicating that for the targumist, this passage is a reflection of a prophet on his prophetic vocation. Moreover, instead of רוח אדני יהוה עלי, the Targum has רוח נבואה מן קדם אדני אלהים עלי, a reading which reinterprets the Spirit of God from the biblical text as the spirit of prophecy. Also, instead of יען משח יהוה אתי, the Targum has חלף דרבי יהוה יתי. With this, the targumist eliminated the idea of anointing and replaced it with the idea of appointing.

The Dead Sea Scrolls contain various allusions to Isa 61:1–3.[245] Among them, the appropriations of Isa 61:1–3 in 1QH and 11Q13 are especially instructive. In 1QH^a 23.14–15, the speaker apparently takes up the role of the herald from Isa 61. He sees himself as a bearer of God's goodness who is sent to proclaim the abundance of God's mercies to the poor. Even though the identity of the speaker is not revealed, proposals have been made that this person might be the Righteous Teacher.[246]

More explicit allusions to Isa 61 can be found in 11Q13.[247] Various scriptural quotations (Lev 25:13, Deut 15:2, Ps 7:8–9, 82:1–2, Isa 52:7, Dan 9:25) are all related to Isa 61:1, which is interwoven into the text of the

---

[242]For a succinct sketch of "a history of function of Isa 61:1–3 from its appearance in the Tanak to its role in the Lukan account of Jesus' appearance and sermon in the Nazareth synagogue," see J. A. Sanders, "From Isaiah 61 to Luke 4," in *Christianity, Judaism and Other Greco-Roman Cults*, part 1, ed. J. Neusner, FS M. Smith, SJLA 12 (Leiden: E. J. Brill, 1975), 73–106; the quotation is from the opening sentence on p. 75.

[243]Cf. D. Michel, "Zur Eigenart Tritojesajas," *ThViat* 10 (1966): 213–230; W. A. M. Beuken, "Servant and Herald of Good Tidings: Isaiah 61 as an Interpretation of Isaiah 40–55," in *The Book of Isaiah: Le livre d'Isaïe*, ed. J. Vermeylen, BETL 81 (Leuven: Peeters and Leuven University Press, 1989), 411–442; P. Hanson, *The Dawn of Apocalyptic: The Historical and Sociological Roots of Jewish Apocalyptic Eschatology* (Philadelphia: Fortress, 1975), 65–68; Sanders, "From Isaiah 61 to Luke 4," 83.

[244]Cf. K. Elliger, "Der Prophet Tritojesaja," *ZAW* 49 (1931): 112–141; C. Westermann, *Isaiah 40–66: A Commentary*, trans. D. M. G. Stalker (Philadelphia: Westminster, 1969), 366.

[245]4Q171 (4QpPs^a) frgs. 1–10 2.9–10; 1QS 9.21–23; 1QM 7.4–5.

[246]D. Flusser, "Blessed are the Poor in Spirit . . ." *IEJ* 10 (1960): 10; Collins, "A Herald of Good Tidings," 231.

[247]Cf. P. J. Kobelski, *Melchizedek and Melchireša'*, CBQMS 10 (Washington: Catholic Biblical Association, 1981), 3–23; J. T. Milik, "*Milkî-sedeq* et *Milkî-reša'* dans les anciens écrits juifs et chrétiens," *JJS* 23 (1972): 95–144; A. S. van der Woude, "Melchisedek als himmlische Erlösergestalt in den neugefundenen eschatologischen Midraschim aus Qumran Höhle XI," *OTS* 14 (1965): 354–373.

interpretation.[248] Melchizedek, an enigmatic priestly figure mentioned in Gen 14:18 and Ps 110:4, is the main character in the eschatological scenario which this document describes. He is a heavenly deliverer called אל and אלוהים, who proclaims the year of Jubilee in which the captives, i.e. the members of the Qumran Community, will be released from the burden of their sins. He is also a judge of Belial and his followers. In 2.15–16, this description of the end-time events is supplemented by the quotation of Isa 52:7 and its interpretation. In 2.18, the pesher identifies "the messenger" (מבשר) from the scriptural text as "the anointed of the spir[it]" (משיח הרו[ח]) about whom Daniel spoke. Even though the designation משיח הרוח is not a term taken from the biblical text, it is probably construed under the influence of Isa 61:1. Its function is to serve as a link between Isa 52:7 and Dan 9:25b, which was probably quoted in the second half of line 18 after the introductory clause [אשר אמר דנ[יאל], because it contains the reference to the "anointed one." If this reconstruction of the text is correct, "the anointed of the spirit" could be identified as "the anointed prince" from Dan 9:25. Unfortunately, the fragmentary state of the text prevents any certainty regarding the identity of משיח הרוח in this document, so that other interpretations are also possible, such as Melchizedek himself,[249] a prophetic figure different than Melchizedek,[250] the Prince of Light,[251] the Danielic "one like a son of man,"[252] or the Righteous Teacher.[253]

In none of these interpretations of Isa 61 is the herald of good news identified as the Messiah. Even in 4Q521, the tasks that the biblical text assigns to this figure, such as preaching good news to the poor, are detached from his personality and presented in a wider context of the eschatological blessings whose ultimate executor is God himself. Yet the fact that within this context the Messiah is mentioned, despite not having a clearly defined function, marks 4Q521 frg. 2 2.1–15 as a messianic passage.

We can thus conclude that the messianic reading of Isa 61:1, to which Matthew apparently subscribes, was one possible reading among several other ways this text was appropriated in the extant Jewish writings of the time. If the unusual correspondence between Jesus' answer to the Baptist's questions and 4Q521 frg. 2, col. 2 indicates the presence of a common tradition, Matthew's messianic reading of Isa 61:1 no longer appears extraordinary. It represents a logical step in drawing the implications from the text that speaks about an

---

[248]See Miller, "The Function of Isa 61:1–2 in 11Q Melchizedek," 467–469.

[249]Sanders, "From Isaiah 61 to Luke 4," 91; P. Stuhlmacher, "Das paulinische Evangelium," in *Das Evangelium und die Evangelien: Vorträge vom Tübinger Symposium 1982*, ed. P. Stuhlmacher, WUNT 28 (Tübingen: Mohr Siebeck, 1983), 171, 173; idem, *Biblische Theologie des Neuen Testaments*, vol. 1, 112.

[250]Collins, "A Herald of Good Tidings," 230.

[251]Kobelski, *Melchizedek and Melchireša'*, 36.

[252]Puech, *La croyance*, 554–558.

[253]Milik, *"Milkî-sedeq et Milkî-reša'*, " 126.

individual who declares that God anointed him with the spirit. The fact that in the original text, this might have been an anointed prophet or an anointed priest was irrelevant for the first-century exegetes. Like his contemporaries, Matthew saw in it only what his interpretative framework enabled him to see – the messianic anointing of a person who has been sent to open the eyes of the blind, heal the sick, and proclaim good tidings to the poor.

4.3.4 Conclusions

The data studied in this chapter lead to the conclusion that the intelligibility of Matthew's presentation of the Davidic Messiah who acts as a healer of the sick is provided through its scriptural basis. Since, however, no scriptural passage assigns this duty to the expected deliverer of the Davidic line, the author of the Gospel achieves his goal by applying certain midrashic techniques to the selected texts from Isaiah that speak either about the servant of Yahweh or an anointed bearer of good tidings. Methodologically, this reconstruction of the Matthean argument presupposes a prior confession of Jesus as the Messiah. It cannot be, in my view, convincingly demonstrated that Matthew came to the conviction that Jesus is the royal Messiah who heals by confessing him first as the "Servant" or "Herald." But it can be shown that he could have applied the Isaianic passages to Jesus on the basis of his belief that Jesus is indeed the expected Messiah whose entire career represents the fulfillment of ancient prophecies.

We have seen that in two instances Matthew asserts that Jesus' healings represent a direct fulfillment of Scripture. In 8:16–17, Matthew quotes Isa 53:4a. His version of the citation, however, differs from the LXX or any other known Greek translation, and most likely represents his own free rendering of the Hebrew text. Through a careful choice of words and the omission of the reference to the redemptive suffering of the servant, the Matthean version of the citation provides a scriptural proof that Jesus is a mighty healer who takes away the illnesses of the sick and with this fulfills his duty as the ideal shepherd/king of the Davidic line. The quotation of Isa 42:1–4 that appears in Matt 12:15–21 has been similarly adapted through a targumizing translation of the Hebrew text with the purpose of conforming it to Jesus' career and demonstrating that his healings do belong to the realm of his messianic responsibilities.

The analysis of Jesus' response to the question of John the Baptist has uncovered several traditional layers. The question itself betrays the influence of Hab 2:3 because it contains a recognizable temporal aspect that is typical for all subsequent adaptations of this text. However, it also bears an unmistakable personal aspect, which is to be expected in a Christian adaptation of this tradition and its application to a distinct historical person, Jesus. Jesus' answer, however, responds only to the implied temporal aspect of the query. By enumerating the extraordinary events that are already taking place, Jesus' logion evokes the memory of similar promises from Isaianic salvation oracles, which some Jews, though not many, associated with the dawn of the messianic time. 4Q521 allows at least this conclusion, even though it leaves many questions open, such as the manner and agency of the actual execution of these wonderful eschatological happenings.

Matthew's redactional phrase τὰ ἔργα τοῦ χριστοῦ secures a reply to the personal aspect of John's inquiry. I have tried to show that this expression represents an outcome of Matthew's midrashic interpretation of Isa 61:1. This can be also seen in Matthew's choice of the word χριστός, a nominalized form of the verb χρίω. In this way, the messianic interpretation of Isaianic oracles is given a scriptural justification. It should be kept in mind, however, that for Matthew, "Christ" is a royal title whose functional equivalent in the narrative is the designation "Son of David." There is no reason to doubt that, at least for his Jewish Christian readers, Matthew's scriptural proof for a healing Davidic Messiah procured a firm and incontestable conviction.

Chapter 5

A Summary of Conclusions

The aim of this study was to discover the inner logic of the intrinsic connection between the royal messianic title "Son of David" attributed to Jesus in the Gospel of Matthew and his healing ministry. My approach was based on the assumption that the link between the Davidic Messiah and healing cannot be found as such in the extant early Jewish literature. It is most likely that Matthew imported it from Mark's Gospel and then developed it further with a definite raison d'être. Yet, I did not consider satisfying the usual solution that merely declares that Matthew modified or redefined the traditional Jewish messianic expectations. This is not the answer to the problem but only the first step in a search for an answer. There is no doubt that Matthew, similar to other New Testament writers, firmly believed that Jesus was the expected Davidic Messiah. However, it would be too simplistic to assume that this inner conviction could have been sufficiently persuasive if he had merely insisted that Jesus' non-messianic career was after all the career of the Davidic Messiah because he and his Christian audience simply believed him to be that. Matthew's Gospel testifies to the fact that this belief needed a rationale, and the foregoing investigation proposes that the latter had been provided through a skillful interpretation of Scripture.

Whether Matthew's evidence for Jesus' messiahship could have also served apologetic purposes is an issue that must remain open at this point. The evidence presented here confirms the conclusion that Matthew's way of arguing follows the rules of scriptural interpretation that were used by both early Jewish and Christian interpreters. However, since the use of an inductive methodology does not grant results, it rarely has the ultimate persuasive power. The exegetical outcomes depend on the constraints set up by a given tradition, which depend on a number of *apriori* beliefs and convictions. On a positive side, a shared methodology can create a context for a dialogue, if other conditions exist. On the basis of what we can deduce from the Gospel of Matthew, his community was engaged in an ongoing identity struggle over against formative rabbinic Judaism. It is quite possible that Matthew's narrative played an important role in this debate, especially for apologetic purposes. However, this and similar speculations regarding the historical circumstances in which the Gospel was written were not treated in this study. Its objective was purely textual, and the events "behind the text" were largely ignored.

The analysis of the framing portions of Matthew's narrative, which assign the title "Son of David" to Jesus, has shown that this designation stems from the tradition that has its basis in Nathan's oracles from 2 Sam 7:12–16. Matthew appears to understand this denomination in a twofold sense – as a messianic title and an indication of a Davidic descent. The purpose of the genealogy and its "enlarged footnote" in Matthew 1 is to demonstrate that Jesus belongs to the Davidic family tree despite the fact that Joseph is not his biological father. The discontinuity in the Davidic lineage points to Jesus' divine sonship, which should also be understood within the framework of Nathan's oracle. In this way, Matthew links a specifically Christian understanding of Jesus' divine origin to the promise tradition rooted in 2 Samuel 7. This fundamental conclusion is not altered by the observation that Matthew reverses the relationship between the Davidic and divine sonships. Even though the act of adoption is in his Gospel associated with Jesus' Davidic lineage and does not serve to explain his relationship with God, the final outcome is unaffected. Jesus, like the promised David's "seed" in 2 Sam 7:12–16, is the son of both David and God. In this way, Jesus' divine sonship receives a clearly defined function within the framework of the promise tradition and serves the purpose of demonstrating that Jesus possesses the prerequisites expected from the Davidic Messiah. One should add, however, that such an argument probably had only limited validity, because even those Jews whose eschatological hopes were associated with the expectations of the Messiah of the Davidic line only occasionally linked these hopes to the idea of God being the father of the Messiah. Yet, those who did so could have certainly claimed the most immediate scriptural support, as 4Q174 clearly shows.

Both aspects of Jesus' origin, his Davidic and divine descent, are again addressed in Matt 22:41–46, the concluding episode of the narrative segment in which Jesus is called the Son of David. It has been argued that Jesus' question about the sonship of the Messiah follows the rabbinic pattern of an apparent contradiction between two scriptural passages. The analysis of the argumentative structure of the dialogue has indicated that in Matthew's Gospel, the solution to this problem should be sought not only in exegetical distinction – i.e. in the application of both designations, David's son and David's lord to Jesus of Nazareth – but also in the sphere of the Messiah's descent. Since the initial question suggests that more than one sonship is possible, the final resolution of the conflicting statements appears to be a distinctively Christian understanding of Jesus' divine and Davidic origin.

In the final section of the first chapter of this study I have argued that the salvation from sins (Matt 1:21) represents Matthew's application of the third major element of the promise tradition, the perpetuity of the Davidic dynasty, to Jesus' ministry. It seems that Matthew's text presupposes a conditional understanding of Nathan's promise, which is discernible in many biblical and post-biblical texts. In this tradition, not only the sins of the Davidic kings, but also the individual and national sins are seen as a hindrance of the realization of the promise to David. Yet, despite this dominant feature, a trust in God's faithfulness still appears in various forms, most notably in the form of hope that God will after all send the promised Davidic king who will deliver his people from the calamities caused by their transgressions. Matthew's explanation of the meaning of Jesus' name seems to be a conscious reference to the sin-consequence schema that lies at the core of this tradition, as well as an expression of hope that the reversal of present circumstances will take place through Jesus the Davidic Messiah.

If the title "Son of David" in Matthew's Gospel is the messianic designation rooted in the traditions based on Nathan's promise to David in 2 Samuel 7, the oddity of its association with Jesus' healing ministry appears in its full force. A survey of the passages in which this title is applied to Jesus has shown that the link between the Davidic title and Jesus' healing is remarkably compelling. Jesus is either asked to heal in his capacity as the Son of David or is identified as the Son of David after he performed the healing(s). In chapter 3, I explored two attractive solutions to this problem, both of which have the advantage of finding an already established link between a certain type of a miracle worker and his ability to heal in the extant Jewish writings.

The first solution explains the link between the "Son of David" and healing in Matthew's Gospel with the help of certain traditions about Solomon, the biological son of David, who possessed the power to exorcise demons and, through this, to heal. There is strong evidence that these traditions pre-date Christianity and continued long thereafter. To which extent they were applied to the Jesus of history and his massive exorcistic activity is a question that can only be speculated upon. Matthew's evident attempt to dissociate Jesus from these traditions might be taken as a support for their existence. What can be observed, however, is that Matthew's presentation of Jesus as the Son of David is lacking all the elements that are constitutive for these traditions. He never directly confronts a demon, he does not possess a secret knowledge of exorcisms, he does not have a seal-ring, and he is addressed as the "Son of David" in a titular sense.

The second solution explores a possible influence of the expectations of the eschatological prophet like Moses. There are several features of Matthew's narrative that support this line of investigation. Matthew often uses the Moses typology in his presentation of Jesus, and he lets some of his characters, regularly the crowd, identify Jesus as the prophet. The most intriguing passage in this regard is the description of Jesus' entry into Jerusalem. Matthew is the only evangelist who lets the crowd exclaim that the coming one in the name of the Lord is the "Son of David," and he is the only evangelist who adds that the crowd introduced Jesus to the citizens of Jerusalem as "the prophet from Nazareth of Galilee." The main difficulty here, however, represents the phenomenon that in Matthew's Gospel, like in other Synoptics, Jesus' miracles do not function as legitimating prophetic signs. Since they are never announced in advance, they are not given the proper context of interpretation. They have ambiguous nature and therefore evoke different responses.

The vagueness of Jesus' miracles led me to investigate the phenomenon of ambiguity of Jesus' healings in a larger literary context. The analysis has shown that the elusiveness exists only on the level of the plotted story. Thus only certain characters in the narrative have difficulties to "see" and "understand" the meaning of Jesus' miracles. On the level of the narrative, Matthew provides a series of interpretative comments, which are meant to create the literary context in which the reader can gain certainty that those characters that identified Jesus as the messianic Son of David indeed were right. The analysis of the so-called healing summaries suggests that the dominant forces, which pervade the commentaries of the narrator, are either scriptural quotations or scriptural allusions. Such a conclusion, taken by itself, is not surprising, because Matthew's Gospel contains numerous scriptural quotations and allusions, most notably the so-called formula quotations, which explicitly claim that Jesus' career represents the fulfillment of certain scriptural predictions. Nevertheless, the most interesting feature within the context of Matthew's claim that Jesus is the Davidic Messiah whose primary activity consists in healing, is the fact that scriptural quotations that do not have a prior history of informing the early Jewish messianic expectations provide the major evidence within a complex exegetical argument for Jesus' messiahship.

Matthew claims that Jesus' healings represent the explicit fulfillment of Scripture in two instances, in Matt 8:16–17 where he quotes Isa 53:4a, and Matt 12:15–21 where he quotes Isa 42:1–4. Matthew's citation of Isa 53:4a differs from all other extant Greek versions of this text. In contrast to the LXX, which spiritualizes the meaning of this verse, Matthew's version is closer to the Hebrew text, which speaks about physical infirmities. Also, the second part of the verse that speaks about the suffering servant of Yahweh is not quoted. Through an occasionally forced translation of the Hebrew text and the atomistic use of Scripture, Matthew achieves the goal of demonstrating that the servant is not a sick person who voluntarily suffers on behalf of others, but a mighty healer who takes away the illnesses of the people and releases them from their sufferings.

The crucial question, however, is whether or not Matthew understands this verse as a messianic prophecy. Isa 53:4a, after all, originally refers to Yahweh's servant and neither the quotation itself nor its introduction in Matt 8:17 mention any Christological title. Even if Jesus himself, or his followers at the earliest stages of Christian tradition, might have understood his mission in terms of the atoning death of the servant of Yahweh, the New Testament writings show that an elaborate application of the imageries of the servant to

Jesus presupposes a firm confession of Jesus' messiahship. The justification for this association can be found in Scripture, which contains certain verbal links between God's Anointed and His servant. Once these associations were made, they themselves became part of the rich Christian tradition and provided the language to speak about Jesus the Messiah. There are, therefore, good reasons to presume that Matthew's application of Isa 53:4a to Jesus was facilitated through his belief in Jesus' messiahship, as the preliminary explanation that Jesus is the one who is called Christ/Messiah (Ἰησοῦς ὁ λεγόμενος χριστός – Matt 1:17) clearly indicates. Additionally, certain expressions and motifs that appear in Matthew betray the influence of traditions based on Ezekiel 34, which liken the ideal Davidic king to the ideal shepherd who cares for and cures his flock.

The quotation of Isa 42:1–4 in Matt 12:15–21 follows Jesus' command for secrecy that he gave to those whom he has just healed. Jesus' request for silence does not appear to be a contingent component in Matthew's narrative, whose mere purpose is to provide a suitable link with the citation, but an integral part of Matthew's presentation of Jesus' attempt to avoid the Pharisaic hostility, which is consistently provoked by the public recognition of his messianic identity. Further, the citation itself, despite being long, fits well its present context and in all its elements elucidates Jesus' messianic engagement on behalf of the sick. The analysis of the text of the citation has revealed a similar targumizing technique that Matthew used in his quotation of Isa 53:4a, which is most likely motivated by his desire to conform the biblical quotation to Jesus' career. Moreover, I have tried to demonstrate that every clause of the citation can be related either to Jesus' messianic identity or to his messianic activity. The main weight in this argument bears the interpretation of the term "my servant" that appears at the beginning of the quotation, which gives it an unmistakable messianic connotation. This is accomplished through the introduction of the term "beloved" from the baptismal tradition. With this addition, the servant in the citation is identified as the beloved son, whom God confirmed as the Messiah at his baptism.

In the last section of this study I have investigated Jesus' dialogue with the disciples of John the Baptist, which is reported in Matt 11:2–6. I have accepted and further developed the thesis of August Strobel that Hab 2:3 provides the scriptural foundation of this exchange. The relatedness between these texts is strengthened by Matthew's wording of the question of John the Baptist, which is especially close to Aquila's translation of Hab 2:3b. The problem of the delay of the end-time events, which this verse addresses, is in some Jewish texts understood as the problem created by the delay of the advent of the Messiah. These passages regularly contain the phrases which express the duration of time, and the verbs which denote keeping and preservation. The cause for delay is regularly ascribed to God's predetermined design, which the humans fail to comprehend. The objectivity of the delay is thus systematically denied, and the entire dilemma is attributed to the subjective and ultimately inaccurate human perception of the events that are taking place. Seen in this light, the question of John the Baptist is characterized by a temporal component, which refers to human failure to recognize the appearance of the messianic time. It possesses, on the other hand, an explicit personal aspect visible through his desire to recognize the Messiah.

By enumerating the miraculous events that are currently taking place, Jesus directly responds to the implied temporal aspect of John's question. His logion contains several recognizable allusions to Isaianic salvation oracles, some of which came to be associated with the commencement of the messianic time in the post-biblical period. A crucial role in this reconstruction plays 4Q521, a Qumran document which, similarly to the Q-material incorporated in Matt 11:5, goes beyond Isa 61:1 by adding the reference to the resurrection of the dead in front of the reference to preaching good news to the poor. This extraordinary similarity suggests a common tradition behind both texts. Jesus' answer thus points to some observable events that were in this tradition expected to characterize the messianic time. With this, he gives an implicit response to the experience of the delay of the eschatological blessings recognizable in John's answer. The remaining ambiguity between the signs of the time and the person of the Messiah is removed through Matthew's editorial comment that these happenings are the "works of the Messiah," an expression that most likely represents the outcome of Matthew's midrashic interpretation of Isa 61:1.

Matthew's Gospel shows that the dominant feature of Jesus' miracles, especially his miracles of healing, is their eschatological significance. They demonstrate the presence of God's reign within the realm of human history. Matthew's exegetical activity and clarifying comments show that although Jesus' healings cannot authenticate his messianic vocation, they can facilitate human recognition of the messianic character of the time in which they take place and through this contribute to the revelation of Jesus' messianic identity.

Bibliography of Works Cited

Biblical Texts

Aland, K., J. Karavidopoulos, C. M. Martini, and B. M. Metzger, eds. *Novum Testamentum Graece*. 27th ed. Stuttgart: Deutsche Bibelgesellschaft, 1993.

Elliger, K. and W. Rudolph, eds. *Biblia Hebraica Stuttgartensia*. Editio funditus renovata. Stuttgart: Deutsche Bibelgesellschaft, 1967/77.

May, H. G. and B. M. Metzger, eds. *The New Oxford Annotated Bible with the Apocrypha. Revised Standard Version Containing the Second Edition of the New Testament and an Expanded Edition of the Apocrypha*. New York: Oxford University Press, 1973.

Rahlfs, A., ed. Septuaginta. *Stuttgart: Deutsche Bibelgesellschaft, 1979*.

Jewish Sources

Barthélemy, D. "Règle de la Congrégation (1QSa)," in *Qumran Cave I*. Ed. D. Barthélemy and J. T. Milik, 108–118 and pl. XXIV. DJD 1. Oxford: Clarendon Press, 1955.

___. *Les devanciers d'Aquila: Première publication intégrale du texte des fragments du Dodécaprophéton trouvés dans le désert de Juda, précédée d'une étude sur les traductions et recensions grecques de la Bible réalisées au premier siècle de notre ère sous l'influence du rabbinat palestinien*. VTSup 10. Leiden: Brill, 1963.

Braude, W. G., trans. *Pesikta Rabbati*. 2 vols. YJS 18. New Haven and London: Yale University Press, 1968.

Brooke, G. J. "4QCommentary on Genesis A," in *Qumran Cave 4*. Vol. 18: *Parabiblical Texts*. Part 3. Ed. VanderKam, 185–207. DJD 22. Oxford: Clarendon Press, 1997.

Carmignac, J. "Le document de Qumran sur Melkisédek," *RevQ* 7 (1969–1971): 343–378.

Cathcart, K. J. and R. P. Gordon, trans. *The Targum of the Minor Prophets*. Trans. ArBib 14. Wilmington: Michael Glazier, 1989.

Charles, R. H. *The Apocrypha and Pseudepigrapha of the Old Testament in English: With Introductions and Critical and Explanatory Notes to the Several Books*. Oxford: Clarendon Press, 1913.

Charlesworth, J. H., ed. *Dead Sea Scrolls: Hebrew, Aramaic, and Greek Texts with English Translations*. Vols 1, 2, 4A, 4B, and 6B. Tübingen: J. C. B. Mohr (Paul Siebeck), 1994–2002.

___. ed. *The Old Testament Pseudepigrapha*. 2 vols. ABRL. New York/London/Toronto/Sydney/Auckland: Doubleday, 1983, 1985.

Discoveries in the Judean Desert. Vols. 1–38. Oxford: Clarendon Press, 1955–2000.

Duling, D. C. "Testament of Solomon: A New Translation and Introduction," in *OTP* 1 Ed. J. H. Charlesworth, 935–987. Garden City, NY: Doubleday, 1985.

Eisenman, R. H. and M. O. Wise. *The Dead Sea Scrolls Uncovered: The First Complete Translation and Interpretation of 50 Key Documents Withheld for Over 35 Years*. Shaftesbury/Rockport/Brisbane: Element, 1992.

García Martínez, F. and E. J.C. Tigchelaar, ed. *The Dead Sea Scrolls Study Edition*. 2 vols. Leiden/ Boston: Brill; Grand Rapids: Eerdmans, 2000.

Gordon, C. H. "Aramaic Magical Bowls in the Istanbul and Baghdad Museums," *ArOr* 6 (1934): 319–334.

Harrington, D. J. "Pseudo-Philo: A New Translation and Introduction," in *OTP* 2. Ed. J. H. Charlesworth, 297–377. New York: Doubleday, 1985.

Horgan, M. P. *Pesharim: Qumran Interpretations of Biblical Books*. CBQMS 8. Washington, D.C.: The Catholic Biblical Association of America, 1979.

Isbell, C. D. *Corpus of the Aramaic Incantation Bowls*. SBLDS 17. Missoula, Mont.: Scholars Press, 1975.

Josephus in Nine Volumes. LCL. Cambridge: Harvard University Press; London: William Heinemann, 1956–69.

Klijn, A. F. J., with G. Mussies, eds. *Der lateinische Text der Apokalypse des Esra*. TUGAL 131. Berlin: Akadamie Verlag, 1983.

Lauterbach, J. Z. *Mekilta de-Rabbi Ishmael: A Critical Edition on the Basis of the Manuscripts and Early Editions, with an English Translation, Introduction, and Notes*. 3 vols. Philadelphia: Jewish Publication Society of America, 1933-1935.

Lévi, I., ed. *The Hebrew Text of the Book of Ecclesiasticus*. SSS 3. Leiden: E. J. Brill, 1904.

McCown, C. C., ed. *The Testament of Solomon*. Edited from manuscripts at Mount Athos, Bologna, Holkham Hall, Jerusalem, London, Milan, Paris, and Vienna. UNT 9. Leipzig: J. C. Hinrichs'sche Buchhandlung, 1922.

Metzger, B. M. "The Fourth Book of Ezra," in *OTP* 1. Ed. J. H. Charlesworth, 517–559. Garden City, NY: Doubleday, 1985.

Montgomery, J. A. *Aramaic Incantation Texts from Nippur*. Philadelphia: The University Museum, 1913.

Puech, É. "4QApocalypse messianique," in *Qumrân Grotte 4*. Vol. 18. Ed. É. Puech, 1–38 and pls. I–III. DJD 25. Oxford: Clarendon Press, 1998.

Sanders, J. A. "A Liturgy for Healing the Stricken (11QPsAp^a)" in *The Dead Sea Scrolls: Hebrew, Aramaic, and Greek Texts with English Translations*. Vol. 4A: *Pseudepigraphic and Non-Masoretic Psalms and Prayers*. Ed. J. H. Charlesworth and H. W. L. Rietz, 216–233. Tübingen: J. C. B. Mohr (Paul Siebeck), 1997.

____. *The Psalms Scroll of Qumran Cave 11 (11QPs^a)*. DJD 4. Oxford: Clarendon, 1965.

Stenning, J. F., ed. and trans. *The Targum of Isaiah*. Oxford: Clarendon Press, 1949.

Sukenik, E. L. *The Dead Sea Scrolls of the Hebrew University*. Jerusalem: Magnes, 1955.

The Talmud: The Steinsaltz Edition. Vols. 20–21: *Tractate Sanhedrin*. Parts 6–7. New York: Random House, 1999.

Yamauchi, E. M. "Aramaic Magic Bowls," *JAOS* 85 (1965): 511–523.

Pagan Sources

Delatte, A. *Anecdota atheniensia*. 2 vols. Liége: Faculté de philosophie et lettres; Paris: É. Champion, 1927.

Preisendanz, K. *Papyri Graecae Magicae: Die griechischen Zauberpapyri*. Vol. 1. Ed. A. Henrichs. Stuttgart: Teubner, 1973–1974; English translation: *The Greek Magical Papyri in Translation*. Ed. H. D. Betz. Trans. W. C. Grese. Chicago: University of Chicago Press, 1986.

Secondary Literature

Abrams, M. H. *A Glossary of Literary Terms*. 6th ed. Fort Worth: Harcourt Brace Jovanovich, 1993.

Allegro, J. M. *Die Botschaft vom Toten Meer: Das Geheimnis der Schriftrollen*. Frankfurt/Hamburg: Fischer Verlag, 1957.

____. "Further Messianic References in the Qumran Literature," *JBL* 75 (1956): 174–187.

Allen, L. C. "The Old Testament Background of (*pro*)*horizein* in the New Testament," *NTS* 17 (1970–71): 104–108.

___. *Psalms 101–150.* WBC 21. Waco, TX: Word Books, 1983.

Allen, W. C. "Matthew xii.19 – Isaiah xlii.2," *ExpTim* 20 (1908/1909): 140–141.

Allison, D. C. "Elijah Must Come First," *JBL* 103 (1984): 256–258.

___. *The New Moses: A Matthean Typology.* Minneapolis: Fortress Press, 1993.

Attridge, H. W. *The Interpretation of Biblical History in the Antiquitates Judaicae of Flavius Josephus.* HDR 7. Missoula, MT: Scholars Press, 1976.

Ådna, J. "Der Gottesknecht als triumphierender und interzessorischer Messias. Die Rezeption von Jes 53 im Targum Jonathan untersucht mit besonderer Berücksichtigung des Messiasbildes," in *Der leidende Gottesknecht: Jesaja 53 und seine Wirkungsgeschichte mit einer Bibliographie zu Jes 53.* Ed. B. Janowski and P. Stuhlmacher, 129–158. FAT 14. Tübingen: J. C. B. Mohr (Paul Siebeck), 1996.

Bacon, B. W. *Studies in Matthew.* New York: H. Holt, 1930.

Barth, G. "Matthew's Understanding of the Law," in *Tradition and Interpretation in Matthew.* Ed. G. Bornkamm, G. Barth, and H. J. Held. Trans. P. Scott, 58–164. London: SCM Press, 1963.

Bauckham, R. "Tamar's Ancestry and Rahab's Marriage: Two Problems in the Matthean Genealogy," *NovT* 37 (1995): 311–329.

Bauer, W. "The 'Colt' of Palm Sunday," *JBL* 72 (1953): 220–229.

Beare, F. W. *The Gospel according to Matthew. A Commentary.* Oxford: Basil Blackwell, 1981.

Beaton, R. "Messiah and Justice: A Key to Matthew's Use of Isaiah 42.1–4?" *JSNT* 75 (1999): 5–23.

Becker, J. *Jesus von Nazaret.* Berlin/New York: Walter de Gruyter, 1996.

___. *Messianic Expectation in the Old Testament.* Trans. D. E. Green. Edinburgh: T.&T. Clark, 1980.

Becker, M. "4Q521 und die Gesalbten," *RevQ* 18 (1997): 73–96.

___. *Wunder und Wundertäter im frührabbinischen Judentum: Studien zum Phänomen und seiner Überlieferung im Horizont von Magie und Dämonismus.* WUNT II/144. Tübingen: Mohr Siebeck, 2002.

Bellinger, W. H. and W. R. Farmer, eds. *Jesus and the Suffering Servant: Isaiah 53 and Christian Origins.* Harrisburg: Trinity Press International, 1998.

Berger, K. "Die königlichen Messiastraditionen des Neuen Testaments," *NTS* 20 (1973/74): 1–44.

___. *Qumran und Jesus: Wahrheit unter Verschluss?* Stuttgart: Quell, 1993.

Bergmeier, R. "Beobachtungen zu 4Q521 f2, II, 1–13," *ZDMG* 145 (1995): 38-48.

Betz, O. "Das Problem des Wunders bei Flavius Josephus im Vergleich zum Wunderproblem bei den Rabbinen und im Johannesevangelium," in *Josephus-Studien: Untersuchungen zu Josephus, dem antiken Judentum und dem Neuen Testament.* Ed. O. Betz, K. Haacker, and M. Hengel, 23–44. FS O. Michel. Göttingen: Vandenhoeck & Ruprecht, 1974.

___. and R. Riesner. *Jesus, Qumran and the Vatikan: Clarifications.* Trans. J. Bowden. New York: Crossroad, 1994.

Beuken, W. A. M. "Servant and Herald of Good Tidings: Isaiah 61 as an Interpretation of Isaiah 40–55," in *The Book of Isaiah: Le livre d'Isaïe.* Ed. J. Vermeylen, 411–442. BETL 81. Leuven: Peeters and Leuven University Press, 1989.

Bittner, W. J. *Jesu Zeichen im Johannesevangelium: Die Messias-Erkenntnis im Johannesevangelium vor ihrem jüdischen Hintergrund.* WUNT II/26. Tübingen: J. C. B. Mohr (Paul Siebeck), 1987.

Blass, F. and A. Debrunner. *A Greek Grammar of the New Testament and Other Early Christian Literature.* A Translation and Revision of the ninth-tenth German edition incorporating supplementary notes of A. Debrunner by R. W. Funk. Chicago and London: The University of Chicago Press, 1961.

Boer, P. A. H. de. *Second-Isaiah's Message*. OTS 11. Leiden: E. J. Brill, 1956.

Bonnard, P. *L'Évangile selon Saint Matthieu*. 3rd ed. CNT. Genève: Labor et Fides, 1992.

Bornkamm, G. "End-Expectation and Church in Matthew," in *Tradition and Interpretation in Matthew*. Ed. G. Bornkamm, G. Barth, and H. J. Held. Trans. P. Scott, 15–57. London: SCM, 1963.

___. *Jesus of Nazareth*. Trans. I. and F. Mcluskey. New York/Evanston/London: Harper & Row, 1960.

Box, G. H. "Adoption (Semitic)," in *Encyclopaedia of Religion and Ethics*. Vol. 1. Ed. J. Hastings, 114–115. Edinburgh: T.&T. Clark, 1908.

___. "The Gospel Narratives of the Nativity and the Alleged Influence of Heathen Ideas," *ZNW* 6 (1905): 80–101.

Braun, H. *Qumran und das Neue Testament*. 2 vols. Tübingen: J. C. B. Mohr (Paul Siebeck), 1966.

Breech, E. "These Fragments I have Stoned Against my Ruins: The Form and Function of 4 Ezra," *JBL* 92 (1973): 267–274.

Brierre-Narbonne, J.-J. *Exégèse talmudique des prophéties messianiques*. Paris: Librairie Orientaliste Paul Geuthner, 1934.

Bright, J. *Covenant and Promise: The Prophetic Understanding of the Future in Pre-Exilic Israel*. Philadelphia: Westminster Press, 1976.

Broer, I. "Versuch zur Christologie des ersten Evangeliums," in *The Four Gospels 1992*. Vol. 2. Ed. F. Van Segbroeck, C. M. Tuckett, G. Van Belle, and J. Verheyden, 1251–1282. FS F. Neirynck. BETL 100. Leuven: University Press, 1992.

Brooke, G. J. "Luke-Acts and the Qumran Scrolls: The Case of MMT," in *Luke's Literary Achievement: Collected Essays*. Ed. C. M. Tuckett, 72–90. JSNTSup 116. Sheffield: Academic Press, 1995.

Brown, R. E. *The Birth of the Messiah: A Commentary on the Infancy Narratives in Matthew and Luke*. Garden City, NY: Doubleday & Company, 1979.

Brown, S. "The Matthean Community and the Gentile Mission," *NovT* 22 (1980): 193–221.

Brownlee, W. H. *The Midrash Pesher of Habakkuk*. SBLMS 24. Missoula: Scholars Press, 1979.

Buchanan, G. W. *The Gospel of Matthew*. 2 vols. The Mellen Biblical Commentary New Testament Series. Lewiston, NY: Mellen Biblical Press, 1996.

Bultmann, R. *The History of the Synoptic Tradition*. Trans. K. Grovel. Oxford: Basil Blackwell, 1963.

___. *Theology of the New Testament*. Trans. K. Grobel. 2 vols. New York: Charles Scribner's Sons, 1954, 1955.

Burger, C. "Jesu Taten nach Matthäus 8 und 9," *ZTK* 70 (1973): 272–287.

___. *Jesus als Davidssohn: Eine traditionsgeschichtliche Untersuchung*. FRLANT 98. Göttingen: Vandenhoeck & Ruprecht, 1970.

Byrskog, S. *Jesus the Only Teacher: Didactic Authority and Transmission in Ancient Israel, Ancient Judaism and the Matthean Community*. ConBNT 24. Stockholm: Almqvist & Wiksell International, 1994.

Cadbury, H. J. "The Titles of Jesus in Acts," in *The Beginnings of Christianity*. Part 1: *The Acts of the Apostles*. Ed. F. J. F. Jackson and K. Lake. Vol. 5: *Additional Notes to the Commentary*. Ed. K. Lake and H. J. Cadbury, 354–375. London: Macmillan, 1933.

Callan, T. "Ps 110,1 and the Origin of the Expectation that Jesus will come again," *CBQ* 44 (1982): 622–635.

Charlesworth, J. H. "Challenging the *Consensus Communis* Regarding Qumran Messianism (1QS, 4QS MSS)" in *Qumran-Messianism: Studies on the Messianic Expectations in the Dead Sea Scrolls.* Ed. J. H. Charlesworth, H. Lichtenberger, and G. S. Oegema, 120–134. Tübingen: Mohr Siebeck, 1999.

___. "The Concept of the Messiah in the Pseudepigrapha," in *ANRW* II.19.1. Ed. H. Temporini and W. Haase, 188–218. Berlin/New York: Walter de Gruyter, 1979.

___. "From Jewish Messianology to Christian Christology: Some Caveats and Perspectives," in *Judaisms and Their Messiahs at the Turn of the Christian Era.* Ed. J. Neusner, W. S. Green, and E. S. Frerichs, 225–264. Cambridge: University Press, 1987.

___. "From Messianology to Christology: Problems and Prospects," in *The Messiah: Developments in Earliest Judaism and Christianity.* Ed. J. H. Charlesworth, 3–35. Minneapolis: Fortress, 1992.

___. "Messianology in the Biblical Pseudepigrapha," in *Qumran-Messianism: Studies on the Messianic Expectations in the Dead Sea Scrolls.* Ed. J. H. Charlesworth, H. Lichtenberger, and G. S. Oegema, 21–52. Tübingen: Mohr Siebeck, 1999.

___. "Solomon and Jesus: The Son of David in Ante-Markan Traditions (Mark 10:47)," in *Biblical and Humane.* Ed. L. B. Elder, D. L. Barr, and E. S. Malbon, 125–151. FS J. F. Priest. Atlanta: Scholars Press, 1996.

___. H. Lichtenberger, and G. S. Oegema, eds. *Qumran-Messianism: Studies on the Messianic Expectations in the Dead Sea Scrolls.* Tübingen: Mohr Siebeck, 1998.

___. and L. T. Stuckenbruck. Introduction to the *"Rule of the Congregation* (1QSa)," in *Dead Sea Scrolls: Hebrew, Aramaic, and Greek Texts with English Translations.* Vol. 1: *Rule of the Community and Related Documents.* Ed. J. H. Charlesworth, 108–109. Tübingen: J. C. B. Mohr (Paul Siebeck), 1994.

Chatman, S. *Story and Discourse. Narrative Structure in Fiction and Film.* Ithaca/ London: Cornell University Press, 1978.

Clark, K. "The Gentile Bias of Matthew," *JBL* 66 (1947): 165–172.

Collins, J. J. "A Herald of Good Tidings: Isaiah 61:1–3 and its Actualization in the Dead Sea Scrolls," in *The Quest for Context and Meaning: Studies in Biblical Intertextuality.* Ed. C. A. Evans and S. Talmon, 225–240. FS J. A. Sanders. BIS 28. Leiden: Brill, 1997.

___. "Jesus, Messianism and the Dead Sea Scrolls," in *Qumran-Messianism: Studies on the Messianic Expectations in the Dead Sea Scrolls.* Ed. J. H. Charlesworth, H. Lichtenberger, and G. S. Oegema, 100–119. Tübingen: Mohr Siebeck, 1998.

___. "A Pre-Christian 'Son of God' Among the Dead Sea Scrolls," *BRev* (1993): 34–38.

___. *The Scepter and the Star: The Messiahs of the Dead Sea Scrolls and Other Ancient Literature.* ABRL. New York: Doubleday, 1995.

___. "The 'Son of God' Text from Qumran," in *From Jesus to John: Essays on Jesus and New Testament Christology in Honour of Marinus de Jonge.* Ed. M. C. de Boer, 65–82. JSNTSup 84. Sheffield: JSOT, 1993.

___. "The Works of the Messiah," *DSD* 1 (1994): 98–112.

Comber, J. A."The Verb *therapeuô* in Matthew's Gospel," *JBL* 97 (1978): 431–434.

Conzelmann, H. "Jesus Christus," in *Die Religion in Geschichte und Gegenwart: Handwörterbuch in gemeinverständlicher Darstellung.* Vol. 3. Ed. K. Galling, H. F. von Campenhausen, and W. Werbeck, 619–653. 3rd ed. Tübingen: J. C. B. Mohr (Paul Siebeck), 1959.

Cope, O. L. *Matthew: A Scribe Trained for the Kingdom of Heaven.* CBQMS 5. Washington: The Catholic Biblical Association of America, 1976.

Cranfield, C. E. B. *A Critical and Exegetical Commentary on the Epistle to the Romans.* 2 vols. ICC. Edinburgh: T.&T. Clark, 1975.

Cross, F. M. *Canaanite Myth and Hebrew Epic.* Cambridge, MA: Harvard University Press, 1973.

Cullmann, O. *The Christology of the New Testament.* Trans. S. C. Guthrie and C. A. M. Hall. Rev. ed. NTL. Philadelphia: Westminster, 1963.

Culpepper, R. A. *Anatomy of the Fourth Gospel: A Study in Literary Design.* New Testament Foundations and Facets. Philadelphia: Fortress Press, 1983.

Dahl, N. A. "Contradictions in Scripture," in *Studies in Paul: Theology for the Early Christian Mission*, 159–177. Minneapolis: Augsburg, 1977.

___. *The Crucified Messiah and Other Essays.* Minneapolis: Augsburg, 1974.

Daly-Denton, M. *David in the Fourth Gospel: The Johannine Reception of the Psalms.* AGJU 47. Leiden/Boston/Köln: Brill, 1999.

Daube, D. "Four Types of Question," in *The New Testament and Rabbinic Judaism*, 158–169. The Jewish People: History, Religion, Literature. New York: Arno Press, 1973.

Davenport, G. L. "The 'Anointed of the Lord' in Psalms of Solomon 17," in *Ideal Figures in Ancient Judaism: Profiles and Paradigms.* Ed. J. J. Collins and G. W. E. Nickelsburg, 67–92. SBLSCS 12. Chico: Scholars Press, 1980.

Davies, W. D. "The Jewish Sources of Matthew's Messianism," in *The Messiah.* Ed. J. H. Charlesworth, 494–511. Minneapolis: Fortress, 1992,.

___. and D. C. Allison. *The Gospel According to Saint Matthew.* 3 vols. ICC. Edinburgh: T.&T. Clark, 1988, 1991, 1997.

Davis, C. T. "Tradition and Redaction in Matthew 1:18–2:23," *JBL* 90 (1971): 404–421.

Deissmann, G. A. *Bible Studies: Contributions chiefly from Papyri and Inscriptions to the History of the Language, the Literature, and the Religion of Hellenistic Judaism and Primitive Christianity.* Trans. A. Grieve. Edinburgh: T.&T. Clark, 1901.

Dewes, B. F. "The Composition of Matthew 8–9," *SEAJT* 12 (1972): 92–101.

Dexinger, F. "Reflections on the Relationship between Qumran and Samaritan Messianology," in *Qumran-Messianism: Studies on the Messianic Expectations in the Dead Sea Scrolls.* Ed. J. H. Charlesworth, H. Lichtenberger, and G. S. Oegema, 83–99. Tübingen: Mohr Siebeck, 1998.

Dodd, C. H. *According to the Scriptures: The Substructure of New Testament Theology.* London: Nisbet, 1952.

Duling, D. C. "The Promises to David and Their Entrance Into Christianity – Nailing Down a Likely Hypothesis," *NTS* 20 (1973–74): 55–71.

___. "Solomon, Exorcism, and the Son of David," *HTR* 68 (1975): 235–252.

___. "The Therapeutic Son of David: An Element in Matthew's Christological Apologetic," *NTS* 24 (1977–78): 392–410.

Dunn, J. D. G. *Christology in the Making: A New Testament Inquiry into the Origins of the Doctrine of Incarnation.* 2nd ed. London: SCM, 1989.

___. *Romans 1–8.* WBC 38A. Dallas: Word Books, 1988.

Dupont, J. "Introduction aux Béatitudes," *NRTh* 108 (1976): 97–108.

Edwards, R. A. *Matthew's Story of Jesus.* Philadelphia: Fortress Press, 1985.

Ehrman, B. D. *The New Testament: A Historical Introduction to the Early Christian Writings.* New York: Oxford University Press, 1997.

Eisenman, R. H. "A Messianic Vision," *BAR* 17.6 (1991): 65.

Eissfeldt, O. "The Promises of Grace to David in Isaiah 55:1–5," in *Israel's Prophetic Heritage.* Ed. B. W. Anderson and W. Harrelson, 196–207. London: Harper & Brothers, 1962.

Elliger, K. "Der Prophet Tritojesaja," *ZAW* 49 (1931): 112–141.

Elliott, N. "The Silence of the Messiah: The Function of 'Messianic Secret' Motifs across the Synoptics," in *SBL 1993 Seminar Papers*. Ed. E. H. Lovering, 604–633. SBL Seminar Papers Series 32. Atlanta: Scholars Press, 1993.

Ellis, P. F. *Matthew: His Mind and His Message*. Collegeville: Liturgical Press, 1974.

Evans, C. A. "Are the 'Son' Texts at Qumran Messianic? Reflections on 4Q369 and Related Scrolls" in *Qumran-Messianism: Studies on the Messianic Expectations in the Dead Sea Scrolls*. Ed. J. H. Charlesworth, H. Lichtenberger, and G. S. Oegema, 135–153. Tübingen: Mohr Siebeck, 1998.

___. "Jesus and the Dead Sea Scrolls from Qumran Cave 4," in *Eschatology, Messianism, and the Dead Sea Scrolls*. Ed. C. A. Evans and P. Flint, 91–100. SDSSRL 1. Grand Rapids, Michigan: William B. Eerdmans, 1997.

___. *Jesus and His Contemporaries: Comparative Studies*. AGJU 25. Leiden: Brill, 1995.

Evans, G. "Reference and Contingency," *The Monist* 62 (1979): 161–184.

Faierstein, M. M. "Why do the Scribes Say that Elijah Must Come First?" *JBL* 100 (1981): 75–86.

Farmer, W. R. "Reflections on Isaiah 53 and Christian Origins," in *Jesus and the Suffering Servant: Isaiah 53 and Christian Origins*. Ed. W. H. Bellinger and W. R. Farmer, 260–280. Harrisburg: Trinity Press International, 1998.

Fisher, L. R. "Can This Be the Son of David?" in *Jesus and the Historian*. Ed. F. T. Trotter, 82–97. FS E. C. Colwell. Philadelphia: Westminster, 1968.

Fitzmyer, J. A. "The Contribution of Qumran Aramaic to the Study of the New Testament," in *A Wandering Aramean: Collected Aramaic Essays*, 85–113. SBLMS 25. Missoula: Scholars Press, 1979.

___. *The Gospel According to Luke I–IX*. AB 28. Garden City: Doubleday, 1981.

___. "More About Elijah Coming First," *JBL* 104 (1985): 295–296.

___. "The Son of David Tradition and Matthew 22,41–46 and Parallels," *Concilium* 20 (1967): 75–87.

___. "4Q246: The 'Son of God' Document from Qumran," *Bib* 74 (1993): 153–174.

Flusser, D. "Blessed are the Poor in Spirit . . ." *IEJ* 10 (1960): 1–13.

___. "Healing Through the Laying-on of Hands in a Dead Sea Scroll," *IEJ* 7 (1957): 107–108.

___. "The Hubris of the Antichrist in a Fragment from Qumran," *Imm* 10 (1980): 31–37.

Fohrer, G. "σῴζω and σωτερία in the Old Testament," in *TDNT* 7. Ed. G. Friedrich. Trans. G. W. Bromiley, 970–980. Grand Rapids, Michigan: Wm. B. Eerdmans Publishing Company, 1971.

France, R. T. "Exegesis in Practice: Two Samples," in *New Testament Interpretation: Essays on Principles and Methods*. Ed. I. H. Marshall, 252–281. Exeter: Paternoster, 1977.

___. "The Formula-Quotations of Matthew 2 and the Problem of Communication," *NTS* 27 (1980/1981): 233–251.

___. *Matthew: Evangelist and Teacher*. Exeter: The Paternoster Press, 1989.

François, F. "Kontext und Situation," in *Linguistik: Ein Handbuch*. Ed. A. Martinet. Trans. I. Rehbein and S. Stelzer, 42–48. Stuttgart: J. B. Metzler, 1973.

Frankemölle, H. *Jahwebund und Kirche Christi: Studien zur Form- und Traditionsgeschichte des "Evangeliums" nach Matthäus*. NTAbh 10. Münster: Aschendorff, 1974.

___. "Jesus als deuterojesajanischer Freudenbote? Zur Rezeption von Jes 52,7 und 61,1 im Neuen Testament, durch Jesus und in den Targumim," in *Vom Urchristentum zu Jesus*. Ed. H. Frankemölle and K. Kertelge, 34–67. FS J. Gnilka. Freiburg: Herder, 1989.

Frankfurter, D. M. "The Origin of the Miracle-List Tradition and Its Medium of Circulation," in *SBL 1990 Seminar Papers*. Ed. D. J. Lull, 344–374. SBL Seminar Papers Series 29. Atlanta: Scholars Press, 1990.

Frenz, A. "Mt. XXI 5.7," *NovT* 13 (1971): 259–260.

Fuller, R. H. "The Conception/Birth of Jesus as a Christological Moment," *JSNT* 1 (1978): 37–52.

___. *The Foundations of New Testament Christology.* New York: Scribner's Sons, 1965.

Furlani, G. "Aram. Gazrin = scongiurotori," *Anti della accademia nationale et filogiche,* Serie Ottava IV (1948): 177–196.

Gagg, R. "Jesus und die Davidssohnfrage: Zur Exegese von Markus 12,35–37," *TZ* 7 (1951): 18–31.

García Martínez, F. "Messianische Erwartungen in den Qumranschriften," in *Jahrbuch für Biblische Theologie.* Vol. 8: *Der Messias,* 171–208. Neukirchen: Neukirchener Verlag, 1993. English translation: "Messianic Hopes in the Qumran Writings," in *The People of the Dead Sea Scrolls.* Ed. F. García Martínez and J. Trebolle Barrerra, 159–189. Leiden: Brill, 1995.

___. and J. T. Barrera. *The People of the Dead Sea Scrolls: Their Writings, Beliefs and Practices.* Trans. W. G. E. Watson. Leiden: Brill, 1995.

Gärtner, B. "The Habakkuk Commentary (DSH) and the Gospel of Matthew," *ST* 8 (1955): 1–24.

Gaston, L. "The Messiah of Israel as Teacher of the Gentiles: The Setting of Matthew's Christology," *Int* 29 (1975): 24–40.

Geist, H. *Menschensohn und Gemeinde: Eine redaktionskritische Untersuchung zur Menschensohnprädikation im Matthäusevangelium.* FB 57. Würzburg: Echter Verlag, 1986.

Gerhardsson, B. *The Mighty Acts of Jesus According to Matthew.* Scripta Minora Regiae Societatis Humaniorum Litterarum Lundensis 1978/79:5. Lund: CWK Gleerup, 1979.

Gibbs, J. M. "Purpose and Pattern in Matthew's Use of the Title 'Son of David'," *NTS* 10 (1963/64): 446–464.

Good, D. "The Verb ΑΝΑΧΩΡΕΩ in Matthew's Gospel," *NT* 32 (1990): 1–12.

Gordon, C. H. *Adventures in the Nearest East.* London: Pnoenix House, 1957.

Gourgues, M. *A la Droite de Dieu. Résurrection de Jésus et Actualisation du Psaume 110,1 dans le Nouveau Testament.* EtB. Paris: Lecoffre/Gabalda, 1978.

Grimm, W. *Weil ich dich liebe: Die Verkündigung Jesu und Deuterojesaja.* ANTJ 1. Bern: Herbert Lang; Frankfurt: Peter Lang, 1976.

Grindel, J. "Matthew 12:18–21," *CBQ* 29 (1967): 110–115.

Grundmann, W. *Das Evangelium nach Matthäus.* Berlin: Evangelische Verlagsanstalt, 1968.

Gundry, R. H. *Matthew: A Commentary on His Handbook for a Mixed Church under Persecution.* 2nd ed. Grand Rapids, Michigan: William B. Eerdmans Publishing Company, 1994.

___. *The Use of the Old Testament in St. Matthew's Gospel with Special Reference to the Messianic Hope.* NovTSup 18. Leiden: E. J. Brill, 1967.

Gunkel, H. *Genesis,* 8th ed. Göttingen: Vandenhoeck & Ruprecht, 1969.

Hagner, D. A. *Matthew 1–13.* WBC 33A. Dallas, TX: Word Books, 1993.

Hahn, F. *The Titles of Jesus in Christology: Their History in Early Christianity.* Trans. H. Knight and G. Ogg. London: Lutterworth Press, 1969.

___. *Das Verständnis der Mission im Neuen Testament.* WMANT 13. Neukirchen-Vluyn: Neukirchener Verlag, 1963.

Hanson, P. *The Dawn of Apocalyptic: The Historical and Sociological Roots of Jewish Apocalyptic Eschatology.* Philadelphia: Fortress, 1975.

Hare, D. R. A. and D. J. Harrington. "'Make Disciples of all the Gentiles' (Mt 28:19)," *CBQ* 37 (1975): 359–369.

Hay, D. M. *Glory at the Right Hand: Psalm 110 in Early Christianity.* SBLMS 18. Nashville: Abingdon, 1973.

Hayes, J. H. "The Resurrection as Enthronement and the Earliest Church Christology," *Int* 22 (1968): 333–345

Hegermann, H. *Jesaja 53 in Hexapla, Targum und Peschitta*. BFCT II/56. Gütersloh: C. Bertelsmann Verlag, 1954.

Heitmüller, W. "Jesus Christus: II. Einzelne Fragen des Lebens Jesu," in *Die Religion in Geschichte und Gegenwart: Handwörterbuch in gemeinverständlicher Darstellung*. Vol. 3. Ed. F. M. Schiele, 362–382. Tübingen: J. C. B. Mohr (Paul Siebeck), 1912.

Held, H. J. "Matthew as Interpreter of the Miracle Stories," in *Tradition and Interpretation in Matthew*. Ed. G. Bornkamm, G. Barth, and H. J. Held. Trans. P. Scott, 165–299. London: SCM Press, 1963.

Hengel, M. "Jesus, the Messiah of Israel," in *Studies in Early Christology*, 1–72. Edinburgh: T&T Clark, 1995.

___. "'Sit at My Right Hand!' The Enthronement of Christ at the Right Hand of God and Psalm 110:1," in *Studies in Early Christology*, 119–225. Edinburgh: T&T Clark, 1995.

___. "Zur matthäischen Bergpredigt und ihrem jüdischen Hintergrund," in *Judaica, Hellenistica et Christiana: Kleine Schriften II*, 219–292. WUNT 109. Tübingen: Mohr Siebeck, 1999.

___. "Zur Wirkungsgeschichte von Jes 53 in vorchristlicher Zeit," in *Der leidende Gottesknecht: Jesaja 53 und seine Wirkungsgeschichte mit einer Bibliographie zu Jes 53*. Ed. B. Janowski and P. Stuhlmacher, 49–91. FAT 14. Tübingen: J. C. B. Mohr (Paul Siebeck), 1996.

Hill, D. *The Gospel of Matthew*. NCB. London: Marshall, Morgan and Scott, 1972.

___. "Son and Servant: An Essay on Matthean Christology," *JSNT* 6 (1980): 2–16.

Hogan, L. P. *Healing in the Second Tempel Period*. NTOA 21. Göttingen: Vandenhoeck & Ruprecht, 1992.

Hooker, M. *Jesus and the Servant: The Influence of the Servant Concept of Deutero-Isaiah in the New Testament*. London: SPCK, 1959.

Horbury, W. *Jewish Messianism and the Cult of Christ*. London: SCM Press, 1998.

Horsley, R. A. "'Like One of the Prophets of Old': Two Types of Popular Prophets at the Time of Jesus," *CBQ* 47 (1985): 435–463.

Howell, D. B. *Matthew's Inclusive Story: A Study in the Narrative Rhetoric of the First Gospel*. JSNTSup 42. Sheffield: JSOT Press, 1990.

Hubbard, B. J. *The Matthean Redaction of a Primitive Apostolic Commissioning: An Exegesis of Matthew 28:16–20*. SBLDS 19. Missoula: Scholars Press, 1974.

Hummel, R. *Auseinandersetzung zwischen Kirche und Judentum im Matthäusevangelium*. 2nd ed. BEvT 33. München: Christus Kaiser, 1966.

James, M. R. "Citharismus regis David contra daemonum Saulis," in *Apocrypha Anecdota*, 83–85. TS 2/3. Cambridge: University Press, 1893.

Janowski, B. and P. Stuhlmacher, eds. *Der leidende Gottesknecht: Jesaja 53 und seine Wirkungsgeschichte mit einer Bibliographie zu Jes 53*. FAT 14. Tübingen: J. C. B. Mohr (Paul Siebeck), 1996.

Jastrow, M. *A Dictionary of the Targumim, the Talmud, Babli and Yerushalmi, and the Midrashic Literature*. New York: Jastrow Publishers, 1967.

Jeremias, J. "Ἀμνὸς τοῦ θεοῦ – παῖς θεοῦ," *ZNW* 34 (1935): 115–123.

___. *Jerusalem zur Zeit Jesu: Kulturgeschichtliche Untersuchung zur neutestamentlichen Zeitgeschichte*. Göttingen: Vandenhoeck & Ruprecht, 1962.

___. *Jesus' Promise to the Nations*. SBT 24. London: SCM, 1958.

___. "Μωυσῆς," in *TDNT* 4. Ed. G. Kittel. Trans. G. W. Bromiley, 848–873. Grand Rapids, Michigan: Wm. B. Eerdmans Publishing Company, 1967.

___. "παῖς θεοῦ," in *TDNT* 5. Ed. G. Friedrich. Trans. G. W. Bromiley, 677–717. Grand Rapids, Michigan: Wm. B. Eerdmans Publishing Company, 1967.

Johnson, M. D. *The Purpose of Biblical Genealogies, with Special Reference to the Setting of the Genealogies of Jesus.* SNTSMS 8. Cambridge: Cambridge University Press, 1969.

Jones, J. M. "Subverting the Textuality of Davidic Messianism: Matthew's Presentation of the Genealogy and the Davidic Title," *CBQ* 56 (1994): 256–272.

Jonge, M. de. "The Expectation of the Future in the Psalms of Solomon," *Neot* 23 (1989): 93–117.

___. "The Psalms of Solomon," in *Outside the Old Testament.* Ed. M. de Jonge, 159–177. CCWJCW 4. Cambridge: University Press, 1985.

___. "The Use of the Word 'Anointed' in the Time of Jesus," *NovT* 8 (1966): 132–148.

Juel, D. *Messiah and Temple: The Trial of Jesus in the Gospel of Mark.* Missoula, Mont.: Scholars Press, 1977.

___. *Messianic Exegesis: Christological Interpretation of the Old Testament in Early Christianity.* Philadelphia: Fortress Press, 1992.

Kilpatrick, G. D. *The Origins of the Gospel according to St. Matthew.* Oxford: Clarendon Press, 1946.

Kingsbury, J. D. "The Figure of Jesus in Matthew's Story," *JSNT* 21 (1984): 3–22.

___. *Matthew as Story.* Philadelphia: Fortress Press, 1986.

___. *Matthew: Structure, Christology, Kingdom.* Philadelphia: Fortress Press, 1975.

___. "Observations on the 'Miracle Chapters' of Matthew 8–9," *CBQ* 40 (1978): 559–573.

___. "The Significance of the Cross within the Plot of Matthew's Gospel: A Study in Narrative Criticism," in *The Synoptic Gospels: Source Criticism and the New Literary Criticism.* Ed. C. Focant, 263–279. BETL 110. Leuven: University Press, 1993.

___. "The Title 'Son of David' in Matthew's Gospel," *JBL* 95 (1976): 591–602.

___. "The Title 'Son of God' in Matthew's Gospel," *BTB* 5 (1975): 3–31.

Klausner, J. *The Messianic Idea in Israel: From Its Beginning to the Completion of the Mishnah.* Trans. W. F. Stinespring. New York: Macmillan, 1955.

Kloppenborg, J. S. *The Formation of Q.* Philadelphia: Fortress, 1987.

Klostermann, E. *Das Matthäusevangelium.* 4th ed. HNT 4. Tübingen: J. C. B. Mohr, 1971.

Knox, W. L. *The Sources of the Synoptic Gospels.* Vol. 2: *St. Luke and St. Matthew.* Ed. H. Chadwick. Cambridge: University Press, 1957.

Kobelski, P. J. *Melchizedek and Melchireša'.* CBQMS 10. Washington: Catholic Biblical Association, 1981.

Kuhn, H.-W. *Enderwartung und gegenwärtiges Heil: Untersuchungen zu den Gemeindeliedern von Qumran mit einem Anhang über Eschatologie und Gegenwart in der Verkündigung Jesu.* SUNT 4. Göttingen: Vandenhoeck & Ruprecht, 1966.

___. "Röm 1,3f und der davidische Messias als Gottessohn in den Qumran-texten," in *Lese-Zeichen für Annelis Findeiss zum 65. Geburtstag am 15. März 1984.* Ed. C. Burchard and G. Theissen, 103–113. Heidelberg: Carl Winter, 1984.

Kuhn, G. "Die Geschlechtsregister Jesu bei Lukas und Matthäus, nach ihrer Herkunft untersucht," *ZNW* 22 (1923): 206–228.

Kühner, R. and B. Gerth. *Ausführliche Grammatik der Griechischen Sprache.* Vol. 2. Part 2. Hanover: Hahnsche Buchhandlung, 1904.

Kvalbein, H. "The Wonders of the End-Time: Metaphoric Language in 4Q521 and the Interpretation of Matthew 11.5 par." *JSP* 18 (1998): 87–110. German original: "Die Wunder der Endzeit: Beobachtungen zu 4Q521 und Matth 11,5 par." *ZNW* 88 (1997): 111–125.

Lagrange, M. J. *Évangile selon Saint Matthieu.* 4th ed. EtB. Paris: Lecoffre/Gabalda, 1927.

Leske, A. M. "Isaiah and Matthew: The Prophetic Influence in the First Gospel," in *Jesus and the Suffering Servant: Isaiah 53 and Christian Origins.* Ed. W. H. Bellinger and W. R. Farmer, 152–169. Harrisburg: Trinity Press International, 1998.

Levenson, J. D. *Creation and the Persistence of Evil: The Jewish Drama of Divine Omnipotence.* San Francisco: Harper & Row, 1988.

Levine, A.-J. *The Social and Ethnic Dimensions of Matthean Salvation History: "Go nowhere among the Gentiles ..." (Matt. 10:5b).* SBEC 14. Lewiston/Queenston/ Lampeter: The Edwin Mellen Press, 1988.

Levison, J. R. *Portraits of Adam in Early Judaism from Sirach to 2 Baruch.* JSPSup 1. Sheffield: JSOT Press, 1988.

Lewis, A. S. *Light on the Four Gospels from the Sinai Palimpsest.* London: Williams & Norgate, 1913.

Lindars, B. *New Testament Apologetic: The Doctrinal Significance of the Old Testament Quotations.* London: SCM Press, 1961.

Linton, O. "The Demand for a Sign from Heaven (Mark 8,11–12 and Parallels)," *ST* 19 (1965): 112–129.

Loader, W. R. G. "Christ at the Right Hand – Ps. CX in the New Testament," *NTS* 24 (1978): 199–217.

___. "Son of David, Blindness, Possession, and Duality in Matthew," *CBQ* 44 (1982): 570–585.

Lohfink, N. "Der Messiaskönig und seine Armen kommen zum Zion: Beobachtungen zu Matt 21,1–17," in *Studien zum Matthäusevangelium.* Ed. L. Schenke, 179–200. FS W. Pesch. Stuttgart: Verlag Katholisches Bibelwerk, 1988.

Lohmeyer. E. *Das Evangelium des Markus.* 4th ed. Göttingen: Vandenhoeck & Ruprecht, 1954.

___. *Das Evangelium des Matthäus.* Ed. W. Schmauch. 3rd ed. MeyerK. Göttingen: Vandenhoeck & Ruprecht, 1962.

Lövestam, E. "Die Davidssohnfrage," *SEÅ* 27 (1962): 72–82.

___. "Jésus Fils de David chez les Synoptiques," *ST* 28 (1974): 97–109; Swedish original: "David-son-kristologin hos synoptikerna," *SEÅ* 15 (1972): 198–210.

___. *Son and Savior.* ConBNT 8. Lund: C. W. K. Gleerup, 1961.

Luomanen, P. *Entering the Kingdom of Heaven: A Study of the Structure of Matthew's View of Salvation.* WUNT II/101. Tübingen: J. C. B. Mohr (Paul Siebeck), 1998.

Luz, U. "Eine thetische Skizze der Matthäischen Christologie," in *Anfänge der Christologie.* Ed. C. Breytenbach and H. Paulsen, 221–235. FS F. Hahn. Göttingen: Vandenhoeck & Ruprecht, 1991.

___. "Fiktivität und Traditionstreue im Matthäusevangelium im Lichte griechischer Literatur," *ZNW* 84 (1993): 153–177.

___. "Die Jünger im Matthäusevangelium," *ZNW* 62 (1971): 141–171.

___. *Das Evangelium nach Matthäus.* 4 vols. EKK I/1-4. Zürich, Düsseldorf: Benziger; Neukirchen-Vluyn: Neukirchener, 1985-2002.

___. *Matthew 1–7: A Commentary.* Trans. W. C. Linss. Minneapolis: Augsburg Fortress, 1989.

___. *Matthew 8–20: A Commentary.* Ed. H. Koester. Trans. J. E. Crouch. Hermeneia. Minneapolis: Fortress Press, 2001.

___. "Die Wundergeschichten von Matt 8–9," in *Tradition and Interpretation in the New Testament.* Ed. G. F. Hawthorne and O. Betz, 149–165. FS E. E. Ellis. Grand Rapids, Michigan: William B. Eerdmans, 1987.

Lyons, J. *Language, Meaning, and Context.* London: Fontana, 1981.

Martin, F. "The Image of Shepherd in the Gospel of Saint Matthew," *ScEs* 27 (1975): 261–301.

McCasland, S. V. "Matthew Twists the Scriptures," *JBL* 80 (1961): 143–148.

McKenzie, J. L. "The Dynastic Oracle: II Samuel 7," *TS* 8 (1947): 187–218.

___. "Royal Messianism," *CBQ* 19 (1957): 25–52.

McNeile, A. H. *The Gospel According to St. Matthew: The Greek Text with Introduction, Notes, and Indices*. Thornapple Commentaries. London: Macmillan and Company, 1915.

Meadors, E. P. "The 'Messianic' Implications of the Q Material," *JBL* 118 (1999): 253–277.

Meeks, W. A. *The Prophet-King: Moses Traditions and the Johannine Christology*. NovTSup 14. Leiden: E. J. Brill, 1967.

Meier, J. P. "Nations or Gentiles in Matthew 28:19?" *CBQ* 39 (1977): 94–102.

___. *The Vision of Matthew: Christ, Church and Morality in the First Gospel*. Theological Inquiries. New York: Paulist Press, 1979.

___. *Textual Commentary on the Greek New Testament: A Companion Volume to the United Bible Societies' Greek New Testament*. 3rd ed. London: United Bible Societies, 1971.

Michaelis, W. "Die Davidssohnschaft Jesu als historisches und kerygmatisches Problem," in *Der historische Jesus und der kerygmatische Christus*. Ed. H. Ristow and K. Matthiae, 317–330. Berlin: Evangelische Verlagsanstalt, 1961.

Michel, D. "Zur Eigenart Tritojesajas," *ThViat* 10 (1966): 213–230.

Michl, J. "Sündenvergebung in Christus," *MTZ* 24 (1973): 25–35.

Milik, J. T. "*Milkî-sedeq* et *Milkî-reša'* dans les anciens écrits juifs et chrétiens," *JJS* 23 (1972): 95–144.

Miller, M. P. "The Function of Isa 61:1–2 in 11Q Melchizedek," *JBL* 88 (1969): 467–469.

Milton, H. "The Structure of the Prologue to St. Matthew's Gospel," *JBL* 81 (1962): 175–181.

Moiser, J. "The Structure of Matthew 8–9: A Suggestion," *ZNW* 76 (1985): 117–118.

Morgenstern, J. "The Suffering Servant – A New Solution," *VT* 11 (1961): 292–320.

Mowinckel, S. *The Psalms in Israel's Worship*. Vol. 1. Nashville: Abingdon, 1962.

Mullen, E. T. "The Divine Witness and the Davidic Royal Grant: Ps 89:37–38," *JBL* 102 (1983): 207–218.

Neirynck, F. "Q 6,20b–21; 7,22 and Isaiah 61," in *The Scriptures in the Gospels*. Ed. C. M. Tuckett, 27–64. BETL 131. Leuven: University Press, 1997.

Nestle, E. "Matthew xii.19 – Isaiah xlii.2," *ExpTim* 20 (1908/1909): 92–93.

Neusner, J. *Messiah in Context: Israel's History and Destiny in Formative Judaism*. The Foundations of Judaism: Method, Teleology, Doctrine. Part 2: Teleology. Philadelphia: Fortress, 1984.

Neyrey, J. H. "The Thematic Use of Isaiah 42,1–4 in Matthew 12," *Bib* 63 (1982): 457–473.

Nickelsbug, G. E. W. *Jewish Literature Between the Bible and the Mishnah*. Philadelphia: Fortress, 1981.

Niebuhr, K.-W. "4Q521, 2 II – Ein Eschatologischer Psalm," in *Mogilany 1995: Papers on the Dead Sea Scrolls Offered in Memory of Aleksy Klawek*. Ed. Z. J. Kapera, 151–168. Kraków: The Enigma Press, 1996.

___. "Die Werke des eschatologischen Freudenboten (4Q521 und die Jesusüberlieferung)," in *The Scriptures in the Gospels*. Ed. C. M. Tuckett, 637–646. BETL 131. Leuven: University Press, 1997.

Nineham, D. E. "The Genealogy in St. Matthew's Gospel and Its Significance for the Study of the Gospels," *BJRL* 58 (1975–76): 421–444.

Nolan, B. *The Royal Son of God*. OBO 23. Göttingen: Vandenhoeck & Ruprecht, 1979.

Nolland, J. "No Son-Of-God Christology in Matthew 1.18–25," *JSNT* 62 (1996): 3–12.

Pesch, R. "Der Gottessohn im matthäischen Evangelienprolog (Matt 1–2). Beobachtungen zu den Zitationsformeln der Reflexionzitate," *Bib* 48 (1967): 395–420.

Philonenko, M. "Remarques sur un hymne essénien de caractère gnostique," *Sem* 11 (1961): 43–54.

Plastaras, J. *The God of Exodus: The Theology of the Exodus Narratives.* Impact Books. Milwaukee: The Bruce Publishing Company, 1966.

Ploeg, J. P. M. van der. "Un petit rouleau de psaumes apocryphes (11QPsAp^a)," in *Tradition und Glaube: Das frühe Christentum in seiner Umwelt.* Ed. G. Jeremias, H.-W. Kuhn, and H. Stegemann,, 128–139. FS K. G. Kuhn. Göttingen: Vandenhoeck & Ruprecht, 1971.

___. "Le Psaume XCI dans une Recension de Qumran," *RB* 72 (1965): 210–217.

Pomykala, K. E. *The Davidic Dynasty Tradition in Early Judaism: Its History and Significance for Messianism.* SBLEJL. Atlanta: Scholars Press, 1995.

Porter, J. R. *Moses and Monarchy: A Study in the Biblical Tradition of Moses.* Oxford: Basil Blackwell, 1963.

Powell, M. A. "The Plots and Sublots of Matthew's Gospel," *NTS* 38 (1992): 187–204.

Puech, É. "Une apocalypse messianique (4Q521)," *RevQ* 15 (1992): 475–522.

___. *La croyance des Esséniens en la vie future: Immortalité, résurrection, vie éternelle? Histoire d'une croyance dans le Judaïsme ancien.* 2 vols. EtB.NS 21-22. Paris: Lecoffre/ Gabalda, 1993.

___. "Fragment d'une apocalypse en araméen (4Q246 = pseudo-Dan^d) et le 'Royaume de Dieu'," *RB* 99 (1992): 98–131.

___. "Messianism, Resurrection, and Eschatology at Qumran and in the New Testament," in *The Community of the Renewed Covenant: The Notre Dame Symposium on the Dead Sea Scrolls.* Ed. E. Ulrich and J. VanderKam, 235–256. CJAS 10. Notre Dame, IN: University of Notre Dame Press, 1994.

___. "Quelques aspects de la restauration du Rouleau des Hymnes (1QH)," *JJS* 39 (1988): 38–55.

Qimron, E. *The Hebrew of the Dead Sea Scrolls.* HSS 29. Atlanta: Scholars Press, 1986.

Rad, G. von. *Old Testament Theology.* Vol. 1: *The Theology of Israel's Historical Traditions.* Trans. D. M. G. Stalker. London: SCM Press, 1975.

Rahlfs, A. "Über Theodotion-Lesarten im Neuen Testament und Aquila-Lesarten bei Justin," *ZNW* 20 (1921): 186–189.

Ratzaby, Y. "Remarks Concerning the Distinction Between *Waw* and *Yodh* in the Habakkuk Scroll," *JQR* 41 (1950–51): 155–157.

Richardson, A. *The Miracle-Stories of the Gospels.* London: SCM Press, 1941.

Riessler, P. *Altjüdisches Schrifttum ausserhalb der Bibel.* 2nd ed. Darmstadt: Wissenschaftliche Buchgesellschaft, 1966.

Roberts, J. J. M. "The Old Testament's Contribution to Messianic Expectations," in *The Messiah: Developments in Earliest Judaism and Christianity.* Ed. J. H. Charlesworth, 39–51. Minneapolis: Fortress, 1992.

Robinson, H. W. *Redemption and Revelation In the Actuality of History.* London: Nisbet & Co., 1942.

Robinson, J. M. "The Sayings Gospel Q," in *The Four Gospels 1992.* Ed. F. Van Segbroeck, C. M. Tuckett, G. Van Belle, and J. Verheyden, 361–388. FS F. Neirynck. BETL 100. Leuven: University Press, 1992.

Rose, M. "Names of God in the OT," in *ABD* 4. Ed. D. N. Freedman, 1001–1011. New York: Doubleday, 1992.

Rothfuchs, W. *Die Erfüllungszitate des Matthäus-Evangeliums: Eine biblisch-theologische Untersuchung.* BWANT 88. Stuttgart: W. Kohlhammer Verlag, 1969.

Sakenfeld, K. D. *The Meaning of Hesed in the Hebrew Bible: A New Inquiry.* HSM 17. Missoula, Montana: Scholars Press, 1978.

Sanders, E. P. *Jesus and Judaism.* Philadelphia: Fortress Press, 1985.

___. *Paul and Palestinian Judaism: A Comparison of Patterns of Religion.* Philadelphia: Fortress Press; London: SCM Press, 1977.

Sarna, N. "Psalm 89: A Study in Inner Biblical Exegesis," in *Biblical and Other Studies.* Ed. A. Altmann, 29–46. Cambridge: Harvard University Press, 1963.

Satterthwaite, P. E. "David in the Books of Samuel: A Messianic Hope?" in *The Lord's Anointed: Interpretation of Old Testament Messianic Texts.* Ed. P. E. Satterthwaite, R. S. Hess, and G. J. Wenham, 41–65. Exeter: Paternoster Press; Grand Rapids: Baker, 1995.

Sayler, G. B. *Have the Promises Failed? A Literary Analysis of 2 Baruch.* SBLDS 72. Chico, CA: Scholars Press, 1984.

Schaberg, J. *The Illegitimacy of Jesus: A Feminist Theological Interpretation of the Infancy Narratives.* San Francisco: Harper & Row, 1987.

Schaper, J. *Eschatology in the Greek Psalter.* WUNT II/76. Tübingen: J. C. B. Mohr (Paul Siebeck), 1995.

Schäfer, P. *Der Bar Kokhba-Aufstand: Studien zum zweiten jüdischen Krieg gegen Rom.* TSAJ 1. Tübingen: J. C. B. Mohr (Paul Siebeck), 1981.

Schlatter, A. *Der Evangelist Matthäus: Seine Sprache, sein Ziel, sein Selbständigkei.* 6th ed. Stuttgart: Calwer, 1963.

Schmidt, W. H. "Gott und Mensch in Ps. 130: Formgeschichtliche Erwägungen," *TZ* 22 (1966): 241–253.

Schneider, G. "Die Davidssohnfrage (Mk 12,35–37)," *Bib* 53 (1972): 65–90.

Schniewind, J. *Das Evangelium nach Matthäus.* 11th ed. NTD 2. Göttingen: Vandenhoeck & Ruprecht, 1964.

Schoeps, H. J. *Paul: The Theology of the Apostle in the Light of Jewish Religious History.* Trans. H. Knight. London: Lutterworth Press, 1961.

Schüpphaus, J. *Die Psalmen Salomos: Ein Zeugnis Jerusalemer Theologie und Frömmigkeit in der Mitte des vorchristlichen Jahrhunderts.* ALGHJ 7. Leiden: E. J. Brill, 1977.

Schweizer, E. *The Holy Spirit.* Trans. Reginald H. and I. Fuller. Philadelphia: Fortress Press, 1980.

Seidelin, P. "Der 'Ebed Jahwe' und die Messiasgestalt im Jesajatargum," *ZNW* 35 (1936): 194–231.

Sigal, P. "Further Reflections on the 'Begotten' Messiah," *HAR* 7 (1983): 221–233.

Sjöberg, E. *Der verborgene Menschensohn in den Evangelien.* Lund: C. W. K. Gleerup, 1955.

Smith, M. "'God's Begetting the Messiah' in 1QSa," *NTS* 5 (1958–59): 218–24.

Skehan, P. W. "Two Books on Qumrân Studies," *CBQ* 21 (1959): 71–78.

___. "The Divine Name at Qumran, in the Masada Scroll, and in the Septuagint," *BIOSCS* 13 (1980): 14–44.

Soares Prabhu, G. M. *The Formula Quotations in the Infancy Narrative of Matthew: An Inquiry into the Tradition History of Matt 1–2.* AnBib 63. Rome: Biblical Institute Press, 1976.

Starcky, J. *et al.* "Le travail d'édition des fragments manuscrits de Qumrân," *RB* 63 (1956): 49–67.

Stegemann, H. "'Die des Uria': Zur Bedeutung der Frauennamen in der Genealogie von Matthäus 1,1–17," in *Tradition und Glaube: Das frühe Christentum in seiner Umwelt.* Ed. G. Jeremias, H.-W. Kuhn, and H. Stegemann, 246–276. FS K. G. Kuhn. Göttingen: Vandenhoeck & Ruprecht, 1971.

___. *Die Essener, Qumran, Johannes der Täufer und Jesus: Ein Sachbuch.* Freiburg: Herder, 1994.

Stendahl, K. "Matthew," in *Peake's Commentary on the Bible.* Ed. M. Black, 769–798. London: Thomas Nelson and Sons, 1962.

____. "Quis et Unde? An Analysis of Mt. 1–2," in *Judentum, Urchristentum, Kirche*. Ed. W. Eltester, 94–105. FS J. Jeremias. BZNW 26. Berlin: Alfred Töpelmann, 1960.

____. *The School of St. Matthew and Its Use of the Old Testament*. ASNU 20. Lund: C. W. K. Gleerup, 1954.

Steudel, A. *DerMidrasch zur Eschatologie aus der Qumrangemeinde (4QmidrEschat^{a.b}): Materielle Rekonstruktion, Textbestand, Gattung und traditionsgeschichtliche Einordnung des durch 4Q174 ("Florilegium") und 4Q177 ("Catena A") repräsentierten Werkes aus den Qumranfunden*. STDJ 13. Leiden, New York, Köln: E. J. Brill, 1994.

Stone, M. E. *Features of the Eschatology of IV Ezra*. HSS 35. Atlanta: Scholars Press, 1989.

____. *Fourth Ezra*. Hermeneia. Minneapolis: Fortress, 1990.

____. "The Question of the Messiah in 4 Ezra," in *Judaisms and Their Messiahs at the Turn of the Christian Era*. Ed. J. Neusner, W. S. Green, and E. S. Freirichs. Cambridge: Cambridge University Press, 1987, 209–224.

Strack, H. L. and P. Billerbeck. *Kommentar zum Neuen Testament aus Talmud und Midrasch*. Vols. 1–4. München: C. H. Beck'sche Verlagsbuchhandlung, 1924–1928.

Strecker, G. *Der Weg der Gerechtigkeit: Untersuchung zur Theologie des Matthäus*. 3rd ed. FRLANT 82. Göttingen: Vandenhoeck & Ruprecht, 1971.

Strobel, A. *Untersuchungen zum eschatologischen Verzögerungsproblem*. NovTSup 2. Leiden/Köln: E. J. Brill, 1961.

Stuhlmacher, P. *Biblische Theologie des Neuen Testaments*. 2 vols. Göttingen: Vandenhoeck & Ruprecht, 1992, 1999.

____. "Jes 53 in den Evangelien und in der Apostelgeschichte," in *Der leidende Gottesknecht: Jesaja 53 und seine Wirkungsgeschichte mit einer Bibliographie zu Jes 53*. Ed. B. Janowski and P. Stuhlmacher, 93–105. FAT 14. Tübingen: J. C. B. Mohr (Paul Siebeck), 1996.

____. "Das paulinische Evangelium," in *Das Evangelium und die Evangelien: Vorträge vom Tübinger Symposium 1982*. Ed. P. Stuhlmacher, 157–182. WUNT 28. Tübingen: Mohr Siebeck, 1983.

____. *Wie treibt man Biblische Theologie*. BThSt 24. Neukirchen-Vluyn: Neukirchener Verlag, 1995.

Suhl, A. "Der Davidssohn im Matthäus-Evangelium," *ZNW* 59 (1968): 57–81.

____. *Die Funktion der alttestamentlichen Zitate und Anspielungen im Markusevangelium*. Gütersloh: Gerd Mohn, 1965.

Tabor, J. D. and M. O. Wise. "4Q521 'On Resurrection' and the Synoptic Gospel Tradition: A Preliminary Study," *JSP* 10 (1992): 149–162; reprinted in *Qumran Questions*. Ed. J. H. Charlesworth, 151–163. The Biblical Seminar 36. Sheffield: Sheffield Academic Press, 1995.

Talmon, S. *King, Cult and Calendar in Ancient Israel*. Jerusalem: Magnes Press; Leiden: Brill, 1986.

____. "Notes on the Habakkuk Scroll," *VT* 1 (1951): 33–37.

Tatum, W. B. "'The Origin of Jesus Messiah' (Matt 1:1, 18a): Matthew's Use of the Infancy Traditions," *JBL* 96 (1977): 523–535.

Taylor, V. *The Gospel according to St. Mark*. London: Macmillan, 1959.

____. *The Names of Jesus*. London: Macmillan, 1954.

Teeple, H. M. *The Mosaic Eschatological Prophet*. SBLMS 10. Philadelphia: Society of Biblical Literature, 1957.

Theissen, G. *The Miracle Stories of the Early Christian Tradition*. Ed. J. Riches. Trans. F. McDonagh. Philadelphia: Fortress, 1983.

Thompson, W. G. *Matthew's Story: Good News for Uncertain Times*. New York: Paulist Press, 1989.

___. "Reflections on the Composition of Matt 8:1–9:34," *CBQ* 33 (1971): 365–388.

Tiede, D. L. *The Charismatic Figure as Miracle Worker.* SBLDS 1. Missoula, Mont.: Scholars Press, 1972.

Tillborg, S. van. *The Jewish Leaders in Matthew.* Leiden: Brill, 1972.

Tov, E. "The Unpublished Qumran Texts from Caves 4 and 11," *JJS* 43 (1992): 101–136.

Tödt, H. E. *The Son of Man in the Synoptic Tradition.* Trans. D. M. Barton. Philadelphia: Westminster Press, 1965.

Trafton, J. L. Introduction to "*Commentary on Genesis A* (4Q252 = 4QPBless)," in *Dead Sea Scrolls: Hebrew, Aramaic, and Greek Texts with English Translations.* Vol. 6B: *Pesharima and Related Documents.* Ed. J. H. Charlesworth and H. W. L. Rietz, 203–207. Tübingen: J. C. B. Mohr (Paul Siebeck), 2002.

Trilling, W. *Das wahre Israel: Studien zur Theologie des Matthäus-Evangeliums.* SANT 10. München: Kösel, 1964.

Tromp, J. "The Sinners and the Lawless in Psalm of Solomon 17," *NovT* 35 (1993): 344–361.

Trunk, D. *Der Messianische Heiler: Eine redaktions- und religionsgeschichtliche Studie zu den Exorzismen im Matthäusevangelium.* HBS 3. Freiburg/Basel/Wien: Herder, 1994.

Tuckett, C. M. *Q and the History of Early Christianity: Studies on Q.* Edinburgh: T.&T. Clark, 1996.

VanderKam, J. "Messianism in the Scrolls," in *The Community of the Renewed Covenant: The Notre Dame Symposium on the Dead Sea Scrolls.* Ed. E. Ulrich and J. VanderKam, 211–234. CJAS 10. Notre Dame, Indiana: University of Notre Dame Press, 1994.

Veijola, T. *Die ewige Dynastie.* Helsinki: Academia Scientiarum Fennica, 1975.

Vermes, G. "Qumran Forum Miscellanea I," *JJS* 43 (1992): 299–305.

___. *Scripture and Tradition in Judaism.* 2nd ed. Leiden: E. J. Brill, 1973.

Verseput, D. J. "Davidic Messiah and Matthew's Jewish Christianity," in *SBL 1995 Seminar Papers.* Ed. E. Lovering, Jr., 102–116. SBL Seminar Papers Series 34. Atlanta: Scholars Press, 1995.

___. *The Rejection of the Humble Messianic King: A Study of the Composition of Matthew 11–12.* EHS.T 291. Frankfurt am Main: Peter Lang, 1986.

___. "The Role and Meaning of the 'Son of God' Title in Matthew's Gospel," *NTS* 33 (1987): 532–556.

Vögtle, A. "Die Genealogie Mt 1,2–16 und die matthäische Kindheitsgeschichte," *BZ* NF 8 (1964): 45–58, 239–262; 9 (1965): 32–49.

___. *Messias und Gottessohn: Herkunft und Sinn der matthäischen Geburts- und Kindheitsgeschichte.* Theologische Perspektiven. Düsseldorf: Patmos, 1971.

Waard, J. de. *A Comparative Study of the Old Testament Text in the Dead Sea Scrolls and in the New Testament.* STDJ 4. Leiden: Brill, 1965.

Waetjen, H. C. "The Genealogy as the Key to the Gospel according to Matthew," *JBL* 95 (1976): 205–230.

Wainwright, E. M. *Towards a Feminist Critical Reading of the Gospel according to Matthew.* BZNW 60. Berlin: Walter de Gruyter, 1991.

Walker, R. *Die Heilsgeschichte im Ersten Evangelium.* FRLANT 91. Göttingen: Vandenhoeck & Ruprecht, 1967.

Westermann, C. *Isaiah 40–66: A Commentary.* Trans. D. M. G. Stalker. Philadelphia: Westminster, 1969.

Wieder, N. "The 'Law-Interpreter' of the Sect of the Dead Sea Scrolls: The Second Moses," *JJS* 4 (1953): 158–175.

Wieser, F. E. *Die Abrahamvorstellungen im Neuen Testament.* EHS.T 317. Bern: Peter Lang, 1987.

Wise, M. O. and J. D. Tabor, "The Messiah at Qumran," *BAR* 18.6 (1992): 60–65.

Woude, A. S. van der. "Melchisedek als himmlische Erlösergestalt in den neugefundenen eschatologischen Midraschim aus Qumran Höhle XI," *OTS* 14 (1965): 354–373.

___, *Die messianischen Vorstellungen der Gemeinde von Qumrân.* SSN 3. Assen: Van Gorcum. 1957.

___. "Messias," in *Biblisch-Historisches Handwörterbuch: Landeskunde, Geschichte, Religion, Kultur, Literatur.* Vol. 2. Ed. B. R. Reicke and L. Rost, cols. 1197–1204. Göttingen: Vandenhoeck & Ruprechet, 1964.

Wrede, W. "Jesus als Davidssohn" in *Vorträge und Studien*, 147–177. Tübingen: J. C. B. Mohr, 1907.

___. *Das Messiasgeheimnis in den Evangelien: Zugleich ein Beitrag zum Verständnis des Markusevangeliums.* Göttingen: Vandenhoeck & Ruprecht, 1901. English translation: *The Messianic Secret.* Trans. J. C. G. Greig. Cambridge/London: James Clarke, 1971.

Wright, R. B. "Psalms of Solomon," in *OTP* 2. Ed. J. H. Charlesworth, 639–670. Garden City, NY: Doubleday, 1985.

Yadin, Y. "A Midrash on 2 Sam. vii and Ps. i–ii (4Q Florilegium)," *IEJ* (1959): 95–98.

Zahn, T. *Das Evangelium des Matthäus.* 3rd ed. KomNT 1. Leipzig: A. Deichert, 1910.

Zakowitch, Y. "Rahab als Mutter des Boas in der Jesus-Genealogie," *NovT* 17 (1975): 1–5.

Ziegler, J. *Untersuchungen zur Septuaginta des Buches Isaias.* ATA 12/3. Münster: Aschendorff, 1934.

Zimmermann, J. *Messianishe Texte aus Qumran: Königliche, priesterliche und prophetische Messiasvorstellungen in den Schriftfunden von Qumran.* WUNT II/104. Tübingen: Mohr Siebeck, 1998.

___. "Observations on 4Q246 – The 'Son of God'" in *Qumran-Messianism: Studies on the Messianic Expectations in the Dead Sea Scrolls.* Ed. J. H. Charlesworth, H. Lichtenberger, and G. S. Oegema, 175–190. Tübingen: Mohr Siebeck, 1998.

Reference Index

Contents: 1. Old Testament; 2. New Testament; 3. Apocrypha and Pseudepigrapha; 4. Dead Sea Scrolls; 5. Philo and Josephus; 6. Rabbinic and Other Jewish Texts; 7. Early Christian Writings; 8. Greek Texts.

1. Old Testament

3. Apocrypha and Pseudepigrapha

4. Dead Sea Scrolls

7. Early Christian Writings

8. Greek Texts

Author Index

Abrams, M. H. 8
Allegro, J. M. 16, 64
Allen, L. C. 25, 67
Allen, W. C. 139
Allison, D. C. 64, 66, 75, 80–82, 84, 89, 92, 95, 108–109, 112, 117–118, 149, 153, 161–162
Attridge, H. W. 31
Ådna, J. 129
Bacon, B. W. 141
Barrera, J. T. 111
Barth, G. 133, 136, 140, 143, 145
Barthélemy, D. 22–23, 55
Bauckham, R. 42–43
Bauer, W. 86
Beare, F. W. 108
Becker, J. 13, 163
Becker, M. 116, 169, 171, 178
Berger, K. 4, 97, 100–103, 106, 117
Bergmeier, R. 168–169, 171–173
Betz, O. 114, 173–174
Beuken, W. A. M. 181
Billerbeck, P. 41–42, 121, 163–164
Bittner, W. J. 93, 113–114, 116, 120–121, 163
Blass, F. 58, 82, 85
Boer, P. A. H. de. 139
Bonnard, P. 145
Bornkamm, G. 51, 60
Box, G. H. 40, 44,
Braun, H. 64
Breech, E. 158
Brierre–Narbonne, J.–J. 157
Bright, J. 29
Broer, I. 59
Brooke, G. J. 16, 177
Brown, R. E. 21, 35, 42–44, 46–49
Brown, S. 151
Brownlee, W. H. 154
Buchanan, G. W. 63
Bultmann, R. 35, 51
Burger, C. 4, 37, 39, 51, 77, 79–80, 82, 87
Byrskog, S. 83, 89

Cadbury, H. J. 128
Callan, T. 56
Carmignac, J. 17
Charles, R. H. 99
Charlesworth, J. H. 4–5, 8, 12, 16–17, 19, 22, 69, 71–72, 77, 97, 103, 105, 107, 155, 158
Chatman, S. 8–9
Clark, K. 78
Collins, J. J. 12, 19, 22–24, 66, 109, 168–169, 171, 173–178, 181–182
Comber, J. A. 105
Conzelmann, H. 37–38
Cope, O. L. 146, 148–149
Cranfield, C. E. B. 20, 25–26
Cross, F. M. 14, 22, 74
Cullmann, O. 47, 50–51, 145
Culpepper, R. A. 9
Dahl, N. A. 5–6, 52, 59, 147
Daly–Denton, M. 21, 55
Daube, D. 51–52, 60
Davenport, G. L. 66
Davies, W. D. 46, 48–49, 64, 66, 75, 80–82, 84, 89, 92, 95, 108, 149, 153, 161–162
Davis, C. T. 35
Deissmann, G. A. 126
Dewes, B. F. 79
Dexinger, F. 110
Dodd, C. H. 128, 130, 136
Duling, D. C. 4, 12–14, 16, 19–20, 26, 28, 59, 97–103, 105–106, 108–109, 120
Dunn, J. D. G. 20, 25–27, 47
Dupont, J. 180
Edwards, R. A. 8
Ehrman, B. D. 78
Eisenman, R. H. 168, 173
Eissfeldt, O. 28
Elliger, K. 181
Elliott, N. 135–136
Ellis, P. F. 81
Evans, C. A. 22–23, 25, 47, 162
Evans, G. 88

Subject Index

Wissenschaftliche Untersuchungen zum Neuen Testament

Alphabetical Index of the First and Second Series

Bosman, Philip: Conscience in Philo and Paul. 2003. *Volume II/166.*

Brocke, Christoph vom: Thessaloniki – Stadt des Kassander und Gemeinde des Paulus. 2001. *Volume II/125.*

Brunson, Andrew: Psalm 118 in the Gospel of John. 2003. *Volume II/158.*

Büchli, Jörg: Der Poimandres – ein paganisiertes Evangelium. 1987. *Volume II/27.*

Bühner, Jan A.: Der Gesandte und sein Weg im 4. Evangelium. 1977. *Volume II/2.*

Burchard, Christoph: Untersuchungen zu Joseph und Aseneth. 1965. *Volume 8.*

– Studien zur Theologie, Sprache und Umwelt des Neuen Testaments. Ed. von D. Sänger. 1998. *Volume 107.*

Burnett, Richard: Karl Barth's Theological Exegesis. 2001. *Volume II/145.*

Byron, John: Slavery Metaphors in Early Judaism and Pauline Christianity. 2003. *Volume II/162.*

Byrskog, Samuel: Story as History – History as Story. 2000. *Volume 123.*

Cancik, Hubert (Ed.): Markus-Philologie. 1984. *Volume 33.*

Capes, David B.: Old Testament Yaweh Texts in Paul's Christology. 1992. *Volume II/47.*

Caragounis, Chrys C.: The Son of Man. 1986. *Volume 38.*

– see *Fridrichsen, Anton.*

Carleton Paget, James: The Epistle of Barnabas. 1994. *Volume II/64.*

Carson, D.A., O'Brien, Peter T. and *Mark Seifrid* (Ed.): Justification and Variegated Nomism: A Fresh Appraisal of Paul and Second Temple Judaism. Volume 1: The Complexities of Second Temple Judaism. *Volume II/140.*

Ciampa, Roy E.: The Presence and Function of Scripture in Galatians 1 and 2. 1998. *Volume II/102.*

Classen, Carl Joachim: Rhetorical Criticsm of the New Testament. 2000. *Volume 128.*

Colpe, Carsten: Iranier – Aramäer – Hebräer – Hellenen. 2003. *Volume 154.*

Crump, David: Jesus the Intercessor. 1992. *Volume II/49.*

Dahl, Nils Alstrup: Studies in Ephesians. 2000. *Volume 131.*

Deines, Roland: Jüdische Steingefäße und pharisäische Frömmigkeit. 1993. *Volume II/52.*

– Die Pharisäer. 1997. *Volume 101.*

Dettwiler, Andreas and *Jean Zumstein (Ed.):* Kreuzestheologie im Neuen Testament. 2002. *Volume 151.*

Dickson, John P.: Mission-Commitment in Ancient Judaism and in the Pauline Communities. 2003. *Volume II/159.*

Dietzfelbinger, Christian: Der Abschied des Kommenden. 1997. *Volume 95.*

Dobbeler, Axel von: Glaube als Teilhabe. 1987. *Volume II/22.*

Du Toit, David S.: Theios Anthropos. 1997. *Volume II/91*

Dunn, James D.G. (Ed.): Jews and Christians. 1992. *Volume 66.*

– Paul and the Mosaic Law. 1996. *Volume 89.*

Dunn, James D.G., Hans Klein, Ulrich Luz and *Vasile Mihoc* (Ed.): Auslegung der Bibel in orthodoxer und westlicher Perspektive. 2000. *Volume 130.*

Ebertz, Michael N.: Das Charisma des Gekreuzigten. 1987. *Volume 45.*

Eckstein, Hans-Joachim: Der Begriff Syneidesis bei Paulus. 1983. *Volume II/10.*

– Verheißung und Gesetz. 1996. *Volume 86.*

Ego, Beate: Im Himmel wie auf Erden. 1989. *Volume II/34*

Ego, Beate and *Lange, Armin* with *Pilhofer, Peter (Ed.):* Gemeinde ohne Tempel – Community without Temple. 1999. *Volume 118.*

Eisen, Ute E.: see *Paulsen, Henning.*

Ellis, E. Earle: Prophecy and Hermeneutic in Early Christianity. 1978. *Volume 18.*

– The Old Testament in Early Christianity. 1991. *Volume 54.*

Endo, Masanobu: Creation and Christology. 2002. *Volume 149.*

Ennulat, Andreas: Die 'Minor Agreements'. 1994. *Volume II/62.*

Ensor, Peter W.: Jesus and His 'Works'. 1996. *Volume II/85.*

Eskola, Timo: Messiah and the Throne. 2001. *Volume II/142.*

– Theodicy and Predestination in Pauline Soteriology. 1998. *Volume II/100.*

Fatehi, Mehrdad: The Spirit's Relation to the Risen Lord in Paul. 2000. *Volume II/128.*

Feldmeier, Reinhard: Die Krisis des Gottessohnes. 1987. *Volume II/21.*

– Die Christen als Fremde. 1992. *Volume 64.*

Feldmeier, Reinhard and *Ulrich Heckel* (Ed.): Die Heiden. 1994. *Volume 70.*

Fletcher-Louis, Crispin H.T.: Luke-Acts: Angels, Christology and Soteriology. 1997. *Volume II/94.*

Förster, Niclas: Marcus Magus. 1999. *Volume 114.*

Forbes, Christopher Brian: Prophecy and Inspired Speech in Early Christianity and its Hellenistic Environment. 1995. *Volume II/75.*

Fornberg, Tord: see *Fridrichsen, Anton.*

Fossum, Jarl E.: The Name of God and the Angel of the Lord. 1985. *Volume 36.*

Fotopoulos, John: Food Offered to Idols in Roman Corinth. 2003. *Volume II/151.*

Frenschkowski, Marco: Offenbarung und Epiphanie. Volume 1 1995. *Volume II/79* – Volume 2 1997. *Volume II/80.*

Frey, Jörg: Eugen Drewermann und die biblische Exegese. 1995. *Volume II/71.*

– Die johanneische Eschatologie. Volume I. 1997. *Volume 96.* – Volume II. 1998. *Volume 110.*

– Volume III. 2000. *Volume 117.*

Freyne, Sean: Galilee and Gospel. 2000. *Volume 125.*

Fridrichsen, Anton: Exegetical Writings. Edited by C.C. Caragounis and T. Fornberg. 1994. *Volume 76.*

Garlington, Don B.: 'The Obedience of Faith'. 1991. *Volume II/38.*

– Faith, Obedience, and Perseverance. 1994. *Volume 79.*

Garnet, Paul: Salvation and Atonement in the Qumran Scrolls. 1977. *Volume II/3.*

Gese, Michael: Das Vermächtnis des Apostels. 1997. *Volume II/99.*

Gheorghita, Radu: The Role of the Septuagint in Hebrews. 2003. *Volume II/160.*

Gräbe, Petrus J.: The Power of God in Paul's Letters. 2000. *Volume II/123.*

Gräßer, Erich: Der Alte Bund im Neuen. 1985. *Volume 35.*

– Forschungen zur Apostelgeschichte. 2001. *Volume 137.*

Green, Joel B.: The Death of Jesus. 1988. *Volume II/33.*

Gregory, Anthony: The Reception of Luke and Acts in the Period before Irenaeus. 2003. *Volume II/169.*

Gundry Volf, Judith M.: Paul and Perseverance. 1990. *Volume II/37.*

Hafemann, Scott J.: Suffering and the Spirit. 1986. *Volume II/19.*

– Paul, Moses, and the History of Israel. 1995. *Volume 81.*

Hahn, Johannes (Ed.): Zerstörungen des Jerusalemer Tempels. 2002. *Volume 147.*

Hannah, Darrel D.: Michael and Christ. 1999. *Volume II/109.*

Hamid-Khani, Saeed: Relevation and Concealment of Christ. 2000. *Volume II/120.*

Hartman, Lars: Text-Centered New Testament Studies. Ed. von D. Hellholm. 1997. *Volume 102.*

Hartog, Paul: Polycarp and the New Testament. 2001. *Volume II/134.*

Heckel, Theo K.: Der Innere Mensch. 1993. *Volume II/53.*

– Vom Evangelium des Markus zum viergestaltigen Evangelium. 1999. *Volume 120.*

Heckel, Ulrich: Kraft in Schwachheit. 1993. *Volume II/56.*

– Der Segen im Neuen Testament. 2002. *Volume 150.*

– see *Feldmeier, Reinhard.*

– see *Hengel, Martin.*

Heiligenthal, Roman: Werke als Zeichen. 1983. *Volume II/9.*

Hellholm, D.: see *Hartman, Lars.*

Hemer, Colin J.: The Book of Acts in the Setting of Hellenistic History. 1989. *Volume 49.*

Hengel, Martin: Judentum und Hellenismus. 1969, ³1988. *Volume 10.*

– Die johanneische Frage. 1993. *Volume 67.*

– Judaica et Hellenistica. Kleine Schriften I. 1996. *Volume 90.*

– Judaica, Hellenistica et Christiana. Kleine Schriften II. 1999. *Volume 109.*

– Paulus und Jakobus. Kleine Schriften III. 2002. *Volume 141.*

Hengel, Martin and *Ulrich Heckel* (Ed.): Paulus und das antike Judentum. 1991. *Volume 58.*

Hengel, Martin and *Hermut Löhr* (Ed.): Schriftauslegung im antiken Judentum und im Urchristentum. 1994. *Volume 73.*

Hengel, Martin and *Anna Maria Schwemer:* Paulus zwischen Damaskus und Antiochien. 1998. *Volume 108.*

– Der messianische Anspruch Jesu und die Anfänge der Christologie. 2001. *Volume 138.*

Hengel, Martin and *Anna Maria Schwemer* (Ed.): Königsherrschaft Gottes und himmlischer Kult. 1991. *Volume 55.*

– Die Septuaginta. 1994. *Volume 72.*

Hengel, Martin; Siegfried Mittmann and *Anna Maria Schwemer* (Ed.): La Cité de Dieu / Die Stadt Gottes. 2000. *Volume 129.*

Herrenbrück, Fritz: Jesus und die Zöllner. 1990. *Volume II/41.*

Herzer, Jens: Paulus oder Petrus? 1998. *Volume 103.*

Hoegen-Rohls, Christina: Der nachösterliche Johannes. 1996. *Volume II/84.*

Hofius, Otfried: Katapausis. 1970. *Volume 11.*

– Der Vorhang vor dem Thron Gottes. 1972. *Volume 14.*

– Der Christushymnus Philipper 2,6-11. 1976, ²1991. *Volume 17.*

– Paulusstudien. 1989, ²1994. *Volume 51.*

– Neutestamentliche Studien. 2000. *Volume 132.*

– Paulusstudien II. 2002. *Volume 143.*

Hofius, Otfried and *Hans-Christian Kammler:*
Johannesstudien. 1996. *Volume 88.*

Holtz, Traugott: Geschichte und Theologie des
Urchristentums. 1991. *Volume 57.*

Hommel, Hildebrecht: Sebasmata. Volume 1 1983.
Volume 31 – Volume 2 1984. *Volume 32.*

Hvalvik, Reidar: The Struggle for Scripture and
Covenant. 1996. *Volume II/82.*

Joubert, Stephan: Paul as Benefactor. 2000.
Volume II/124.

Jungbauer, Harry: „Ehre Vater und Mutter".
2002. *Volume II/146.*

Kähler, Christoph: Jesu Gleichnisse als Poesie
und Therapie. 1995. *Volume 78.*

Kamlah, Ehrhard: Die Form der katalogischen
Paränese im Neuen Testament. 1964. *Volume 7.*

Kammler, Hans-Christian: Christologie und
Eschatologie. 2000. *Volume 126.*

– Kreuz und Weisheit. 2003. *Volume 159.*

– see *Hofius, Otfried.*

Kelhoffer, James A.: Miracle and Mission. 1999.
Volume II/112.

Kieffer, René and *Jan Bergman (Ed.):* La Main de
Dieu / Die Hand Gottes. 1997. *Volume 94.*

Kim, Seyoon: The Origin of Paul's Gospel.
1981, [2]1984. *Volume II/4.*

– "The 'Son of Man'" as the Son of God.
1983. *Volume 30.*

Klauck, Hans-Josef: Religion und Gesellschaft
im frühen Christentum. 2003. *Volume 152.*

Klein, Hans: see *Dunn, James D.G..*

Kleinknecht, Karl Th.: Der leidende Gerechtfer-
tigte. 1984, [2]1988. *Volume II/13.*

Klinghardt, Matthias: Gesetz und Volk Gottes.
1988. *Volume II/32.*

Köhler, Wolf-Dietrich: Rezeption des Matthäus-
evangeliums in der Zeit vor Irenäus. 1987.
Volume II/24.

Kooten, George H. van: Cosmic Christology in
Paul and the Pauline School. 2003.
Volume II/171.

Korn, Manfred: Die Geschichte Jesu in
veränderter Zeit. 1993. *Volume II/51.*

Koskenniemi, Erkki: Apollonios von Tyana in
der neutestamentlichen Exegese. 1994.
Volume II/61.

Kraus, Thomas J.: Sprache, Stil und historischer
Ort des zweiten Petrusbriefes. 2001.
Volume II/136.

Kraus, Wolfgang: Das Volk Gottes. 1996.
Volume 85.

– see *Walter, Nikolaus.*

Kreplin, Matthias: Das Selbstverständnis Jesu.
2001. *Volume II/141.*

Kuhn, Karl G.: Achtzehngebet und Vaterunser
und der Reim. 1950. *Volume 1.*

Kvalbein, Hans: see *Ådna, Jostein.*

Laansma, Jon: I Will Give You Rest. 1997.
Volume II/98.

Labahn, Michael: Offenbarung in Zeichen und
Wort. 2000. *Volume II/117.*

Lambers-Petry, Doris: see *Tomson, Peter J.*

Lange, Armin: see *Ego, Beate.*

Lampe, Peter: Die stadtrömischen Christen in
den ersten beiden Jahrhunderten. 1987,
[2]1989. *Volume II/18.*

Landmesser, Christof: Wahrheit als Grundbe-
griff neutestamentlicher Wissenschaft. 1999.
Volume 113.

– Jüngerberufung und Zuwendung zu Gott.
2000. *Volume 133.*

Lau, Andrew: Manifest in Flesh. 1996.
Volume II/86.

Lawrence, Louise: An Ethnography of the
Gospel of Matthew. 2003. *Volume II/165.*

Lee, Pilchan: The New Jerusalem in the Book of
Relevation. 2000. *Volume II/129.*

Lichtenberger, Hermann: see *Avemarie,
Friedrich.*

Lieu, Samuel N.C.: Manichaeism in the Later
Roman Empire and Medieval China. [2]1992.
Volume 63.

Loader, William R.G.: Jesus' Attitude Towards
the Law. 1997. *Volume II/97.*

Löhr, Gebhard: Verherrlichung Gottes durch
Philosophie. 1997. *Volume 97.*

Löhr, Hermut: Studien zum frühchristlichen und
frühjüdischen Gebet. 2003. *Volume 160.*

– : see *Hengel, Martin.*

Löhr, Winrich Alfred: Basilides und seine
Schule. 1995. *Volume 83.*

Luomanen, Petri: Entering the Kingdom of
Heaven. 1998. *Volume II/101.*

Luz, Ulrich: see *Dunn, James D.G.*

Maier, Gerhard: Mensch und freier Wille. 1971.
Volume 12.

– Die Johannesoffenbarung und die Kirche.
1981. *Volume 25.*

Markschies, Christoph: Valentinus Gnosticus?
1992. *Volume 65.*

Marshall, Peter: Enmity in Corinth: Social
Conventions in Paul's Relations with the
Corinthians. 1987. *Volume II/23.*

Mayer, Annemarie: Sprache der Einheit im
Epheserbrief und in der Ökumene. 2002.
Volume II/150.

McDonough, Sean M.: YHWH at Patmos:
Rev. 1:4 in its Hellenistic and Early Jewish
Setting. 1999. *Volume II/107.*

McGlynn, Moyna: Divine Judgement and Divine Benevolence in the Book of Wisdom. 2001. *Volume II/139.*

Meade, David G.: Pseudonymity and Canon. 1986. *Volume 39.*

Meadors, Edward P.: Jesus the Messianic Herald of Salvation. 1995. *Volume II/72.*

Meißner, Stefan: Die Heimholung des Ketzers. 1996. *Volume II/87.*

Mell, Ulrich: Die „anderen" Winzer. 1994. *Volume 77.*

Mengel, Berthold: Studien zum Philipperbrief. 1982. *Volume II/8.*

Merkel, Helmut: Die Widersprüche zwischen den Evangelien. 1971. *Volume 13.*

Merklein, Helmut: Studien zu Jesus und Paulus. Volume 1 1987. *Volume 43.* – Volume 2 1998. *Volume 105.*

Metzdorf, Christina: Die Tempelaktion Jesu. 2003. *Volume II/168.*

Metzler, Karin: Der griechische Begriff des Verzeihens. 1991. *Volume II/44.*

Metzner, Rainer: Die Rezeption des Matthäusevangeliums im 1. Petrusbrief. 1995. *Volume II/74.*

– Das Verständnis der Sünde im Johannesevangelium. 2000. *Volume 122.*

Mihoc, Vasile: see Dunn, James D.G..

Mineshige, Kiyoshi: Besitzverzicht und Almosen bei Lukas. 2003. *Volume II/163.*

Mittmann, Siegfried: see Hengel, Martin.

Mittmann-Richert, Ulrike: Magnifikat und Benediktus. 1996. *Volume II/90.*

Mußner, Franz: Jesus von Nazareth im Umfeld Israels und der Urkirche. Ed. von M. Theobald. 1998. *Volume 111.*

Niebuhr, Karl-Wilhelm: Gesetz und Paränese. 1987. *Volume II/28.*

– Heidenapostel aus Israel. 1992. *Volume 62.*

Nielsen, Anders E.: "Until it is Fullfilled". 2000. *Volume II/126.*

Nissen, Andreas: Gott und der Nächste im antiken Judentum. 1974. *Volume 15.*

Noack, Christian: Gottesbewußtsein. 2000. *Volume II/116.*

Noormann, Rolf: Irenäus als Paulusinterpret. 1994. *Volume II/66.*

Novakovic, Lidija: Messiah, the Healer of the Sick. 2003. *Volume II/170.*

Obermann, Andreas: Die christologische Erfüllung der Schrift im Johannesevangelium. 1996. *Volume II/83.*

Öhler, Markus: Barnabas. 2003. *Volume 156.*

Okure, Teresa: The Johannine Approach to Mission. 1988. *Volume II/31.*

Oropeza, B. J.: Paul and Apostasy. 2000. *Volume II/115.*

Ostmeyer, Karl-Heinrich: Taufe und Typos. 2000. *Volume II/118.*

Paulsen, Henning: Studien zur Literatur und Geschichte des frühen Christentums. Ed. von Ute E. Eisen. 1997. *Volume 99.*

Pao, David W.: Acts and the Isaianic New Exodus. 2000. *Volume II/130.*

Park, Eung Chun: The Mission Discourse in Matthew's Interpretation. 1995. *Volume II/81.*

Park, Joseph S.: Conceptions of Afterlife in Jewish Insriptions. 2000. *Volume II/121.*

Pate, C. Marvin: The Reverse of the Curse. 2000. *Volume II/114.*

Peres, Imre: Griechische Grabinschriften und neutestamentliche Eschatologie. 2003. *Volume 157.*

Philonenko, Marc (Ed.): Le Trône de Dieu. 1993. *Volume 69.*

Pilhofer, Peter: Presbyteron Kreitton. 1990. *Volume II/39.*

– Philippi. Volume 1 1995. *Volume 87.* – Volume 2 2000. *Volume 119.*

– Die frühen Christen und ihre Welt. 2002. *Volume 145.*

– see Ego, Beate.

Pöhlmann, Wolfgang: Der Verlorene Sohn und das Haus. 1993. *Volume 68.*

Pokorný, Petr and *Josef B. Souček:* Bibelauslegung als Theologie. 1997. *Volume 100.*

Pokorný, Petr and *Jan Roskovec* (Ed.): Philosophical Hermeneutics and Biblical Exegesis. 2002. *Volume 153.*

Porter, Stanley E.: The Paul of Acts. 1999. *Volume 115.*

Prieur, Alexander: Die Verkündigung der Gottesherrschaft. 1996. *Volume II/89.*

Probst, Hermann: Paulus und der Brief. 1991. *Volume II/45.*

Räisänen, Heikki: Paul and the Law. 1983, ²1987. *Volume 29.*

Rehkopf, Friedrich: Die lukanische Sonderquelle. 1959. *Volume 5.*

Rein, Matthias: Die Heilung des Blindgeborenen (Joh 9). 1995. *Volume II/73.*

Reinmuth, Eckart: Pseudo-Philo und Lukas. 1994. *Volume 74.*

Reiser, Marius: Syntax und Stil des Markusevangeliums. 1984. *Volume II/11.*

Richards, E. Randolph: The Secretary in the Letters of Paul. 1991. *Volume II/42.*

Riesner, Rainer: Jesus als Lehrer. 1981, ³1988. *Volume II/7.*

– Die Frühzeit des Apostels Paulus. 1994. *Volume 71.*

Rissi, Mathias: Die Theologie des Hebräerbriefs. 1987. *Volume 41.*

Roskovec, Jan: see *Pokorný, Petr.*

Röhser, Günter: Metaphorik und Personifikation der Sünde. 1987. *Volume II/25.*

Rose, Christian: Die Wolke der Zeugen. 1994. *Volume II/60.*

Rüegger, Hans-Ulrich: Verstehen, was Markus erzählt. 2002. *Volume II/155.*

Rüger, Hans Peter: Die Weisheitsschrift aus der Kairoer Geniza. 1991. *Volume 53.*

Sänger, Dieter: Antikes Judentum und die Mysterien. 1980. *Volume II/5.*

– Die Verkündigung des Gekreuzigten und Israel. 1994. *Volume 75.*

– see *Burchard, Christoph*

Salzmann, Jorg Christian: Lehren und Ermahnen. 1994. *Volume II/59.*

Sandnes, Karl Olav: Paul – One of the Prophets? 1991. *Volume II/43.*

Sato, Migaku: Q und Prophetie. 1988. *Volume II/29.*

Schaper, Joachim: Eschatology in the Greek Psalter. 1995. *Volume II/76.*

Schimanowski, Gottfried: Die himmlische Liturgie in der Apokalypse des Johannes. 2002. *Volume II/154.*

– Weisheit und Messias. 1985. *Volume II/17.*

Schlichting, Günter: Ein jüdisches Leben Jesu. 1982. *Volume 24.*

Schnabel, Eckhard J.: Law and Wisdom from Ben Sira to Paul. 1985. *Volume II/16.*

Schutter, William L.: Hermeneutic and Composition in I Peter. 1989. *Volume II/30.*

Schwartz, Daniel R.: Studies in the Jewish Background of Christianity. 1992. *Volume 60.*

Schwemer, Anna Maria: see *Hengel, Martin*

Scott, James M.: Adoption as Sons of God. 1992. *Volume II/48.*

– Paul and the Nations. 1995. *Volume 84.*

Shum, Shiu-Lun: Paul's Use of Isaiah in Romans. 2002. *Volume II/156.*

Siegert, Folker: Drei hellenistisch-jüdische Predigten. Teil I 1980. *Volume 20* – Teil II 1992. *Volume 61.*

– Nag-Hammadi-Register. 1982. *Volume 26.*

– Argumentation bei Paulus. 1985. *Volume 34.*

– Philon von Alexandrien. 1988. *Volume 46.*

Simon, Marcel: Le christianisme antique et son contexte religieux I/II. 1981. *Volume 23.*

Snodgrass, Klyne: The Parable of the Wicked Tenants. 1983. *Volume 27.*

Söding, Thomas: Das Wort vom Kreuz. 1997. *Volume 93.*

– see *Thüsing, Wilhelm.*

Sommer, Urs: Die Passionsgeschichte des Markusevangeliums. 1993. *Volume II/58.*

Souček, Josef B.: see *Pokorný, Petr.*

Spangenberg, Volker: Herrlichkeit des Neuen Bundes. 1993. *Volume II/55.*

Spanje, T.E. van: Inconsistency in Paul? 1999. *Volume II/110.*

Speyer, Wolfgang: Frühes Christentum im antiken Strahlungsfeld. Volume I: 1989. *Volume 50.*

– Volume II: 1999. *Volume 116.*

Stadelmann, Helge: Ben Sira als Schriftgelehrter. 1980. *Volume II/6.*

Stenschke, Christoph W.: Luke's Portrait of Gentiles Prior to Their Coming to Faith. *Volume II/108.*

Stettler, Christian: Der Kolosserhymnus. 2000. *Volume II/131.*

Stettler, Hanna: Die Christologie der Pastoralbriefe. 1998. *Volume II/105.*

Strobel, August: Die Stunde der Wahrheit. 1980. *Volume 21.*

Stroumsa, Guy G.: Barbarian Philosophy. 1999. *Volume 112.*

Stuckenbruck, Loren T.: Angel Veneration and Christology. 1995. *Volume II/70.*

Stuhlmacher, Peter (Ed.): Das Evangelium und die Evangelien. 1983. *Volume 28.*

– Biblische Theologie und Evangelium. 2002. *Volume 146.*

Sung, Chong-Hyon: Vergebung der Sünden. 1993. *Volume II/57.*

Tajra, Harry W.: The Trial of St. Paul. 1989. *Volume II/35.*

– The Martyrdom of St.Paul. 1994. *Volume II/67.*

Theißen, Gerd: Studien zur Soziologie des Urchristentums. 1979, ³1989. *Volume 19.*

Theobald, Michael: Studien zum Römerbrief. 2001. *Volume 136.*

Theobald, Michael: see *Mußner, Franz.*

Thornton, Claus-Jürgen: Der Zeuge des Zeugen. 1991. *Volume 56.*

Thüsing, Wilhelm: Studien zur neutestamentlichen Theologie. Ed. von Thomas Söding. 1995. *Volume 82.*

Thurén, Lauri: Derhethorizing Paul. 2000. *Volume 124.*

Tomson, Peter J. and Doris Lambers-Petry (Ed.): The Image of the Judaeo-Christians in Ancient Jewish and Christian Literature. 2003. *Volume 158.*

Treloar, Geoffrey R.: Lightfoot the Historian. 1998. *Volume II/103.*

Tsuji, Manabu: Glaube zwischen Vollkommenheit und Verweltlichung. 1997. *Volume II/93*

Twelftree, Graham H.: Jesus the Exorcist. 1993. *Volume II/54.*

Urban, Christina: Das Menschenbild nach dem Johannesevangelium. 2001. *Volume II/137.*

Visotzky, Burton L.: Fathers of the World. 1995. *Volume 80.*

Vollenweider, Samuel: Horizonte neutestamentlicher Christologie. 2002. *Volume 144.*

Vos, Johan S.: Die Kunst der Argumentation bei Paulus. 2002. *Volume 149.*

Wagener, Ulrike: Die Ordnung des „Hauses Gottes". 1994. *Volume II/65.*

Walker, Donald D.: Paul's Offer of Leniency (2 Cor 10:1). 2002. *Volume II/152.*

Walter, Nikolaus: Praeparatio Evangelica. Ed. von Wolfgang Kraus und Florian Wilk. 1997. *Volume 98.*

Wander, Bernd: Gottesfürchtige und Sympathisanten. 1998. *Volume 104.*

Watts, Rikki: Isaiah's New Exodus and Mark. 1997. *Volume II/88.*

Wedderburn, A.J.M.: Baptism and Resurrection. 1987. *Volume 44.*

Wegner, Uwe: Der Hauptmann von Kafarnaum. 1985. *Volume II/14.*

Weissenrieder, Annette: Images of Illness in the Gospel of Luke. 2003. Volume II/164.

Welck, Christian: Erzählte ‚Zeichen'. 1994. *Volume II/69.*

Wiarda, Timothy: Peter in the Gospels . 2000. *Volume II/127.*

Wilk, Florian: see *Walter, Nikolaus.*

Williams, Catrin H.: I am He. 2000. *Volume II/113.*

Wilson, Walter T.: Love without Pretense. 1991. *Volume II/46.*

Wisdom, Jeffrey: Blessing for the Nations and the Curse of the Law. 2001. *Volume II/133.*

Wucherpfennig, Ansgar: Heracleon Philologus. 2002. *Volume 142.*

Yeung, Maureen: Faith in Jesus and Paul. 2002. *Volume II/147.*

Zimmermann, Alfred E.: Die urchristlichen Lehrer. 1984, ²1988. *Volume II/12.*

Zimmermann, Johannes: Messianische Texte aus Qumran. 1998. *Volume II/104.*

Zimmermann, Ruben: Geschlechtermetaphorik und Gottesverhältnis. 2001. *Volume II/122.*

Zumstein, Jean: see *Dettwiler, Andreas*

For a complete catalogue please write to the publisher
Mohr Siebeck • P.O. Box 2030 • D–72010 Tübingen/Germany
Up-to-date information on the internet at www.mohr.de